URY

THE RESIDENCE OF THE BARCLAY FAMILY

Taken down 1855

A HISTORY OF THE

BARCLAY FAMILY

WITH PEDIGREES FROM 1067 TO 1933

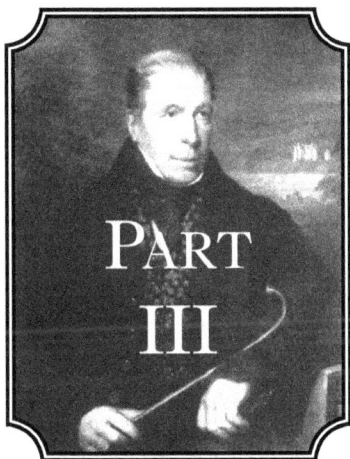

PART
III

THE BARCLAYS IN SCOTLAND AND ENGLAND FROM
1610 TO 1933

COMPILED BY

LIEUT.-COLONEL HUBERT F. BARCLAY
AND ALICE WILSON-FOX

HERITAGE BOOKS
2015

HERITAGE BOOKS

AN IMPRINT OF HERITAGE BOOKS, INC.

Books, CDs, and more—Worldwide

For our listing of thousands of titles see our website
at
www.HeritageBooks.com

A Facsimile Reprint
Published 2015 by
HERITAGE BOOKS, INC.
Publishing Division
5810 Ruatan Street
Berwyn Heights, Md. 20740

Originally published
LONDON
THE ST. CATHERINE PRESS
STAMFORD STREET, S.E.
1934

International Standard Book Numbers
Paperbound: 978-1-58549-860-4
Clothbound: 978-0-7884-6135-4

FOREWORD TO PART III

IN placing before the family this, the third and final Part of the Barclay History, I must express my regret that the completion of the work has been so long delayed. A short perusal will, however, inform the reader of the immense amount of research rendered necessary if the records were to be, as far as possible, complete, and of the impossibility of compressing the History into two Parts, as originally intended by my uncle, The Rev. Charles Wright Barclay, Compiler of Part I.

The work has been prolonged and arduous, and I have gladly availed myself of the assistance of Mrs. Wilson-Fox, author of the *Life of Lord Halsbury* and other books, herself a connection by marriage of the Barclays of Bury Hill. She has dealt in masterly fashion with such outstanding characters as Colonel David Barclay (Urie I) and his son, Robert, the famous " Apologist " for the Quakers. I take this opportunity of tendering to her my most grateful thanks.

I desire also to place on record my appreciation of the work of the Printers' Readers, whose knowledge and care have been of the greatest help.

I cannot claim that the work is exhaustive : more information may be available to future historians extracted from charter chests of other families. Since the issue of Part II I have received extracts from sundry charters at Glamis Castle, which serve as additional proofs to statements already set forth. Recently two valuable deeds have been discovered by Messrs. Kinnear and Falconer, Solicitors, of Stonehaven, whose forebears were factors to the Urie estates. One of

FOREWORD

these original documents is the contract of the purchase of East New Jersey, in 1685, from the executors of Sir George Carteret, first owner. The other is the Fundamental Constitution of the Province, as laid down by the first proprietors under the Governorship of Robert Barclay " the Apologist." These deeds, with the original seals attached, are now at Bury Hill.

I desire once more to record my deep gratitude to my wife, who has been my devoted collaborator throughout.

H. F. B.

Orchards,
    Letty Green,
        Hertford :
December, 1933.

CONTENTS

CONTENTS

viii

LIST OF ILLUSTRATIONS

LIST OF PRINCIPAL
AUTHORITIES CONSULTED
FOR PART III

Genealogical Account of the Barclays of Urie, together with Memoirs of the life of Colonel David Barclay and of his eldest son, the late Robert Barclay of Urie. Robert Barclay. 1740.

The Court Book of the Barony of Urie. 1604–1747. Douglas Gordon Barron.

The Genealogy of the Earls of Sutherland and Gordon.

Theological Review, 1874, " The Great Laird of Urie." Alexander Gordon.

Theological Review, 1875, " The Marrow of Barclay." Alexander Gordon.

History of the Carnegies, Earls of Southesk. William Fraser.

Earldoms of Strathearn, Menteith and Airth ; with a report on the claim of Robert Barclay-Allardice. Sir Harris Nicholson, G.C.M.G.

Pedestrianism, with a full account of Captain Barclay's Public and Private Matches. Walter Thom.

The Memorials of Hope Park.

Life of Gustavus Adolphus. Chapman.

Life of Gustavus Adolphus. Spence.

Earl of Callender.

Gordon of Salleach.

Calder.

PRINCIPAL AUTHORITIES CONSULTED

The Thirty Years War. Anton Gindeley.

Civil War in Dorset. Robert Baillie.

Memorialls of the Trubles in Scotland. Spalding Club.

The Army and the Covenant, 1644–1645.

History of the Great Rebellion. Tout and Powell.

History of Scotland. Wishart.

Outline of Scottish History. Mackenzie.

Scotland and the Protectorate. Firth.

Historical Associations of My Native Country. David Scott.

The Pentland Rising.

The Black Book of Kincardineshire. James Anderson.

Trew and Perfyt Account.

East Coast of Scotland. Francis Douglas.

Dictionary of National Biography.

The Building of the Empire. Alfred Story.

Scottish Colonial Schemes. George Pratt Insh.

Pennsylvania Magazine, Volume V.

Pennsylvania Gazette, January 17th, 1771.

Agricultural Tour in the United States and Upper Canada. Captain Robert Barclay-Allardice.

Life of Richard Blair.

Secretary's Papers, Register House, Edinburgh, 1688.

The Lauderdale Papers, Camden Society, Edited by Osmond Airy.

Register of the Privy Council of Scotland.

Acta Parliamentorum Regni Scotiae.

Supplementary Parliamentary Papers, being Warrants of Parliament during the interregnum found subsequently. Original MSS. in the Register House, Edinburgh.

Convention of Royal Burghs.

Clarendon State Papers.

Thurloe Papers.

PRINCIPAL AUTHORITIES CONSULTED

Calendar of State Papers.

Fraser Papers.

Nicholas Papers. Camden Society.

Records of the Secretary's Office, Windsor.

Sufferings of the Church in Scotland. Woodrow.

Sufferings of the Quakers. Joseph Besse.

History of the Friends. William Sewel.

Early Quakerism. W. C. Braithwaite.

Story of Quakerism. Mrs. Emmott.

History of the Quakers. Gough.

Rise of Quakerism in Yorkshire. Rowntree.

The Quakers. Clarkson.

Memoirs of the Rise of the Quakers in the North of Scotland.

Life of William Penn, Prefixed to Penn's Works. Joseph Besse.

Life of William Penn. William Sewel.

Life of Penn. Clarkson.

Life of William Penn. Graham.

Quaker and Courtier : the Life and Work of William Penn. Mrs. Colquhoun Grant (one of his descendants).

Life of George Fox. Dr. Thomas Hodgkin.

The Journal of George Fox, Cambridge University Press.

Diary of Alexander Jaffray, with Memoirs of the Rise, Progress and Persecutions of the People called Quakers. John Barclay.

Robert Barclay, his Life and Work. E. Christabel Cadbury.

A Short Account of the Life and Writings of Robert Barclay. David Barclay (of Walthamstow).

The Letters of Lydia Ann Barclay, 1862.

Piety Promoted : A Quaker Record, 1701–1829, Reprinted Edition, 1854.

PRINCIPAL AUTHORITIES CONSULTED

A Man of Plain Speech. M. E.

Deeds and Letters at Bury Hill.

Manuscript Life of Robert Barclay, by Arthur Kett Barclay (1843).

Rachel Gurney of the Grove. Sir Alfred Pease, Bart.

Barclay's Bank, Limited. F. W. Mathews.

Annals of an East Anglian Bank. W. H. Bidwell.

PEDIGREE I.

The Barclays of Urie

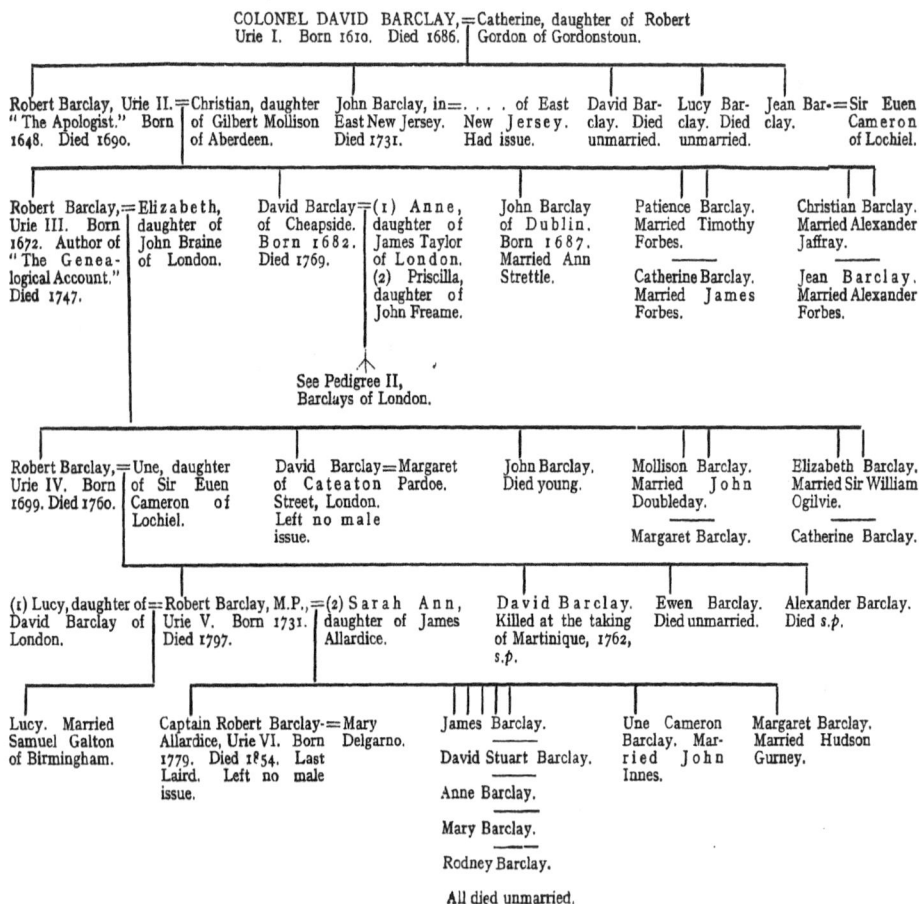

COLONEL DAVID BARCLAY,＝Catherine, daughter of Robert
Urie I. Born 1610. Died 1686. | Gordon of Gordonstoun.

Robert Barclay, Urie II.＝Christian, daughter	John Barclay, in＝. . . . of East	David Bar-clay. Died unmarried.	Lucy Bar-clay. Died unmarried.	Jean Bar-clay. ＝Sir Euen Cameron of Lochiel.
"The Apologist." Born	of Gilbert Mollison	East New Jersey. New Jersey.			
1648. Died 1690.	of Aberdeen.	Died 1731. Had issue.			

Robert Barclay,＝Elizabeth, | David Barclay＝(1) Anne, | John Barclay | Patience Barclay. | Christian Barclay.
Urie III. Born | daughter of | of Cheapside. | daughter of | of Dublin. | Married Timothy | Married Alexander
1672. Author of | John Braine | Born 1682. | James Taylor | Born 1687. | Forbes. | Jaffray.
"The Genea- | of London. | Died 1769. | of London. | Married Ann | |
logical Account." | | | (2) Priscilla, | Strettle. | Catherine Barclay. | Jean Barclay.
Died 1747. | | | daughter of | | Married James | Married Alexander
| | | John Freame. | | Forbes. | Forbes.

See Pedigree II,
Barclays of London.

Robert Barclay,＝Une, daughter | David Barclay＝Margaret | John Barclay. | Mollison Barclay. | Elizabeth Barclay.
Urie IV. Born | of Sir Euen | of Cateaton | Pardoe. | Died young. | Married John | Married Sir William
1699. Died 1760. | Cameron of | Street, London. | | | Doubleday. | Ogilvie.
| Lochiel. | Left no male | | | |
| | issue. | | | Margaret Barclay. | Catherine Barclay.

(1) Lucy, daughter of＝Robert Barclay, M.P.,＝(2) Sarah Ann, | David Barclay. | Ewen Barclay. | Alexander Barclay.
David Barclay of | Urie V. Born 1731. | daughter of James | Killed at the taking | Died unmarried. | Died s.p.
London. | Died 1797. | Allardice. | of Martinique, 1762, | |
| | | s.p. | |

Lucy. Married | Captain Robert Barclay-＝Mary | James Barclay. | Une Cameron | Margaret Barclay.
Samuel Galton | Allardice, Urie VI. Born | Delgarno. | ——— | Barclay. Mar- | Married Hudson
of Birmingham. | 1779. Died 1854. Last | | David Stuart Barclay. | ried John | Gurney.
| Laird. Left no male | | | Innes. |
| issue. | | Anne Barclay. | |

Mary Barclay.

Rodney Barclay.

All died unmarried.

THE BARCLAYS OF URIE

COLONEL DAVID BARCLAY

Colonel David Barclay, third son of David Barclay (Mathers XI), was born in 1610 at Kirktounhill, on the estate of Mathers, which had been in the possession of his line since the year 1351. This property was not yet sold to meet the family embarrassments, as related in Part II of this History.

Although in the seventeenth century the bitter ecclesiastical controversies of Tudor times had died down, and material prosperity was clearly increasing, great religious questions still held a dominant place in men's minds both in England and Scotland.

In the year 1618 the Scottish nation was deeply stirred by the revolt of the Protestant nobles of Bohemia against their Catholic Ruler, the Emperor Mathias, and their refusal to accept as his successor his cousin Ferdinand of Styria, a rigid Catholic. They chose in his place, as their King, the Protestant Frederick V, Elector Palatine of the Rhine, son-in-law of James VI and I, the leader of the South German Calvinists, and the conflict was thus intensified between the German Protestants of the Evangelical Union and the Romanist Princes of the Catholic League.

King James, torn between his horror of religious war and his duty to support his son-in-law, was too cautious and niggardly to side openly with the spirited Elector, and when the Catholic forces of the Emperor Ferdinand overran and conquered the Palatinate in 1622, and the Elector and his wife had to take refuge at her father's Court, all Protestants in England and Scotland were warmly indignant on their behalf.

His son-in-law's loss of dominions roused James, however, and he gave permission for a force of 12,000 men to be raised

III.—A   I

COLONEL
DAVID
BARCLAY,
1610–1686,
Urie I. in England to serve under the Protestant adventurer Count Mansfield, in an attempt to win back the Palatinate. The expedition was half-hearted and ill organised, and proved a complete failure. The King was unable to obtain further supplies from Parliament, and when he died in 1625 the matter was still in abeyance.

David Barclay went to King's College, Aberdeen, to pursue his studies, in 1628, but his name does not appear among those who graduated there, and we read in the Memoir of his life by his grandson Robert (Urie III): " He no sooner went through his education in the schools than he went abroad on his travels in Germany, where he went a volunteer into the Swedish Genealogical
Account.
p. 27. Army, under Gustavus Adolphus, King of Sweden, in which he served and was made a Captain."

Robert Barclay tells us that David's commission as Captain was, in the Swedish language, still extant in the family when he wrote in 1740. The date of this commission appears to have been 1630.

Many younger members of Scottish and English nobility were at this time seeking useful employment and adventure in the standing armies of the Continent, and it may be that the financial embarrassments of his family turned the thoughts of David Barclay to a similar course. We may suppose also that the Protestant cause had been a subject of constant discussion in his home, and that there would have been a strong attraction for the brave and serious youth in the character of the young King of Sweden.

The eyes of Europe were focused upon Gustavus Adolphus, "the Lion of the North," whose heroic stand, as upholder of Protestantism against the overwhelming Catholic forces of the Emperor Ferdinand, had raised the hopes and courage of the persecuted Protestants throughout Central Europe.

When he succeeded to the throne at the age of eighteen he found his kingdom worn out and demoralised by fifty years of civil war, and by his firm administration he had in a few years restored Sweden to her position as a power in the Councils of Europe.

2

He had been brought up in a strict Protestant school and when he was appealed to by his co-religionists in the " Thirty Years War " took up their cause with enthusiasm.

He was also stirred to bitter indignation by the cruelties committed, in the name of religion, by the Austrian troops. With a small force of 15,000 men he attacked the huge armies of Ferdinand and by the superiority of his discipline and the bravery of his soldiers soon turned the fortune of war and caused the Imperial troops to retreat before him.

No doubt he welcomed the accession to his forces of the English and Scottish volunteers, including David Barclay and his friends, as he had been disappointed by the hesitation of the German princes to throw in their lot with him, though fighting on their behalf. They were still under the terror inspired by the name of Wallenstein and Tilly, the two great Austrian Generals, whose military successes had raised the Catholic Emperor to a position of supremacy.

Nevertheless Gustavus continued to advance with unbroken successes. Tilly was utterly defeated at Breitenfeld in 1631, and died of wounds, and Wallenstein was reappointed Commander-in-Chief of the Imperial forces. After some preliminary engagements the armies met at Lutzen, where the Swedes were again victorious, but Gustavus Adolphus was killed, it was believed by treachery, in the moment of victory.

David Barclay took part in all this campaign, and showed such conspicuous courage that he was promoted to a Captaincy.

The strong religious principles of Gustavus influenced all ranks, and when the troops were assembled for prayer daily, and advanced to attack to the solemn strains of "Ein feste Berg ist unser Gott" we can imagine how the conviction of Divine support must have inspired the grave young Scottish officer.

The years during which Gustavus Adolphus commanded the Swedish army were an heroic epoch, and the King's tragic death at the age of thirty-eight was a staggering blow to German Protestantism. Though the war continued it had

COLONEL DAVID BARCLAY, 1610–1686, Urie I.

Genealogical Account, p. 27.

COLONEL DAVID BARCLAY, 1610–1686, Urie I. lost its moving spirit and reverted to many of its old barbaric methods.

David Barclay, now promoted to the rank of Major, remained on the Continent for six years. It is thought probable that he transferred his services to the Prussian army after the death of Gustavus, but it is certain that he consistently espoused the cause of the Protestant Powers until 1638, when the serious civil commotions in England and Scotland summoned him home.

The names of several "Barckleis or Barklays" appear in the Swedish Military Archives during this period. Among them William Barclay, "son of the laird of 'Sidgot'" [Seggatt], he was grandson of Walter Barclay (Towie XVI); and another David, stated to have been an ensign in Jacob Seton's regiment in 1624, and afterwards in Alexander Leslie's company of foot, but his identity cannot be established.

We must now review the sequence of events at home during the years of David Barclay's absence.

1638. King James the Sixth of Scotland and First of England had determined that the two countries should have a united Church, combining moderate Protestant doctrine with Episcopal government. On his accession to the English throne he had declared " I will have one doctrine and one discipline, one religion in substance and ceremony. I shall make them conform themselves, or I will harry them out of the land, or do worse."

The Building of the Empire, Alfred Story.

The dour national character of the Scots, however, had been too deeply penetrated by the Presbyterian tenets for them to accept this compromise, and it was against the wish of the majority that, in 1612, Episcopacy had been forcibly established by law in Scotland. The King, a timid man, had been convinced by the Armada, and the Gunpowder Plot, that the Papists were secretly conspiring against him, and felt that a religious alliance and united Church between Protestant England and Presbyterian Scotland would add to the security of the Realm. He was the more desirous of this as certain negotiations had passed between Scotland and France with a

4

view to renewing their ancient alliance, which policy had, COLONEL however, been checked by Cardinal Richelieu.

DAVID BARCLAY, 1610–1686, Urie I.

But when in 1618 the Five Articles had been adopted by the General Assembly at Perth, in which the King was declared to be the absolute Head of the Scottish Constitution, the smouldering flames of religious war were fanned. The devout and political instincts of the Scots began to gather strength, and by 1635 had come to a head. Consequently the introduction of the Liturgy in St. Giles's Church, Edinburgh, in that 1618–1635. year, which seemed to indicate a slight deviation towards the Roman Catholic ritual, provoked an uproar initiated by Jenny Geddes, and her " creepie stool," which had not been equalled since the Reformation.

The Scottish nation rose in wrath. King Charles I, who suc- 1625. ceeded his father in 1625, held to King James's policy, and was overwhelmed with supplications, petitions, and protests. Among these the chief was "The Covenant," prepared by Alexander Henderson, the head of the ministers, and Johnston of Warriston, "For the Defence of the Reformed Religion" (as reformed from Popery). This was enthusiastically accepted by a large number of nobility and gentry, signed by three hundred Ministers, and a great multitude of the people, "many of whom Tout and Powell. signed it with tears, and so intense was the feeling, some in their own blood."

After this the Covenanters held an Assembly in Glasgow, and declared their intention of prosecuting the Bishops, but the King challenged the mode of election to the Assembly, and absolutely forbade the prosecutions. Matters had reached this point when David Barclay was urgently 1638. summoned home by his relatives and friends in 1638. His reputation for courage and military skill was too well known for him to be spared to foreign service when events of such national importance were taking place in Scotland. He kept his rank as Major, and threw in his lot with the moderate Presbyterian party, at that time under the leadership of the young Marquis of Montrose, a nobleman of brilliant qualities, and one of the most accomplished gentlemen of his age. He was supported by all the great north-eastern families, Keiths,

Forbes, Frasers and Crichtons, many of whom were kin to the Barclays.

The Covenanters restored Presbyterian Church government, condemned the Service book, abjured Episcopacy, and put an army into the field, commanded by Alexander Leslie, a General trained in the service of Gustavus Adolphus, under whom he had risen to the rank of Field-Marshal.

He is described thus: "There came out of Germanie hame to Scotland, ane gentleman of base birth, born in Balveny, who had served long and fortunately in the German wars, and called to his name Felt Marschal Leslie, His Excellence."

And "such was his wisdom and authoritie," writes another historian, "that all with ane incredible submission, from the beginning to the end, gave over themselves to be guided by the little old crooked soldier, as if he had been the great Solyman."

He was seconded by another Leslie, called David, but no kinsman of his. He was a Fife man, son of Leslie of Pitcarly, and was afterwards created Lord Newark. He had also served in the Swedish army and had become Major-General. Both these men were personal friends of David Barclay.

A somewhat strange welcome awaited David and the Scots officers with him, who had given up their posts in the Swedish army, and hastened home at the call of their country. Directly they reached the coast of Yorkshire in May 1639, they were attacked by a hostile force, who took from them much of their military gear and carried them off to Newcastle, where they were detained twenty days, and thence to London for three months, as prisoners of war.

This hostile force was most probably a privateer or "pirat" vessel, of which many were manned by Royalists living near the coasts, and haunted the seas near the ports to waylay incoming ships bearing munitions of war. The company of Scottish officers returning to take part in the Rebellion would be a rich prize, and their "saidles and pistoles" and so forth, most welcome booty to the impoverished Cavaliers.

6

HISTORY OF THE BARCLAY FAMILY

The following petition was sent to King Charles, on September 28th, 1641 :

COLONEL DAVID BARCLAY, 1610–1686, Urie I.

" Laig Lotenant Colonell J Barclay, Lt Coll J Stewart, Robert Graem, J Urry, David Barclay.

1641.

" Wee officers of Fortune within the countrie are forced now at last by reason of our great necessitie to have recourse unto y^r Majestie, after so many petitions given in to severall Com^{tees} appointed to that end, but no course as yet being taken for our satisfaction, we are necessitat to show our extreme want unto y^r sacred Majestie."

Acta Parl. Scot. V, p. 674.

This appears to have been only one of several appeals, and is followed by a more detailed account on October 7th, addressed this time to the Committee of Estates (Scottish Parliament).

" Supplication be these officers of War, imprisoned at Newcastle.

" My Lords and others of the Committee of the Estates of Parliament vnto y^r Lordships so humblie meanes and shawis [shows]

Acta Parl. Scot. Vol. v, p. 708.

" Wee your servitors vnder subscryving [under subscribing] That whereas after long and great expenses in comeing from Germanie to O^r native Kingdome in May 1639 yeiris, wee were takin prisoneris upon the coist of England neir to Flamburro heid, Quhair we left the maist part of or gudes, saidles [saddles], pistoles, and other armes. And thairefter to Newcastle, quhair wee remained twentie days upon our owne charges. And from thence carried clois [close] prissoniers to London. And their were detained neir for the space of three mo upon our own chairges, paying fees of the severall prissones. And all other expensis to our utter loss. We humblie thairfor beseek [beseech] your Lo: to tak our foresaid lois to your consideracon. That we may be repayed and yor Lordships anser most humblie wee attend."

Among eighteen signatures appear those of " David Barclay, Lt Colonell," and " Alexander Barclay Lt Coll."

1641.

The hostilities which broke out between the King and the Covenanters in 1639, on the question of Episcopacy, were at first known as " the Bishops War."

1639.

Charles resolved to coerce his rebellious subjects by an English army, and his plan was to advance to the Border, with

COLONEL
DAVID
BARCLAY,
1610–1686,
Urie I.
Hamilton and Huntly combining to attack the Scots in the rear. The Marquis of Hamilton, a weak, self-seeking courtier, had been appointed a special Commissioner to Scotland to deal with the malcontents, and George Gordon, second Marquis of Huntly, with the powerful and numerous Gordon clan at his back, was a valuable though somewhat independent ally.

The King soon found that his " pressed men " made a poor fight against the Scottish army, who had been well drilled and trained by Alexander Leslie. The Covenanters bore on their colours in gold letters " For Christ's Crown and Covenant " with the Royal Arms, maintaining that though against the King's policy, they still supported the Monarchy.

See Part II,
p. 248.
Both parties began ingloriously with a flight of the Covenanters before Huntly, called in derision " The trot of Turriff," and a stampede of Royalist Highlanders at Megray Hill. More serious fighting followed, and Montrose gained a victory at Brig o' Dee, which he consolidated by the occupation of the "prelatic" city of Aberdeen in the Covenanting interest.

The King found that his men would not stand fire, and it was useless to continue the campaign, so, on June 18th, 1639, he signed the Treaty of Berwick, by which it was agreed that the civil and religious grievances of Scotland should be settled by a Free Parliament and Assembly.

When the Assembly met, they declared once more for the abolition of Episcopacy, whereupon Charles broke his word, withdrew his promise, and once more resolved on War.

Scotland then became divided into three great parties— the uncompromising Royalists, the equally extreme Covenanters, of whom the Duke of Argyll had constituted himself leader, and the Moderate Party, under Montrose, with whom David Barclay identified himself.

1640.   For many years the people had submitted to the authority of the priesthood, without protest, but the resistance of the Scots to Laud's Service Book was the spark that fired the train, and as the King persisted in upholding it, all Scotland Colonel David Barclay, 1610-1686, Urie I. fell away from their obedience. The army, under Alexander Leslie, invaded England, crossing the Tweed at Coldstream, his Lowlanders in hodden-grey with blue caps, and his High-landers in their ragged plaids and home-dyed orange-coloured kilts, with bows and arrows, and defeated the English troops August 28, 1640. at Newburn. After which Leslie occupied Northumberland and Durham.

Charles entered into negotiations with him, and promised to leave those counties in the hands of the Scots as a security for the payment of £850 a day, which the King had to promise, to pay the troops until a permanent settlement was effected. This was at last arranged in 1641, and the Scots 1641. army then returned home.

Sir Robert Gordon says: "The Scots armie having stayed Gen. of Earls of Suther-landGordon, p. 508. in England for the space of twelf months, they returned into Scotland with great honour and commendation, to the eternal glory of this nation, having settled religion and liberties to their own content, and also assisted England against the practice of the popish and prelatical faction, having at the time of their being abroad (as an English writter sayeth) behaved themselves ' rather like saints than soldiers.'"

So the discipline of General Leslie carried on the traditions of Gustavus Adolphus, and we may assume that the Scots officers who had returned with David Barclay were mainly responsible for this testimony.

In 1641 Montrose became dissatisfied with the proceedings 1641 of the Covenanting leaders, and resented the preference they showed to the Marquis of Argyll. Also, the Acts passed by the Edinburgh Parliament in that year, which substituted Presbyterian for Episcopal forms of worship, and con-stituted Church government by Burghs instead of Bishops, had been approved and ratified by the King. It seemed that Charles was prepared to act in a constitutional manner; so Montrose gradually became alienated from the Covenanters and ultimately espoused the Royalist cause.

This came as a great blow to the Moderate Party, which

COLONEL
DAVID
BARCLAY,
1610–1686,
Urie I.

was now led by the Earl Marischal, Marr, Southesk, Seaforth and Perth. David Barclay remained unshaken in his allegiance, though he must deeply have regretted the loss of his gallant leader.

Although David Barclay's personal records have unfortunately not been preserved, there are abundant proofs of his active service in the archives of the Scottish Army.

Acta Parl.
Scot. (1644),
Vol. vi, pp.
66–198;
(1645), pp.
134, 366-492;
(1646), p.
628; (1647),
pp. 684, 687.

In "Parliamentary Proceedings" between the years 1641 and 1648, a large number of military orders are recorded, relating to movements of troops, pay of soldiers, promotion of officers, and alteration and remodelling of the Army under Cromwell's system, which are full of references to David Barclay and his kinsmen.

He shared the difficulties of the officers in the matter of the payment of the troops, when the subsidy promised by the King failed to materialise, but he received later substantial sums in reimbursement of the money he had personally advanced when the New Model was organised in 1647.

The Committees of War for the Shires appointed in 1645 contain many names of the Barclay family.

David Barclay's name appears in honourable mention more than once while he served with Lord Montgomerie's regiment

1641–1648.

Acta Parl.
Scot. Vol. vi
(1), pp. 684-5.

of " Hors." In the reorganisation of the forces to form Cromwell's New Model Army, Barclay's " Dragowners " (Dragoons) are often referred to.

When the Parliament made fair promises of repayment in December 1645, their communication was addressed to the Earl of Crawford, " to write to Colonell David Barclay."

The Army
and the
Covenant
(1644-5),
p. xxx
(Intro) and
p. 168.

Lord Montgomerie's regiment of horse is mentioned as having been engaged at Philiphaugh in 1645, and as having been represented at the muster at Newark in January 1646, when Colonel Barclay's troop is described as having been " formed in Scotland."

It was also engaged in the siege of Newcastle in 1644, and, after Philiphaugh, was sent to " lie in Aberdeenshire," while there are numerous entries relating to technical and responsible services entrusted to Major (afterwards Colonel) David Barclay.

He was appointed " Root-master " to the regiment on January 9th, 1647. These officers appeared to hold the equivalent rank of colonels of foot and were nominated by the Committee of Estates.

His grandson, in his Memoirs, frequently refers to a note-book in Colonel David's own handwriting, which related to this period, but which, it is greatly to be regretted, has not been preserved.

The Civil War in England, between the King and the Parliament, broke out when Charles I raised the Royal Standard at Nottingham on August 23rd, 1642, and the campaign opened favourably for the Royalists at the battle of Edgehill.

After many varying fortunes, and a brilliant offensive by Montrose, now of course on the Royalist side, the Covenanters under General Leslie and General Fairfax besieged Newcastle and York, and threatened the north of England.

In both these sieges Lord Montgomerie's regiment was engaged, and Major David Barclay's name again appears in connection with delivery of arms for the regiment.

Montrose was now north of the Border, and the Marquis of Huntly was conducting a somewhat aimless rising in the Lochaber country. The Leslies were recalled from England to deal with the situation, and the following order was issued to the Scottish Army :—

" Edinburgh, 16th April 1644.

" Commn. to Earl Marischal to command the hors in the forces to be sent for suppression of rebellion of Marquis of Huntlie and his adherents in the North.

" The Marquis of Argylle to be Chief Commander of the whole forces of hors and foote to be so employed (w. consent of Earl of Callender commander in chief of all hors and foote in Kingdom).

" A Committee to be appointed ' to go allongis with the forces. These personis or any seven of the saide to be a Committee of the robales [rebels] to go towards the north, headed by the Earls of

Margin notes:

COLONEL DAVID BARCLAY, 1610–1686, Urie I.

Acta Parl. Scot. Vol. vi (1), p. 673. 1641–1648. Genealogical Account, p. 32.

1642.

Feb. 1644.

Acta Parl. Scot. vi (1), p. 90.

1644.

COLONEL
DAVID
BARCLAY,
1610–1686,
Urie I.

Murray and Sinclair, including the Lairds of Penmure, Morphie, Innes, Johnstoun, Barclay, and many more names.' "

It is not quite clear which Barclay is meant here, though David Barclay was certainly in command of his troop of horse in this expedition, and it may have been his kinsman, Sir David Barclay of Collairnie (XII).

Meanwhile things were not going well for the King in England, and on July 2nd was fought the battle of Marston Moor, where the Parliamentary Army, with Cromwell and his Ironsides, won a decisive victory over the Royalist forces. The battle was largely decided by a magnificent charge of the Scots horse, under David Leslie, with whom rode the tried and seasoned troopers of David Barclay's command. They are said to have cut through Prince Rupert's Cavaliers, who were scattered " like a little dust," and so settled the fate of the day. The King's army was hopelessly defeated, and the whole of the north of England fell into the hands of " the godly party."

Cromwell's resolution to reorganise the military forces opposed to the King had a direct bearing on the fortunes of the war at this time. He forced the New Model Ordinance on the Parliament, and by it the various armies were formed into a single whole, as a thoroughly professional and permanent body, under uniform command, stern discipline, and with regular pay, for which new taxes were imposed.

The officers were expected to sign the Covenant, and precedence was given where possible, to men of strict Puritan views. The Army thus formed soon became a practically irresistible machine, and among the first results the Parliament was obliged to pay their long overdue arrears to the soldiers in Ireland, for on September 13th, 1644, in the Calendar of the Proceedings of the Committee for Compounding with Delinquents, 1643-1669, we find this entry :—

" Declaration by the Estates of Parliament of Scotland of the receipt by their Commissaries in London, Robert Barclay [Collairnie

12

XII] and John Campbell, from the Committee of Goldsmith's Hall, of the balance in full of £30,000, due to the Scots army in Ireland, . . . sent by ships in chests." COLONEL DAVID BARCLAY, 1610–1686, Urie I.

And again on May 6th, 1645, by request of Robert Barclay, a further sum of £10,000 and in July 1645, £9,500 is sent, " by persons appointed to carry it " for the Scottish army in Ireland.

The army in Scotland and England had reason to hope that their bill would also be met, though it was not for another two years that " Leven's treasure carts rolled over the Tweed," bringing the necessary funds after the surrender of the King.

Montrose had been offered the post of Captain-General and Viceroy of Scotland by King Charles, but had declined it, preferring to be called the King's Lieutenant-General, and leaving the higher sounding title to the King's nephew, Prince Maurice, son of the Elector Palatine. 1644-5.

In September 1644, with a force of only 3,000 men, and no cavalry, Montrose swept the Covenanters before him at Tippermuir, and the city of Perth surrendered. After this he marched to Aberdeen and gained a second victory there, followed by a pitiless massacre of the defenceless townsmen. He then led the Clan Macdonald into the Campbell country, where they fought fiercely with their hereditary foes, and, joining with the great Gordon Clan under the Marquis of Huntly, he invaded the Eastern Lowlands and captured Dundee.

Sir Robert Gordon wrote :—

" No man being able to withstand him, Montrose crossed the river Dee, and marched to Stonehyve [Stonehaven] which he caused burne, together with Cowie, Fetteroso, and divers other landes belonging to the Earle Marischal, because he refused to joyne with him." Gen. of Earles of Sutherland Gordon, p. 522.

We read also :—

" His [the Earl Marischal] girnelles [meal granaries] sic as were left oncareit to Urie, were pillaged, with the Barronies of Trubles Scotland, Spalding.

13

COLONEL
DAVID
BARCLAY,
1610–1686,
Urie I.
1645.

Dunnotta and Fetteroso, and [Montrose] then merches to Urie," where " he fyres the place, burnis alle to the voltis [roofs] and haill lauche bigging, cornes and barn-yardis, and plunderis the haill grund."

Included in these lands thus devastated was the estate of Urie, soon to become the property of Colonel David Barclay.

Montrose's dashing and successful advance, darkened only by the siege and ruthless sack of Aberdeen which has been described as the only blot on his fair fame, and culminating with his victory at Kilsythe in August, 1645, very nearly recovered the whole of Scotland for the King. But his Highland allies deserted him to take back their booty to their native glens, after their wont, and a rapid movement by the Covenanting army, under David Leslie, down the Vale of Gala, resulted in his being taken by surprise, with but 500 Irish Foot, and about 1,200 cavalry from the Border country. On September 12th, 1645, Montrose found himself compelled to stand and give battle at Philiphaugh, " on the long green meadow that lies beside Ettrick water."

In this engagement, David Barclay had the grief of losing his youngest brother James, who was killed serving as Captain in his Troop of Horse, which rode with Major Lord Middleton's Regiment, and is specially mentioned in despatches.

1645.

David Leslie's army numbered 4,000, and the Covenanters won a notable victory which finally decided the fate of the Royalist cause in Scotland. On June 14th, 1645, Charles I had been defeated at the battle of Naseby, but his followers continued the gallant but hopeless struggle until the news of the disaster at Philiphaugh reached them, and the King realised that with the failure of Montrose, his last hope of success had vanished.

Though triumphant in the field, the Covenanting Army was still in difficulties as to the payment of the troops, and the soldiers were becoming very impatient.

HISTORY OF THE BARCLAY FAMILY

COLONEL DAVID BARCLAY, 1610–1686, Urie I.

The Parliament sent fair promises, and on December 23rd, 1645, the following entry was made in the records :—

"The Estates on pet^n" from the town of Brechin order John, Lord Crawford, Prext [President] of Parliament to write to Colonel David Barclay, to whom and to his regiment 2 months maintenance of October and November are assigned, to forbear exacting payment, which is to be supplied by Parliament."

Acta Parl. Scot. Vol. vi (1), p. 492.

We have no record that this was done, and it would seem that payment was being exacted from the towns where the troops were billeted.

David Barclay had other duties besides his regular military routine, and was occasionally made responsible for the care of important prisoners.

On March 25th, 1646, a warrant was sent to the Constable of Edinburgh Castle

1646.

Supplementary Parliamentary papers, being Warrants of Parliament during the Interregnum, Found subsequently to the binding of the Parliamentary Warrants.

"for the delivery of Sir John Mure of Archindrane, and Sir Michael of Posso, to the keeping of Major David Barclay, until certain fines have been paid, and thereafter till security is given for their good behaviour.

"(Signed) Cassilis. P.T.D. Com :"

Orig. MSS. at Register House, Edinburgh.

Again on April 1st, 1646.

April 1.

"Warrant to David Barclay to apprehend and imprison James Murray of Romanno, Sir John Veitch of Danick, Robert Hunter of Polmood, Andrew Tweedie of Kingsdoors, William Govan of Cardrono, and William Johnstoun of Balmyre, until they pay their fynes, provided to the said David Barclay, for the use of Lord Montgomerie's Regiment.

"(Signed) Cassilis."

This gives another sidelight on the methods employed to support the cost of the Army.

April 29.

After Philiphaugh, the Royalist army of the West capitulated to Cromwell's general, Fairfax, and the King had to choose between flight and surrender. He chose the latter, and as Lord Leven (Alexander Leslie) was now again encamped at Newark, Notts, and had been created an Earl by Charles himself in order to placate the Covenanters, he decided to trust himself in his hands. He was received " with all honour and courtesy " by the old Field-Marshal, and was sent under honourable restraint to Newcastle.

In the next eight months, strenuous attempts were made to force Charles to accept the Covenant *in extenso*. He would not give way on the question of episcopal independence, both from personal conviction and hereditary instinct, and in the meanwhile the remnants of the Royalist party still continued to struggle with Fate, and David Leslie was despatched back to Scotland to deal with them. He shortly afterwards handed over this work to Lord Middleton, who appointed David Barclay as his second in command.

The first time that David Barclay is mentioned as having charge of an independent expedition is at this time, when we find him described as " Crowner " or Colonel of a Regiment of Horse, entrusted with the mission of punishing the Marquis of Huntly,* who had been keeping up a guerilla warfare, and had burnt Fraserburgh. Barclay encountered him in the neighbourhood of Banff, and defeated him with great slaughter. He retreated, closely pursued by Middleton and Barclay.

David Barclay was then sent to relieve the town of Inverness, besieged by the Earl of Seaforth and the Marquis of
Montrose. He forced them to raise the siege and retire. In their pursuit of the enemy, after relieving Inverness, Middleton burnt Montrose's own house, and so cut off his retreat in that direction.

The Marquis of Huntly, who was the chief landowner in those parts, had hitherto refused to support Montrose, but now wrote to say that as " Middleton and Barclay had begun
to oppress and ruin all the Gordon country," he would " joyne with him in putting an end to that business." But he advised him to leave Inverness, " as for the present he was

---

* The Genealogy erroneously speaks of the Earl of Crawford in this place. But he was a Covenanter until 1648, and the Marquis of Huntly is clearly meant.

forced to go and help his friends and tenants, that they were not altogether ruined and undone."

Montrose, thus deserted by Huntly, unwillingly retired, and had " confusedly " crossed the Ness before Middleton arrived there. Middleton sent David Barclay with a Regiment of Horse to pass the ford above the town. They presently dispersed Montrose's forces, and made him and Seaforth fly to the hills, " broke the bagadge," and took two cannon which had been sent to Montrose by the Queen. The followers took refuge in Chanrie of Rosse and in Seaforth's newly built castle at Fortrose.

By this time David Barclay had become full Colonel, but though honours and titles were freely bestowed on the victorious party, he cared nothing for them beyond his military promotion.

He besieged Fortrose for four days and compelled the surrender of the castle, together with the remainder of Montrose's ammunition. In those rough days no doubt the inmates of the castle trembled for their safety, but Colonel Barclay showed Lady Seaforth the utmost courtesy and consideration, and restored the castle to her at once " using her very discretely."

Meanwhile Huntly, seeing Aberdeen but lightly defended, attacked and sacked the city, taking about twenty prisoners, among whom was Colonel Harrie Barclay, son of John Barclay of Johnston.

About this time a deputation from the Estates, consisting of Lords Lanark, Callender and Balmarino, went to Lord Leven's camp at Newark, to hold a conference with the King, from which they returned with this letter to Montrose from Charles :—

" You must disband your forces and go to France, where you shall receive any further instructions. This at first may justly startle you, but I assure you that if, for the present, I should offer to do more for you I should not do so much."

Montrose (who was now on Speyside) called a council of his officers and laid the letter before them, but as Huntly and Sir Alexander Macdonald had received the same commands,

Margin notes:
Colonel David Barclay, 1610-1686, Urie I.

1646.

Gordon of Salleach.

May 19, 1646.

Clarendon State Papers, Vol. ii, p. 224.

there was nothing to be done but obey, and on June 2nd
Montrose replied : " I shall in all humility and obedience
endeavour to perform your Majestie's commands."

A truce was therefore concluded between him and Middleton, and towards the end of July, they met on the banks of the
Isla to arrange conditions of peace.

Middleton's terms were not severe. He granted an amnesty
to Montrose and all the Royalist leaders on condition that they
left the country in a ship to be provided by the Estates. The
ship was to sail from the town of Montrose, but hearing a
rumour of treachery, the Marquis, in disguise, boarded a
September, vessel bound for Bergen, in which several of his friends had
1646. sailed from Stonehaven.

While the Scottish army under Lord Leven lay at Newcastle in January 1647, they became hopeless of success with
the King, and being unable to bring him into Scotland in face
of the refusal of the General Assembly to receive a Sovereign
who would not swear to the Covenant, they accepted £400,000
in discharge of their claims, handed Charles over to a com-
1647. mission of the House, and marched back over the Border.

The Parliament then moved Charles to Holmby House, in
Northamptonshire, and General Lord Leven was enabled,
with the money received, to pay off the arrears due to the
Army.

Though Montrose had obeyed the King's orders, the
Marquis of Huntly still refused to disband his forces, his
excuse being that the King had acted under compulsion, and
Middleton and David Barclay were dispatched again to the
North to reduce him. In this they were entirely successful
and took possession of his two principal strongholds, Middleton becoming governor of the Castle of Bog of Gight (afterwards Castle Gordon) and Colonel Barclay of the Castle of
Strathbogie. So history reversed the friendship of previous
centuries between the Gordons and the Barclays.

Though Middleton was still employed on active warfare,
David Barclay, as governor of the Castle of Strathbogie,
found himself in a more settled position, and began to consider the question of a home of his own. Although he had

seen so much service, he was but in his thirty-seventh year, a fine, stately figure, with modest and courteous manners. He was no doubt received with civility by the gentry of the district, in spite of his appearance among them having been somewhat violent and uninvited, and he shortly became attracted by a young lady of the Gordon family, whose admiration for him overcame her wounded family pride. COLONEL DAVID BARCLAY, 1610–1686, Urie I.

On Christmas Day 1647 a contract of marriage was con- December, cluded between him and Katherine Gordon, daughter of Sir 1647. Robert Gordon, of Gordonstoun, younger son of Alexander, twelfth Earl of Sutherland, and his wife Lady Jean Gordon, daughter of George, fourth Earl of Huntly. Lady Jean had previously been the wife of James Hepburn, Earl of Bothwell.

Sir Robert Gordon, the first Knight Baronet of Scotland, was a man of great parts and honour. He was second cousin to King James VI, his grandmother having been Lady Helen Stewart, sister of Matthew fourth Earl of Lennox, the father of the ill-fated Darnley. He was much esteemed at Court, was Vice-Chamberlain of Scotland, Privy Councillor and Gentleman of the Bedchamber both to King James and his son Charles I.

Though his forces had recently devastated the Gordon country and defeated their " Chief," it is interesting to note that Lord Middleton was an honoured guest at the wedding, and wrote his name as one of the " cautioners " and " sureties " in the contract of marriage. This document states that the Colonel was obliged to bestow for jointure to the said Katherine Gordon about five thousand pounds sterling to be settled by the advice of both their fathers. As David's father's estate was almost all sold off or embarrassed, he contracted with the Earl Marischal for the property of Urie. Baron Court, The estate was properly styled " Urie and Monquich," Book of Urie " situated in the county of Kincardineshire, and in the p. xlx. Parish of Fetteroso, and in the vicinity of Stonehaven, the County Town."

Robert Barclay says in his Memoirs that :—

" The half of the estate happening to be mortgaged, till that was cleared, David Barclay unluckily laid out the money in securities in

COLONEL
DAVID
BARCLAY,
1610–1686,
Urie I.
Ireland, and the rest at interest. The persons he trusted almost all became insolvent, so he was obliged to rest satisfied with the Manor Place, and only the half of the Barony."

The estate was not actually erected into a free barony until 1679.

It may be asked why Colonel David Barclay, returning from Germany with sufficient capital to buy an estate, did not repurchase the old family property of Mathers, just at that moment struggling under the financial difficulties which resulted in its sale. But it had practically all been parted Part II,
p. 198. with in small lots, under the agency of that John Barclay (Johnston III) to whom we find Colonel David writing with such severity on the occasion of his father's funeral. Although the house itself was not sold until 1651, there was not enough left of the land to make it a profitable purchase.

1648. It is generally accepted by the family that when the Earl Marischal's estates were ravaged by Montrose in 1645, his own castle at Fetteroso was plundered and burnt, so that he was left in dire straits for funds. Colonel Barclay lent him money, and by way of security was " infeft " or made heir to the estate of Urie.

BB. 37, 59. This is corroborated by the existence of two documents at Bury Hill, of which one is a " Summons of poinding and apprising in Implement of Contract " owing to failure to pay the sum agreed to be paid. The summons or writ is issued by " Colonel Barclay of Urie, lawful son of David Barclay of Mathers (XI), and Catherine Gordon his wife," and sets forth that a contract dated 29 July, 1648, was entered into between them and " William Earl Marshall, Lord Keith and Altyre," under which the sum of 23,000 merks Scots was " borrowed by the said William Earl Marshall from the said Colonel David Barclay and Catherine Gordon, and that the said William Earl Marshall should convey his lands to them and the longest liver of them and their lawful heirs, whom failing, to Colonel David Barclay's nearest lawful Heir, his lands of Urie, with Manor House, salmon fishing in the water of Cowie, the lands of Magray, Woodhead, Powbair, Balnagight 1646. and Glithnow, said lands within the parish of Fetteroso and

Sheriffdom of Kincardine, and should pay to the same Colonel David Barclay and Catherine Gordon his wife the sum of 1,840 merks yearly, together with the sum of 200 merks as expenses." COLONEL DAVID BARCLAY, 1610–1686, Urie I.

This summons or writ was served because of the failure of William Earl Marischal to repay the 23,000 merks. Dated 29 July, 1652.

On the same day a second summons is issued. " Summons of poinding and apprising issued by Colonel David Barclay of Urie and Katherine Gordon his wife, narrating that by contract dated 29 July 1648, between William Earl Marshall on the one part, and the said Colonel David Barclay of Urie and Katherine Gordon his wife, on the other part, of which the sum of 23,000 merks was borrowed by the said William Earl Marischall, and he conveyed in security the Lands mentioned in BB. 37. No. 59." Dated 29 July, 1652.

[This is only a portion of the summons, but it makes clear that William Earl Marischal failed to repay the sum of 23,000 merks.]

Another fragment of an inhibition issued by Colonel David Barclay of Urie against "William Earl Marshal, Principal, and John Keith of Quhitrigen, as Cautioners," interdicting them from selling, alienating, or disponing certain lands, particulars of which are narrated in the missing portion, is also dated July 29th, 1652. 1648.

There are also in existence at Bury Hill several deeds and summonses to prevent tenants from selling or alienating their lands, and to explain that the rents therefrom are now due to Colonel Barclay instead of to the Earl Marischal. It is not advisable to quote these in full, though they are interesting for their archaic wording. The originals are all at Bury Hill, Dorking. There are also " Summons' " directed to the Earl Marischal himself, and his representatives and cautioners, warning them of the consequences of selling lands, which he seems disposed to do, in order to pay the yearly rent due to the Colonel. But these appear to be purely formal documents, and their lifelong friendship does not seem to have been impaired thereby. The only serious B.B. 38–39 40, 34–42, 25.

threat is one addressed to Sir Alexander Irving of Drum, who is warned that he will be " put to the Horn " for a similar offence.

No doubt the many absences of the Colonel left his tenants to do pretty much what they pleased, and as all the unlucky Royalist gentry were at their wits' end to make both ends meet, they were not over scrupulous as to their methods of raising money.

The Colonel does not appear to have foreclosed this mortgage for some years, probably out of consideration for his old friend, though he was practically the owner of the property, while it was only technically in the Earl Marischal's possession.

This made it the more unjust that his claim as a creditor should have been put aside on a mere legal quibble, as will be seen.

The details of negotiations entered into by Colonel David Barclay with William, seventh Earl Marischal, for the purchase of the estate and lands of Urie, will be of interest here.

He concluded the purchase on his own wedding day, January 26th, 1648, though, unfortunately for him, the final settlement was not signed until the following July, which caused a most serious complication and delay in his obtaining possession.

He is described in the deed as " being designed in all the conveyances Colonel David Barclay of Mathers, as he is also in his own marriage contract dated at Bog of Gight (now Castle Gordon) and Gordonstoun, and likewise in his sister Anne's contract of marriage with her last husband, Strachan afterwards Bishop of Brechin, when her father, David Barclay of Mathers, and her brother, Colonel David Barclay, were ' consenters ' in 1649."

The Earl Marischal had bought the property from the Earl of Errol, in 1647 " for 2,000 merkes for ilk chalder of victual, and ilk hundreth merkes of silver " (equalling about £3,000 sterling).

He redeemed the wadset (mortgage) on the lands of Urie, and resold them in the following year to Colonel David

Barclay, with a considerable part of his estates in the adjoining parish of Dunnottar.

The property had been in the possession of the " gryte Covenanter " John Forbes, when it had been so ruthlessly plundered by the Royalist troops under Montrose. It is said that the Earl Marischal was a spectator of the destruction of his castle of Fetteroso from the tower of Dunnottar, but found small comfort in the pious consolations offered him by the minister of the parish on that occasion.

The great Covenanter, doubtless finding the lands of small value after the passing of the Royalist troops, left the country, and the property reverted to the over-lord, the Earl Marischal.

When David Barclay began to consider its purchase with the view of replacing his old family estate of Mathers, the place must have been practically a wilderness. Farms, cottages and buildings had been levelled to the ground. Growing crops had been ruthlessly trampled, and stores of hay and corn burned in their barns and granaries. Any of the wretched peasantry who had escaped the savagery of the soldiers, and crept back to their ruined homes, had had no spirit to till or plant the land, beyond the few roods necessary for their maintenance and that of their few sheep, or half-starved goats or cattle.

Plantations had been cut down, and where the rotting trunks of trees had fallen into the stream, they had dammed it so that it had spread into swamps, with here and there huddles of whitening bones of drowned beasts. The whole aspect of the country was deplorable, and may well have seemed hopeless.

But Colonel Barclay looked with a discerning eye on the gently undulating ground, the " little hills " from which the shire of the Mearns derived its name, the sunny southern slopes where the young saplings were already beginning to spring again, the Cowie River with its fresh and salt water, and excellent salmon and trout fishing. We may conclude from the many references to the rights, that both the Colonel and his son were keen fishermen. The easy approach to the

1648.

seaport of Stonehaven was also of great importance in those days, when the roads were but deeply furrowed tracks, quagmires in winter, and high ridges of baked clay with deep ruts between in summer, all the more impassable now for the military operations during the Civil War, when troops of horse and clumsy heavy camp wagons had cut them up. It was said that a regiment of Royalist Horse had been so hopelessly bogged in one of these so-called roads that they had been taken prisoners without striking a blow.

Sea transport was of the utmost value, which David thoroughly realised. He inspected the blackened rafters of the old house of the Hayes, which had been burnt down by Montrose, but considered a new site, facing southwards towards the bay which was less than two miles distant, and sheltered from the keen north winds by the remains of a belt of fir trees. It stood on the top of a steep bank, sloping down to a burn which still runs with musical chatter, though doubtless in less volume. The price was reasonable, with consideration of the state of the land, and as he rode in his weather-stained buff coat and great horseman's boots over the wide, neglected fields, where the only signs of life were the gliding curlew and the plover circling overhead, and planned how to clear and restore the land, he may well have said to himself : " Here will I build my home. Here shall be the abiding place of my race."

David Barclay's decisions, once made, were not easily overset.

It has always seemed perplexing that Colonel Barclay, who had left Scotland as a lad and joined the Swedish Army as a soldier of fortune with probably little or nothing besides his pay, had returned home in a position to purchase the

Urie Estate, besides building the house, and also to be able to settle so large a sum on his wife. He was always open-handed. An acknowledgment of a loan to Sir John Innes of " Two thousand merkes guid and usuall money of Scotland in friendlie borrowing," on January 28th, 1648, together with a list of names of creditors to whom he had advanced sums of varying amounts, show that not only was he a man of substantial financial position, but that his friends and neighbours knew where to apply when they were in need of help.

The matter may be explained by reference to the terms of service at that time under Gustavus Adolphus. Anton Gindeley, in his *History of the Thirty Years' War*, says :

"Adam von Waldstein, incorrectly called Wallenstein, gave splendid rewards on behalf of the Emperor Ferdinand, to those who distinguished themselves at Lützen and elsewhere. Several warriors received large sums of money, and one a Memorial Estate."

What Ferdinand could do Gustavus was not likely to fail in, and he was in a position to be generous, as France, which was disturbed by the territorial ambitions of the Emperor of Austria, gave him considerable financial assistance. Gustavus undertook to enter Germany with an army to check the Austrian advance, if Louis would support him to the extent of 3,000,000 thalers annually. The amount was finally fixed at 1,000,000 francs a year, and the Swedish Army invaded Germany on May 20th, 1630, just after David Barclay had joined it.

Chapman says, "If the temptation of booty added, as doubtless it did, a spur to the valour of the soldier, the Imperial troops fighting against the Swedes could have little of this incentive, whereas to urge on the Swedish Army to conquer, they had before them camps filled with all manner of wealth, and armies rich with the spoils of Germany."

And further, in Sir James Spence's account, written in 1667, we read :

"In the Swedish Army there were of colonels and other inferior officers above the rank of a sergeant, at that time, of English and Scottish 500 and more. No portion of the King's troops were more conspicuous for their zeal and fidelity, and no portion received more signal testimonies of the approbation and confidence of their illustrious Chief."

We can, therefore, assume that David Barclay accepted his share of the material benefits conferred by the generous Gustavus on those who, like David himself, as described

COLONEL DAVID BARCLAY, 1610–1686, Urie I.

Anton Gindeley, The Thirty Years' War, Vol. ii, p. 157.

Life of Gustavus Adolphus, Chapman, p. 200.

Spence's Life of Gustavus Adolphus.

III.—D

Colonel
David
Barclay
1610–1686,
Urie I.
on his memorial stone, " rose high in the favour of the King."

Though the Colonel had been in occupation of Strathbogie for some time, his formal occupation was not " ordained " until June, 1648, as follows :

"Octavi Junii 1648

Acta Parl.
Scot.
Caroli I,
Vol. vi,
p. 98.
" Item, the parliament ordaines that the charge of the hous of Bog of Geight be continewed with Major-General Middletone. And do thereby continew the same with him. And allowes 39 sojours and a Lewtenant keep^t p^r in. And that Colonell David Barckley have the chairge of the hous of Strathbogie, and allowis 50 souldiore [soldiers] and a Captain to be keep^t pr in, (both upon the publicke charge) And ordaines the rest of the soldiores in these two houses to goe to their Regimentis.

" And the Estates declairis this article and ordinance above written, to be alwayes but without prejudice to any manis rightes to the forseidis [aforesaid] houses *rexue prout de fine.*"

When David Barclay gave up the governorship of Strathbogie Castle, he returned to live at his wife's home, Gordonstoun, with her parents, and there his son Robert, afterwards famous as the Apologist for the Quakers, was born in 1648. Colonel David's wife, who was known as " The White Rose of Gordonstoun," was greatly loved and respected, and her memory was long treasured in the country-side. In the unsettled state of the country it was doubtless well for her to have the protection and shelter of her father's roof, and Gordonstoun was a real mediæval stronghold, with walls eight feet thick, and full of secret passages and hidden staircases. It was a gloomy enough building seen from the outside, with small windows, high pitched roofs, and " pepper-pot " turrets, but it stood in a sheltered hollow, looking towards the blue ranges of the Grampian Hills, and David spent much of his free time there in his later years, while his children were growing up.

His wife bore him three sons, Robert, John, and David, and two daughters, Lucy and Jean. David and Lucy died unmarried, Jean married Sir Euan Cameron of Lochiel, to whom she bore eight children. John married in East New Jersey, and left children.

HISTORY OF THE BARCLAY FAMILY

Public events were now moving rapidly, and David Barclay Colonel David Barclay, 1610–1686, Urie I. was not long to be left to enjoy the peace he had hoped for, and so well earned.

When, in 1647, King Charles had been sent to Holmby House, under charge of the Parliament, Cromwell sent a force of cavalry under Cornet Joyce there, to secure the King's person for the Army. It was a high-handed and illegal proceeding, and the story is well known how, when the King asked to see the warrant for his arrest, the officer in charge merely pointed to the soldiers. Charles observed drily that the warrant was written in too legible characters to be misunderstood, and accompanied his captors without protest.

The Parliament was very angry at his abduction and, still being at odds with the soldiers, prepared to resist them by force, counting on the Scots Army and the London trainbands for support.

But the " New Model " Army, under Cromwell, marched up to London, occupied the capital, and had both King and Commons at their mercy.

The military leaders, however, still hoped to win Charles, and offered him better terms than the Presbyterians had suggested. He was offered freedom to worship in his own way, provided he allowed similar freedom to others. He rejected their offers, and escaped to the Isle of Wight, where, however, he was recaptured and imprisoned in Carisbrooke Castle. 1648.

Here he secretly "engaged" with Commissioners sent from London to look after Scottish affairs and promised to be the Covenanted Monarch of a Presbyterian people. At the same time he rejected four Bills sent to him by Parliament, whereupon they passed a vote of " No Addresses," in which they solemnly renounced any further negotiations with him.

The famous " Engagement " was meanwhile accepted and ratified by the Moderate Party in Scotland, who thereupon commissioned an army to support the King.

Sir Robert Gordon thus describes the position :

" In Merch one thousand six fourty eight, there was a parlament Genealogy of the Earles of Sutherland, Gordon, pp. 508–9. held at Edinburgh. . . . It was then concluded that a warr should be undertaken against the parlament of England, for relief of our

27

COLONEL
DAVID
BARCLAY,
1610–1686,
Urie I.
King. . . . Great armies of hors and foote were raised out of all the Shyres, and besydes five months maintenance was imposed upon this nation, ane insupportable burden. . . . This was mightilie opposed by the Church. . . . so that State and Church now directlie stood opposed to each other.

1648.
"This moved manie to be slow in advancing these levies . . . and many Commanders of the former Armie refused charges at this tyme, including the Earl of Sutherland, General Leslie (Leven), Lt General Leslie, and others."

Had Lord Leven, that great soldier and most experienced general, accepted the post of Commander-in-Chief, the history of England might have been changed ; but "Duke Hamilton" was made General, and the Earl of Callendar Lieutenant-General of the Horse, and the army marched into England in July, 1648.

Sir Robert Gordon continues :

"Att this Parlament the whole kingdome of Scotland for hors and foote, was devided among severall Colonels ; every one had his own particular devision for his regiment.

"Collonell David Barclay (Att this tyme a Colonell of Hors) hade his devision for uplifting [recruiting] his hors-men in Sutherland, Cateynes [Caithness] and a part of Rosse."

Thus David Barclay had to leave his newly-married wife and his newly-acquired estate and turn his attention to the administration and pacification of this large district, which must have exercised his experience and organising powers to the full.

1648.
In July his responsibilities were increased, for there was a rumour that the Prince of Wales was coming to Scotland from Holland, and disturbances might be expected in consequence.

"A verie just and impartial historian " says : " So there was a new leavie of hors in this kingdome, to the number of fifteen hundred, pretended to be raised to guard the Prince's person . . . and also pretendyn that these should keep our borders from incursions, whilst our armie [conducted by Duke Hamilton] was marching into England. But in effect these hors were appointed to stay at home, to keep this Kingdome from any stur in the Duke's absence.

" These hors were devided amongst three commanders.

28

The Earl of Lanark [Duke Hamilton's brother] was to have Colonel David Barclay, 1610–1686, Urie I. five hundredth, Collonell David Barclay was to have the command of five hundredth, and the Laird of Garthland was to have five hundredth."

" Colonell Barclay his locality was appointed to be north-ward from Saint Johnstoun to Dungesby."

" Which Commission," adds Sir Robert Gordon, " those three Commanders executed with vigour and fidelitie." Gen. of Earles of Sutherland, p. 543.

So began the second Civil War in 1648. On the approach of this large and menacing Scots force in aid of the King, the 1648. English Parliament and the Army agreed to sink their dif-ferences and unite to meet the common danger.

The Royalist Party found it impossible to excite fresh enthusiasm among the war-weary country folk, and could only depend on the Scots. Unfortunately, the Scottish coun-cils were divided. Churchmen and Presbyterians could not work together, and no common plan or unity of purpose existed among them. However, they joined with the northern insurgents in England and advanced in considerable force as far as Preston. But here Cromwell, with his New Model August 17, 1648, Preston. veterans, met and utterly defeated them. A desperate remnant held out a little longer, but eventually the leaders, including the Duke of Hamilton, were all taken and executed, and the triumphant soldiers believed that the special Pro-vidence of God was indeed with them.

When this attempt had completely failed, the eight Com-missioners for Scotland met and drew up an agreement which directly affected David Barclay's fortunes as, though he had not taken up arms in the " Engagement," he had been employed in " a publict place of trust " and as such rendered himself liable to penalty.

Articles agreed upon by the Commissioners appointed by the noblemen, gentlemen, and burgesses who protested against the late " Engagement " :—

" It is agreed that for easing the burdens of the Kingdome, and to 1648. prevent famine and desolation, all the forces under the respective Thurloe commands of the Earls of Crawford and Lanerk, George Monro, and Papers, Vol. i, p. 99, all forces having commission from any of the Committee of Estates, Sept. 27.

that were for the Engagement, and all others whom they can stop or lett, whether in the fields or garrisones of Berwicke and Carleil [Carlisle] or other garrisones within this kingdome, on this syde of Tay, be disbanded betwixt [now] and the first of October next, and that none of them be seene after the said day in troupes, companies, or regiments. . . .

" That to prevent the imminent danger to religion, and a quarell with our neighbour nation, in the mean tyme until the meeting of a Parliament, that all such as have been employed in publict place or trust, and have been accessory to the late Engagement, shall forbear the exercise of their places, and not come to the Committee of Estates, to the end the Committee of Estates may only consist of such members of Parliament, as dis-assented from and protested in Parliament against the said Engagement.

" Subscribed at Edinburgh 27 Sept 1648."

The reply to this was :

" We agree to the above written Articles, and doe declare that most of our garrisones this syde Tay shall be disbanded betwixt [this day] and the 1st October next to come, and all of these on the other side of Tay, betwixt [this day] and the 10th day of the said month.
    " W. Keith.   J. Hamilton.   · J. Lyone.   J. Borth.
" Subscribed at Stirling the 27th day of September 1648."

The defeat and imprisonment of Duke Hamilton, followed by his execution, and Cromwell's coming to Scotland after the battle of Preston, " gave a turn and new face to all the affairs
there," says Robert Barclay (Urie III), " for all those who gave assistance, or by any manner of way favoured the Engagement, were by Oliver's desire, turned out of all their posts, civil and military, and among others Colonel David Barclay ran the same fate, having his Regiment either broke or taken from him, and was never after that engaged in the military, which gives me an opportunity of contradicting as notoriously false, a piece of low, ignorant, as well as impotent malice, viz., a report that the Colonel served under Cromwell against the King, whereas it was at Oliver's instance for that very service that he was turned out of his Regiment."

David Barclay received his dismissal not only from his office but also from his Regiment, which must have been a serious blow to him. His grandson adds : " Neither had he afterwards any Command in the Army, which he thus lost for his loyalty in joyning with those who designed to free their distressed Sovereign."

The year 1648 was a momentous one for David Barclay, but notwithstanding all his political business, and the vexations and disappointments consequent upon his loss of office, he never lost sight of the religious questions that guided his life. " In the welter of ecclesiastical dogma at this time, earnest men were striving to fix standards to satisfy the uneasy minds of countless seekers after truth. But there were various schismatic forces at work within the Protestant camp. The sacerdotalism of Archbishop Laud had roused the spirit of opposition on both sides of the Tweed, and many new sects sprang to life. The Assembly of Divines at Westminster had, in 1645, drawn up the Confession of Faith, the longer and shorter Catechisms, the Directories for worship, and the form of Presbyterian Church Government." David Barclay, in common with many other thinkers, felt they did not satisfy their aspirations nor answer their questions. They asked for bread, and he felt these official utterances were but a stony substitute.

But the tenets of a new sect, called in derision Quakers, appeared to satisfy most of David Barclay's ideals, and when George Fox began his ministry in this year he heard him preach, and read and thought much on the subject. George Fox wrote in his Journal, " Justice Bennett of Derby was the first to call us Quakers, because I bade him quake and tremble at the Word of the Lord."

It seemed to David Barclay that the practice and principles of these people " were most agreeable to the teaching of Jesus Christ, and that if He hath followers, disciples, or a visible Church on earth, these must be they." Being himself a sincere and convinced Christian, he desired to join himself to a society of like-minded men, and weighed their conflicting claims " with the utmost anxiety and earnestness, studying closely the New Testament as the ultimate source of information as to the foundations of Christianity."

Meanwhile, great events had been taking place in England. When the second Civil War had come to its inglorious conclusion, Cromwell at last gave way to the insistent cry of the

Colonel David Barclay, 1610–1686, Urie I.

1648.

History of the Great Rebellion, Tout and Powell.

1648.

Gough's History of the Quakers.

Army, that Charles Stewart, " that man of blood," must be brought to justice. The Independent minority in the House of Commons were entirely under the domination of the soldiers, and after the expulsion of the Presbyterian members by Colonel Pride, in 1648, voted that a High Court of Justice should be set up to bring the King to trial. Every legal and constitutional obstacle was set aside, and Charles was condemned to death as a murderer and traitor to the Common-

wealth. On January 30th, 1649, he was beheaded at Whitehall.

" A treacherous, treasonable, and bloody act," wrote the chroniclers, and though the nation recoiled, aghast and horror-stricken, it was helpless under the iron rule of Oliver Cromwell.

In April 1649 Montrose made one more desperate effort to restore the Monarchy, and returned to Scotland with about 1,500 men. David Leslie met and defeated him with much slaughter, at Carbisdell, after which the great Marquis was apprehended, hiding in the mountains, and conveyed to Edinburgh, where he was barbarously executed on the charge of high treason, on May 21st, 1650.

David Barclay's grandson quotes from the manuscript he so constantly refers to " as wrote with the Collonell's own hand,

giveing account of his conduct, which I have by me," that " being rendered incapable of further service to my Prince in the Army, for having joyned Duke Hamilton," he lived quietly for several years at Gordonstoun.

The wording of this phrase would certainly suggest that the Colonel was at heart a Royalist, which indeed his actions go far to prove ; but it would seem that it was with him as with Montrose, and many others of the leaders in the Rebellion, that he was torn between his faith and his loyalty. His religious convictions, which inclined him strongly to Presbyterianism, and his dread of Episcopacy as a first step to " Popery " outweighed the personal devotion to " his Prince," though even so, as we shall see, his sympathy with the Royalist cause involved him in serious loss.

It was not until that cause was hopelessly defeated that he

threw in his lot with Cromwell, whose stern and fanatical religious views agreed in many points with his own, and whose statesmanlike conduct of affairs compelled his admiration.

In the meanwhile he proceeded with his own affairs, and entered into preliminary negotiations for taking possession of the estate of Urie.

Though the actual charter of the " enfeoffment " of the property to " Colonell David Barclay of Mathers, and to Katherine his spouse, of the lands of Ury " was signed on September 1st, 1649, and it would have seemed probable that he would devote these peaceful years to rebuilding the house and restoring the land, an alarming and serious obstacle prevented his taking final possession of the property.

William Keith, seventh Earl Marischal, the over-lord, had been prominent amongst the Covenanting leaders. He had raised a regiment from his estates and, as we have seen, his lands had been devastated by the Royalist troops in 1645.

But he had joined with the Duke of Hamilton in the ill-fated Engagement to rescue Charles from the English Army, and openly welcomed Charles II on his arrival in Scotland in 1649, thus finally severing his connection with the Covenanters. He had escaped the fate of the other leaders in the army of the Engagement, and had evidently found a temporary refuge, but it must have been clear to everyone that if the Royalists were defeated in the field, retribution must fall upon him. The usual form of penalty was the forfeiture of estates, and David Barclay, though personally already penalised by the loss of his office and command, was probably well aware of possible complications in the matter of Urie as well, in which anticipation he was soon justified.

The actual blow fell in 1651, after the battle of Worcester, when Cromwell had defeated the Scottish Army and had all three kingdoms at his mercy. The Earl Marischal was engaged at a meeting of the Committee of Estates, described by Richard Blair as " a ragged body which professed to be the Government of Scotland," at Alyth (Eliot), in the company of the Earl of Crawford, General Leslie, Lords Ogilvy and Bargeny, the lairds of Humby, Lees, Collington, Powie, and others,

Margin notes:

COLONEL DAVID BARCLAY, 1610–1686, Urie I. 1649.

Bury Hill U, 55.

Calendar of State Papers, Vols. 1654, p. 283, and 1656, pp. 44, 360.

1651.

Life of Richard Blair

engaged in concocting measures for raising forces on behalf of the King, when the whole party was surprised and arrested by a troop of General Monk's Scouts, who took them prisoners, with their clerks, attendants, and followers, and shipped them all off to London. The Earl Marischal was committed to the Tower, where, with occasional liberty *en parole*, he remained until the Restoration, doubtless thankful to have escaped execution.

He was one of those excepted from Cromwell's Act of Grace in 1654. His whole estates, comprising eleven Baronies, " of which David Barclay was wont to speak," were forfeited, together with the lands of Urie, owing to the unfortunate delay in completing the legal transfer.

" The Estates were vested in Trustees, under burden of his creditors rights, and of certain modest provision for his four daughters. Full advantage was taken of this provision. But a certain check was placed on the manufacture of claims by the provision that no debts incurred after April 18th, 1648, would be recognised." Therefore David Barclay found himself excluded from the rights of the creditors and unable to establish his claim to the estate.

There is a contemporary document at Bury Hill, entitled " The trew and perfyt relation of Colonell David Barclay's deportment since the King's Majestie's coming to Scotland in anno 1649," which sets forth that " David Barclay having in 1648 lent the Earl Marischal a considerable soume upon ane improper wadset of the lands of Ury, was at muche truble, paines, and charge to get his annual rent payed. Manie precepts on merchands being given him, and few of them answerid until a great part of the annuall was expendit by him.

" The Earl Marischal being taken prisoner at Eliot (1651) and thereafter impowering the Countess his mother, and the Laird of Morphie and others, to manage his Estate to the best advantage, the Colonell desyred of them to be possessed of the lands of Ury, for sattisfying his bygon and futour anwells, and offered to be accomptable for the superplus, unto those intrusted with the saide Earle's affairs.

" But was denyed by them."

The document goes on to explain that "the Earle Mari- COLONEL DAVID BARCLAY, 1610–1686, Urie I. schal's estate (with manie others being sequestrat), whereon the said Colonell had ane improper wadset [mortgage] he caused his agent desyre libertie from the Commrs [Commissioners] for Sequestration at Leith to possess the wadset lands, which they had granted to manie, bot refused the same to the said Coll for being imployed in Duk Hamilton's Armie in the yeire 1648."

It would therefore appear that the Dowager Countess and her co-trustees, under the terms of forfeiture, refused to grant Colonel David the possession of the lands of Urie, though the transaction had been a perfectly straightforward one, and they must have understood the position. The delay of the final signatures put it in their power to deprive him of his rights and withhold the property, though David had accepted it in lieu of the " considerable soume " advanced to the Earle Marischal, and was in all equity the real owner before the estate had been sequestrated.

His second application to the Sequestration Commissioners had no better fortune, though their refusal was more comprehensible than that of his personal friends.

The " considerable soume " he had paid to the Earl 1649. Marischal was 23,000 merkes, equalling about £3,000, and the charter bound the Earl to " enfeoff " (give possession) to David and Katherine in return. The actual deed was not officially drawn up until 1652, and was doubtless intended to strengthen his position, as it was dated before his petition to Cromwell for restitution of his property had been granted.

The original charter and deed are still in the archives at Bury Hill Papers, No. Ua, 2c, 58. Bury Hill.

This difficult position David Barclay dealt with in statesmanlike fashion.

His wife, Katherine Gordon, had many influential friends and relations, and Robert Barclay (Urie III) says in his Memoirs : " By advyce of the Earle and his other friends, he laid hold of the interest he had by his wife's cousin germane, the Earle of Sutherland, and other relations there, and gott himself elected Member of Parliament for that shire, and in the next Parliament by his own interest, for the Shires of

COLONEL
DAVID
BARCLAY,
1610–1686,
Urie I.

1649.

Angus and Mearns which was reckoned the only method to gett possession of his own estate." He also adds that, in addition to the Colonel's desire to get possession of his estate, he "wished as well to doe service to his counntrey and friends, particularly to the family of Marischal, for whom he bore a great respect."

The Scots, who had upheld Charles I to the day of his death, proclaimed Charles II without delay at Edinburgh on February 3rd, 1649, and after a Committee of the Scottish Parliament had debated the matter they sent over Commissioners to the new King, who was then in the Isle of Jersey, to treat with His Majesty, and having produced a copy of the Proclamation, invited him to come over and take possession of his hereditary Kingdom of Scotland. Whereupon the King, after consultation with such as were about him, appointed three Commissioners to meet him at the Hague, where he was then invited by his brother-in-law, the Prince of Orange.

Wishart's
History of
Scotland,
p. 172.

Wishart writes of this interview: "When the Commissioners or Deputies of the States had first access to the King Charles II in Holland, to invite him home, their slow pace, grave habit, and dejected countenance had all the appearance imaginable of humility." It was, of course, a serious occasion, but hardly an encouraging reception for the young King, who, however, decided to agree to the terms the Commissioners offered. He accepted both the National Covenant and the Solemn League and Covenant, promised to do nothing without the goodwill of Parliament, and pledged himself to set up Presbyterianism. In June 1650 he landed at Speymouth and in January 1651 was crowned at Scone.

Bury Hill
Papers.

In February 1651 David Barclay took the precaution of procuring a Crown charter from King Charles II, "to Colonel David Barclay of Ury and spouse, of the lands of Ury

1651.
"Historical
Associations
of My Native
Country,"
David Scott.
From the
Library at
Urie, now at
Bury Hill.

and others," which he doubtless hoped would secure his position in the event of the success of the Royalist party.

But "att this time the Party who had murdered the King in England, having taken to themselves the title of the Commonwealth's men, they by proclamation commanded:

"That no person whatsoever should presume to declare or call

Charles Stewart, son to the late Charles, commonly called Prince of Wales, or any other person, King or Chief Magistrate of England or Ireland, or any other Dominion belonging to them, by Pretence of Inheritance, Succession, or any right whatsoever, without the free consent of the People and Parliament, by a particular Act or Statute to that purpose. COLONEL DAVID BARCLAY, 1610–1686, Urie I.

And whosoever should, contrary to that Act, proclaim the said Charles Stewart, should be deemed and judged a Traitor, and suffer accordingly."

This being the position, Colonel David saw small chance of the legal restitution of his property, and had to take the matter into his own hands.

His formal application for liberty to stand for Parliament was granted by the Commissioners of Assembly at Perth on November 23rd, 1650, as follows :

" The Commission of Assembly being convinced of the evidence of the Repentance of John Lord Lister, Colonel David Barclay, and Colonel William Lockhart, for their accession to the late unlawful Engagement against the Kingdome of England, and having proof of their affection to the cause of God in former times, and being now verie confident that they shall hereafter cary themselves faithfully and zealously in the Cause, and give real evidence of the sincerity of their affection thereunto in all tyme coming. 1650. Thurloe Papers.

" Therefore they doe seriously recommend them to the Honourable Estates of Parliament, or Committee of Estates, that they may be looked upon by their Lordships accordinglie."

This annulled the sentence passed by the English Commissioners at Dalkeith in 1649, which had " denied him liberty to possess the wadset lands, for being imployed in Duk Hamilton's Armie in 1648."

If it had not been for the delay which had placed his claim beyond the date fixed for creditors, he might have entered into possession of Urie without further trouble, but that day was still postponed.

The Royalist cause was now hopelessly lost in Scotland. David Leslie, in command of the Scots Army, had made an ill-fated attempt to restore the monarchy at Dunbar in 1650, and had been defeated, but the next year had rallied his forces and invaded England, hoping to stir up a Royalist revolt. At

HISTORY OF THE BARCLAY FAMILY

COLONEL
DAVID
BARCLAY,
1610–1686,
Urie I.

1651.

Mackenzie's
Outline of
Scottish
History.

Worcester on September 3rd, 1651, Cromwell had met and overwhelmed the Scots Army of 13,000 men, and with his trained troops had utterly routed them. Charles II, who had accompanied Leslie, only just escaped and, after many romantic adventures, got safely away into France.

After this, the first intention of the English Parliament was simply to annex Scotland and abolish the name ; but this idea was given up, and the country was placed under eight English Commissioners, and afterwards under a Council of State which included some Scots. In place of the Committee of Estates, Scotland was given thirty representatives in the House of Commons, among whom appears the name of David Barclay as Deputy for Sutherlandshire.

1652.
Acta Parl.
Scot.
1644–56,
pp. 781–782.

" At the Committee of Parliament appoynted to conferre with the Deputies sent from Scotland, October 14, 1652, the Declaracon of Parliament intituled ' A Declaracon of the Parliament of England in order to the Uniting of Scotland into one Parliament,' is read. It was resolved to informe them what Shires and Burroughs in Scotland, have chosen to send Deputies to Edinburgh, and what Deputies have subscribed to the Union, according to the said Declaraçon."

" The Committee are informed that of the said 30 Shires, twenty Shires only sent Deputies to Edinburgh who subscribed to the Union."

The twenty Deputies who had subscribed to the Union, according to the Declaration of Parliament, therefore took their seats, and among them was David Barclay.

It was not long before he asserted his independence, for

1652.

" An Order of Parliament committing a Bill for continuing severall Comissions granted by the Commissioners of the Parliament of the Commonwealth of England, for ordering and managing affairs in Scotland, unto this Committee was voted."

Among the names of the Deputies who signed to the Commission, Colonel David Barclay is noted alone as " signed not," with no excuse of " sicknesse," or " poverty " as many gave as their reasons for abstaining or non-attendance. A question being put to the Deputies as to their members who assented or refused to vote, they stated that " for the Shire of Sutherlandshire it was represented by one Com[r.] (Colonel

38

David Barclay) who was fully impowered, and was at the COLONEL
Meeting, subscribed the tender, and voyced in the Election." DAVID
BARCLAY,
" So that there are 24 Shires who assent to the Commission. And 1610–1686,
by the Parlts Declaraçon Warrant is given to the Deputies present Urie I.
by vote of the major part to elect 14 persons to represent the Shires."

It was not altogether surprising that so many of the Deputies from Scotland should have failed to appear at the first meeting of Parliament at Westminster, for the travelling in those days was very difficult. In addition to the absence of any made roads outside the four great high roads, the country was infested with bands of masterless men, the result of the Civil War, who roamed in marauding parties ready to rob or even murder travellers.

The houses of call were few and far between, and often 1652. themselves without adequate means of entertainment for travellers. The distance from the north of Scotland to London took at least a fortnight to accomplish on horseback, and even if they went by sea, the coasts were rendered dangerous by the " pirats " or privateers, who were often dispossessed and desperate Royalists. No travellers dared to adventure alone, and armed parties were formed for mutual protection.

Colonel David Barclay was not one of the absentees. He was in his place at the meeting of Parliament and though, as in duty bound, he subscribed the all-important Act of Union, he alone among his colleagues stood out against the Commission for ordering and managing affairs in Scotland, though he was outvoted, and perforce had to acquiesce.

It was in this year that the deed was drawn up by the 1652. Notary Public, which legalised the charter of sasine of the Bury Hill
Papers, No. lands of Urie. The attorney presented the charter to the U 2c, 58. bailiff of the Earl Marischal, who took it and handed it to the Notary Public to read to those present, but the Colonel had still a long time to wait before his ownership was acknowledged.

Ever since David Barclay had heard the great Quaker 1653. George Fox preach in 1648, he had been meditating on the religious problems of the day, and in 1653 he took a definite

COLONEL
DAVID
BARCLAY,
1610–1686,
Urie I.

step. Though he had not yet decided to adopt the tenets of the Friends, he made a frank admission that he was not convinced of the soundness of the doctrine and discipline of the Kirk of Scotland, and the Records of Moray have this entry :

"David Barclay, sonne in law to Sir Robert Gordon, has professedlie declined from the doctrine and discipline of the Kirk, denying it to be a Kirk. The Synod orders him to be processed."

We have no further record of this procedure, which was presumably the ecclesiastical form of prosecution, and no doubt the Colonel had many discussions and arguments to encounter, as so important a Kirk member would not be lightly relinquished ; but he was not to be shaken, and by preserving this independent outlook in ecclesiastical matters, he finally severed his connection with the Covenanting Party in the State.

1654.
Scotland
and the Protectorate,
Firth, p. 329.

1654.
Scottish
History
Society.

The year 1654 saw the power of the Parliament of England vested in Oliver Cromwell, under the title of Lord Protector of the Commonwealth of England, Scotland and Ireland ; and on May 4th, 1654, the Protectorate and the Union were proclaimed with fitting pomp at Edinburgh.

The Ordinance of April 12th, 1654, had again fixed Scotland's representation in the United Parliament at thirty members. It remained to determine how so small a number could be distributed among the Scottish constituencies. Upon June 2nd, General Lambert reported the re-grouping of twenty-nine constituencies, each, save Edinburgh, having a single member. The name of Colonel David Barclay of Ury appears first upon the list, as representing Forfar and Kincardineshire.

"Save that the scheme of distribution made some effort to secure geographical symmetry, and, for the most part, every burgh that had secured the right to be represented in the Scottish Parliament was included in the Council's scheme, Scotland had little cause to regard either the proportion of members allotted to her, or the way in which they were distributed, with particular favour. To the Council, however, the scheme presented itself as a reasonable if not the only way to apportion thirty members among nearly three times that number of Constituencies."

Colonel Barclay's selection, therefore, points to the influential position he had attained to in Scotland.

His arresting personality set him above ordinary men, as did his great height and dignity of manner. Fraser relates that he could appreciate these characteristics in others, as Barclay observed when he saw Robert Arbuthnot, the Earl Marischal, and Alexander Arbuthnot walking together, " I never saw three such people for figure and stature." As they were all intimate personal friends of his own, they must have looked a distinguished group when together.

The " Trew and Perfyt Account " gives a detailed description of Colonel David Barclay's actions in 1654. " That in 1654 in the beginning thereof the said Colonell Barclay heiring of acts of forfaultrie, and fynes comeing out from Cromwell and his then Counsell, with qualifications (excluding such creditors from that sattisfactione as had incumbrance on the forfaulted persons estates) for their accessione to the Ingadgement in 1648, did goe to London, to gett himself freed of forsaide qualifications. But was necessitat to returne *re injecta*, the saide Actes being past the Counsell before his arrival into the Citie. That the said Colonell was, without his desyre or knowledge, named in ane ordinance for settling of landes on the wyffes and childring of forfaulted persones, and sattisfying their creditors. That he was necessitat to officiat, that he might get possession of his owne wadset he hade on the Earle Marshall's estate, which was then, and still is all his livelihood."

The statement of Robert Barclay (Urie III) here conflicts with that given us in the " Trew and Perfyt Account," as whereas that document maintains that the Colonel was " without his desyre or knowledge," named in the ordinance for settling of forfeited lands on the wives and children of the landowners, his grandson writes : " David Barclay, maintaining all through one definite and consistent purpose, succeeded in securing for himself an appointment as Trustee for administering the Estates of those Noblemen and Gentle-

COLONEL DAVID BARCLAY, 1610–1686, Urie I.

1654.

Fraser Papers, p. 81.

Bury Hill Papers.

1654.

41

COLONEL
DAVID
BARCLAY,
1610–1686,
Urie I.
men whose property had been forfeited for their participation in the Engagement."

The appointment was so obviously the most direct method, both of recovering his own property, and also of befriending the family of the Earl Marischal, and many more Royalist friends, that it seems hardly probable that he was entirely unaware that it was to be offered to him.

Acta Parl.
Scot. Vol. vi,
p. 821.
It is dated April 12th, 1654, and is headed : " An Ordinance for settling the Estates of severall excepted Persons in Scotland in Trustees to the uses herein expressed."

After the usual long preamble, it sets forth :—

" WHEREAS . . . diverse persons and their Estates are excepted and reserved out of the said Ordinance, and all benefits thereof, and yet nevertheless the Estates of the said diverse persons are thereby left subject to diverse debts, charges, and Incumbrances . . . and lykewise several proportions of lands, Tenements, and Hereditaments are by the said Ordinance appointed to be settled for a Provision for their wives and children. . . . And it is ordained by His Highness the Lord Protector that with the advice and consent of his Council, that all and every the Honours, Manors, etc., etc., which upon the 18th of April 1648 did belong to

[Here follows the long list of names]

and were lawfully used and enjoyed by them, are hereby invested and settled on

[Names of Commissioners, including David Barckly, Esq.]

and the survivors of them, their heirs and assigns, for the Uses, Purposes, etc., hereafter in and by this Ordinance expressed, untill the Sale, disposition, and Conveyance thereof, or of such part thereof as shall be requisite for the Purposes aforesaid, . . . and the Remainder to the use of His Highness the Lord Protector and his successors for the benefit of the Commonwealth."

[Here follow detailed instructions as to the methods to be pursued.]

It might appear inconsistent with the policy of the Protector to appoint a man of David Barclay's known Royalist sympathies to a post giving him power to improve the conditions of the suffering Cavaliers ; but Carlyle says in his " Cromwell " :

"Little over a year before, Cromwell, a man of a magnanimity far greater than that of his associates—when criticising the Rump's arbitrary rule, had spoken with indignation of the victimisation of Royalist squires. 'Poor men,' he said, 'under this arbitrary power, were driven like flocks of sheep by forty in a morning, to the confiscation of goods and estates, without any man being able to give a reason why two of them had deserved to forfeit a shilling.'"

COLONEL DAVID BARCLAY, 1610–1686, Urie I.

We can therefore understand that Colonel Barclay's acceptance of the appointment was not unwelcome to Oliver Cromwell.

After this matter had been settled we find a petition from David Barclay to the Protector, which deals in a brief, business-like way with his personal grievance.

Cal. of State Papers, p. 361, August 2, 1654.

"Aug. 2, 1654

1654.

"I am a Creditor to the Earl Marshall (of Scotland) for £1,500 borrowed by him in July 1648, to pay debts contracted before 1648, but he being one of the persons exempted from pardon, his estate is not to be charged with anything done by him since April 1648, therefore this sum being the most of my subsistence, I shall be in a worse case than most of the excepted persons, which I have not deserved by any opposition to the Parliament or you, since 1648, for though frequently urged, I refused to engage in the late War.

Cal. State Papers (Dom.), 1654-5-6. Also Thurloe State Papers, Vols. iv-v (Scottish).

"In 1652 I was a Commissioner for electing the Deputies to perfect the Union of the Nations, I have always been ready to promote the Parliament's interests, applying both to Major-General Deane, and Colonel Lilburne, when Commander-in-Chief.

"I beg your order to the Commissioners for determining the claims on the Estates of exempted persons to allow this debt, though claimed beyond the date allowed by the rules."

With this petition a reference in the Protector's own hand was sent to the Council, in charge of Major-General Lambert, "to take care of it," as follows :—

"Order in Council that the Commissioners at Leith examine the matter, and if they find the Petitioner had no hand in the late war against the Commonwealth, and that the rest of the petition is true, they are to order the debt to be paid."

Holograph Reference, Cal. State Papers (Scottish), August 2, 1654.

As Colonel Barclay's Commission had been only to keep

COLONEL
DAVID
BARCLAY,
1610–1686,
Urie I.
1654.

order in Scotland while the Army marched into England to rescue the King, he could not be said to have taken part in the war, and Cromwell accepted his statement, adding at the end of the order :—

> " The Committee for determining claims on Scotch Estates to observe what the Leith Committee shall order."

This put the matter beyond a doubt, and the petition was, therefore, fully successful.

As is related in the Baron Court Book of Urie, " This done, infeftment in the lands of Ury followed readily, though not till 1679 did he obtain that formal Charter which, combining the various subjects he had purchased from the Earl Marischal, erected them into Ane haill and free Barony, called ' The Barony of Urie.' "

Thus, after nearly six years of injustice, Colonel Barclay obtained his own property.

Scotland and
the Protec-
torate, Firth,
p. 164.

Some of the Royalist party appear to have been disturbed at what they called " David Barclay's Capitulation to the Protector," but they awaited the result with anxiety, being by now themselves despairing of success, and only desirous of a peaceful conclusion to their hopeless opposition.

A letter from the Earl of Glencairne shows this feeling. He was one of the King's most loyal supporters, lost his whole fortune in his service and at the Restoration was appointed High Chancellor of Scotland.

It is addressed to the Earl of Atholl :—

1654.

> " Ile of Inchmerrin,
> "Aug. 28, 1654.

" My Lord,

" I have bin since I parted with you most part bed-fast, and am so still, els I had not been so long in writing to you. . . .

" My Lord, I finde wee are not the firste who hes capitulated, for Middletone has sent Colonel David Barclay to Cromwell to make his peace. This is sent me from England from one [who] spoke with David Barclay.

" This is so much trouble, but I hope you will forgive it among the rest of the troubles [which] hes been occasioned you by Your Lordship's humble servant

> " GLENCAIRNE."

44

As we have seen, Colonel Barclay had gone to England COLONEL
entirely on his own affairs, and not to negotiate for Middleton ; DAVID
indeed, Lord Middleton never actually capitulated, but he 1610–1686,
escaped to the Continent in 1654, where he remained till the Urie I.
Restoration in 1660.

Another letter from the Earl of Glencairne to the Earl of
Atholl was written from his sick bed, in great depression of
spirits, two days later :

" MY LORD,   " Aug. 30, 1654.   Scotland and
     the Protec-
" I find Lieutenant-General Middletone is put to begin the play torate,
anew, and hee says hee hopes to see it shortly in a better condition Firth, p. 165.
than ever it was since hee came to Scotland. I wish it may be so,
but it is none of my beleife. . . . I pray God direct you arighte :
my great respects to you makes mee thus dash out my opinion to you,
and now poore Sir Arthur Forbes is beatt, it makes busyness hopeless, nay I feare so much of hope as that Colonel David Barclay will
obtayne a capitulation for the General. . . .

" I make it my last suite to you that you will wreate to me and let
me know your resolutions and intentions that I may bless them the
best prayers of, my Lord,

       " Your faithfull obedient servant and cousen,

                  " GLENCAIRNE."

" My opinion is your lordship hasten one quickly to Middletone
that he may know the true condition of busyness here, lest he (be)
abused with fancying forces to be heire whilst their is none.
    " Directed for the Right Honble The Earl of Atholl."

When this rumour reached Charles II in Holland it 1655.
disturbed other Royalists in exile there, who, it is observed, Nicholas
by now regarded David Barclay as one of themselves, and one lished for the
Captain Peter Mews writes to Mr. Secretary Nicholas, ex- Society,
pressing incredulity in it :—   1652–8.

" HONOURABLE SIR,   " Rotterdam, Jan. 28, 1655.   1655.
" I finde a sad and an uncomfortable account of our affaires in
general, and more particular in Scotland : but I must profess I doe
no more beleive anything of Middletone's capitulation now than I
did of my Lord Glencairne's story about David Barclay's making
his Peace. Whatever it is, I am resolved to see the uttermost, and
give His Majesty a just and faithfull account so far as I am able to
advance, which shall bee (if my endeavours feyle not) as farr as he
hath a man in Arms.

" Sir, I have no tyme to see what I desyred, and perhaps it is wel I have not, but pray beleive my passion. My designes, my interest, are all at His Majestie's commands, and I cannot doe anything which may make mee otherways than his subject, and, Sir,

" Your servant,

" PETER MEWS."

In October 1655 we find the respect and esteem in which David Barclay was held testified to by this Commission on behalf of the leading men in his constituency :—

" At Conveth the twentie twa day of October, in the yeir of God 1655, the whilk day the noblemen, barones, gentilmen and heretores of the Sheir of Kincardin, being mett and convenient, and finding it necessar to have ane of their number as Commissioner for them and their sheir, at the Councill of State upon the second day of November instant, to represent their grievances and just desyres to the Honourable Councill, and wheris in powar have w^t unanimous consent nominat, electit, and choysen Colonel David Barclay, Commissioner for them, and in behalf of the said sheir to compeir for them and in their names, before the said Honourable Councill, to the effect above w'rin [written], and to joyne w^t Commissioners of uther sheiris in the leik caices, to [voyte] vote, treat, rasone, and review uther things neidfull to doe for the good weill and behowe [behoof] of the said sheir w^{lk} they might doe themselffis if they were personally present, or q^{lk} [which] is knawin to appertaine to Commissioner or com^{rs} of sheirs in the leik conditions.

Promitten firme and stable to hould all and qt somewir [whatsoever] laws ther said Commissioner shall doe in the premises.

In witness of

Arbuthnott	A^r Carnegy Pittars
Harie Barclay	G. Ramsay
William Naper	Jo Barclay
J. Grahame	W. Rait of Halgrein
Halcartoune	— Raitt

William Ramsey.

[Colonel Harie or Harrie Barclay of Johnston and John, his son.]

In David Barclay's official position as Trustee of confiscated estates, he produced businesslike and convincing arguments against the wholesale forfeiture of properties. The so-called " Malignants " had been gradually stripped of all their possessions, the luckiest of them only preserving part of their lands by paying heavy compositions which drained their resources, and left their unfortunate creditors unpaid. So effective was his mediation that the Report from the Leith Committee, so anxiously awaited, was wholly favourable to his claims on behalf of the distressed Royalists, and reported from the Commissioners in Scotland to the Protector :—

COLONEL DAVID BARCLAY, 1610–1686, Urie I.

1656.

Cal. State Papers (Dom.), 1656, p. 1.

" It is our duty to present to you the charges, by debts and donatives on forfeited Estates in Scotland, that you may consider it when applications are made.

"On April 12, 1654, you ordered that what came short to pay lawful creditors from one estate, by reason of donatives, should be paid from another, after its debts and incumbrances were satisfied, but many estates then forfeited are since discharged by capitulation with General Monck, e.g. Earls seaforth, Lowdoun, Athol, Glencairn, Lords Kenmure, Lorne, Macklin, and the Laird of Womatt, whose estate would have afforded great relief to creditors. If particular persons receive grants out of the forfeited estates, the creditors will be great sufferers.

" 1. That the estates will not answer the intended objects, which were three :—

" (1) To pay the creditors of each estate, and provide for the wives and children of excepted persons. 1656.

" (2) To do the same for other estates, which are overburdened with donatives.

" (3) The overplus to His Highness.

"But overplus is impossible, as by reason of donatives estates hardly bear their own incumbrances, and those that should have yielded relief are released from forfeiture.

" 2. That the Commissioners should have full release as to the disposal of those estates discharged from forfeiture, or the creditors may complain with reason of prejudice. . . .

" We would be far from restraining your favour, or disputing your commands, yet as the condition of the forfeiture stands we leave it to you.

" Leith, 16 December 1655."

Even General Monck, to whom Cromwell had given the chief command in Scotland, was glad to avail himself of David Barclay's services, and writes on February 12th, 1656, to Major-General Lambert :—

" Edinburgh.

" MY LORD

" Understanding that Collonel David Barclay is gone up to London, to Move His Highnesse and Council about the forfeited 1656.

lands heere, (for sattisfying of creditors) I desire your Lordship will be pleased that before any order be given concerning them by His Highness and Council that there may be consideracion taken of the lands that were given to some officers by the Parliament, and since sould to other people. As for mine in particular which Captain Bressie bought of mee, and since Collonel Cooper, Mr. Bilton, Mr. Saltonshall and some others have taken the land for as much moneys more as it is worth for their debts (with Capt Bressie's consent) soe that I cannot see how His Highnes and Council can well take off all those engagements from that estate, which I thought fitt to acquaint your Lordship withall that you might prevent further trouble to the Councill in case they should not be rightly informed in it (and I shall desire your lordship to stand my friend, that in case the Councill shoulde thinke fitt to dispose of the land for debts, that both my own engagements to make it good to him, and the engagements made to others since, may be discharged, and those that have now bought it may receive sattisfaction for what they have disburst for itt, before they part with the land)

" I have one thing more to trouble your Lordship withall, that wee are quite out of moneyes, and unless the Treasurers please to give orders to their Deputies heere to return moneyes, we shall suddenly bee in want, which I thought fitt to acquaint your Lordship withall.

" For news heere is none. All things are quiette. The Lord Cranston is now bringing in his officers to give engagement for their peacable deportment and for raising men for the King of Sweden which are to be shipt in March. I remaine your Lordshippe's most humble servant.

" GEORGE MONCK."

Although the Leith Committee had issued its report on December 16th, 1655, there appears to have been some delay in carrying out its enactments, for on June 10th, 1656, we find Colonel Barclay presenting two more petitions to Cromwell, one dealing with the question of the forfeited estates, and the other on his own behalf.

Petition of Colonel Barclay to the Protector :—

" The Commissioners entrusted by you with the estates of the excepted persons in Scotland, finding by the release of so many of them, that the remnant will not answer the ends for which they were invested in them, represent the condition thereof to you, by me, and request your speedy order."

48

Annexing Instructions by the said Commissioners in Scotland to Colonel Barclay, to be presented to His Highness.

Petition of Colonel David Barclay to the Protector :—

" In 1648 I paid large sums to the creditors of the Earl Marshall in Scotland, who had lands made over to them by mortgage, which they thereupon conveyed to me, but by the Ordinance of Grace and Pardon to the people of Scotland, it is provided that no deeds on the estates shall be allowed unless made before 18 April 1648, wherefore the Commissioners for allow[ing] claims on forfeited estates refuse to allow mine.

" I beg an order for allowance, as the moneys were not paid to the Earl Marshall, but to the creditors who had the lands before the said 18 April 1648."

Annexing two forms of proposed letters to the said Commissioners for the allowance.

The reply to these petitions and the reference thereon by Council to the Committee for Scotland, to report July 24th, 1656.

President Lawrence to the Council in Scotland, " Council on considering Colonel Barclay's Petition wishes you to examine the case, and what sums have been paid for redemption of any of the Earl Marshall's lands, and whether the debts were contracted before April 18, 1648, and to certify meanwhile as much of the Estate as will pay Barclay, and he is to hold what is now in his possession."

We learn from his grandson (Urie III) that Colonel David Barclay's efforts on his own behalf and that of the distressed Royalists were successful.

" In the end he got the Government then in power to restore all the Nobility and Gentrey to their fortunes, which made him so popular in the Countrey that he was again in the year 1656 elected Member of Parliament for the two Shires, from whom he had their publick thanks signified by their letter to him, still in my custody, subscribed by the Vicount of Arbuthnott, the Lord Halcarton, and the principall Gentlemen, for his great services done the Country."

Conspicuous among those who benefited by his disinterested advocacy were the Countess Marischal and her chil-

COLONEL DAVID BARCLAY, 1610-1686, Urie I.

1656.

Bury Hill Papers, No. 77.

III.—G

49

COLONEL
DAVID
BARCLAY,
1610–1686,
Urie I.

Genealogical
Account

dren, who had so far appealed in vain for payment of the allowance granted them by the Commissioners for their support, and had been reduced to penury by the Earl's forfeiture.

Consequently, by the Colonel's good offices, the Countess was given "Ane easy tack of the whole Estate and good provision for the children so that there was little or nothing made by that forfeiture, or the others."

When the Dowager Countess Marischal had received the good news that her son's old friend Colonel Barclay had been successful on his behalf, she wrote to a friend of her own.

1656.

Letter in
possession of
Sir Patrick
Keith
Murray.

"To my verie loving freind Patrick Rankine advocat, dualling [dwelling] at the foot of the Kirkheughe in Edinburgh.

"I did not intend to have sent this bearer until I had heard from you. But having within these two nights receaved a letter from David Barklay showing that severall claimes on my sone's estate are cleared, and it is his advyce that I shall enter my childrine's claimes, and also that some adresses be maid to the Trustes for allowance to my grandchildrine, I resolve to send the bearer with the best instructions I could give him. Trewlie, Colonell Barclay writes verie kindlie, and promises all the assistance that is within his reatch. Soe that I have derected the bearer that after he has spoken with Maister John Nesbit and you, he shall goe to him with my letter, and ask his advyce."

A strong personal friendship as well as the tie of kinship had existed for generations between the two families, and in the Fraser Papers two anecdotes are related which show the pleasant and familiar terms they were on.

During the interregnum the care and concealment of the Regalia of Scotland had fallen to the Earl Marishal by right of his hereditary office, and the secret of their whereabouts was only divulged to a very few of his most intimate friends. They were called "The Honours of Scotland," and consisted of the Crown, the Sceptre, and the Sword. In the Fraser letters there is an account of how David Barclay was privileged to see them.

Fraser
Papers, p. 51.

"David Barclay, along with several others, accompanied from Fetteroso, the Earl Marshall with his visitor Earls, Seaforth and Sunderland, to see the Regalia (called The Honours of Scotland) which were kept in a Vault in the Tower of Dunottar Castle, cut out

of the solid rock, and cased or lined with lead, and also mahogany, COLONEL
in which they were kept on a table covered with fine linen, and hung DAVID
with tapestry. BARCLAY,
    "The Governor of the Castle first opened two locks, and the Earl 1610–1686,
Marshall a third, with a key taken from a bag hung from his neck Urie I.
by a silver tripet, on which the door of the Regalia was opened, and
the Earls kneeled on cushions to view it, after which the attendants
got leave by sixes to go and do the same, when the door was locked,
and a salute fired from the Castle."

When the Committee of Estates was seized at Alyth in 1651
the Earl Marischal was in possession of this important key,
which he wore in the bag round his neck, and must have been
extremely anxious lest it should fall into the wrong hands. In
the confusion consequent upon the arrest and transhipment
of so large a number of people, he was able secretly to send
the key to his wife, by a trusty messenger. She managed to
save the Honours, and only just in time, as the castle was
already surrounded, and was taken by Cromwell a few months
later.

The Countess Marischal arranged with the wife of the Rev. Black Book
James Grainger, minister of Kinneff, a small parish church of Kincar-
within a few miles of the castle, to remove these precious dineshire,
relics. Mrs. Grainger had been obliged to leave her horse in p. 15.
the besieging camp when she was permitted to enter the
castle, approach being only possible on foot. On her return
she carried the crown, rolled up in some linen, and must have
had an anxious moment when the English General in charge
of the blockading Army courteously helped her to mount, and
she took the crown in her lap. Her maid followed her on
foot, bearing the sword and sceptre concealed in bundles of
lint, which Mrs. Grainger pretended were to be spun into
thread. They passed safely through the English army, and
arrived at Kinneff, when her husband took charge of them,
and wrote to the Countess:

    "I, Mr. James Grainger, minister of Kinneff, grant me to have
in my custody the Honours of the kingdom, viz., the Crown,
Sceptre and Sword. For the Crown, and Sceptre, I raised the
pavement stone just before the pulpit (in the church of Kinneff)
in the night tyme, and digged under it ane hole, and layed down

COLONEL
DAVID
BARCLAY,
1610–1686,
Urie I.
the stone just as it was before, and removed the mould that remained, that none would have discerned the stone to have been raised at all, the Sword again at the west end of the church amongst some common seits that stand there. . . . and if it shall please God to call me by death before they be called for, your Ladyship will find them in that place."

Here they remained till the Restoration, safe in their obscure place of concealment, and visited from time to time by the faithful Graingers to renew the cloths in which they were wrapt.

In consideration of their services, an Act of Parliament was passed on January 11, 1661, appointing that they should receive two thousand merks Scots from the King's Treasury ; but it is feared that the payment of this sum remained, as did so many of the debts of Charles II, on paper only.

Another anecdote illustrates the cordial terms existing between David Barclay and the Earl Marischal.

Fraser
Papers, p. 54.
" Once when the Earl was hunting with David Barclay in company, he, on exhausting his firegun colfin (wadding), drew out of his pouch a commission from Charles II for raising the Mearns Militia, which, on getting some colfin from Barclay, he threw at him."

Another time, hunting with General James Keith, the Colonel got a present of a powder horn richly carved. Both the commission and the powder horn came later into the hands of John Napier, formerly tenant of Mains of Allardice, afterwards merchant in Stonehaven, who married a descendant of David Barclay's, and were by him presented to Lord Keith.

1656.
The elections were held throughout Scotland for the most part on August 20, 1656, and the second Parliament of the Protectorate was summoned for September 17.

Thurloe
Papers,
p. 322.
" Great efforts were made to secure the return of Englishmen, or at least Scotsmen on whom the Government might rely. The Protector was likely to require ' friends,' and the Scottish Council, almost to a man, offered itself for re-elec-
Life of
Robert Blair,
tion."   Colonel Barclay was re-elected for Angus and Mearns.
p. 327.
The representatives elected were described by Monk as

" honest and peaceable Scotsmen, and I believe will be all right for my Lord Protector."

In the beginning of 1656 a list of Justices of the Peace was drawn up, and the name of Colonel Barclay appears for Kincardineshire.

In June we find a further testimonial to his public services.

COLONEL DAVID BARCLAY, 1610–1686, Urie I.

Bury Hill Papers.

"For Coll David Barclay. [*Endorsed*]

" Sir,

" Having so much experience of yor former favours, and great paines you [have] taken manie tymes in promoteing the good of the Shy^r of whereof wee are verie sensible Qr uponn [whereupon] we have maid bold to put you to a furder trouble in recommending to you these inclosed imperfect instructionnes to be better digested and rectified by yor self as you shall finde convenient efter deliberat.

" We are Sr Your very faithfull friends and servantes,

Arbuthnott	H. Carnegy Pitcarrn	Grame of Morphie
G. Ramsay	J° Barclay	(?) Stuardes
Robertt Douglas		Harie Barclay

Conveth. Junii 1656.

"Anie farder we would say in further busyness of the shy^r we remitted to ye Laird of Glenfargt for his further information."

A letter written by General Monk, who had been appointed a member of the Council of State and had assumed supreme authority in Scotland, is another testimony to David Barclay's influence.

He writes on behalf of the Protector's Council in Scotland, to Colonel Ralph Cobbett, Military Governor of Dundee, on December 3, 1656.

The letter deals with a bond given by the collector of the monthly assessments in the Shire of Kincardineshire, " for the payment of the moneys exacted from the said shire, to the persons authorized by the Council to dispose of these moneys in defraying the public engagements of the Shire. Colonell David Barclay being satisfied on behalf of the Shire with the security offered, and desiring the release of the Collector, the Council have set him at liberty."

Notwithstanding David Barclay's military record in the past, he was always a strong advocate for peace in the realm, whatever Government was in power, and after having been

COLONEL
DAVID
BARCLAY,
1610–1686,
Urie I.

appointed to protect the person of the Prince of Wales in 1649, in 1656 we find him in a similar position towards the Lord Protector.

Acts and
Ordinances
of the Inter-
regnum.

On Nov. 27, 1656, " An Act for the Security of His Highness The Lord Protector His Person, and Continuance of the Nation in Peace and Safety " was passed, and an order " to guard against Divers wicked Plots and meanes that have of late been devised and laid, as well in Foreign parts beyond the seas, as also within this Nation. . . . The Lord Chancellor, Lords Commissioners of the Great Seal of England," are authorized to issue Commissions to. . . a long list of names, including that of David Barclay, " who shall by virtue of this Act have authority to examine, hear, and determine, all the matters, crimes, and offences aforesaid, and . . . also to hear and determine all Misprisons of the Treasons in this Act mentioned, and to take order for charging the Offender or Offenders with all or any of the crimes, etc., and to take examination of persons upon Oath (which the said Commissioners are hereby authorized to administer), and to proceed to Conviction and final sentence."

1656.

Among the Commissioners appears the name of " David Barckley," who was always called upon when any important public duty was needed—as we have seen—by both parties in the State.

When David Barclay was re-elected to Parliament in 1656 for Angus and Mearns, there are several indications that he was an active and influential member.

Thurloe
Papers,
Vol. v,
p. 322.

Lord Broghill, writing to Secretary Thurloe on August 19, 1656, says, " Since my last, Colonell Nath Wetham is chosen for all the burroughes of Fife, and Sᵣ John Weems for the Shire. Sᵣ Jas. McDowell (one of our Commissioners for excise and customs) is chose for Galloway, and Col. Barcklay for Angus. All the rest will be chosen to-morrow, and so will be all stanch men."

In this year Colonel Barclay invested the sum of £100 sterling on " store and stocking " of land in Ireland. Robert Barclay (Urie III) speaks of the mortgage on the Baronie of Ury not being quite cleared, and that he " unluckilie lay'd out the money upon securities in Ireland." which does not seem to have been a wise investment, and reduced the value of the estate.

Although Cromwell had been so complaisant in the matter of the forfeited estates, David Barclay retained his independence of opinion, and was one of the four members who " vigorously opposed and voted against Cromwell's being made King." COLONEL DAVID BARCLAY, 1610-1686, Urie I. Genealogical Account.

Thurloe writes to Lockhart on March 2, 1657: " Debates in Parliament on the proposal about Cromwell ; the House is most desirous of the Kingship. . . ." 1657.

In the debates four of their countrymen dissented from the rest, *viz* : Lord Cradell (?), Newton Carr, Sir James McDougall, and Colonell Barclay."

It must have required considerable moral courage to run counter to the opinion of 396 members, who were convinced that Cromwell's best policy for securing permanent power lay in his assuming hereditary rank, and presented " ane humble Petition and Advyce " strongly urging that course upon him.

The City also were anxious that Cromwell should assume royal rights, and went so far as to set up his portrait, crowned and sceptred, in the London Exchange, with the inscription :

> " Ascend three thrones great Captain and Divine
> I' th' Will of God, old Lion, they are thine."

The poet Waller wrote in fulsome style,

> " Let the rich ore forthwith be melted down
> And the State fixed by making him a crown.
> With ermine clad, and purple, let him hold
> A royal sceptre made of Spanish gold."

But though Cromwell allowed himself to be installed, in 1657, in something approaching Waller's description of royal state, he was more influenced by the Republican Army, who were horrified at the idea of his accepting the abhorred title, and he eventually declined the advice of his Parliament and remained the Lord Protector. 1657.

There were certain people, probably disappointed Royalists, who criticised David Barclay's action in entering Cromwell's Parliament, and his grandson warmly defends him. Genealogical Account.

He says :

" If any object it as a Reflection upon the Colonell to have been a Member of Parliament during the Usurpation, let them remember that many have got themselves elected to serve their own ends only in such times, and always voted as directed, whereas he, as hath been observed, laid himself out both to serve it [the country] and his friends the oppressed Loyalists as well as himself, as is evident by what he did, and his directly voting against Cromwell's being made King. Which, if it had taken effect, as Clarendon observes in his history, it would have pulled up by the roots all hopes from the Royalist Cause, this noble author mentioning, ' that none were att first more forward to have Cromwell crowned, than some who were supposed to have a warm side to the Royal Family,' but the more thinking trembled at such ane overturn, foreseeing that if the Kingly Government was again established, though out of the right line, yet, it being agreeable to the antient Constitution, people being already wearied out with so many unsuccessful attempts and hard oppressions, would sit down contented. Of which mind the Colonell was, as plainly appears by his voting as he did."

1658.

In 1658 Colonel Barclay had to apply for the refunding of certain expenses he had incurred on his public business. So a meeting was called at Drumlithie by his " affectionate freinds and servantes," who sent him this reply :

" For the Right Honble Coll David Barclay of Urie thees."
Conveth the 16th 1658. [No month given.]
"SIR,

"The Meeting at Drumlithie did order that yor concernement should bee discussed, and determined heir this day. And thees heir convened have concludit and ordered that thair be thrittie thrie pund sterling raised of the scheir, for peyment of yor laitt parliament charges, and for the expenses you are to be att for the laitt commissiones you have from the schyre, the twentie pairt of ane monies being thairwith includit. You shall also receave ane summondes here inclosit, anent the Laird of Morphie's fischings, whereby the collector is citted to compeir befor the Com^r for administration of justice, wch we entreatt you may attend and gett ane sight of the Laird of Morphie his wreitte [writ] where his seasing is taken, and in what schyre it is locallie lying. We remitt it to your consideracione to do yairinto [hereunto] as you think fitt, either to bring before the Counsell or Sessione.

"Which is all Sir, from yor affectionate freinds and servantes
Arbuthnott.
Halcartoune
Carnegy Pitarro (?)
Stratton of that Ilk."

There is no further record of Colonel Barclay having taken any prominent part in politics. His name does not appear in the House of Commons list for 1658, and he evidently gave up his Parliamentary work now that his double object had been achieved, and returned to his home and family.

COLONEL DAVID BARCLAY, 1610–1686, Urie I. 1658.

On September 3rd, 1658, Oliver Cromwell died, and his eldest living son, Richard, was proclaimed Lord Protector. The Parliament were on the whole friendly to him, hoping to form an alliance with him against the Army, but the soldiers did not wish for a civilian leader, and were mutinous and restless. Richard, who had no ambition and could not control them, resigned his office in May 1659. The Army, under General Lambert, assumed authority, expelled the Rump Parliament, and attempted, unsuccessfully, to govern the country.

Whereupon General Monk, who had kept Scotland in submission, and had of old served with the Royalist forces in Ireland, marched upon London with his troops, receiving a cordial welcome from the City, and declared a free and full Parliament to settle the destiny of the nation. This Parliament not being summoned by Royal Writ, after the lawful fashion, was called The Convention of Estates. When it met, it voted that " According to the Ancient and Fundamental laws of this Kingdom, the government is, and ought to be by King, Lords and Commons," and decided to invite Charles II to return and resume his birthright.

While these great events were impending, David Barclay continued quietly in his work for his county, and took no part in public affairs.

In March 1659 the Convention of Royal Burghs resolved to oppose a claim pursued by certain noblemen and gentlemen for repayment from the public purse of £30,000 advanced by them in respect of public obligations, and drew up a document empowering Colonel Barclay to approach Richard Cromwell on their behalf.

1659.

" The present Commissioners taking to consideration the damnage the borrowis ar in by the persuit of the thertie thousand pund sterling perserved by some noblemen and wthers who have payed the

Convention of Royal Burghs, p. 483.

COLONEL
DAVID
BARCLAY,
1610–1686,
Urie I.

publict debt to be levied off the natione, which the general conven-
tione did find themselves oblidged to oppose by thair act of dait the
13 day of July last, and now being informed that at the next sessione
it is probable the bussienes may be discussed befoir the judgis
to thair great prejudice, except cours be takin to procuir from His
Hienes [Highness] and Parliament some warrant for interrupting the
said proces, and wnderstanding that the gentlemen of the several
schyres have maid choyse of Colonell David Barclay to repair to
London for that effect, and the Commissioners being weall satisfied
with the fidelitie and abilitie of the said gentleman, concurred in his
election, and impowered him to act for the Burghs, allowing him £50
sterling as their proportion of his charges.

"Anent £1600. 10.

" Ordained the Burghs to send to next general convention their shares of
£1000 Scots disbursed by the agent, and of £50 sterling advanced to Colonell
Barclay, conform to the preceding Act.

July, 1659.

In July following, Colonel Barclay desired to have his
commission renewed, " in respect of the alteration in the
Government," but the Restoration changed many things, and
the matter seems to have been dropped.

Bury Hill
Papers,
No. 56.

There appears to have arisen a decided coolness between
the Dowager Countess Marischal and the Colonel, notwithstanding all his efforts and " straining of his trust," to obtain
for her daughter-in-law a lease of her husband's lands in
1652. She must have been an autocratic dame to venture to
dispute a point of law with so redoubtable an adversary, but
it was not the first time she had disputed David Barclay's
claims, as we have seen. She endeavoured, having established her position (presumably as trustee for the estate) " to
remove all creditors that have been posest by the Trusties, or
any part of it, for payment of their interests."

" Trew and
Perfyt
Account."

The Colonel endeavoured to persuade her to forbear from
this injustice, " bot she persisting, he was forced to get ane
order from the trusties, discharging her from troubling the
said creditors."

This angered both the Dowager Countess and her co-
trustee the Laird of Morphie, and both of them were " pleased
to aspersse (most unjustlie) the said Colonell, as if he had not
endeavoured to do them service." Colonel Barclay was
naturally hurt and annoyed, and returned to the Countess " a

58

ring, set with five diamonds, which shee was pleased to send
him for obtaining unto her the Laice on her sonne's estate."

There may have been other reasons for this quarrel, and the old friendship between the families was interrupted for a time, when the following letter from the Earl Marischal appears to have restored their friendly relations.

" Directed for the Right Hon David Barclay. Bury Hill Papers, No. 80.

"Bervie. March 12th, 1659.

" COUSIN,

" I have received so many favours from you, especially the late evidence ye have given of your kindness and respects to me at this time, before your Committee at Leith, engages me to return my hearty acknowledgements for the same. And that I may in some measure express it, and make a difference of my respects to you and others, I have thought fit to signify that I shall be very willing to strengthen your conveyance by all that is in my power, as ye shall desire the same, with jovial heartiness. And I do intreat, that when anything relating to me shall come before you, that you will own the same for my interest and good, and in special I desire that the tack-duty of Boddam, which is but three pounds sterling, may not be disponed to any, it being a thing so much concerning me, or if it shall be assigned to a creditor that I may know to whom it is, that I may know how to recover. Something I have desired Arbuthnott to write to you, which I desire you will advert to, and any letters ye send to me, send them still to my son at Bervie. My wife remembers her service to you, and we both to your lady and little Robin.

" I am, Your faithfull Friend and servant

" MARISCHAL."

Alexander Gordon, in the *Theological Review* of 1874, says " the ' little Robin ' whom his father's courtly correspondents found room to include in their complimentary remembrances became the great and celebrated Apologist of the Quakers."

In 1660 David Barclay's father, the old Laird of Mathers, died at the age of 80. As has already been related in Part II, he was interred in the church in the Canongate, Edinburgh.

On May 29, 1660, Charles II was received with extra-ordinary enthusiasm by the whole country.

He had issued on April 4th the Declaration of Breda, which by its full acknowledgment of the dependence of the Crown on Parliament, cleared the way to the Restoration, and was eagerly welcomed by both Houses. It had become inevitable, as the only alternative to military tyranny. The people were tired of the rule of " Saints or Soldiers," and the one great break in the continuity of modern English History came to an end by the return of the Monarchy.

Shortly after the Restoration, David Barclay " disentangled himself from all public affairs, living very private, sometimes at Edinburgh, and sometimes at Gordonstoun with his mother-in-law, Lady Lucie Gordon, much to his ease and satisfaction, until the month of March 1663, when he suffered the loss of his excellent wife, Catherine Gordon, aged 43 years."

Her last desire had been to bring home her eldest son, Robert (then in Paris with his uncle, the Rector of the Scots Theological College there), which request Colonel Barclay most religiously performed.

In this resolve he was strengthened by the warm support of his mother-in-law, the Lady Lucie Gordon. She was a woman of remarkable character and strong religious convictions. Her father, the Dean of Sarum, was descended from a long line of distinguished and scholarly divines, and the affection and respect that she inspired is testified to by the name universally bestowed upon her of " Auld Maa " or " Auld Maman."

A letter from her, which has fortunately been preserved, expresses her satisfaction with his decision to bring back his son Robert from Paris, in accordance with the wish of his wife.

" The Lady Gordonstoune to David Barclay of Urie.

" DEAR SON,   " Gordonstoune, July 17, 1663.

" I receaved yours from London the 13 Aprill. I was exceedingly glad to hear that you were well, for I did long much to hear from you, all the things that you have sent to Edinborough, I shal use the best means I can to bring them hear. Both your little boys have had the pox, but very favourably. David was not sick at all with them, but John had three days a fever, but it has done him much good, for he is now very lusty, and beginns to find his tongue.

" I bless God for the resolution you have taken to fetch your son, although your brother would not send him to you to the Rhine, yet I cannot believe he will keep him against your will. You shal do well to walk wisely to get your son with the consent of his uncle, but if he will not then you were better want his kindnes than buy it with the loss of your son. Lett not therefore the hope of worldly gain perswade you, but remember who hath said, I will never leave nor forsake you, which certainly He will make good to all that walk in His Commandments.

"I am old, and although I praise God in health for the present, yet I know not wherever I shall see you. I desire you to see your little ones bread in the ways of God, and I shall pray the Lord to continue you to them and that they may be comforts to you. This is the prayer of Your affectionate Mother to serve you

"LUCI GORDON."

David Barclay therefore took the long journey to Paris, the account of which follows in the Life of his son Robert, and brought him home.

In the year 1665 a sudden and most unjust blow fell upon Colonel David, when he was, "att the instigation of malicious persons, committed to the Castle of Edinburgh, by order of the Government."

This must have been a great shock to him and his friends, for it might have been expected that the services he had rendered to the Royalists who had suffered for their devotion to Charles I would at least have been acknowledged with gratitude by Charles II.

But, though Robert Barclay in his Memoirs denies warmly that the Colonel ever supported Cromwell against the King, and points out how he had voted against his assumption of Royal Honours, and moreover how he had had his posts cancelled, and his estate withheld from him for many years by the orders of the Protector, he was now indicted for having been a Trustee under Cromwell.

Though this was technically true, it should have been taken into consideration that he had employed the powers then given him wholly on behalf of the Royalists, and the accusation seems to have been a singularly unjust and ungracious one.

He was not taxed with any crime in the Committal Order, but there was cause for serious anxiety to his family and

COLONEL DAVID BARCLAY, 1610–1686, Urie I.

1665. Baron Court Book of Urie.

Mackenzie's History of Scotland.

COLONEL
DAVID
BARCLAY
1610–1686,
Urie I.
friends, as it was suspected that " there was a design of forfeiting him both of estate and life," which might have succeeded had it not been for the strong interposition of his old friend General, now Earl of, Middleton, who had received high promotion at the Restoration, and was the King's Commissioner to Parliament. Though the records do not give favourable accounts of his administration of that office, and shortly after this he was disgraced and exiled for misconduct, yet it must be put to his credit that he could not permit his old friend and comrade to be unjustly accused, without protest.

The fact that Lauderdale was then Secretary of State for Scotland, and that " in order to gain the favour of the King and Court he became a most merciless persecutor of the D.N.B.,
Vol. xii,
p. 153. Covenanters . . . and was deeply implicated in all the arbitrary and unconstitutional acts of the Government at this period," may be some explanation.

This seems the more remarkable as Lauderdale was himself brought up as a Presbyterian. Desiring to stand well with the King, he consulted him as to which religion he would prefer him to adopt. Charles's characteristic reply, that Presbyterianism was no religion for a gentleman, was sufficient for the time-serving courtier. He was made a Duke in 1672.

The reason for David Barclay's imprisonment has never been officially explained, though his grandson attributes it to 1665. " mere jealousy." This treatment was the more extraordinary in that the Royalist Government was actually in debt to him for a considerable sum he had advanced out of his own pocket, to pay his regiment.

This fact was acknowledged, but he never recovered this Records of
Secretary's
Office,
Windsor,
July 30,
1688. expenditure in his lifetime, though in July 1688, " James II caused re-imburse his sonne Robert £400, as the order upon the Receiver General remarks, in my grandfather's pocket book," says Robert Barclay (Urie III).

There is a family legend that sundry old parchments and manuscripts were put away in a garret at Urie House. Their value and interest were not suspected, until a visitor observed fragments of torn papers, nibbled and destroyed by mice, scattered on the floor, but it was too late to restore them. Possibly this manuscript book so constantly referred to in Robert Barclay's Memoirs may have been among them, and would have cleared up many difficulties and filled up many gaps in the history of David Barclay. COLONEL DAVID BARCLAY, 1610–1686, Urie I.

The order for his Committal to Edinburgh Castle was made out as follows. 1665.

" August 23 1665.
    " CHARLES R. From original in British Museum.
        " Our Will and pleasure is that you cause apprehend the persons of Colonel David Barclay, and Sir James Stewart, sometime Provost of Edinburgh, and ——— Wallace, sometime Lieutenant Colonel of our foot guard in Scotland. And them and every one of them you commit into sure prison in some of our castles of Edinburgh, Sterlin, or Dumbarton there to remaine until you receave our further orders.
    " For which this shall be your warrant.
  " Given att our Court att Salisbury the 23rd day of August 1665, & of our reign the 17th yeare.
           To these alle
        Sr George Maxwell of Nether Rock
        Sr Hugh Campbell of Lesnock
        The Lairds of Cunninghamhead, Rorallan, Dunlop,
        Sr Jas Chester, Rowallan, Robert Harker, Major Moore.
" By His Majestie's Command   " LAUDERDAILL."

The Court had removed to Salisbury, for fear of the Great Plague, which was raging in London at that time.

There is a letter to the Secretary of the Privy Council, which refers to this affair, but does not throw much light upon it, nor the real reasons for his imprisonment. It says " Anent Colonel Barclay and one Lennox, both prisoners for being concerned in the late Rebellion.—underwrytten by order of Councill direct to the Lord Secretary." Register of the Privy Council of Scotland.

" MY LORD, 1666.
    " The Councill has desyred me in their name to transmitt to your Lordship the copy of a petition [This refers to a sale of horses] . . and Lykeways a petition presently presented the last Councill day in name of Colonell Barclay for his liberty, and seeing he was imprisoned by the King's order, the Councill desyres to know His Majestie's pleasur anent it.

" There is also a signatour herewith sent for a remission to one Lennox for his accession to the late Rebellion, which they desyre may be offered by your Lordship to the King.

" Of these the Council expects an accompt, which they have desyred me to signifie in their name.

" I am your Lordship's most humble servant.

" LINLITHGOW."

The first year of the Colonel's incarceration passed without official record, and there is no evidence that he was kept in " close prison " all the time. It is probable that he may have negotiated a " bond of union," undertaking to make certain payments as " caution money." It seems that Lauderdale encouraged this form of penalty and no doubt benefited thereby. We find an entry in the Register of the Privy Council, January 1, 1670, where he is ordained to remain at his own house, and to find caution " as formerly " for £100 sterling. The practice varied according to the quality of the prisoner, and the political situation, and was often accepted in the case of prisoners able to pay for their liberty.

When he was consigned to Edinburgh Castle it happened that the place was unusually crowded, and he found he had to share a cell with a fellow Member of Parliament, one John Swinton, of Swinton. This man had been a judge of the Court of Session under the Commonwealth and, though originally a Royalist, had become one of Cromwell's most trusted and influential agents in Scotland. He was a man of great natural ability and eloquence, and had joined the

Society of Friends. In prison Swinton talked with Barclay on the theme that most interested them both, and " David Barclay was strengthened and assisted towards an open avowal of himself as a believer in the principles and practice of the Quakers. He had always meditated much and deeply on religious matters, and having himself had much experience on the uncertainty of life, and the evils of malice, envy and persecution, from which neither innocency nor justice could protect a man, he turned to their teaching, which seemed to him to most closely resemble the principles laid down by the Founder of the Christian religion."

No doubt his imprisonment and enforced inactivity gave COLONEL him more opportunity for consideration of these questions. DAVID BARCLAY, Swinton's proselytising tendencies resulted in an order for 1610–1686, him to be placed in solitary confinement, but his eloquence Urie I. had so strongly influenced David Barclay that we find in 1666. the Journal of the Society of Friends that " David Barclay of Urie, in the Kingdome of Scotland, received the truth in 1666, being the fifty sixth year of his age, about the seventh month, and abode in it, and in constant unity with the faithful Friends thereof, having suffered the spoiling of goods cheerfully, and many other indignities he was formerly unaccustomed to bear, and several tedious imprisonments after the sixty-fifth year of his age."

It is not easy to define shortly the doctrines of a body which never accepted any creed nor employed any liturgy, which denied the sacraments and refused to acknowledge an ordained Ministry. But their teaching was

That there is a direct revelation of the Spirit of God to each individual soul, that this light comes to all, heathen or Christian, and that thereby the love and grace of God to all mankind is universal.

That the sacraments were inward and spiritual and not dependent on material manifestations.

That liberty of preaching and prayer should be common to all and not restricted to men specially ordained and paid.

That litigation, oaths, and war were absolutely unlawful, and that the use of weapons, even in self-defence, was contrary to Christian teaching.

That women were entitled to equal rights with men in all matters, and many minor regulations, as to the use of bad or coarse language, the denial of outward forms of respect to men of worldly position, strictness and purity of life, and so forth.

This teaching appealed strongly to David Barclay, but brought George Fox, its principal exponent, into direct conflict with all the religious bodies in England and Scotland, Anglicans, Presbyterians, Independents, Baptists, and the more extreme sects of Fifth Monarchy men, Ranters, Seekers and Muggletonians, who all resented this claim to direct inspiration " from within " without ecclesiastical sanction.

A furious opposition arose to the new doctrines, but thousands of people full of devout enthusiasm, crowded to the meetings, and the leaders of religious thought became seriously alarmed.

In 1646 and 1648 ordinances had been passed by Parliament for the prevention of " Blasphemies and Heresies," which covered several of the Quaker doctrines, notably their denial of the sacraments and an ordained priesthood. Also their refusal to pay tithes raised a legal point, which was placed in the hands of justices of the peace.

In 1654 Cromwell declared in a speech in the House of Commons that liberty of conscience was a natural right, and the Quakers breathed more freely. But other pretexts for persecution were soon found. They were accused of being Sabbath-breakers because they travelled to their meetings. They were fined for non-attendance at church services, were called " brawlers " when they spoke in churches, were guilty of breaches of the peace when they preached in the streets, refused to pay tithes, or take off their hats to men, or declined to take any Oath in Courts of Law, which latter rule had a serious result in Colonel Barclay's own case at this time.

He had for so long seriously considered the question, and made up his mind to accept all its drawbacks and dis-
advantages, that his first step was to disembarrass himself of all worldy concerns and devote his life to the religion in which he found true peace and happiness.

Robert Barclay says that " having cleared accounts with Barclay of Johnston, his father's Factor, concerning his intromissions, which clearance I have by me, and having finished all transactions with the Earle Marischal, and his brother-in-law, Charles Gordon, his Trustee, about the lands of Urie, and being now at liberty from all worldly encumberances, the uncertainty whereof he had seen both in prosperity and adversity, upon a serious and mature reflection he joined himself to the people called Quakers, about the year 1666."

"Surprise, incredulity, ridicule, dislike, resentment, and even fury, were awakened by David Barclay's profession of Quakerism. A Barclay, whose coat armorial still bore the shining mitre of Aberbrothwick,* a staunch King's man— a gallant and distinguished soldier—brother-in-law to a bishop—and own brother to the dignified Rector of the Scots College ! The thing was impossible, not to be credited." _{COLONEL DAVID BARCLAY, 1610–1686, Urie I. Alex. Gordon in Theological Review, 1874.}

David Barclay pursued his way unmoved. The date of his "convincement" conflicts with the statement that David was actually in "close prison" at the time, as this involved imprisonment in a cell with a warder, and no communication with the outside world. There must have been certain formalities connected with his election to the Society, and they could hardly have taken place in Edinburgh Castle. The rules were so severe against the Quakers gathering themselves together, or holding meetings of any kind, that the only safe places for such functions were in private houses, and under conditions of extreme secrecy. _{1666.}

But "open imprisonment" permitted of occasional leave and some of the amenities of civilised life on payment of caution money.

This points to the likelihood of his having returned to Urie, if only for a time, and this probability is increased by the fact that in 1667 Colonel Barclay reconstituted the Baron Court of Urie, which had lapsed since 1637. _{1667.}

It may have been merely a formality which did not require his personal attendance at Urie, but it probably involved a gathering of the tenants and crofters, and certain ceremonies to reinstate the feudal system, so it seems that at any rate in the beginning of the year 1667, his imprisonment was not "close."

The establishment of the Baron Court in Scotland may be regarded as an essential growth of feudalism, coincident with _{Baron Court Book of Urie.}

---

* "The shining mitre of Aberbrothwick." This statement, though frequently made, is without foundation. The origin of the "mitre" cannot be traced, but it dates back to Gloucestershire days. The Earls of Berkeley, of Berkeley Castle, bear the same crest.

67

the tenure of the land by military service. The early kings recognised in it a ready means of increasing the influence of the Crown over turbulent subjects, through the grant of power to the feudal lords to enforce respect for law and order. For as he did homage for his land, so must his sub-vassals recognise a similar duty to him as their overlord.

Their authority in the earlier days was absolute, extending to jurisdiction over all crimes except treason, and the right of " pit and gallows." As things improved, these privileges were curtailed, but the landowner could still pursue for debt, punish for theft or contumacy, and settle disputes over land and tenancy. He might call a jury, consisting of fifteen in most cases in Scotland, though the useage of the Court of Urie was not limited to that number, and could summon fewer or more if desired by him, but his authority and judgment could not be disputed.

Such in its main outlines was the Baron Court, on which the comfort and self-respect of the rural population rested. They were held in Scotland until 1747, when their jurisdiction was by law curtailed to an extent which rendered them no longer indispensable, and they gradually fell into complete disuse.

Even the partial freedom that Colonel Barclay was allowed was to be curtailed. The restoration of the bishops with the return of the Monarchy was still resented in Scotland, and the legal dispersal of hillside meetings, or " conventicles," was a never-ending grievance. In 1667 a little band of about a thousand stern Covenanters, or Cameronians, as they were called, after their leader, Richard Cameron, took up arms against the Government, believing that " God was able to save by few as by many." They were routed and dispersed in a fight with the soldiers among the Pentland Hills. There is no reason to suspect that David Barclay had any hand in this revolt, but Woodrow, the historian, writes in April, 1668:—

" I find David Barclay prisoner in the Castle of Edinboro, for some concern I suppose in Pentland, upon his declining to sign the Bond, is sent to the Tolbooth of Montrose."

Though there seems to have been no foundation for the charge, the authorities were evidently suspicious of him, no doubt increasingly so after his profession of Quakerism, and the terms of his imprisonment became more severe. His implication in this rising was the more improbable since his severance from the Kirk in 1653, and the pretext was a lame one. The Bond referred to by Woodrow was called The Bond of Peace, and was drawn up by the authorities and presented to all political prisoners for signature, without which they could not be given their freedom.

There had been many such Bonds of Peace during these times of rebellion and unrest, and the terms offered do not seem to have been unduly harsh. The wording of this particular bond ran :—

" I, A.B. bind and oblige me that I shall Keep the Public peace, and that I shall not rise in arms against or without His Majesty's authority, under all highest pains that may follow, in case I shall do anything to the contrary : and for further security C.D. doth bind and oblige himself as Cautioner for me for my keeping of the Peace, and performance of the obligement aforesaid under the pain of . . . . to be paid in case I contravene the same."

There was another version, which was " the shape in which it was offered up and down the country " :

" I, A. B. do bind and oblige me to keep the public peace, and, if I fail, that I shall pay a year's rent : likewise that my tenants and men-servants shall keep the public peace, and in case they fail, I oblige myself to pay for every tenant his year's rent, and for every servant his year's fee. And for more security I am content these presents be registered in the books of Council."

It does not appear that the wording of either of these Bonds need have offended any man with David Barclay's Royalist sympathies. It could only have been the strict tenets of the Society of Friends forbidding the taking of oaths that stood between him and his liberty. He steadfastly refused to sign the bond, and remained in prison. It must have been no light deprivation, for though being considered a political prisoner he was probably allowed to see his family and friends, he was cut off from his home and private affairs which urgently demanded his presence at Urie.

COLONEL
DAVID
BARCLAY,
1610–1686,
Urie I.
1667.

Council's
Act anent
the
Indemnity
with the
Bond of
Peace, Oct.
9, 1667,
Woodrow,
Vol. 11,
p. 93.

COLONEL
DAVID
BARCLAY,
1610–1686,
Urie I.
1667.

There is a vaulted chamber in the Castle of Edinburgh which is pointed out as the cell where both Montrose and Argyll spent their last hours. Montrose may have been there in 1641, when he was imprisoned on the representation of Argyll that he was a traitor to the Commonwealth, but, as we know, the great Marquis's last hours were spent in the Tolbooth. Argyll was, however, imprisoned there, and only left it to suffer death on the gallows in 1685. This cell was used chiefly for the safekeeping of the Covenanting leaders, so one of Colonel Barclay's importance would most probably have been put there, and shared it with John Swinton, as the room itself is of tolerable size. It can, however, be partitioned in two through a long slit in the floor, through which the great portcullis could be raised or lowered, the room being immediately above the main entrance to the castle. It was without light or air, beyond what filtered through one narrow arrow-slit in the wall, which affords a very limited glimpse of the roofs and pinnacles of Edinburgh far below, with the steel grey waters of the Firth of Forth behind them, and beyond the faint blue distance of the opposite shore.

The prisoners were allowed to take exercise on the ramparts, which are little altered to-day, and we can picture Colonel Barclay's commanding figure and military stride, as he paced to and fro, either alone, or with his fellow-prisoners.

Looking over to the north, he could see the huddle of smoky roofs of the " auld toun " below, dominated by the stately crown tower of St. Giles's church. He must often have stood to gaze into the grey distance, thinking of his wide and desolate fields lying untilled and waiting for the master's eye.

He had sent his son Robert to live at Urie, but he was unversed in estate management, and, even at this early period of his life, already deeply engaged in writing his world-famous " Apology." David's other children were still at Gordonstoun, where their grandmother Lady Gordon gave them a mother's care. Robert no doubt sent his father reports, but to a man of his energetic temperament the enforced idleness must have been irksome indeed, and needed all the patient endurance enjoined by his creed.

COLONEL DAVID BARCLAY, 1610–1686, Urie I.

1668.

He sent up a petition for the release of himself and his friend Thomas Lennox, but only received this reply from Lauderdale, speaking for the King.

March 30, 1668.

Register of the Privy Council of Scotland, 1665-1669, Vol. 11, p. 424, 428.

" Wee did see the petition of David Barclay, which though it bee of unusual straine, yet if he will signe such a bond and security as the uther persons did who were committed with him, wee do allow you to grant him his liberty, bot if he refuse, then you shall remove him to some other prison, for we will not have our Castle of Edinburgh made a prison.

Received here inclosed the remission you desyred for Thomas Lenox.

Given at our Court at Whithall the 30 day of March 1668, and of our reigne the 20th year.

Subscribitur by His Majestie's Command,

LAUDERDALE."

Thomas Lennox was restrained by no religious scruples, and on taking the Bond for Peace was released at once under this order :—

" The Lords of His Majes^ties Privy Councill ordaines His Majesties Remission in favour of Thomas Lenox to be delyvered up to him, and ordaines the Magistrates of Edinburgh to sett him to liberty, he first subscryving the band for the peace, and having his remission past the great Seall.

Appoyntes the Lord Register to call for David Barclay, and to offer him the band for the peace, that he may sign the same, and to report."

But David still refused to sign. Possibly the next order sent by the Council on April 9, 1668, was not altogether unwelcome to the Colonel, as it brought him to Montrose, which was nearer Urie, though the accommodation and comfort of the actual quarters were even inferior to those in Edinburgh Castle, and were indeed sordid, cramped and insanitary beyond description.

Edinburgh, April 9, 1668.

Register of the Privy Council of Scotland, Vol. 11, p. 282.

" The Lords of His Maj^ties Privy Councill having considered His Maj^ties letter anent David Barclay, and finding that he is unwilling to subscryve the band for the peace, doe ordaine him betwixt

COLONEL
DAVID
BARCLAY,
1610–1686,
Urie I.
1668.
(now) and the first of May nixt, to remove and transport himself from the Castle of Edinburgh, and enter himself prisoner within the Tolbooth of Montrose, under the payne of five thousand Scots merks, and that he find caution for that effect, and ordaines the keeper of the Castle of Edinburgh to sett him to liberty to the effect forsaid, and the Magistratts of Montrose to receave and detean him prisoner until further order, and discharges the said Magistratts not to suffer any Quaikers to have access to him, except his own sonne."

Though it seems strange to us that a prisoner should be ordered to arrange his own transfer from one prison to another, David Barclay transported himself as commanded ; but he addressed another " supplication " to the Lords of the Council in a month's time, which shows the hardship and injustice of his treatment. Montrose lies some twenty-five miles distant from Urie, and he could probably communicate with his friends there, but was rendered so uneasy by their reports of the condition of the place, that he wrote :—

Reg. of
Privy
Council,
Vol. 11, p.
457.
" Colonel David Barclay reports that by the Council's order he has removed himself a prisoner from the Castle of Edinburgh to the Tolbooth of Montrose, bot by reason of his effaires and family, which are in much disorder and straites, that unless he have some farder tyme to make some shift for his and his children's maintenance, he or they shall starve ; besides there is no roume in that prison wherein any persone can stay, and so craves some relief."

May 9, 1668.

The Lords thereupon ordained him to have " the liberty of the town of Montrose till further orders, on finding caution in 5000 merkes, to confine himself within the same, and not remove without license."

They again recommended the magistrates of the burgh " that they be carefull no quaikers frequent his company, except his owne sonne."

The repetition of this caution throws some light on the severity of his treatment, he being still accused of no offence.

However time went on, and it was not until the 3rd of December 1668, that an answer was vouchsafed to the first part of his petition.

Ibid.
" The Lords of His Majestie's Privy Council having considered a petition presented be David Barclay desyring that in respect of his

72

urgent affaires he might be liberat of the confynement putt upon him to the towne of Montrose, doe hereby change the place of the petitioners confynement from Montrose to his house at Urie, and three myles about the same, the petitioner finding caution under the payne of five thousand merkes that he shall keep his confynement and return to Montrose against the first day of June, nixt, to which time they allow him to reseid at his house, as said is, whilk caution is found accordingly."

The references to " his own house at Urie " are rather perplexing, for we know he did not finally build " the old Castle " until 1670. There must have been some sort of habitation there, possibly a farm house, or maybe the old manor house of the Hayes may not have been entirely destroyed, where Robert could live and prosecute his studies, as we are told he did during these years.

Another grudging extension of leave was granted in April 1669.

" The Lords of the Council having considered a petition presented by Colonell David Barclay supplicating that the former liberty allowed him to reseid at his house of Urie with the licence of three myles about the same, to goe about his affaires might be prorogat for some further tyme, notwithstanding of his former confynement to the towne of Montrose, do hereby contnow [continue] the petitioners confynement to his house of Urie, and three myles about the same, untill the last day of July nixt, he finding caution under the payne of five thousand merkes, to keep his confynement, and to return to the burgh of Montrose immediately after the said last day of July."

Again on July 29, 1669, a permit extended his liberty for another six months.

It must have been during this time when the Colonel was permitted to live at Urie that one of his earliest acts in connection with the reconstituted Baron Court of the estate took place. " It was one which probably stands unique in the history of such tribunals."

We can easily understand how, after so long a period of practical exemption from authority, there had grown up in the Barony a race of tenants ill-disposed to brook the will of a superior, however considerately and wisely it might be imposed. Accordingly on May 7th, 1669, we have the curious

Margin notes: COLONEL DAVID BARCLAY, 1610–1686, Urie I. — 1669. — *Ibid.* — July 29, 1669. — Baron Court of Urie. — 1669.

COLONEL
DAVID
BARCLAY,
1610–1686,
Urie I.
1669.
incident of the Laird voluntarily surrendering himself at
the bar of his own Court, in answer to the charge of being
an oppressor and exactor.

The question narrowed itself to one of the rendering of
certain services, and the matter was amicably settled by the
refusal of the tenants to prosecute, confessing " in regaird to
them that they had no reasons soe to doe." David Barclay
met them half way, by proposing to discontinue the exaction
of service for the future, on payment of a small yearly equivalent of six pounds Scots.

Notwithstanding this action on his part it is not difficult to
see how, in discharging his duties as a landlord, the Colonel's
religious opinions must have caused him, for a time at all
events, to be ill thought of and misjudged. " In his hands a
Court of legal justice is transformed, as far as may be, into a
tribunal of religious equity, and doubtless there were few
among his vassals that rightly appreciated the change." It
upset their notions, and disturbed their equanimity. It frequently overwhelmed with rebuke and penalty those who had
not calculated to meet a moral element in the preferment of
their often-times vexatious and ill-considered claims.

The Colonel did not always " suffer fools gladly " if a tradition about him is true. Though his religion was the leading
and absorbing interest of his life, he did not altogether neglect
his practical concerns. His strenuous life had left him little
opportunity for learning agricultural lore, and when he set
about improving his estate, he found his lack of practical
knowledge laid him open to criticism and even imposition.
But for all that the Colonel meant to be master on his own
property, and when he differed with one of his ploughmen as
to the correct method of ploughing, and the man ventured to
disagree, the Colonel addressed him in these words : " Thou
knowest, friend, that I feed and pay thee to do my work in a
proper manner, but thou art wise in thine own eyes, and
regardest not the admonitions of thine employer. I have
hitherto spoken to thee in a style thou understandest not, for
verily thou art of a perverse spirit. I wish to correct thy
errors, for my own sake and for thine, and therefore thus tell

74

thee that I am thy master, and must be obeyed." These
moderate words were followed by a properly administered
castigation, and it is related that he had no more trouble
with insubordinate servants, who had been under the impression that "the old Quaker" could be defied with impunity.

His longed-for liberty was granted to him at last, on
August 23, 1670. The Lords of His Majesty's Privy Council,
sitting at Edinburgh, once more

" haveing considered a petition presented on behalf of Colonel David
Barclay, supplicating that the former restraint put upon him, con-
fyning him to his own house, might be taken off, and he permitted to
goe about his necessar affaires as he shall have occasion, doe thereby
take off and discharge the restraint and confynement putt upon the
Petitioner, and notwithstanding thereof grants him liberty to goe
about his own affaires in any place of the Kingdome."

We can imagine with what thankfulness of heart David
Barclay set to work to build his house and restore his property.

He erected a long, low, solidly built mansion out of great
blocks of the local granite, on the top of a steep bank, at the
foot of which ran the burn. It faced south-east, so the morning sun shone on its steep roofs and whitewashed walls.
He built it with two " pepper-pot " turrets, a sign of the
occupancy of the owner, and small deep-set windows,
characteristic of those times, when the possibilities of defence
were more considered than beauty of architecture. A battle-
mented porch was later erected over the front entrance, but
the house was built as a manor house, not a fortified
dwelling, though capable of standing a siege if need be.

He planted young trees behind it to shelter it from the cold
north winds, and began to restore the land. The damage
had gone deep; the uprooting of the gorse, the clearing out
of the heather and bracken, and the thinning and replanting
of the scattered woodland was the task of years, and even so
late as 1760, we find the fifth Robert Barclay of Urie complaining that the estate was still " in the rudest condition "
when he inherited it.

The Colonel also built a meeting house in the grounds,
close to the house, in spite of having been expressly for-

COLONEL
DAVID
BARCLAY,
1610–1686,
Urie I.
1670.

bidden by the magistrates to " keep Quaiker Meetings." As ever, his conscience was his only guide.

As soon as the house was completed he handed over the whole property to his son Robert, who had married in 1669, making certain business-like arrangements as to his continued residence there.

Of the Colonel, his grandson writes : " He became as eminent for his religious and exemplary life as formerly among others for his bravery, resolving now to suffer indignitys and injurys for conscience sake, a virtue he was before unacquainted with." His strong example encouraged others, and a little group of converts to the Society of Friends gathered round him, many of them his kinsmen : Alexander Jaffray, five times Provost of Aberdeen in the old campaigning days, the wife of Baillie Gilbert Molleson, the Gellie Family, the Forbes of Achorties, Patrick Livingstone, in whose marriage contract to Sarah Hyfield of Nottingham, in 1675, the name of David Barclay of Urie appears as " consenter," and many other people of rank and family were among the early friends in and about Aberdeen.

Urie from henceforth became the centre of the Quakers in the north, and the meetings there held first monthly, and then weekly, were attended by increasing numbers of tenants and neighbours, though the Synod of Aberdeen had issued a sentence of excommunication against " Papists, Quakers, and other scandalous persons," and all Christian people were enjoined to hold no communication with them.

Colonel Barclay, however, was not under that ecclesiastical jurisdiction, and the Bishop of the neighbouring diocese of Brechin was his brother-in-law, and his very good friend ; but the peace and order of his later years were rudely broken, and he suffered with many of his friends from the bitter intolerance of the Restoration period.

The ancient " prelatic " City of Aberdeen was still strongly opposed to any form of religious dissent and persecuted the Society of Friends with the utmost harshness. Where there was pretext that they had broken the law, it was used to excuse the greatest cruelty of prosecution, and even though many of its members were people of good position, and living peaceful charitable lives, all were treated the same. A party of Quakers was driven out of the town by town sergeants, and the inhabitants were forbidden to harbour them or succour them in any way. The humbler members were roughly handled, refused medical or other aid, and for the smallest offences subjected to heavy fines, and even personal chastisement. George Keith, a cousin of David Barclay, a rather aggressive ring-leader, was imprisoned for ten months. The clergy were especially vindictive, and at their instigation the magistrates ordered all male Quakers to be apprehended at a meeting and committed to gaol, while their meeting house was closed. Some interments having taken place in the Friends' private burial ground without religious ceremony, the magistrates ordered the bodies to be exhumed and removed to the churchyard.

David Barclay therefore made a burial ground on the top of a steep hill in the Urie " policies " which he purposed to surround with a stone wall and locked gate, so that no un-authorised person could break in. He left the building of the wall to his son Robert, in his last directions. Here lie the Colonel himself, his son Robert and his wife, with the successive members of his family who inherited Urie, down to the year 1853.

A small mausoleum was later erected to cover their graves, and the walls are hung with plain slate tablets, inscribed with their names and dates only. No further inscriptions are added, nor even a text of scripture.

This mausoleum, or " Howff " as it is locally called, has been added to by the present owners of Urie and used as their private burying ground. It should be said that this addition was not approved of by the country people, who still hold the name of Barclay in veneration.

It must be admitted that, as in so many religious move-ments, there was some truth in the accusations made by their opponents that the extremist followers of the new sect brought it into disrepute.

The Quakers were accused of carrying religious excitement

to the verge of frenzy, and their very nickname was popularly, though erroneously, attributed to their shaking and trembling under the influence of excessive religious fervour. Though they forbade the use of weapons, they employed the power of the pen, and issued great numbers of controversial tracts and pamphlets, which possibly inflamed the passions of their persecutors quite as much, though until Penn and Robert Barclay began to write nothing of much literary value appeared. They did not meddle with politics, and obeyed George Fox's exhortation, " Keep out of the powers of the earth."

Meanwhile David Barclay was suffering many things for his faith. He was never one to hide his opinions, and on his occasional visits to Aberdeen, he wore the rather conspicuous garb of black cloak, and severely plain garments, with a broad brimmed hat set on his straight cut grey hair, which in those days of brightly coloured and fantastically cut clothes, left the passers by in no doubt as to his profession.

The citizens of Aberdeen were given to the throwing of unsavoury missiles, and the utterance of coarse abuse of their religious opponents, and assuredly this dress must have attracted notice which it would have been pleasanter to avoid. David was still a noticeable figure, and those who remembered him in the scarlet tunic, white plumed hat, full trunks, high black boots and gilt spurs of his Swedish campaign, or in later days in the workmanlike steel breastplate and helmet, leather belt, and plain basket-hilted sword of the great Rebellion, may have regretted the change.

The Laird of Urie, as he was now called, rode through the jeering crowds, indifferent to their conduct, and no doubt with a prayer on his firm lips that they might receive the truth.

The American poet Whittier has described the scene in a poem which may be quoted here.

THE LAIRD OF URIE.

Up the streets of Aberdeen, by the Kirk and College Green
Rode the Laird of Urie
Close behind him, close beside, foul of mouth and evil-eyed
Pressed the mob in fury.

HISTORY OF THE BARCLAY FAMILY

Flouted him the drunken churl, jeered at him the servant girl
Prompt to please her master,
And the begging carlin, late fed and clothed at Urie's gate,
Cursed him as he passed her.

COLONEL
DAVID
BARCLAY,
1610–1686,
Urie I.

Yet with calm and stately mien, up the streets of Aberdeen
Came he slowly riding
And to all he saw and heard, answering not with bitter word,
Turning not for chiding.

Came a troop with broadswords swinging, bits and bridles sharply
    ringing
Loose and free and froward.
Quoth the foremost " Ride him down. Push him, prick him
    through the town.
Drive the Quaker coward."

But from out the thickening crowd, cried a sudden voice and loud,
"Barclay ! Ho ! A Barclay !"
And the old man at his side saw a comrade, battle-tried,
Scarred and sunburned darkly.

Who, with ready weapon bare, fronting to the troopers there,
Cried aloud, " God save us !
Call ye coward him who stood ankle deep in Lutzen's blood,
With the brave Gustavus !"

" Nay I do not need thy sword, comrade mine," said Urie's lord,
" Put it up, I pray thee.
Passive to His Holy Will, trust I in my Master still
Even though He slay me.

" Pledges of thy love and faith, proved on many a field of death,
Not by me are needed."
Marvelled much that henchman bold that his Laird, so stout of old,
Now so meekly pleaded.

" Woe's the day ! " he sadly said, with a slowly shaking head,
And a look of pity.
" Urie's honest lord reviled, mock of knave and sport of child,
In his own good city.

79

HISTORY OF THE BARCLAY FAMILY

COLONEL
DAVID
BARCLAY,
1610–1686,
Urie I.

" Speak the word, and, Master mine, as we charged on Tilly's line,
And his Walloon Lancers,
Charging through their midst, we'll teach civil look and decent
   speech
To these boyish prancers."

" Marvel not, mine ancient friend, like beginning, like the end,"
Quoth the Laird of Urie,
" Is the sinful servant more than his gracious Lord, who bore
Bonds and stripes in Jewry ?

" Give me joy that in His name I can bear with patient frame
All these vain ones offer,
While for them He suffereth long, shall I answer wrong with wrong
Scoffing with the scoffer ?

" Happier I with loss of all, hunted, outlawed, held in thrall
With few friends to greet me
Than when squire and reeve were seen, riding out from Aberdeen,
With bared heads to meet me.

" When each goodwife, o'er and o'er, blessed me as I passed her
   door
And the snooded daughter,
Through her casement glancing down, smiled on him who bore
   renown
From red fields of slaughter.

" Hard to feel the strangers scoff, hard the old friends falling off,
Hard to learn forgiving,
But the Lord His own rewards, and His love with them accords
Warm and fresh and living.

" Through this dark and stormy night, Faith beholds a feeble light
Up the blackness streaking,
Knowing God's own time is best, in a patient hope I rest
For the full day-breaking."

Thus the Laird of Urie said, turning slow his horse's head
T'wards the Tolbooth prison,
Where through iron gates he heard poor disciples of the Lord
Preach of Christ arisen.

80

Not in vain, Confessor old, unto us the tale is told
Of thy day of trial,
Every age on him who strays from its broad and beaten ways,
Pours its seven-fold Vial.

Happy he, whose inward ear angel comfortings can hear
O'er the rabble's laughter,
And while Hatred's faggots burn, glimpses through the smoke dis-
cern
Of the good hereafter.

Knowing this, that never yet share of truth was vainly set
In the World's wide fallow.
After hands shall sow the seed, after hands from hill and mead
Reap the harvest yellow.

Thus, with somewhat of the Seer, must the moral pioneer
From the future borrow,
Clothe the waste with dreams of grain, and on midnight's sky of
rain
Paint the golden morrow.

David Barclay lived unmolested at Urie with his family for 1676. five or six years, when new troubles fell upon him. In March 1676 the Council of Edinburgh put forth a declaration recommending the execution of former Acts of Parliament against conventicles. No doubt the meetings of the Society of Friends in his grounds and their increasing success had been watched with jealous eyes by the ecclesiastical authorities, who had no power over him outside the county of Aberdeen, and seized the opportunity of employing the civil law.

In *The Sufferings of the Quakers* this is thus described, "Now, though this Proclamation was expressly relative only to such persons as had been outlawed by the Council, yet the Priests and Rulers of Aberdeen made a Handle of it to oppress the Quakers, and coming to the Meeting, arrested all the Leaders, and committed them to prison in the new Tolbooth." So eager were they that this was done before the Declaration had been actually received. On March 19th they took George Keith, and on the 21st, David Barclay with

Sufferings of the Quakers, Joseph Besse, Vol. II.

COLONEL DAVID BARCLAY, 1610–1686, Urie I.

Andrew Jaffray and five others. The Prisoners were all accused of " not only having absented themselves from Divine Worship, but had kept House Conventicles, and presumptuously dared and presumed to preach, pray, and expound Scripture and were all condemned to all Paines and Penalties due to the wilful disobeyers and contemners of His Majes^{ties} just Authorities."

1676.

After being detained in the Tolbooth for over two months, in June they came up for trial. The witnesses produced were mostly students of divinity, many of them mere boys, and David Barclay was appointed the spokesman for the accused. The three commissioners were Lord Errol, George Earl Marischal (brother to David's old friend, who had died in 1671) and Sir John Keith.

The Laird of Urie was at the head of the body of Friends, who were all men noted for learning, culture and public spirit. He stood, tall, dignified, and impressive, and made the only public speech of which any clear record remains.

The lawyers of Aberdeen, to their honour, had refused to take any part in the case, and only one, " a needy pettifogger " called Patrick Hay, appeared against them. Urie made short work of his lame arguments, and taking the legal points one by one showed the weakness, cruelty and injustice of the prosecution, in words that could not be gainsaid, except by the simple method of overruling his objections. This was accordingly done. He said " That though it was usual for people in like case with them, to keep lawyers to plead their cause, yet they, having an Advocate in the Father, who could and would prove their innocency in the consciences of their opposers, did not think it proper to employ any man to speak for them."

He desired that " no advantage might be taken of the prisoners for their lack of knowledge of the intricacies of the Law ; and that the Court would consider that maxim of the Law, which says *Summum jus est summa injuria* [the extremity of the Law is the extremity of injustice] and would not extend the utmost rigour of the Law against them."

A written defence was then handed in, to the effect that the prisoners were not among the persons against whom the Conventicle Acts were directed ; that they had been imprisoned, contrary to the Law, for nearly three months ; that they had only done their duty to God, and dared not forsake the assembling of themselves together, but that this was not done in contempt of those in authority ; that the charge against the prisoners in general of having met three times a week ever since the month called March, 1674, could not be true, because divers of them had been out of the nation beyond the seas, and others in England, and many of them had not been within the town of Aberdeen for several months during the time mentioned in their charge.

These arguments were scornfully rejected, and the prisoners were separately asked if they would obey, and as they all refused, they were all penalised.

" To wit, Each of the said David Barclay and other Ilk ane, the fourth part of their valued rents for their keeping of Conventicles, and an eighth part for withdrawing from public worship, and others in lesser amounts."

This must have been a considerable loss to David Barclay, with his encumbered estate and unproductive land. He had hardly yet restored it from the devastation of the Montrose campaign, owing to his enforced absences, and the rebuilding, restocking, and replanting his farms, woods, and arable land, was an expensive business. He appears to have found it impossible to pay at once, so was sent to prison.

We have a letter which tells the story in his own words, written from the Tolbooth, Aberdeen, to his son Robert, who had just returned from Holland,

DEAR CHILD,—

I had thine from London to Friends, to myself and likewise from Harwich, which was 20 days a'coming. G. K₁ [George Keith.] had thine from London, who wrote to thee to Holland, with Alexander Simwell, & I wrote on the side of his letter, who got out to go his voyage & enter here on his return. There are in prison 31 of us, and 4 out on bond, Alex^dr Harper, who is going as is informed, to build in the country, being recovered. Robert Burnet of Muchells, for whom the Clerk here gave bond, that he should not keep meetings, which as yet he has not done, no, not at my house on the first days,

Margin notes: COLONEL DAVID BARCLAY, 1610–1686, Urie I.

1676.

Bury Hill papers.

COLONEL
DAVID
BARCLAY,
1610-1686,
Urie I.

pretending his wife causes lock doors on him, as he told me this week himself. The other is Alex: Patin's servant, called John King, we are all in health and refreshed daily by the Lord's powerfully appearing in & amongst us, & in a wonderful and unexpected way visiting us by His overcoming love to the gladning of our hearts, & making us willing not only to believe but to suffer for his name's sake, to whom be ever living Praises. There was ane address sent from Friends to David Falconer to be given to the King's Council, & as he informs us ane other from Friends, prisoners at Leith, but neither were read, yet the Magistrates at Leith set Friends at liberty the next day on the account that there was nothing against them, without engaging them to enter again, but the most of the Magistrates here continue their wonted enmity & have manifested this this day by causing lead-nail all the Prison windows, because And: Jaffray declared to the people in the streets out at them, so that we are barred from breathing the free air, & these here deputed by the Council are to meet on the 26th of this month to proceed against us, in order to which they are drawing inditements against us, & have appointed an Advocate to pursue us, as Criminalls in the King's name, though the King's Councill at Leith hath not as yet, as is informed, done anything against the Presbyterians on whose account their declaration was emitted, so that we are like to be the butt of all their malice here, if the Lord restrain them not, if thou had freedom to move Lauderdale for a letter to the Council that (wee being a peaceable pecople from whom there can be no inconvenience arise to the Government) that our Meetings may be untroubled, it would mightilie discourage our opposers, for after we are fined & set at Liberty, they intend to imprison us again in the high Tolbooth repenting they have given us so good a house at this time.

Fraser his nephew was with me before I had thine from Hariche, & inquired if I had heard from thee out of London, but signified nothing of what thou wrote, for he had (been) warned.

From thy affectionate Father

DA BARCLAY.

Aberdeen Tolbooth . 12th of the $\frac{1}{mo.}$ 1676.

Sufferings
of the
Quakers,
Joseph
Besse,
Vol. II.

The Provost of Aberdeen, perceiving that the loss of their goods did not deter this people from returning to their meetings, which his aim was to prevent, determined to render their confinement as incommodious as he possibly could, for which purpose they would cause the prisoners frequently to remove their utensils and bedding out of one room into another. They also made a proposition for

petitioning the Commissioners to give order for the close COLONEL DAVID BARCLAY, 1610–1686, Urie I.
shutting up of all the prisoners in the higher part of the gaol, but could not obtain their concurrence in that piece of cruelty. Bailie Barnet tried to urge the Commissioners to prevent the Quakers speaking to the people out of the prison windows, and they, willing to prevent this supposed danger, gave the said Bailie Barnet an order to remove Patrick Livingstone, George Keith, Robert Barclay (who had recently been arrested, on his return from abroad), John Skene and Andrew Jaffray, out of the prison to a place out of the town, called "the Chapel," where they thought they would have better accommodation. But the Provost and Bailie, whose aim was to incommode the prisoners, not ease them, were not well pleased, and delayed to execute the order. Such was the bitterness of their opponents, that Bailie Barnet (or Burnet) Theological Review, Alex. Gordon.
is reported to have said, " He would pack them as salmon in a barrel, and though they stood as close as the fingers on his hands, yet they should have no more room."

A few days later, observing some of the prisoners out of the High Prison preaching to the people who stood in great numbers in the street to hear them with much attention, they were angry, and immediately employed workmen to nail up the windows in the Upper Prison, and the very chinks that were to let in light upon the stairs, after which the Provost with Bailie Barnet went into the Low Council House (a place divided from that where the prisoners were only by a thin partition) where they cursed and swore, raved and foamed, in the hearing of the prisoners.

Alexander Gordon says:

" From the windows of the Tolbooth, Aberdeen, the Quakers Theological Review, 1874.
observed Ministers who were attending the Synod of the Diocese, staggering from drunkenness in the streets, and boldly warned the people. The clergy wrote to the Bishop, complaining that the Quakers were so insolent and abusive that they could not move along the streets. This may be some reason for what appears to be meaningless cruelty in boarding up the windows."

At length the magistrates decided to execute the last order of the Commissioners, only instead of Patrick Livingstone, they determined to move David Barclay in his place, which was accordingly done. Those who were sent to "the Chapel" were then placed in a cold narrow building, which had a great door opening on to the Eastern Ocean, where there was very little room, and only one little window, so that the prisoners could not see to eat their food except by candle light, or the door being opened by the keeper. At those times a servant coming to sweep out the floor, the prisoners used to make way for him by standing a few paces outside the door, when the Provost sharply rebuked the keeper for letting them have a few minutes' breathing.

The little room had a chimney, but it smoked so that they could not light the fire. When they asked for a little space 1676. to lay some peats or fuel in, the gaoler durst not give it, without consent of the Provost, who, when appealed to, rudely chid the man who kept the key.

This dreary imprisonment was cheered by sympathising letters from George Fox, William Penn and Isaac Pennington, but it seems extraordinary to our modern ideas that an old and distinguished gentleman like the Colonel, and a celebrated author like his son, should have been subjected to such indignities.

The unhappy prisoners kept in the Tolbooth higher prison in Aberdeen were in even worse case, without light or air, or room even for their beds, which had to be piled up one above another by day. "But at last their relations and acquaintance applied to the Magistratts to prevent the death of the prisoners, which the Physicians did declare them to be in danger of."

Before they were removed an order of the Council arrived, in reply to letters written by Robert Barclay to the Lords of the King's Council, that the Council granted that " A Missive be sent to the said Commissioners to enquire into the Quality and Condition of the several prisoners. . . and in the mean time ordains the Magistrats of Aberdeen to provide the 1677. prisoners with convenient Rooms for their imprisonment April 3rd. so that they may be accommodated with necessaries."

This was followed by another order from the Council, which

ordained that the said Quakers be removed from the Tolbooth of Aberdeen to the Tolbooth of the Borough of Banff.

COLONEL DAVID BARCLAY, 1610–1686, Urie I.

The irregularity of the posts caused the two decrees to be delivered at the same time and the contradictory orders caused some confusion, during which Robert Barclay with five others were released, and several of them went to Edinburgh, whence further petitions were issued by Robert on behalf of the remaining prisoners.

These resulted in another order from the Commissioners of the Council, which ordained that David Barclay and those with him be removed from the said prison of Aberdeen and " hereby confines them to their Countrey respective Dwelling Places and Parochies, wherein the same lie, straitly charging and prohibiting them during their said confynement from permitting within their houses or frequenting any unlawful Meetings, wherein if they fail they are to be imprisoned and fined according to the Acts of Parliament, and the said Magistrats are to apprehend and imprison them in case of their transgression within these bounds."

Pursuant to this decree, the prisoners were set at liberty, and told the purport of the Council's order as to their confinement in their own parishes, to which they answered that " they did accept of their liberty, but as to the restrictions imposed on them, they should act as they thought proper."

April 16th, 1677.

The restrictions were not insisted on, and they were all released, David Barclay returning home.

The magistrates, however, " vexed because they could not have further access to his person att that time," procured a warrant to distrain his goods, which they sent to be executed by one Captain Melvill, formerly in the Colonel's troop.

Genealogical Account.

On December 29th, 1677, George Melvill went into the country to " poynd " David Barclay, but upon producing his warrant from the Council Commissioners, David Barclay pointed out that he could not lawfully take anything of his by virtue of that warrant, because the shire of Mearns, in which he dwelt, was not within the bounds of the Commissioners authority, which extended only to the shire of Aberdeen.

Sufferings of the Quakers, Besse, Vol. II.

Melvill, regarding not any such point of law, proceeded to execute his purpose by committing yet a greater act of injustice, for he took from the said David Barclay ten labouring oxen, which was by Act of Parliament forbidden to be done, even in case of a just debt, in the ploughing season. He took also two kine and a young bull and a quantity of corn. Having driven the beasts to Stonehaven, he could not get them appraised so low as he desired, but had them valued at the lowest rate he could, which was £20 (Scots.)

Captain Melvill, having levied the fines in that part of the country, returned home with his plunder ; but the cattle he had taken from David Barclay became burdensome to him, for he could find no man that would buy them, and they, continually feeding, put him to so much expense for pasturage that he had much ado to keep them from starving until the spring. At which time the means of his getting rid of them being somewhat observable, we shall here mention it.

1677.

Some time before this the students of divinity at Aberdeen had held a public dispute with the Quakers, of which that people had published an account. The students in reply to that account thought it necessary for their own reputation to publish an answer to them which they composed, and made a fairly large book of it, but such as they could not find a printer who would publish it at his own charge and hazard the sale of it, wherefore they were obliged either to let their performance lie dormant, or print it at their own expense. Having with some difficulty raised the money among them, in hopes of being reimbursed by the sale of their book, they were grievously disappointed by having almost the whole impression left on their hands, which nobody would purchase. Seeing their labour thus neglected, and their money lost, they had recourse to the following expedient.

They drew up a petition representing their loss to the Commissioners, and requesting some relief out of the Exchequer, and through the influence of the Archbishop (Andrew Sharpe) obtained their request so far, that the Commissioners issued a precept upon Captain Melvill to pay them a certain part of the Quakers' fines in his hand, and he having nothing else left gave them those oxen of David Colonel Barclay's, which had long lain heavy on his hands Thus David Barclay, those cattle became the students' property, and at length were 1610–1686, sold to raise the money they wanted. Urie I.

David Barclay took no steps to recover his property, even though so illegally taken from him, and beyond lodging a formal protest with a notary public, in the interests of law and order, suffered the loss with dignity and patience.

His antagonists were not yet satisfied, and in June 1677 he and his son Robert were again arrested at a meeting, but were soon liberated, as Robert Barclay (Urie III) says : " As I have heard from good authority, by ane order from Court, with a Reprimand for medling with either of them considering their relations and alliances, and so the good old man mett with no further trouble to the end of his days."

The last religious meeting of the Aberdeen Quakers which 1679. was disturbed by the authorities took place on November 9th, 1679, when all the leaders were once more arrested and sent to prison, but in about three hours were all set at liberty.

" From which time their religious assemblies were held at Sufferings Aberdeen without molestation from the Magistrates, who of the Quakers, having abundantly proved the Patience and Constancy of Besse. this people, in religiously assembling to worship God, to be such as their utmost Force and Cruelty could not conquer, forebore at length to repeat their fruitless attempts, and quietly to permit what they were fully convinced their Power was unable to prevent."

After this the persecution of the Quakers moderated, and in a few years ceased, Woodrow regretfully reporting " some of them being even in close friendship with the Judges." We need have little doubt that the Laird of Urie was one of these, and that after his stormy life, he was at last permitted to find peace. He devoted his leisure to the improvement of his house and estate, and in 1679 employed one James Smith, an architect, who despite his English name was bred in Italy, to cover with freestone the house of Urie, " which he hand- The Great somely compleated." Alexander Gordon tells us that " It Laird of Urie. was decorated inside by frescoes in the Italian fashion."

III.—M   89

COLONEL
DAVID
BARCLAY,
1610–1686,
Urie I.

In 1680 David Barclay drew up a deed, making provision for his children, as follows :—

David Barclay his Divisione of his children's provision in the year 1680.

1680.

Bury Hill
Papers
No. 89.

Be it kend till all men be their p[rese]nt l[ett]ers me David Barclay of Urie, forsamerlie as be ye disposition and right of the dait at Edinburgh the 14 March 1668, made by the deceased Master Charles Gordon, brother german to Sir Ludovick Gordon of Gordonstoun . . . to me in lyf-rent, and Robert Barclay my eldest lawful sone in ffie [fee] and to his aires and assignes therein expressed heritable and irremedablie of the Lands and Barronie of Urie and others therein rehersed. And which right of ffie is granted to my said sone & his forsaids with and under the particulars, reservations etc therein mentionat. And particularlie with the burthen of the payment of the some of 20.000 merks Scots money . . . to Jhon, David, Lucie, and Jeanes Barclayes my childrine at the terms herein specified, and with interest and aliment as is therein exprest. And that according as I shall please to proportion and devyd [divide] the same at any time in my lifetime in manner specified in the said right and disposition, as the same in itself mair fullie is contained.

And I, . . . by declaring my pleasur to prevent all contraversie and seed of plea amongst them, therefor make the devision of the said somme of 20.000 merks, as followeth, viz : 6.000 merks each to his [my] sons Jhone and David, 4.500 to Lucie, my eldest daughter and 3.500 marks to my youngest daughter Jeane Barclay.

In case any of my daughters decease unmarried or within yeare and day of her marriage without any living child lawfully procreat in marriage, within yeare and day, I apoint and order the propertie of the daughter or daughters so deceasing to accrue and appertaine and belong also to the said Robert (my eldest sone).

Witnesses, Robert Sandiland brother germane to Patrick Sandiland of Cotton [Corton ?] and Alexander Paterson, my present servant.

DA. BARCLAY.

1683.

Genealogical
Account.

" He went once after this to London, accompanied with his old friend and acquaintance, John Swinton of Swinton, chiefly to visit his friends, and sometimes to Edinburgh, upon that account, particularly in April 1683, being accompanied with his friend, Andrew Jaffray of Kingswells, his eldest son and his wife, and their eldest son, whom they were carrying to a boarding-school at Theobalds, within twelve miles of London : but for the most part he staid at his own COLONEL DAVID BARCLAY, 1610–1686, Urie I. house at Urie enjoying great satisfaction in a country life, being much respected by gentry and nobility wherever he was known. . ."

We are told that " the baser sort only resented his religious views " and even they after a time were compelled to respect his consistency and courage, and took full advantage of his unfailing kindness and charity when in need.

David Barclay was as thorough in his desire for peace as he had been in the past for success in his war-like operations, and left no stone unturned that might encourage good will amongst those he loved, both during his lifetime and afterwards. He was, however, not easily imposed upon, as the following anecdote, related in a correspondence some hundred years later, seems to show us. A certain William Tuke writes from York to George Miller, speaking of an attack in print made by the Memorials of Hope Park, 1790, pp. 40, 41. Rev. George Markham, D.D., which tried to prove that the " Society of Friends " were ready to defend their property by force of arms rather than submit to injustice. William Tuke says that the pamphlet abounds with abuse and scurrility, and he quotes the annexed anecdote.

" Colonel Barclay, father of the famous ' Apologist ' for the Quakers, who in his earlier youth served under Gustavus, King of Sweden, appears to have been wiser in his generation than certain high and mighty authorities, civil and ecclesiastical, in our times and country.

" A neighbour of the Colonel's in the county of Mearns, in Scotland, had built a temporary hut on a barren mountain for the use of those who tended his cattle, a few hundred yards beyond the Marches, on the land belonging to the Colonel. Barclay sent the gentleman notice to remove the hut, signifying that if he did not he would come and throw it down.

" No regard being paid to the message the Colonel called together a number of his tenants in arms and marched to the spot. The other gentleman, who had heard of his intentions, came also, prepared to repel force by force. When they approached each other at the head of their respective corps a halt was commanded on both sides.

" ' Friend,' said Colonel Barclay, ' I have long renounced the wrathful principle, and wish not to quarrel with anybody, but if

COLONEL
DAVID
BARCLAY,
1610–1686,
Urie I.
thou hast a right to build within the marche line between us, here, it is but extending that right to build within my arable fields, which are also unenclosed. Let our people stand by, whilst thou and I pull down this hut, injurious to my property, but of no consequence to thee.'

" The other affirmed he had a right to build the hut where it stood, that his neighbour's claim was unjust and ill-founded, and that he would be the death of the first man who should dare to touch it.

" ' Friend,' said the Colonel, ' the time was when thou wouldst not have dared to speak to me in this style, but though I am only the withered remains of what I once was, thou had better not stir up the old man within me, as if thou dost he will soon be too much for thee. Be thy threats unto thyself. I shall throw down the first stone, and do you my people resist this unjust encroachment of my property.'

" The hut was thrown down, without the least opposition, and both parties returned in peace to their respective abodes."

Dr. Markham was a bitter opponent of the " Friends," and took every opportunity of vilifying them, and caused several of them to be imprisoned for a number of years for non payment of tithes. Knowing the character of David Barclay, this anecdote, it must be admitted, bears the stamp of truth.

Bury Hill
Deeds.
We have seen his careful and orderly arrangements in his will for his children, and how he settled all outlying debts and claims that might disturb them. In 1684 he wrote another deed in which he explains how he used the 2,000 merks of his daughter-in-law's dowry for the benefit of the estate, but had in return made over to his eldest son, Robert, his life-rent, or ownership of the house and lands. He says, " I make and constitute the said Robert Barclay and his foresaides [heirs] my undoubted and irrevocable cessioners and assignees in and to all right that I have in any manner of way to the said lands of Urie, either by virtew of my lyf rent so reserved or otherways, and to all cowes, horses, oxen, sheep or other moveable in or about the lands of Urie, to which I can in the least pretend righte, which are now and were few and of small value. hardlie worth to be mentioned, & all the household plenishing, . . . with full powre to him and his foresaides
Bury Hill
Deeds.
to intromett with and uplift from the tennants all rents of the lands and others whatsumever due to me."

In return for which he was to be maintained in " meat, COLONEL DAVID BARCLAY, 1610-1686, Urie I.
bed, and clothes, and spending money " as he had been since
1670. The deed is long and complicated, with every possible
contingency provided for, and we can realise how the old
Laird was happy to relieve his mind of all earthly cares and 1684.
responsibilities, and devote his declining years to the things of
the Spirit.

But there was still something to be provided for, and in the Bury Hill Papers.
same year he drew up another document, dealing with the
arrangements for his own burial.

As has been related, David Barclay had appointed the top
of a steep hill, in the policies of Urie, as a resting place for
Friends, and left instructions with his son to build a strong
stone wall round it.

The instructions left by him were that he wished " to be
buried in that buriall place upon Carentowe long ago destined
by me, and that without any of the customary and superstitious ceremonies of the world. . . . that no person be
invited to my buriall except the professed friends of truth and
my own tenants. . . . My eldest son to see my will herein
answered, and I also recommend him to cause sufficiently fence
the said buriall place.

" Next as to other things I have not much to say since there
is not the least occasion for me to make any testament. In
respect that though I made no written agreement with my
eldest son upon his marriage, (we having always lived so
together in that love and unity as needed no such thing) yet I
took up and made use of 2000 marks he received with his
wife, and shortly after his marriage, about 13 years ago, I really
and effectively denuded myself of my estate or life-rent in his
favour, being willing to be freed of the trouble of my debts,
and contenting myself cheerfully with an aliment with him,
having at all times what I thought meet to call for, and since
that time he has freed me of all engagements I lay under, so
that no person alive or dead, has my bond of obligation for a
farthing, and therefore since that time I never meddled with
the rent. . . . and as for my moveables either without or
within the house. . . . I have not these many years looked

upon them, nor understood them to be mine, but as belonging to his [my?] son and daughter in law. And as for what relates to my other children, I have declared my division of their portions according to the tenor of the disposition made by Charles Gordon, my brother-in-law, to me and to my son in a paper all written with my own hand, and dated on 12th March 1680, and subscribed by me before Robert Sandilands and Alex Paterson, as witnesses. . . . These things I thought necessary to leave as a true declaration under my hand written by my second son John, and subscribed by me (before these witnesses : Gilbert Molleson late Bailie of Aberdeen and Thomas Mercer, and Andrew Gallaway, merchants there, and Andrew Jafra [Jaffray] of Kingswell, and John Barclay, writer hereof,) the 17th day of January, 1684."

Almost the last record we have of the esteem in which David was held by all who knew him, and how, notwithstanding the disapproval felt for his religious opinions by " the baser sort," he was regarded as an authority and a present help in trouble by his own friends, is in a letter from the Earl of Sutherland, which has been preserved, and is at Bury Hill.

His wife's cousin, the Earl of Sutherland, to whom he had been so much indebted in the matter of his election to Parliament in 1652, wrote to him from Perth in 1685 for help and advice. Lord Sutherland's daughter was married to my lord Arbuthnott, and her father and mother were in very real anxiety as to her welfare.

The letter is a touching one, and expresses their parental feelings in a way that must have affected the kindly Laird of Urie. We are not told the result of his mediation, but Lord Sutherland appeals to their old friendship, and " kyndnes," speaks moderately of ingratitude and harsh words from Lord Arbuthnott, and implores David to influence him " not to use so harshly one yᵗ he once pretended to love, and is young wᵗ child to him." He goes on, " therefore dear freind, I attest you, for to owne and befriend my poor girle. Let her not be tied upon or made a slave, as not to dar to wreat [write] to us or her other relations, or that she cannot command a servant to go about her necessary adoes without being threatened to be badly used, which I hope your friendship will cause to be prevented."

He continues to explain some delay in payment of the tocher [dowry], which gives Lord Arbuthnott an excuse for blaming and " putting affronts upon " his young wife, though not in any case her fault, and only a matter of some " twentie pieces," and ends, " But y' prudence will so order matters that you will rather be a Healer than a weydner [widener] of breaches betwixt them, and blissid be the peace-makers ; and this I will hold of, and owe to our old friendship which shall not be diminished but rather increased on my side.

" I do recommend my poor broken-hearted daughter to you that you may own her, counsell her, & protect her as if she were your own, which will add to the favor and kyndnes I have of long tyme experienced from you to

Dear Friend

Your reall freind and coussine and servant

SUTHERLAND."

At last the end came. In September 1686 David Barclay, " being past the 76th year of his age, took a fever, which kept him about a fortnight and then carried him off." He made a " most religious and edifying departure," almost his last words being to Robert, " you are my witness, in the presence of God, that the Lord is nigh " ; and later, " The perfect dis-covery of the Day-spring from on high, how great a blessing it has been to me and my family "; and finally " The Truth is over all."

" Upon the 12th of October he was buried in the new burying place he had made upon his own ground, having ordered the manner of his interment himself some time before while in perfect health."

It is easy to visualise Colonel David in his old age from the description written by his grandson, Urie III, the compiler of "The Genealogical Account of the Barclays of Urie." Though only a lad of fourteen at the time of the Colonel's

Margin notes: COLONEL DAVID BARCLAY, 1610–1686, Urie I. 1685. 1686. Piety Promoted. Genealogical Account.

COLONEL
DAVID
BARCLAY,
1610–1686,
Urie I.

death his grandfather had made so deep an impression on his young mind that he is able to give us the following clearly drawn picture :

" His humility and sincerity in his religion was most remarkable and exemplary in his whole conduct particularly in the time of public prayer. He was a proper, tall, personage of a man, as could be seen among many thousands : his hair, white as the flax, but quite bald upon the top of his head, which obliged him to wear, commonly, a black sattin cap under his hat. It was observable, that he always kneeled in time of public prayer, pulled off his hat with one hand, and his cap with the other, and so continued during the whole time of prayers : I have often seen it, and it made such an awful impression upon me, that I shall never forget it."

He had been further described as having left

" the impress of a distinctive personality of singular elevation, and strongly marked individuality of character, tenacity, and inflexibility of purpose, and a deep and strong religious spirit. In his thought and character he had much self-reliance. He was a born pioneer, and the original qualities of his strong character found scope and exercise in the early struggles and triumphs and in the deeper aspirations of the new religious Society of which he was one of the Apostles."

Over two centuries have passed, but even now, it is impossible to study the records of Colonel David without feeling the influence of the singular purity and force of his personality, and the strength of the religious convictions upon which his every action was based. The courage of the gallant soldier, the lion-cub of Gustavus Adolphus, remained unshaken in the Man of Peace ; the tender ardour with which he wooed and won the " White Rose of Scotland " from the enemy's camp, remained undimmed to the last. His great qualities did not change with the altered environment of his life, they were transmuted by the alchemy of a calm yet stalwart godliness. His example was, and is, far-reaching and it " lives on without visible symbol woven into the stuff of other men's lives."

Colonel David Barclay (Urie I) and his wife Katherine Gordon had issue three sons: Robert, John and David ; and

96

two daughters: Lucy, who died unmarried; and Jean, who married Sir Euen Cameron of Locheil.

We learn from a deed in the records of " The General Proprietors of the Eastern Division of New Jersey," that Colonel David Barclay gave to his son David (designated as merchant) certain moneys, which in the event of the said David dying without issue were to revert to his brother Robert. With part of those moneys David Junior bought a propriety in the Province of East New Jersey, and goods to the value of £150, all of which goods, together with seven or eight servants, he took in August 1685 on board the ship " America " bound from Aberdeen to East New Jersey. David Barclay died at sea during the voyage, and the land and property thereupon reverted to his brother Robert. Robert with the consent of his father, Colonel David, and out of love and affection for his brother John, conveyed all the said property to John Barclay (described as planter and inhabitant of the said Province), on condition that if John should die without issue, everything should revert to Robert, his heirs, executors, &c.

Colonel David Barclay, 1610–1686, Urie I.

JOHN BARCLAY OF PERTH AMBOY

John Barclay (Urie IIB), second son of Colonel David Barclay, was born in 1659, and at the age of about twenty-five years migrated to America.

His elder brother, Robert, was appointed Governor of East New Jersey, as we shall see, and although John did not go out as his deputy, there is no doubt that his brother's interests drew him to the Colony.

In July 1685 John Barclay received from his brother Robert an estate of 500 acres in East New Jersey, called "Plainfields," and in the following year, as has been stated, he received the portion which had belonged to his brother David.

John Barclay died in 1731, having married Catherine, whose surname is unknown, and left issue, one son, John.

The history of John Barclay (Urie IIB) and his descendants has been fully dealt with by Mr. R. Burnham Moffat, in his able work *The Barclays of New York : Who They Are and Who They Are Not—and Some Other Barclays*, published in 1904.

ROBERT BARCLAY, " THE APOLOGIST "

Robert Barclay (Urie II), known as " The Apologist," was born at Gordonstoun on December 23rd, 1648. From very early days he showed remarkable promise, and the circumstances of his education gave him a broader view and greater opportunities of acquiring knowledge than most boys of his age, especially in religious matters.

His childhood was spent at Gordonstoun, the home of his maternal grandfather, Sir Robert Gordon. His father was constantly absent on military and political business, and his mother and grandmother brought him up in strict Presbyterian principles. Though the Gordon atmosphere, he tells us, was " that of the strictest sort of Calvinism," the intellectual and tolerant outlook of his grandfather and his friends and the charm and intelligence of his grandmother and his beautiful mother, modified the harshness of their creed and opened the boy's mind to a wider vision. He was sent to the best schools available near Gordonstoun, but when his eager mind began to outstrip his teachers, his parents sent

him to Paris to be further instructed by his uncle and namesake, Robert Barclay, who was in a position to give him the best education possible, being Rector of the Scots Theological College there.

Young Robert was an engaging child. We find in Sir Robert Gordon's will of 1656 an entry in which he appoints " six faithfull and loving friends," among whom is Colonel Barclay, to the special charge of his wife and children, and adds, " Item, I doe leave to my grandchyld, Robert Barcklay, my silver pieces and purse pennies, as a small token from me, and doe appoint his mother to keep them for him as long as she lives."

The special message to " little Robin " in the Earl Marischal's letter to Colonel David in 1658, already recorded, shows us that he was popular with his father's friends.

Gordonstoun was a happy home for David Barclay's children. Though their mother died in 1658 while they were all young, they had tender affection and care from her mother, the Lady Gordon, and the long stone corridors and gloomy vaulted chambers of the Castle were full of young voices and childish laughter, for another of her sons, Sir Ludovic Gordon, with his wife and their eight children, lived there at the same time. Their eldest son was only a few years older than Robert, and the little boy must have carried happy memories with him when he was despatched to his school in Paris, and the care of his uncle. He was younger than the other pupils, probably about nine or ten years of age, but his love of knowledge and quick understanding soon made him equal to and even superior to his fellows, and his uncle became very fond and proud of him.

The College had been founded in the Middle Ages by a Bishop of Moray, for the purpose of preparing students to become Roman Catholic Missionaries. Robert's vivacity and keenness in debate seemed to indicate his special fitness for such a vocation, and for some time it seemed that the Church of Rome was destined to claim him. He was very happy in Paris, and studied classics, rhetoric, and divinity with enthusiasm. He also learnt fencing, and " other gentlemanly accomplishments."

Meanwhile, at Gordonstoun, his mother was getting uneasy. Although she had consented to let him go to the College for the advantages of the admirable education there, she was failing in health, and became seriously anxious to remove him from the religious influences which she with her Calvinist convictions could but regard as dangerous. Her anxiety was justified, for Robert Barclay writes himself, in his *Treatise on Universal Love*, in 1666 :—

" My first education, from my infancy, fell among the strictest sort of Calvinists, those of our country being generally acknowledged to be the severest of that Sect, in the heat of zeal surpassing not only Geneva, from whence they derive their pedigree, but all the other Reformed churches abroad, so called. I had scarce got out of my childhood, when I was, by the permission of Divine Providence, cast among the company of Papists, and my tender years, and immature capacity not being able to withstand and resist the insinuations that were used to proselyte me to that way, I became quickly defiled with the pollutions thereof, and continued therein for a time, until it pleased God through his rich love and mercy to deliver me out of those snares and to give me a clear understanding of the evil of that way."

1663. His mother earnestly besought her husband the Colonel to bring Robin home, and when David Barclay promised to do so, she, knowing his unswerving reliability, died in peace. Her death was a most grievous loss to her husband and family, but she had the happiness of knowing that her mother, Lady Gordon, was able and most willing to undertake the charge of the children, whom she loved as her own.

After a few months, David Barclay set out on the long journey to Paris. He had considerable difficulty in persuading his brother to part with his nephew and most promising pupil, but, bound by his promise to his wife, David stood firm against his brother's arguments, even when the Rector offered to make the lad his heir and to advance him to influential positions where his talents would be fully developed and appreciated. Young Robert was sent for, and the position explained to him.

It could not have been an easy choice. His father must have been almost a stranger to him, for we have no record of any previous journey to Paris, while the Rector was a familiar and dearly loved figure.

The young man must have hesitated between the two strong wills, and have thought regretfully of the friends he was leaving, and the happy studious life he loved; but early memories of his mother's teaching must have been in his mind, and possibly some realisation of what that loss meant to Genealogical his father, for "though his uncle endeavoured to dissuade Account. him from returning, pointing out the worldly advantages he could offer him, Robert's repeated reply was 'He is my father, and ought and must be obeyed.' This so disobliged the Rector his uncle, that at his death he bequeathed all his wealth to the College, and other religious houses in France."

The inscription on Father Robert Barclay's grave in Paris runs :—

" Here lieth the body of Robert Barclay, a priest of most blessed memory. Of Royal Extraction, he was lineally descended from the sovereigns of Denmark, Norway, Sweden, Scotland, and England, of a most ancient and most honourable lineage, connected by blood or alliance with every noble family of Scotland. His family was yet more honorably known for the probity, talents, and valour by which it was distinguished during a long course of centuries, nor was he unworthy the stock from which he sprang. His warm attachment to the most holy Catholic Church was the more remarkable, as it was opposed by most of his own countrymen."

There are some records of young Robert's schooldays in *Ibid.* various books that were later in his son's custody, " gott from the Master of the Colledge." There is no doubt that he made many friends there, and one of his biographers says " here was he brought up in good literature, and after a manner that suited to his quality, and those noble youths that were his fellow students."

The change of religious outlook must have been unsettling, even at his early age, but Robert appears to have had the happy disposition that extracts the good from experience and ignores the evil.

Father and son journeyed home together, and Robert took up his life in his native country probably at first at Gordonstoun, where his splendid old grandmother gave him a warm welcome. Robert no doubt discussed with her the great questions that were occupying his mind, and the fine library at Gordonstoun, with its collection of theological and ecclesiastical works, inherited from her ancestors, gave him the opportunity of studying them at first hand. Though he was so young, he was well fitted to examine these matters, for he was already acquainted with French and Latin, and now set himself to master Greek and Hebrew, in order to study the Fathers and religious history in the original text.

The Colonel conscientiously refused to use persuasion *Ibid.* or to bias Robert's mind in any way, but the boy was in daily contact with his father's strong principles and marked individuality, which cannot but have had their effect. David *1663–1665.* Barclay did not openly join the Society of Friends until 1666, three years after Robert had returned home, but his whole practice and principles were so definitely in accord with their tenets, and with that high and noble ideal of Christianity they sought to establish, that his son could not fail to appreciate how much more closely his life agreed with the teaching of Christ than those of many ostensible professors of Christianity.

Robert Barclay (Urie III) says in his Memoirs, " I have beene often informed by persons of great credit that he [the Colonel] used no endeavours to turn him [Robert] that way, being rather desirous he should have his religion from conviction than imitation, which soon proved the case, for having gone throughout the whole Countrey to visit all his friends and Relations of all persuasions, particularly those of the Romish religion, and having strictly examined both their principles and practice, how far consonant to the Scriptures of Truth, he found himself constrained to embrace the opinions of that despised people (so esteemed by the unthinking world) in the defence of whose tenets he wrote several books, the best known being his *Apology*, dedicated to King

1666.
Charles II."

(This is a mistake on the part of the biographer as Robert Barclay expressly states in his preface to the *Apology*, that he neither dedicates it to the King, nor craves his patronage, and that to God alone and to the service of His Truth he dedicates "whatever work He brings forth in me.")

The peaceful family life at Gordonstoun was destined to be rudely interrupted. When Robert was about seventeen, the sudden arrest of his father, with no definite charge against him, and his imprisonment in Edinburgh Castle at the instance of the Royalist party whom he had done so much to serve, must have come as a great shock to his family.

Even though, as we have reason to believe, the Colonel's first year's detention was not much more than a formality, and that he was permitted on the payment of "caution money" to be a good deal at home and to manage his own affairs to a certain extent, the injustice and danger of his position must have been most alarming.

Robert was at first allowed to visit his father in Edinburgh, and there made the acquaintance of John Swinton. He listened to the arguments of that eloquent advocate, and like his father, became convinced that where all other religious sects lived in constant enmity with each other, and bigotry and animosity took the place of Christian Charity, the one sect that maintained the true teaching of Christ, and ruled their lives by the Law of Love, was the small and despised company led by George Fox.

In his *Treatise on Universal Love*, he writes of his early training: "In both these sects I had abundant occasion to receive impressions contrary to this principle of Love, seeing the straitness of several of their doctrines, as well as their practice of persecution, and do abundantly declare how opposite they are to Universal Love. The time that intervened betwixt my forsaking the Church of Rome and joining those with whom I now stand engaged, I kept myself free from joining any sort of people, though I took liberty to hear several, and my converse was most with those that inveigh much against *judging* and such kind of severity, which latitude may perhaps be esteemed the other extreme, opposite to the preciseness of these other sects; whereby I also received an opportunity to know what is usually *pretended* on that side likewise. As for those I am now joined to, I justly esteem them to be the true followers and servants of Jesus Christ."

" Not by strength of argument," he says later in the *Apology*, " or by a particular disquisition of each doctrine, and convincement of my understanding thereby, I came to receive and bear witness of the truth, but by being secretly reached by this Life. . . . For when I came into the silent assemblies of God's people, I felt a secret power among them which touched my heart, and as I gave way to it, I found the evil weakening in me, and good raised up, and so I became thus knit and united unto them, hungering more and more after the increase of this power and life, whereby I might feel myself perfectly redeemed."

Robert's attendance at these secret assemblies was not without danger, for at this time, on March 2, 1665, the Commission

Robert
Barclay,
1648–1690,
Urie II.

Register of
the Privy
Council of
Scotland,
Vol. 2,
p. 36.

for the suppression of Quakers in Edinburgh applied for further authority, and received this warrant:

" The Lords [of the Privy Council] being informed that there are great multitudes of quaikers who frequently and avowedly meet together in Edinburgh, to the high contempt of authority and scandal of the professed religion, grant warrant and commission to the Archbishop of Glasgow, the Earl of Tweedale, the President of the Session, Lord Advocate and Lord Lee, or any two of them, to meet and discover by what means to suppress these disorderly meetings ; and meanwhile they grant warrant to the magistrates of Edinburgh to seize and imprison all quaikers found at any such meetings."

Robert was fortunate enough to escape capture, and went his peaceful way, meditating deeply on these matters.

A mystical phrase he had heard at the first Quaker meeting he had attended remained in his mind. "In stillness there is fullness. In fullness there is nothingness. In nothingness there are all things." We can imagine it was a time of severe mental conflict for him. To stand in open opposition to the young men of his age and class, many of them his own friends, whose habits he could not approve, and whose levity and extravagance in dress and social customs were practically universal, following the example set by the Court, could not have been easy. Robert's own aristocratic traditions could not but jar with the sometimes coarse and uncultivated society of those who principally supported the new movement. George Fox himself was an uneducated man, and the misplaced enthusiasm of his extremist followers went far to discredit the simplicity of his teaching.

Of course there must have been those among his father's relatives and friends who were in sympathy with his views, but on the whole these years must have been full of trial.

In 1666 Robert felt himself "constrained to embrace the same doctrine and course of life" that his father had adopted, and after he had been officially received into the Society of Friends, he never wavered nor looked back. In Sewell's *History of Friends* we read that "Robert Barclay grew so zealous and valiant in the doctrine . . . that he became a public promulgator of it, and often engaged in disputes with the scholars

Sewell's
History of
Friends,
p. 163.

not only verbally, but also by writing, for he was so skilful in ROBERT
school learning, that he was able to encounter the learned with BARCLAY,
their own weapons, and of such quick apprehension as not to Urie II.
be inferior to the most refined wits. His meekness also was
eminent, and these qualifications were accompanied by so
taking a carriage as rendered him very acceptable to others.
Altho his natural abilities were great enough to have made him
surpass others in human learning, and so to have been famous
among men, yet he so little valued knowledge, that he in no
wise endeavoured to be distinguished on that account. His
chief aim was only to advance in real godliness."

.   .   .   .   .

Two years before Robert Barclay and his father had joined 1664.
the Society of Friends, a certain dandified young gentleman
had been sent on a Continental tour by his father, Admiral Sir
William Penn, in the hope that some odd and unpopular
opinions that he had picked up at Oxford, might thereby be
modified or forgotten.

The rigour of the Anglican statutes, and the suppression of
some Puritan heads of Colleges, had roused the indignation of
the students, and it is said they showed their disapproval in the
way common to students, by rioting in the streets. Young
Penn was prominent in these affrays and is reported to have
plucked gowns from the backs of the wearers, as showing
a step towards popery, for which acts he was expelled from the
University. He spent a gay two years abroad, in the best
society at the Court of Louis XIV, where he made many de-
sirable and aristocratic friends, but, to the disappointment of
his father, young William also attended the classes and lectures
of the Protestant College at Saumut, whose President's teaching had stimulated the religious views he already entertained. He returned to England, with his opinions unchanged,
but his outer man was described by Pepys, who was a gossip- 1664-1666.
ing acquaintance, though hardly a friend, of Sir William's, as
" having a great deal, if not too much, of the variety of the
French garb, and an affected manner of speech and gait."
William then became a student at Lincoln's Inn, but the awful

ROBERT
BARCLAY,
1648–1690,
Urie II.

visitation of the Plague again turned his mind to serious matters and the doctrines of the Quakers. His anxious father then despatched him to the Duke of Ormonde's "pure and brilliant Court" in Ireland, and also to manage a family estate in Cork. A mutiny broke out in Carrickfergus, and William volunteered for service. He acted with so much courage that he was offered a Commission in a Company of Foot, but this he declined, though his portrait, in full armour, was painted at this time, and is the earliest likeness that exists of the great Apostle of Peace.

The Quaker movement had by this time reached Ireland, and young Penn fell foul of the Law by attending a meeting in Cork, and helping to eject an unsympathetic soldier. He was consequently sent to gaol, from whence he wrote a letter to Lord Orrery, the President of Munster, making an eloquent and public appeal for liberty of conscience.

He was thereupon released and sent home to his father, but in different guise, for by now he had adopted the distinctive garb and phraseology of the Friends, and firmly refused to

1664–1666.

employ titles of honour or to uncover his head "even for the King, or the Duke of York," which distressed Sir William Penn, who had a very hearty respect for the conventions. Though William's discourtesy so disturbed the Admiral, it only amused the easy-going King Charles. One day, meeting young Penn in the Park, the monarch removed his hat.

"Why dost thou take off thy hat, friend Charles?" enquired the young man.

"Because," said the King, "wherever I am it is customary for only one person to remain covered."

This question of wearing hats may seem a small point to become such a cause of controversy, but "Hat Honour" was more considered then. Hats had been worn everywhere, indoors, at meals, and in church, only being raised at the name of God. The French fashion, which was just being introduced, of doffing the hat to social superiors, or to ladies, was considered an infringement of the honour due only to the Almighty, and as such formed one of the strictest Quaker prohibitions, though it sometimes led to rather paradoxical situations, as when cer-

106

tain Friends were brought before the magistrates, the police
knocked off their hats, and the magistrates had to have them
replaced, in order to furnish a cause for complaint.

William Penn became a member of the Society of Friends in
1668, and he and Robert Barclay became intimate, and we can
imagine how the spirited young man must have delighted the
heart of the brave old Colonel.

The organisation and discipline of the Society had hardly
kept pace with its rapid development, and at this time internal
schisms began to threaten its unity. Penn's gift for controversial writing, with the learning and scholarship of Robert
Barclay, soon averted the danger, and the movement quickly
recovered its stability and cohesion.

Penn's many pamphlets, sometimes couched in violent and
aggressive language, and sometimes powerful and unanswerable, frequently caused him to be imprisoned and fined. He
was not discouraged, and when imprisoned in Newgate in
1670 for holding open-air meetings, he launched a noble defence, entitled *The Great Case for Liberty of Conscience*
which, next to Robert Barclay's *Apology*, did most to open the
eyes of the authorities and justify the teaching of the Quakers.

When David Barclay's imprisonment in Edinburgh Castle
became more stringent, he sent Robert to live at Urie, leaving
the rest of the family under the sheltering care of Lady Gordon.

As the new house of Urie was not built until 1670, there
must have been something left of the old manor-house, which
had been burnt in 1645 by Montrose, or a farm house may
have been available. David Barclay's imprisonment checked
any building operations, and he may have thought that to
put his son into residence there would help to keep order
among the tenants, many of whom shared the popular
prejudice against Quakers, and were not unwilling to try
experiments as to how much their patience would stand.
They were supported by all other religionists, who agreed
that they were, " a damnable sect . . . deluded by Satan,"
though they could not deny their honesty and clean living.

Robert found things there in great disorder, and reported
the same to his father, who, as we have seen, made various

ROBERT
BARCLAY,
1648–1690,
Urie II.

appeals for his release, and was ungraciously allowed short periods of freedom. But Robert was too young, and too unversed in estate management to carry much weight, and spent the years mainly in study and writing. He had a friend to live with him, one David Falconer, a young Quaker, who acted as Factor and took the business of the property off his hands while he was occupied in his literary work.

1667.
Genealogical
Account.

In this year he and David Falconer were able to collect sufficient followers to open the first of the Quaker Meetings, which were to become such a feature of the life at Urie. It was attended by a number of tenants and neighbours, and the gatherings continued weekly, with a monthly assembly, and afterwards two yearly General Meetings, for upwards of 74 years. The first Annual Meeting was held on March 1, 1669, " which day was remarkable for the ' convincement ' of several people of good account."

The success of the Quaker movement at Urie was remarkable, as Scotland as a whole was not very receptive. Presbyterianism was a type of religion well suited to the national character and the people had not the same unsatisfied craving for truth as existed in England which was torn between so many antagonistic opinions and warring sects.

In spite of Robert's difficulties, his life was not without compensations. Urie is within a long day's ride of Aberdeen, and there he found congenial friends with whom he spent much time. A family named Mollison in particular welcomed him, and their encouragement and sympathy must have been a comfort in those lonely years. Bailie Mollison, the father, was a highly respected magistrate, and his wife Margaret, whose family was almost as ancient as that of the Barclays, had been one of the earliest members of the Society of Friends in the north. They had a daughter Christian, and the young people were soon mutually attracted. Robert's letter of proposal to her has been preserved.

1669.

28th of $\frac{1}{mo}$ 1669.

DEAR FRIEND,
Having for some time past had it several times upon my mind to have saluted thee in this manner of writing, and to enter into a

liberal correspondence with thee, so far as thy freedom would ROBERT
allow, I am glad that this small occasion hath made way for the BARCLAY,
beginning of it.   1648–1690,
The love of thy converse, the desire of thy friendship, the Urie II.
sympathy of thy way, and the meekness of thy spirit, have often, as
thou mayest have observed, occasioned me to make frequent opportunity to have the benefit of thy company. But beyond and before
all I can say, in the fear of the Lord, that I have received a charge
from Him to love thee.   I am sure it will be our great gain so to be
kept, that all of us may abide in the pure love of God ; in the sense
of drawing, whereof we can only discern and know how to love one
another.   In the present flowings thereof I have truly solicited thee,
desiring and expecting that in the same thou may'st feel and judge.

ROBERT BARCLAY.

Though his phraseology followed the formal lines of the
Society, and there does not seem much to attract a young girl
in his works, yet the demure young Quaker damsel, whom we
can picture in her quiet grey or dove-coloured dress, pike
bonnet and white tippet, seems to have found it sufficient,
and after a few months Robert Barclay made formal application to her father for her hand.

The Bailie was so well satisfied with the proposed alliance
that in the deed drawn up on the occasion he agrees to give
more to his daughter Christian than to any of his other
children.

Addressed to his much respected friend David Barclay of Urie. Bury Hill
Papers.

Aberdeene.   19th Jan 1670.   1670.

HONOURED SIR,
Yesternight David Falconer did give me to read the draught
drawn up by you wherewith I am verie sattisfied . . . and if it shall
please God to enlairge my worldlie estate considerablie . . . except
my eldest sonne, there shall none of the rest of my children have so
liberal a share as she shall have, for I must confess she hez beine the
most deserving child I have to me. . . . Also, if I may at any tyme
enjoy by my brother, I undertake to allot some part thereof to her.

(Signed) GILBERT MOLLISON.

Though they were so warmly received by the relatives on
both sides the young couple had yet to reckon with the public.
When it became known that the Bailie, a well-known towns-

ROBERT
BARCLAY,
1648–1690,
Urie II.

Pamphlets
XVI.
Record book
of Friends
at Urie,
p. 93.

man and magistrate of Aberdeen, was allowing a Quaker marriage to take place in his own house, without the benefit of clergy, there arose a storm of derision and disapproval.

" In the beginning of the 11th month of 1669, the fury and envy of Magistratts, Priests, and People in and about Aberdeen began to grow very great. So at the monthly [Friends] Meeting, the rabble being stirred up by some envyous spirits, was like to have laid hands upon John Swintoun, P. Livingstone, and some others who were there, which fury was somewhat increased by Robert Barclay's marriage, which had been publickly performed that morning in [his her] father's house . . . where by the priests found their authority so slighted, and were exasperated thereat, that by the Bishop of Aberdeen's means, they procured letters to summons Robert Barclay before the Privy Council, for ane unlawful marriage, which matter was so over-ruled of the Lord, that they never had power to put their summons in execution, so as to do us any prejudice."

1669.

The peaceful little wedding party must have listened anxiously to the " rabble " roaring up and down the streets outside, with no doubt accompaniments of crashing glass, and broken heads ; but Bailie Mollison's home and property were respected, and the civic authorities were too much occupied in defending their own premises from the mob to take much note of their complaints, and the matter passed, as is recorded.

A Quaker wedding was a very simple ceremony. The relatives and friends assembled as for an ordinary Meeting, and sat in silence " for a reasonable time."

Life of
William
Penn
Graham.

Then the two young people stood up, Robert notable by his slender height and noble countenance, clad in his usual black cloth long coat, flapped waistcoat, and neat knee breeches and hose, with the square-toed shoes so often referred to in derision. Though studiously plain, there was no objection to the garments being made of superfine material and excellent cut. He wore his own hair, tied back with a black ribbon, and a broad-brimmed black hat. The bride wore the simple straight dress and fine white lawn cap and fichu, which was

almost a uniform : but the dress could be made of soft rich ROBERT
silk or satin, though in grey or dove-colour only, and her BARCLAY,
hair could appear in neat bands under the cap, though curls Urie II.
or waves were considered " Babylonish."

The bridegroom took her hand in his and said distinctly, 1648-1690,
addressing the company, " Friends, I take this my friend,
Christian Mollison, to be my wife, promising through Divine
Assistance, to be unto her a loving and faithful husband, until
it shall please the Lord by death to separate us."

The bride repeated the words with the necessary variations,
and after Colonel Barclay and the bride's father had each
given a short address of tender exhortation Robert Barclay
and Christian Mollison were man and wife, " in the sight of
God, and this Company."

Colonel David, as we have seen, handed over the property 1670.
of Urie to Robert and his wife, while continuing to live there
himself whenever his affairs permitted. His younger children
found a welcome there until they married and made homes 1670-1686.
of their own.

The household, under the management of Christian Barclay, Genealogical
was conducted on strict rules, with every hour apportioned to Account,
its duty. Early rising, plain food, and exquisite cleanliness p. 42.
were the order of their days. Any severity was balanced
by her kindly and charitable outlook on all, even on those
who most harshly misjudged and ill-treated the Friends,
while the absence of violent language, rancour or resentment,
made the home singularly peaceful.

A descendant of hers writes : " She laid herself out to Life of
assist and give advice to sick people, and supplied their Barclay, by
necessities, especially the poor, many of whom came ten, David
twenty, thirty, and even forty miles and upwards receiving Barclay of
great benefit, for her success was wonderful. She was a stow,
well accomplished woman every way, and of singular virtues, 1802.
which she improved to the praise of the Lord." 1670-1676.

She was indeed a notable housewife, and her book of
household recipes is still preserved in the family, and deserves
more honourable mention than space allows here.

The title-page is headed with her name, and continues,

III

"A Receipt Book, or the fruits of a young Woman's Spare Hours. Into three parts, the first containing several receipts of Physicke, the second concerning Cookrie, and the third of dying very necessary and profitable."

This last item, though at first sight slightly misleading, refers to the art of dyeing and many forgotten secrets are explained.

A short family record is appended, dealing with the children of her daughter Christian Barclay, who married Andrew Jaffray in 1700. This is followed by seventy-nine prescriptions covering every disease or accident, many of which would be new to the College of Physicians.

She used herbs to an immense extent, a short list of which may be interesting now, though by no means exhaustive, such as "coltsfoot, burrage, saffron, scoebius, Dragon's Pimpernell, Agromony, Sweet Marjoram, Rosemary, Tormentil, Spur Mint, Sweet John's Wort, Penny royall, Woodsorrell, Hart's tongue, Cardus, Mugwort, Burnatt, Scordium, Angelico Balsam, Hysop, Tamaris, Mother of Time, Bettony, Rue, Wormwood, Camamile, Liverwort, Sallendine, Pelletony of the wall, Southernwood, Feverfew, Walnut leaves, sage, Grumbell seeds, Fennel seeds, aniseeds, Carey seeds, Nettleseeds;" with fourteen kinds of "drugs," such as "Spanish Angelico, Boots Galingall Cubibs, Jedry rods, Long Peppers, Grains of Paradise, etc., half ane ounce of each to 2 Gallons of Brandy and 1 gallon of sack. The herbs cannot be had together, therefore they that come first must be put into one gallon of brandy, English, till the rest are to be had, and when they are all gott, steep them 24 hours, and then still them, and sweeten them with white sugar candy."

These were all used in one recipe, "A Surfeit Water," which, in those days of heavy meals, was probably often required. The names of the ingredients show an extraordinary range of plants, and the fruits she also mentions, such as "Blew figs," grapes, peaches, lemons, and oranges, seem to indicate a softer climate than the dwellers in northern Scotland now enjoy before the days of glass houses, while spices, long peppers, nutmegs, ginger, cloves, and such, may have been brought to the port of Stonehyve by private venturers.

HISTORY OF THE BARCLAY FAMILY

The vast quantities of wine and brandy used are surprising, and when we read of the gallons of sack, canary, " gascoin wine," " whyt wine " and both English and French brandy that are used to steep the herbs, roots, leaves, or seeds employed, we are tempted to appreciate the popularity of the lady's nostrums, and the crowds of the " poorer sort " that stood outside the door every morning must have gone away warmed and cheered, even though " Foxgloves and Cowslips," with " pelepodie wood " for the " fitts," though well mixed in an earthen " pott " with a gallon of brandy, may not appear to us to be an unfailing remedy.

She gives several recipes for the " dropsie," which seems prevalent, and we find " best Roman vitriolle as much as you please " mixed with honey, for " evil fistulas, cancers and ulcers." There is no disease for which she has no remedy, especially the eye troubles, and she is even reported to have reduced a cataract, while lesser ills, such as the " tooth-ake," " Gandis " (presumably jaundice) and " reums," are included, with more serious complaints, " A Consumption, the Gravell, Rupter, Stone," and so on.

It gives a pleasant glimpse of neighbourly exchanges and " friendlie borrowing " of recipes, for the Countess Marischal is responsible for powders and plaisters, and the newly married daughter recommends an elixir, with a Latin inscription from " Christina Jaffray."

The calendar plays some part in her treatment, as, " A worme ointment has to be composed of herbs gathered 3 days before the change of the moon, & 3 dayes after, or 3 dayes before or after the full moon," though in those superstitious times it shows some strength of mind to exclude supernatural assistance, or " white witchcraft " from her pharmacopœia.

The second part contains many recipes of excellent good cheer, and it was fortunate that the strict Quaker tenets did not forbid moderate pleasures of the table, for to have wasted such a gift as Christian Barclay's for " high Cookrie " would indeed have been a loss. She deals with cakes of all kinds, pickles, candied fruits, preserving of vegetables, fruits, and even oysters. Jams and preserves are made from every kind

HISTORY OF THE BARCLAY FAMILY

of wild and garden fruit: "White and green marmaletts, Apricocks, Jelly of quinces, lemmoms, oringes, cherries, pipings [pippins], gooseberries, and Curebs, elder berries, apples and pears, rassberries, syrup of roses;" and a long list of homemade wines: "Balm wine, Elderberry wine, Birtch wine, Cowslipp wine, Gooseberry wine, and Mead."

She does not say much about meat, though there is a detailed account of how to "coller a fatt young pigg," and Scotch "colips" and Westphalia ham are mentioned. Christian Barclay's table must always have been well served and her larder well stocked.

The third part on "dying" gives lists of the various ingredients employed to produce different colours, most of which are unknown to the general public now. "Ingrain, Reedwood, Copress, to dye ane ingraint grey, to a Weinstone colour." "Sadest blew must have a boyll in fresh blew birsell, to make it sader." Yellows are produced by "Galling Peapings." And so on.

It seems that Christian could have had but few "spare hours," in her life. Andrew Jaffray, the son of the celebrated Alexander Jaffray, whose diary describes the early years of the Society of Friends, writes of the "beauty, good order, and holiness, that shined therein [at Urie], I can say to my refreshment and many others as in a quiet habitation."

He was a constant visitor, and in 1700 married the younger Christian, and had five children. In *A Man of Plain Speech* there is an account of the family, who are described as his greatest friends, and he is said to remember riding up to the straight walled grey house, flanked by two turrets, "standing all by itself in the middle of a field, with a small spinney on the east, and the Cowie flowing away to Stonehaven and the sea."

He was not then a member of the Society of Friends. He is stated to have got "convincement" and joined it in the year 1673.

Robert Barclay was much occupied with writing, but welcomed the visits of his friends, and never failed to attend

114

Meeting or to assist the elders of the Society in whatever charitable plans they had in hand. The " Meeting for Sufferings " found in both Robert and Christian Barclay its most liberal supporters and earnest workers.

ROBERT BARCLAY, 1648–1690, Urie II.

Alexander Gordon, in *The Marrow of Barclay*, says, " Barclay is the Scottish Quaker, scholastic and metaphysical, living so truly above forms that they are nothing to him one way or another—never dreaming of discarding his green silk coat as a qualification for constructing a subtle and elaborate Christology."*

Theological Review, Vol. 12, p. 392, 1874.

To this we may perhaps attribute the fact that we hear no more of public insult beyond that organised in the name of the Law, but troublous times were again in view.

In 1670 the second Conventicle Act confirmed the Act of 1664 and endeavoured to destroy non-conformity by forbidding all meetings. It deprived the accused of trial by jury, and instructed that the Act was to be construed as against the prisoners, which was contrary to the first principles of English justice.

The Act was not specially aimed at the Quakers, but their opponents took advantage of its wording to persecute and harry the unoffending Friends in a most cruel and unjustifiable manner.

Robert Barclay (Urie III) says, " In the north malicious persons laid hold of any occasion of disturbing this peaceable people, expecially at Aberdeen, where they were often mobbed by the dregs of the town, set on by the clergy and other flaming bigots." Robert also says of this time, " Why do they oppose us in our meetings at Aberdeen and elsewhere, and curse and swear, and use all manner of filthy communication and are ready to stone us in the streets ? And none more than that young fry and spawn of the priesthood, who are bred in your nurseries of learning."

1672.

Evidently, though strong language was not countenanced by their rules, Robert was sufficiently human both to feel indignation and express himself with vigour on this

---

* A piece of that same green silk coat is among the family treasures at Bury Hill, together with his walking-stick.

ROBERT
BARCLAY,
1648-1690,
Urie II.

matter, as on others. The trend of public opinion was expressed by the historian Woodrow, who, though connected with the Barclays, opined that " had these good acts been enforced with more vigour, wee might in this land have been free from this dangerous sect."

1672.

Robert Barclay, with his father's friend, John Swinton, made an unfortunate expedition into Montrose, a ride of some 40 miles, in the " dead of winter " in 1672.

A Friends' Meeting was being held there to return thanks for the deliverance of nearly all the members from one of their unjust imprisonments. The Meeting had only just opened, when the loud familiar summons was heard at the door, and the officers of the Law burst their way in to re-arrest all those present. John Swinton's silver tongue and Robert's position and influence had no effect on the magistrates, and the two found themselves included in the number of Quakers who were convicted and were thrown into the dark, noisome Tolbooth of Montrose, where Colonel David had been confined in 1667.

Robert still had his pen, and from the prison wrote to the magistrates of the town, setting forth the wrong he and his fellow prisoners were undergoing. He showed that the law under which they had been committed was really directed only against those who endangered the peace of the realm, and urged that the Friends were loyal subjects, who asked nothing but leave to meet together and worship God in their own way, and concluded, " As for us, we are not afraid of you, nor ashamed of our testimony, and you cannot vanquish us. We are, as regards our testimony and for its sake, well contented, well pleased, well satisfied, to be here : our bonds are not grievous to us."

This letter, which could not be contradicted, had the desired effect, and the prisoners were all released, when Robert returned to Urie, and to his work.

1671-1676.

In 1671 the earliest of Robert Barclay's published works, which bore the title of *Truth Cleared of Calumnies*, caused considerable controversy. The Bishop of Aberdeen had sent to Alexander Jaffray a paper containing thirty queries

116

on the various points at which the Church and the Friends were at variance, and a paper from George Meldrum, minister of St. Nicholas, entitled *The State of the Controversy between the Protestants and the Quakers*, had also been received. Alexander Jaffray was ill, and these questions had been replied to by George Keith. At that time the courtesies of debate were not strictly observed, and Keith's aggressive style probably did not mollify his opponents. A book entitled *Dialogue between a Quaker and a Stable Christian* thereupon appeared, printed at Aberdeen. It purported to have been written by a Member of the Society of Friends, and put forward their side with ingenious misrepresentation, calculated to weaken and damage their cause. The Dialogue took the same line as a sermon previously preached by Meldrum, in which he pretended kindness towards the Friends, with unwillingness to meddle with them, and made a great show of zeal for the truth. Meldrum had been a Regent in Marischal College, and varied between Presbyterianism and Episcopacy. Among other misrepresentations the Dialogue alleged that Barclay had been educated in a Jesuit College.

Truth Cleared of Calumnies has a long sequel to the title, which gives a comprehensive précis of the book : " Wherein the book entitled *Dialogue between a Quaker and a Stable Christian* (printed at Aberdeen, and upon good grounds judged to be written by William Mitchell, preacher, or at least that he had a chief hand in it,) is examined, and the disingenuity of the author in his representing the Quakers is discovered. Here is also their case truly stated, cleared, demonstrated, and the objections of their opposers answered according to Truth, Scripture and right reason."

In this book, Robert Barclay speaks with some freedom on the " so-called ordinance of outward bread and wine," " the outer Baptism used in condescension to the weak," and the " outward Sabbath," which topics were highly controversial. There is an appendix which states that the priests in Aberdeen had begged the magistrates to search for copies of *Truth Cleared of Calumnies* with a view to their destruction, and that Meldrum had likened it to poison and enjoined his people

ROBERT BARCLAY, 1648–1690, Urie II.

1671.

Genealogical Account.

117

ROBERT
BARCLAY,
1648–1690,
Urie II.

1671.

Theological
Review,
1874, Vol. II.

not to read it. To the assertion that he had been educated in a Jesuit College, Robert gives the lie direct, and in plainer language than would be tolerated now, though mildness itself compared with that of some of his assailants.

John Gratton, in his diary, says, " In the controversy over *Truth Cleared of Calumnies*, Robert Barclay's arguments were distinguished by the exceeding keenness of unanswerable logic, which not only unmasked Mitchell, but extinguished him."

Some of these arguments were contained in another controversial pamphlet, entitled *William Mitchell Unmasked*, or " The staggering instability of the pretended stable Christian discovered, his omissions observed, and his weakness unveiled, in his late faint and feeble animadversions by way of reply to a book intituled *Truth Cleared of Calumnies*, wherein the integrity of the Quakers' doctrine is for the second time justified and cleared from the re-iterate, clamorous, but causeless calumnies of this cavilling catechist." This sentence must have been more gratifying to the writer than to the subject.

In a later leaflet called *A Seasonable Warning* Robert directs some pointed shafts at the cautious Aberdonians, who seem disposed to " face both ways " and observes drily that " Notwithstanding their concern to avoid a detestable neutrality, they could now preach under the Bishop, dispense with the Doxology, forbear lecturing, and other parts of the directorial discipline at the Bishop's order, and yet keep a reserve of Presbytery in case it came again into fashion."

William Penn, in his preface to Barclay's works, speaking of this book, observes that " the dispute rises high, and the contest seems sharp and close, but to every impartial reader the advantage evidently runs on our author's side, who appears rather zealous than heated and sharper on his enemy's matter than person, for he rather pities his enemy, than triumphs over his weakness and envy."

The editor of the *Encyclopædia* says, " In this work our author discovers an amazing variety of learning, which shows how good a use he made of his time at Paris, and how thorough

a master he was of the Scriptures, the Fathers, and ecclesias- Robert
tical history, and with how much skill and judgment he applied Barclay,
them. In these two books . . . will be found the buddings of 1648-1690,
Urie II.
much of that sound argument which afterwards grew to so
vigorous a degree of strength in Barclay's famous *Apology*."

Robert Barclay was at this time about 22 years of age,
and had not shown any signs of that fanatical zeal indulged
in by so many of the extremist followers of George Fox, but
soon after his marriage, and no doubt encouraged by the
sympathy of his devout young wife, he experienced a strong
spiritual call that could not be gainsaid. In his own words,
when the command of the Lord came to him to pass through
the streets of Aberdeen clad in sackcloth and ashes, calling
all to repentance, " the burden thereof was very great, yea,
seemed almost insupportable . . . and some whom I called to
declare to them this thing can be witness to the agony of my
spirit . . . how I besought the Lord that this cup might
pass from me, yea, how the pillars of my tabernacle were
shaken, and how exceedingly my bones trembled, until I freely
gave up unto the Lord's Will . . . and this was the end and
tendency of my testimony—to call you to repentance by this
signal and singular step, which I, as to my own will and
inclination, was as unwilling to be found in, as the worst and
wickedest of you can be averse from receiving or laying it
to heart. . . ."

He goes on to ask, " Ye who are called Christians . . .
how you can so confidently array yourself in all manner
of greedy and superfluous apparel and exceed in lustful
powderings and perfumes, and yet are ashamed and amazed
at sackcloth and ashes, which according to your own acknow-
ledgement is so suitable to your state ? "

To the sensitive and scholarly young man it must have been
an ordeal, though fortified by his conviction of the Divine
Command and the support and encouragement of his friends.
We have no record of any bodily harm coming to him,
but his progress through the streets of Aberdeen in such
guise must have called forth the coarse derision of the lowest
element in the population. His action has been condemned

by historians as misplaced enthusiasm, but Robert Barclay had a definite method and practical aim in his remarkable testimony to the people of Aberdeen, and we cannot tell how far his self-sacrifice was justified by the results.

Notwithstanding the half-hearted response of the people of Aberdeen, the Society of Friends persevered in their crusade, and in 1672 a Meeting House for Quakers was established there, to which Robert Barclay contributed the greater part of the purchase money. In the *Genealogical Account of the Barclays of Urie*, he is said to have " posted through all the affairs of life he thought incumbent on him, as if he had a prevision of the shortness of his time in this world, and spent and bestowed his service for the benefit of all he could be helpful to, especially the Church of Christ."

In 1673 he published in Aberdeen *A Catechism and Confession of Faith*, " approved of and agreed by the general assembly of the patriarchs, prophets, and apostles, Christ Himself chief speaker in and among them. Which containeth a true and faithful account of the principles and doctrines which are most surely believed by the Churches of Christ in Great Britain and Ireland, who are reproachfully called by the name of Quakers, yet are found in one faith with the primitive Church and Saints, as is most clearly demonstrated by some plain Scripture testimonies (without consequences or commentaries which are here collected and inserted by way of answer to a few weighty yet easy and familiar questions, fitted as well for the wisest and largest, as for the weakest and lowest capacities)."

This work was intended by Barclay to reply to the recently compiled *Confession and Catechism* of the Westminster Divines. He thought, by using the express language of Scripture for his statements, he gave them Biblical authority, and criticised with some severity the more modern method employed by the Westminster Conclave.

Alexander Gordon, in *The Marrow of Barclay* writes, " The chapter in the ' Confession ' devoted to the treatment of Holy Scripture is perhaps the most strenuous and fearless defence of the living and paramount authority of the Spirit that is anywhere to be found. He deliberately leaves room for the unrestricted play of critical enquiry, and maintains that there is no necessity for believing that Holy Scripture is a ' filled canon.' " ROBERT BARCLAY, 1648–1690, Urie II.

The whole section may be earnestly recommended to all Christian people as a vindication of the Spiritual.

In the following year, 1674, he issued a treatise on Church order, in which he defends " The people of God, called in derision Quakers," from accusations of disorder and confusion on the one hand, and tyranny and imposition on the other, brought against them by every other sect, from the Romanists to the Ranters, who, " divided on all other subjects, are united in their enmity to the true and pure principles of the Gospel." 1674.
Theological Review, 1875.

This treatise called forth the usual animadversions and arguments, but he did not reply to them at once. It was not till 1679 in the prison at Aberdeen that he did so, when no doubt he had abundant leisure. He was constantly called upon to preach, and his persuasive eloquence is referred to in George Fox's journal in October, 1674, as follows : " Some Friends out of Scotland came to visit me, by whom I understood that there were four young men, students of Aberdeen convinced there this year, at a dispute held there by Robert Barclay and George Keith, with some of the scholars of that University."

As these students are constantly mentioned as the most inveterate and bitter opponents of the Quakers, the arguments employed must have been convincing indeed, though Alexander Gordon, in *The Marrow of Barclay*, observes, " In the argument with the students, their impudence and bravado were overcome by the grave logic of their opponents, and they had to conclude the passage of arms by a shower of stones and turf." Theological Review, 1875, Vol. 12.

Robert Barclay did not spend all his time writing books in the peaceful seclusion of Urie, but constantly availed himself of the opportunities of attending the meetings of all religious bodies and of preaching the doctrines of his society. In 1674 he travelled up to London with Patrick Livingstone

ROBERT
BARCLAY,
1648–1690,
Urie II.

and William Hague, and paid a visit to the notorious Ludovick Muggleton, whose teaching, attracting considerable attention, lingered even to the nineteenth century.

The Muggletonians claimed to be the two witnesses of Rev. xi. vv. 3 and 6, denied the Trinity, and held grossly anthropomorphic opinions, with many strange doctrines, such as that the Devil became incarnate in Eve. Robert never spared any effort to strengthen the spiritual life, however misguided ; he took the long journey to discuss these questions, to spread his own doctrines, and reassert his insistence on the power of the heart and conscience to reprove evil, and equally to stir up good impulses.

" This is the Inward Light." " To believe this is Christ."

1676.

Although Robert Barclay wrote so many books and pamphlets during these years, he never lost sight of his intention of writing a book which should secure for the Friends immunity from misrepresentation, liberty of development, and a position of acknowledged respect.

Alex.
Gordon,
The
Marrow of
Barclay.

" He decided to call it *The Apology*, not, as is usually understood, entirely as a vindication of the Quaker tenets, nor as a justifying explanation, but rather a defence in the nature of a fortifying outwork or advanced guard, of the citadel of right belief."

Its full title ran as follows :—

" An Apology for the true Christian Divinity as the same is held forth and preached by the people called in scorn Quakers. Being a full explanation and vindication of their principles and doctrines by many arguments deduced from Scripture and right reason, and the testimonies of famous authors, both ancient and modern. With a full answer to the stringent objections usually made against them."

Apologia was written at first in Latin " for the information of strangers," and published in Amsterdam, but was afterwards translated into English by its author, and published in London. It was a remarkable work for a young man of 27 years of age, and has always been accepted as the text book of Quaker theology. The doctrines of the Quakers had been rather chaotic, as most of the early Friends had been men of little education, held together by their common faith. They had a strong conviction of their immediate relationship with the Deity, and a mystical sense of the revelation of the Divine Will to the human spirit, but their ideas were misty and half-formed, and the words in which they sought to clothe them were often inconsistent and extravagant. Robert Barclay was the first to crystallise these indefinite convictions into coherent language, and to present them in clear and logical words. Macaulay says: "It was a lucky chance for the Quakers that they got Robert Barclay and Willian Penn to make sense of the unintelligible jargon of George Fox and Nayler."

The book shows remarkable ability and deep learning, and its author was, with good reason, described as the St. Paul and the St. Augustine of Quaker theology.

Barclay divides the essence of his teaching into fifteen propositions, which can be briefly summarised as follows :— 1676.

(1) That the true knowledge of God, as the foundation of all happiness, is the supreme necessity.

(2) That this knowledge is still revealed only by the Spirit as it was to the Patriarchs, Prophets, and Apostles, and has a self-widening power.

(3) That the Scriptures are revelations of God's Spirit, as streams from the fountain of Divine Truth, but are not to be esteemed as themselves the primary rule of faith and manners.

(4) That all men are by nature " fallen " and dead to the inward feeling of the Divine testimony.

(5) That God sent His Son as a light to lighten every man.

(6) That Christ's redemption is universal, extending even to those to whom the Gospel is unknown.

(7) That in all who resist not the inward light is produced a holy, pure and spiritual birth—involving both " justification " and " sanctification."

(8) That those who are fully regenerated are free from sin, and in that respect perfect.

(9) That it is possible for those who have made some progress in the Divine life, to fall away, but that an increase and stability in the truth is possible, from which there cannot be a total apostasy.

(10) That all who have received God's gift of Divine light in their hearts may minister in holy things, and must do so without hire.

(11) That all true and acceptable worship comes from the inward and immediate moving of the Holy Spirit.

(12) That Baptism is a spiritual thing, of which the Baptism of John was a figure, and that baptism of infants is a mere human tradition.

(13) That the conversion of the body and blood of Christ is inward and spiritual, of which the breaking of bread by Christ was a figure.

(14) That no human authority has a right to force the conscience, provided that no man under the pretence of conscience does anything inconsistent with the welfare of society.

(15) That, since the end of religion is to redeem man from the spirit of the world, and to lead him to inward communion with God, all vain customs and formalities, and unprofitable amusements are to be abandoned.

The leading and cardinal doctrine which penetrates all Robert Barclay's teaching is the direct revelation of the Divine Will in the hearts of all His creatures. This faith, as defined by him, is described as a system of mystical theism, the same in substance as that which finds a different form of expression in Emerson, and in other words is represented by Maurice, and others of the more spiritual of the Broad Church school.

Barclay was also influenced by the writings of Thomas Baxter, to which he refers in his *Truth Cleared of Calumnies*. He had always protested against the dogmatic spirit that was finding its expression in the teaching of the Westminster Divines, and the *Apology* marks his reaction and revulsion from it. He expounds each of the fifteen propositions in detail, and supports his case with quotations from the Bible and the early Christian writers. The book is written with remarkable breadth of view, and with a modern tone and spirit which is striking, though couched in somewhat laboured and archaic phraseology. It became a subject of bitter disputation and close discussion among men of all sorts and shades of religious opinion, who found it seriously deficient in the matter of orthodoxy.

His insistence upon the doctrine of the Inward Light was ROBERT contrary to the accepted standards, and his condemnation of BARCLAY, 1648–1690, the Sacraments shocked every sect, however mutually anta- Urie II. gonistic. Among the various writers who attacked his con- clusions, one John Brown of Wamphray, a headstrong covenanting divine, who had been banished to Holland in consequence of his anti-prelatic fervour, was one whom Robert Barclay thought worthy of reply. He described Quakerism as " a pathway to Paganism," and as a sample of his intelligent criticism he concluded that " The height of the Quakers' Divinity is but what a natural conscience can teach a man- eater." Robert did not reply for some time, but in his *Vindication* published some years later, he speaks of Brown's pamphlet as a mere " bundle of railing abuse."

Alexander Gordon, in the *Marrow of Barclay* says, " It is Theological his country's loss that Robert Barclay's splendid *Apologia* Review, should be left in the hands of a sect. Here indeed is a genuine 1875. outcome of the inner depth of the nation's worship, something characteristic and her own. A gift to her religious life akin to her profoundest requirements, and if she did but know it, far worthier the thankful acceptance of her people than any religious aid she has ever welcomed from the other side of the Border. . . . One great original theologian, and only one, has Scotland produced, and Robert Barclay was he."

The *Apology* was chiefly admired and valued by the Society inasmuch as it commanded the respect of the world for the Community which could produce such a masterpiece. It shook Calvinism to its core on fundamental principles, and while Calvin's axioms are of the waning past, Barclay's are of the widening future, and time has shown how the wider vision has conquered.

It remains a most remarkable and monumental work, full of erudition and dialectical skill, " such as few other of the sects into which modern Christians are divided, have been able to produce to give account of their particular faith and doctrine."

Among his critics, Robert had to meet the arguments of his friend George Keith, with whom he had collaborated in many meetings and writings. Keith declared the *Apology* should not be made the standard of the Quaker religion, as it, in places, contradicted Barclay's own teaching, and that the quotations from the Fathers were not always supported by their context ; but though he gleaned some small triumphs in argument, on the chief issues Barclay remained unshaken. At last Keith could only lament " that so good a Christian should be found in such bad company," as some of the authors he had quoted.

Barclay's "nobly balanced mind" survived all these attacks. Two years after his death George Keith finally rejected the doctrine of " the Inner Light " and after vainly endeavouring to keep together an independent body of " Christian Quakers," eventually seceded from the Society of Friends and took orders in the Church of England.

There are some quaint doctrines set forth in the *Apology*, but Robert Barclay was a highly educated and cultivated man, and did not fall into the exaggeration sometimes shown by George Fox.

He explained the reasons for their opposition to so many accepted customs and phrases, in direct terms which were literally obeyed by his followers.

" We affirm positively that it is not lawful for Christians to give and receive titles of honour, such as ' Your Excellency,' ' Your Majesty,' ' Your Honour,' ' Your Eminence.'

" 1st. Because these titles are no part of that obedience due to magistrates and superiors.

" 2nd. We find not that in the Scriptures any such titles are used, but in speaking to rulers they only used a simple compellation such as ' O King ' or ' O King Agrippa.'

" 3rd. It lays of necessity a lie upon Christians, because the persons obtaining these titles may have none of the qualifications answering to them. ' Your Excellency ' may be a person of no excellence. ' Your Grace ' may be an enemy to Grace. ' Your Honour ' known to be base and ignoble. What law of man should oblige us to call evil good and good evil ?

" 4th. ' Holiness,' ' Eminence,' used among Papists for Pope and Cardinal, and ' Grace,' ' Lordship ' and ' Worship,' used to the Clergy among Protestants is a blasphemous usurpation. Ought not holiness and grace to be in every Christian, and not peculiarly to themselves, and how can they claim any more titles than were practised by the Apostles and primitive Christians ? We find no such thing in Scripture. The Apostles are not called ' Your Grace ' nor ' Your Worship,' neither ' My Lord Peter,' or ' My Lord Paul,' nor yet ' Master Peter ' or ' Master Paul,' but simply ' Peter ' and ' Paul,' and that not only in the Scriptures but for hundreds of years after." Though we may find it difficult to disagree with his facts, we can understand how these conclusions would offend people accustomed to being addressed with titles of honour, and all the more as they could find no flaw in his argument.

ROBERT BARCLAY, 1648–1690, Urie II.

Robert Barclay had friends in every class of society, and his cheerful spirits, charming manners, and agreeable conversation made him a general favourite, while his talents as a linguist introduced him to people of condition on the Continent.

He and William Penn were received everywhere, and even those who regarded their religious opinions with disapproval or contempt, found the two serious, well-bred young men an acquisition to any company, and we may be sure they did not miss any opportunities of " testifying " in so sympathetic an atmosphere.

The literal interpretation of Scriptural phrases employed by the Friends is shown in George Fox's *Journal*. He says, " The World says, ' Kiss the Book,' but the Book says, ' Kiss the Son, lest he be angry.' "

Journal of George Fox, p. 506.

" And the Son saith, ' Swear not at all, but keep to Yea and Nay in all your communications, for whatsoever is more than this cometh of evil.' " The refusal of Colonel David Barclay to take the oath, or Bond of Peace, in 1667, in Edinburgh Castle, was in literal obedience to these tenets. No Quaker would take a legal oath in the accepted form, and they suffered much persecution in consequence, until in 1688 William of Orange decreed that a form of affirmation would be considered adequate.

ROBERT
BARCLAY,
1648–1690,
Urie II.

Robert Barclay says in the *Apology*, that the refusal to defend oneself is the hardest and most perfect part of Christianity, because it requires the most complete denial of self, and the most entire confidence in God. He had an object lesson in this always before him in the life of his brave old father.

Braith-
waite's
Early
Quakerism.

Another critic writes, referring to the *Apology*, " The permanent value of this work lies not in the imperfect success that attended Barclay's efforts to press the Quaker experience into Calvinistic moulds of thought, but in the sureness of emphasis with which, in spite of them, he is continually asserting that religion is an inward spiritual life received from God, and transforming human nature. . . . Below the scholastic surface of Barclay's writing, we shall seek to penetrate to the deep ocean of Divine Life in which he found peace and strength, and to know for ourselves the secret power which touched his heart."

History of
Quakerism.

This criticism is supported by another authority, E. B. Emmott, who writes, " He had been so thoroughly grounded in Calvinistic doctrine, that he never freed himself from the current conception of the innate depravity of human nature while at the same time he was convinced in his own experience that the life of Christ in the soul is an inward and universal power for the salvation of men. He felt the necessity for harmonising his own new experience with his old beliefs, as well as for defending the Quaker position logically, and by arguments which would appeal to theologians on their own ground. He therefore made a careful study of the writings of the Fathers, and of the history of the Catholic Church, and embodied the results of his researches in the book called *Apologia*."

Genealogical
Account.

" The *Apology* was published in six languages, Latin, French, High Dutch, Low Dutch, Spanish, and our own English tongue, of which there are already six impressions, and is in the Libraries of the Learned throughout Europe," says his grandson. It found most eager acceptance among the English Quakers, and was described as " The great Treatise, which raised Quakerism from being a formless enthusiasm,

128

to be a philosophy, a worthy reply to Calvin, and to Rome." It was read by the great sceptic Voltaire, who wrote of it, " It was surprising to see his *Apologie* only wrote by a private gentleman should have the offset to procure almost a general release to the whole sect from the sufferings they underwent."

It became the standard book of Quaker theory, while Penn's pamphlet *No Cross, No Crown* illustrated their practice, and Fox's *Journal* showed their history and origin.

The Quakers were great travellers. In those days of difficult transport, abominable roads, pirate-infested seas and interrupted communications between warring foreign countries, they penetrated to Eastern Europe, and bore their courageous testimony to places as generally inaccessible as Smyrna, Zante and Constantinople, where they found listeners and left believers. At first they were attacked by footpads and highwaymen, who knew they would offer no resistance, but as they made a practice of travelling without valuables and with little money, they gradually found themselves unmolested. George Fox, who had strange, unconventional ways, when refused shelter at inns, used to sleep under hedgerows and in barns.

"These were great days of high courage, noble sacrifices and rich fruit. Through hills and dales, meadows and moors, narrow streets and broad squares, villages and towns, cities and hamlets, come the children of the light."

Early in 1676 Robert Barclay journeyed to Amsterdam for the purpose of arranging the printing of his *Apology*. While in Holland he visited his kinswoman Elizabeth Princess Palatine, at Herwardine (or Herford). This lady was a daughter of Frederick V, Elector Palatine of the Rhine, whose acceptance of the crown of Bohemia in the Protestant interest had led to the Thirty Years War, and his wife Elizabeth, daughter of James I of England, known as the " Winter Queen."

Princess Elizabeth was Abbess of an ancient religious foundation, which as a Protestant institution had been left undisturbed at the reformation.

Her brother Charles Louis, who had been restored to the Electorate in 1648, was at this time ruler of the Palatinate.

III.—S

Deeply religious from her youth, she had shown her strong Protestant convictions by refusing, when quite a girl, to marry the Roman Catholic King of Poland.

Though she lived removed from the gay world, she kept in touch with the English Court, where her brother, Prince Rupert, was on terms of friendship with their first cousin King Charles.

Robert established a close friendship with her, gave her a copy of his book, and took a letter from her to Prince Rupert, begging him to mitigate the persecution of the Friends, in whom she became deeply interested.

The visit was cut short, for while he was at Herwardine, he received an urgent message from home, telling him of the arrest of his father in Aberdeen, where he had been indicted before a committee of the Privy Council for going to a meeting prohibited by law, with several other prominent Friends.

His defence has been previously given in Colonel Barclay's life, but simple and direct as it was, and based on law and humanity, it was harshly overruled, and he, with his companions, all people of rank and position, were ordered to pay exorbitant fines, or go to prison.

Robert at once returned to England, to be met in London with the information that his father, having declared his inability to pay the fine which amounted to over a fourth of his annual income, had been imprisoned in the Tolbooth of Aberdeen.

In righteous indignation, Robert made up his mind to approach King Charles II and lay his case before him. He was determined to destroy the pretext that the Friends had infringed the Conventicle Act, which was the only legal ground for their prosecution, and he felt also that as their principles were misrepresented, and rendered odious, and they themselves exposed to harm and violence, he was justified in taking the same course that Calvin had taken under similar conditions, and go straight to his Sovereign with his complaint. While he was waiting for an appointment, he wrote this letter to Princess Elizabeth, from whom he had parted rather abruptly :—

1676.

130

HISTORY OF THE BARCLAY FAMILY

London. 24 of $\frac{4}{mo}$ 1676.

[Old style.]

ROBERT
BARCLAY,
1648–1690,
Urie II.

DEAR FRIEND,

The sense and constant remembrance which I entertain in my
spirit of that good opportunity which it pleased the Lord to minister
unto us when together, would long e'er now have engaged me to
write unto thee, but that I was not willing to do anything in the
forwardness of my own spirit. The Lord seems to have laid a
particular care and concern upon me which I shall not adventure
to express lest I might seem to exceed. I shall be glad to hear from
thee as thou finds true freeness to let me know how things are with
thee, let this transmit the remembrance of my true and unfeigned
love to the Countess of Hornes [The Princess's lady in waiting].
I hope she hath held her resolutions of learning to read and understand English, which it may please the Lord to bless unto her.

I delivered thy letter to thy Brother [Prince Rupert] who was
civile to me. I also took occasion from thence to employ him to be
assisting me in ane address I intend to make to the King, in behalf
of my Father, and about forty more of our Friends that are about
some months ago imprisoned in Scotland for conscience sake, in
which he promised his concurrence ; if it prove successful it is well,
if not, it is well also. We must be contented to suffer, and I shall go
home cheerfully willing to partake with them of their bonds. I
intend to send thee some books which I hope may be usefull unto
thee, but above all I recommend thee to that inward word of Grace,
in which thou can read thyself and learn to know the Lord, in which
pure and fruitful knowledge that thou may more and more advance,
is the earnest desire of Thy assured Friend in the love of Jesus.

R. BARCLAY.

Princess Elizabeth replied as follows :—

July 31 1676.

My dear Friend in our Saviour Jesus Christ.

I have received your letter dated the 24th of June, this day.

Your memory is dear to me, so are your lines and your exhortations very necessary. . . I confess that whatsoever I have studied and
learnt heretofore, is but dirt in comparison to the true knowledge of
Christ. I confess also my infidelity to this light heretofore by suffering myself to be conducted by false politick lights, now that I have
sometimes a small glimpse of the True Light, I do not attend it as I
should, being drawn away by the works of my calling which must be
done, and (as your swift English hounds) I often over-run my sent,
being called back when it is too late. Let not this make you less
earnest in prayer for me, for you see I need them, your letters will be
always welcome to me, so will your friends if any choose to visit me.

I should admire God's Providence if my Brother could be a means of releasing your father and forty more in Scotland, having promised to do his best I know he will perform it. He has ever been true to his word, and you shall find me with the grace of the Lord, a true friend. ELIZABETH.

P.S.—The Countess of Hornes sends you her most hearty commendations, she has not had time to learn English, having imployed it in more necessary works, since God hath visited this family with many sick of small-pox, and Contagious feavers, of which she has had a care, not considering the infection, amongst the rest there was a servant of hers very desperately sick of whom she had an especial care, deeming her also a sister in Christ, who did draw great comfort out of the books you left here.

Robert Barclay had no difficulty in gaining access to the King, and presented to him this petition on behalf of the Friends :—

The State of the Case of the People called Quakers, in Scotland, presented unto the King's consideration. The Council of Scotland having about three months ago, emitted a Declaration to re-inforce former Acts of Parliament, against Conventicles, and recommended the execution of them, because of the abuse several persons had made of the King's indulgence as the said Declaration intimates.

Some inferior Magistrates have taken occasion thereby to imprison many of them, and some Deputies of the Council have stretched the law against Conventicles to the highest pitch of severity, by heavy fines and tedious imprisonments, although their practices and principles never gave ground for such procedure.

It is therefore, on behalf of the said suffering people, with all sincere respect desired, that it would please the King favourably to recommend their case to the Council of Scotland, that a difference of character may be put upon them, who have ever lived and behaved themselves peaceably under the present Government, from such that are said to have abused the indulgences, with some present relief to those harmless sufferers to prevent that utter ruin, which in all probability will attend so many of them that live by their labour and trade.   (Signed) R. BARCLAY.

Charles was kind-hearted and shrewd enough to distinguish intellectual power and discern moral force. He good-naturedly recognised his serious young kinsman, even though he refused him the hat-honour that was universally and obsequiously bestowed upon him. The young man must

have been conspicuous among the gaily-dressed courtiers in ROBERT
his sombre garments, for judging by Princess Elizabeth's BARCLAY,
letter to her brother, he appears to have assumed the formal 1648–1690,
Quaker garb for this occasion. When he approached his Urie II.
royal cousin, a roll of paper in his hand, Charles waved
aside the officials that would have checked him, and taking
the roll, threw himself back in his great chair of state to
read it, while Robert stood, courteous, but not subservient,
awaiting his pleasure.

The King is said to have read this appeal attentively, and Life of
to have observed to those around that it appeared a hard case, Wm. Penn,
Sewel.
adding: "What shall we do for this people?" "But some
light-minded persons approached and engaged His Maj^{tie} in
merrie conversation."

The King was thereupon about to put the matter on one
side, when he encountered the patient gaze of the young
Quaker still standing there, and summoned the Duke of
Lauderdale to speak with him. He ordered the Duke to
transmit the said paper to the Council of Scotland, and refer
it to their consideration.

Lauderdale, who was then Commissioner of Scotland, and
very unfavourable to the Society of Friends, could not have
been best pleased, but dared not disobey, so an order was
despatched to the effect that

" His Matie is graciously pleased to refer this paper to Rt. Hon.
the Lords of His Majesty's Privy Council in Scotland, for their
consideration.
"Aug. 7, 1676.   " LAUDERDALE."

This being a tolerably clear intimation of His Majesty's
wishes, after the usual unavoidable delays in transmission,
Robert Barclay had the satisfaction of hearing that his father,
" whom he loved with tender affection," was to be released
with his companions, and the magistrates warned against
undue severity.

He had yet to contend with the animosity of the Duke of
Lauderdale, who was ever Charles's evil genius, and put every
obstacle in the way of his following his naturally generous

impulses. It was said that he had been brought up as a Presbyterian himself, but anxious to stand well with the King, he had consulted him as to which religion he preferred him to practise. Charles's characteristic answer, that "Presbyterianism was no religion for a gentleman," was quite enough for the time-serving courtier, who forthwith became one of the most bigoted opponents of his former co-religionists.

Robert says in another place that he was not able to gain any ground with Lauderdale, in whose hands was the sole management of Scots affairs.

But here the Duke of York stood his friend, being said to be " the only man whom Lauderdale could bear to midle in his province, or was like to do it with any success." Doubtless the self-seeking Minister found it judicious to keep on good terms with the heir-apparent.

Emboldened by the King's kindness, Robert also presented him with a copy of *The Apology*, prefaced by a letter :—

" It is far from me," he wrote, " to use this epistle as an engine to flatter thee, the usual design of such works ; and I can neither dedicate it to thee, nor crave thy patronage, as if thereby I might have more confidence to present it to the world, or be more hopeful of its success. But I found it upon my spirit to take occasion to present this book unto thee ; that as thou hast been often warned by several inhabitants of England, so thou mayest not want a seasonable advertisement from a member of thine ancient kingdom of Scotland."

After again pointing out the peaceableness and loyalty of his Quaker subjects, and their courage under persecution, and the faithfulness with which they had discharged their consciences, even to the risking of his favour, he says,

"If thou wilt allow thyself so much time as to read this, thou mayest find how consonant their principles are both to Scripture, Truth, and right feeling."

He also wrote frankly and boldly, warning Charles against the flattery of court parasites, and begged him, in accordance with the great Quaker principle, to apply himself to " that Light of Christ, which shineth in Thy conscience."

The King did not appear to resent this plain speech,

indeed may have been amused by the reference to the ROBERT
courtiers, and Robert continued to be well received at court, BARCLAY,
where he remained pending the answer to his petition. He Urie II.
wrote to his friend Stephen Crisp, in August, 1676 :—

> " I have at last, after long and tedious attendance, near finished my
> business, for the Duke of Lauderdale tells me yesterday he has received
> orders to give me a letter to the Council in Scotland, in order to
> grant Friends their liberty, which he promised to give me tomorrow,
> so that I propose in two or three days to be going homewards."

However, owing to Lauderdale's opposition or the supine-
ness of the King, no definite action in favour of the Quakers
appears to have been taken at that time, though for some
reason not recorded David Barclay regained his liberty.

On October 28th, 1676, Robert wrote again to the Princess
Elizabeth, to tell her of his ill-success, in spite of court
promises :—

Urie Oct. 28, 1676.

DEAR FRIEND,

I did write to thee about 7 weeks ago from Edinburgh at what
time I presented a paper from the King to the Council here on
behalf of the Prisoners in which I acquainted thee of its proving
unsuccessful, the Council refusing to release them unless they would
pay certain fines, and promise not to meet to worship God again,
unless according to the religion approved by Law, neither of which
because for conscience sake they cannot do. They must remain and
patiently wait untill the Lord in whose hands are the hearts of men,
work their deliverance who will not suffer this exercise to continue
any longer than it is needful for us, therefore I being in daily expectation to hear from thee of the receipt of that letter wherewith I
also wrote one in French to Anna, doe forbear to enlarge at this time,
only thou may know that thou art daily in my remembrance and my
breathing is that the Lord may not suffer His seed to be unfruitful in
thee but raise it and thee over all difficulties that stand in the way
until thou arrive at the blessed end. . . .
I remain Thy assured Friend in the Lord,

R. BARCLAY.

Although Robert must have found the atmosphere of the
court uncongenial, his visit gave him an opportunity of meeting people of standing and influence and of spreading his
testimony wherever he could find a listener.

ROBERT
BARCLAY,
1648-1690,
Urie II.

History of
the Friends,
Sewel,
p. 249.

Among others he met with Heer Adrian Paets, a distinguished Dutchman, who had been Ambassador from the Netherlands to Spain, and had come to London as one of the Commissioners for the Dutch East India Company. He had been in correspondence with Robert since his visit to Holland, and now sought him out at Court, and told him that he readily yielded to his arguments, was greatly impressed by his learning, and admitted that he had been mistaken in his notion of the Quakers, as he found they could make a reasonable plea for the foundation of their religion.

Though it may seem an inconsiderable point, the name " Quakerism," was a stumbling-block to many foreigners. The Rector of the Scots College may well have been horrified when he heard of his nephew's conversion, when conveyed to him through French sources, as " Berclai Ecossois de nation, un des principaux Chefs de Quouackres."

Heer Paets was better informed, and entered into serious argument with Robert, writing to contest the point of the inward revelation of God to the Saints, which was an essential part of the Quaker doctrine. He maintained that the being and substance of the Christian religion consisted in the knowledge of and faith concerning the birth, life, death, resurrection and ascension of Christ, which contingent truth is matter of fact, and that matter of fact cannot be known but by the relation of another, or by the perception of the outward senses, and quoted the text, " Faith cometh by hearing," and that, therefore, there can be no immediate revelation by the simple operation of the Spirit in the mind, unless there be somewhat proposed to the outward senses.

Robert replied on November 24, 1676, from " The Prison of Aberdeen, where I am confined for the sake of the testimony of Jesus."

He argued that though faith and historical knowledge are indeed a part of the Christian religion, they are not such an essential part as that without which the Christian religion cannot exist, as the feet and hands of a man are integral parts of a man, but that he may exist without them. He said that Friends do not contend for a revelation which would beget in

136

their souls historical faith and knowledge, but all can be learnt by study of the Scriptures, and that the inward illumination of God, which is like the sun's light proceeding from the Divine sun, doth shine into the eye of the mind, and by its influence moves the mind to reading or hearing the Scriptures and meditating thereon.

The arguments continued at considerable length, and with great erudition on both sides. That the Apologist's reasoning was convincing can be assumed from the success of the Quaker movement in Holland in the following year.

In the meanwhile, on September 6th, Robert wrote again to the Princess Elizabeth, knowing her deep interest in the sufferings of the Friends, from Edinburgh.

DEAR FRIEND,

Last night thy acceptable letter came to my hands, in which my spirit was refreshed, in a sence that the Lord continueth his love to thee.

I doubt not that thy Brother would have kept his word in speaking to the King on my behalf, but it so happened that at that time he had a sore legg (from which he is since recovered) so that I could not make use of him.

With no small difficulty I obtained a kind of recommendation from the King to the Council of State, but such is the opposition and enmity of the world's spirit against us, and the influence of the chief Bishops who sit in Council, that no release for the Prisoners could be obtained, so that they must patiently suffer till the Lord in His own time work their deliverance, who will suffer them to continue no longer there than is good for their souls and his own glory, and indeed they have great reason to be contented, for the glory and heavenly majesty of the Lord doth singularly every day appear among them, and the virtuous Life of Jesus doth often flow among them as a mighty stream.

Thus are shut up together forty-two men in one great room, who, not of self-will nor their own choice, but by the providence of God are placed for a time together in heavenly community.

I this day take my journey towards them, not doubting that I shall be taken and shut up with them, and with all cheerfulness of spirit am prepared to partake wt them of their bonds, not doubting but I shall also share of their joys. It will be very refreshing and comfortable to me in my Prison, to hear of thee, for thy Prosperity and Increase in the Truth is desired by me, as that of my own soul.

Thy faithful Friend,

R. BARCLAY.

Robert's anticipation was soon realised. He was arrested while attending a meeting in Aberdeen, and was imprisoned with his father, Andrew Jaffray, John Forbes and others, in the Tolbooth of Aberdeen. The account of their ill-treatment has already been recorded in Colonel Barclay's life. He was not released until April 9, 1677.

Though he accepted this treatment in his usual spirit of Christian philosophy, and was described by a fellow prisoner as " a man marked among many for evenness of spirit," his friends were active on his behalf.

When Princess Elizabeth received his letter she was much disturbed, and wrote to remonstrate with Robert. She said :

"It is a cross to me that you will not make use of the liberty that God miraculously gave you, but will return to Scotland to be clapt up again in prison, for which there is neither precept nor example."

Again on December 31, 1676, she wrote :

MY DEAR FRIEND,

I have received your letter from Urie, dated the 28th of October, and at the same time Information from Benjamin Furly that you have been clapt up—though I am sure that the Captivers are more captive than you are, being in the company of Him that admits no bonds and is able to break all bonds. That He may break all bonds is th sything [sic] of your true friend

ELIZABETH.

She also wrote again to her brother Prince Rupert, a letter in which womanly sympathy was mingled with the diplomatic arguments she thought most likely to appeal to King Charles.

Herford, Dec. 19, 1676.

DEAR BROTHER

I have written to you some months ago, by Robert Barclay, who passed this way, and hearing I was your sister, desired to speak with me. I knew him to be a Quaker by his hat, and took occasion to inform myself of all their opinions, and finding they were to submit to Magistrates in real things, ommitting the ceremonial, I wished in my heart the King might have many such subjects : and since I have heard that notwithstanding His Majesty's most gracious letter on his behalf to the Council of Scotland, he has been clapt up in prison, with the rest of his friends, and they threaten to hang them unless they subscribe their own banishment ; and this upon a law made against other sects, that appeared armed for the maintenance of their heresy, which goes directly against the principles of those which are ready to suffer all that can be inflicted, and still love and pray for their enemies.

Therefore dear Brother, if you can do anything to prevent their destruction, I doubt not but you will do an action acceptable to God Almighty, and conducive to the service of your Royal Master, for the Presbyterians are their main enemies, to whom they are an eyesore, as being witnesses against all their violent ways. I care not though His Majesty see my letter : it is written out of no less an humble affection for him than most sensible compassion for the innocent sufferers. You will act herein according to your own discretion, and I beseech you to still consider me as yours

ELIZABETH.

A Monsr le Prince Rupert a Londres.

There appear to have been no restrictions upon the prisoners' correspondence, though the conditions under which it was carried on must have been far from agreeable, and in addition to many letters Robert Barclay passed the time in prison by writing one of his well-known treatises, called *Universal Love, considered and established upon its right foundation*. He also wrote a pamphlet, called *Truth Triumphant*, which points out the inconsistency of the accusations levelled against the Friends.

" Some," he says, " will have us to be Foolish mad creatures ; others to be deep subtle Politicians, others to be learned cunning Jesuits under a mere vizard. . . . Sometimes we are a Disorderly Confused Rabble, leaving everyone to do as they list, against all good Order and Government ; at other times we are so much for Order as we admit not Men to exercise the liberty of their own Judgments. Thus are our Reputations tossed by the envy of our Adversaries, [who] save us the pains while they refute one another."

Though Robert had the solace, denied to most of his friends, of his literary work, the days must have passed slowly, and he was helped and cheered by letters from outside. Princess Elizabeth was one of his most constant correspondents, and he wrote her long exhortations to courage and patience. On December 24, 1676, he sent a very long letter containing much wise advice.

HISTORY OF THE BARCLAY FAMILY

From Aberdeen Prison. 24 Xber 1676

DEAR FRIEND

Thy letter in answer to mine of the 6th of September came yester-night to my hand, and was very acceptable unto me in my present bonds. . . .

He confesses that her material prosperity makes it harder for her to apply herself to that divine grace and light that has shown her her poverty and the need she has to partake of the spiritual riches of Christ's Kingdom.

He admits that the " so needful natural silence " is hard to the natural mind, especially to those who have

enriched their spirits with great variety of notions, and have laboured to deck themselves with the wisdom and knowledge of this world . . . thy eminency wherein though it commendeth thee to the world, renders now that which is most needful so difficult for thee, and makes that thy friend [the Countess of Hornes] because of her greater simplicity and less attainments in these things have a readier access to possess and enjoy the naked truth, which for this cause of old was more readily received by poor fisher-men and simple women than by the great Rabbis and wise Greeks.

He encourages her to persevere, and

to draw near to the Lord in the small appearance of his seed in thy heart, and for that end abstract thyself from the multiplicity of thy outward affairs.

He suggests that after any pressing outward business she should retire for a season and look upon any faithless per-suasion that her temptations and difficulties are too great or too strong, as being " befooled by the Enemy, and kept under his bonds."

He concludes,

1676.

I hope thou wilt take in good part my freedom herein, which proceedeth from pure love and ane earnest desire that thou may go on as not to lose the glorious prize that is set before thee, which is better than an earthly crown. My soul breaths to the Lord for thee that this may be thy portion, for the obtaining thereof I with my brethren do at present contentedly suffer these Bonds, though we see no way of outward deliverance, not doubting that the Lord will bring it about in his own good time.

Thine assured friend

R. BARCLAY.

HISTORY OF THE BARCLAY FAMILY

In January 1677 Robert Barclay wrote from the prison in Aberdeen an eloquent appeal to James Sharpe, the Archbishop of St. Andrews, who was known to be one of the most cruel and tyrannical oppressors of the Friends.

The Protestant Episcopacy of Scotland had been of short duration, but at this time the ecclesiastical government was vested in bishops, and the city of St. Andrews was the Metropolitan See.

The letter has been preserved, and though over long to quote in full, has always been considered an irrefutable charge, and had it been accepted and acted upon would have saved infinite suffering and injustice.

It was addressed to " James Sharpe, Archbishop of St. Andrews (so-called)," and was Robert's last literary production before he gained his liberty in April 1677.

It begins :—

My being personally unknown to thee, hath hindered me to give way to that pressure of mind, whereby I have felt myself oftentimes moved to write to thee, because I was loth to trouble thee : but since there is an address intended to be presented to the Council, at the first sitting on behalf of me and my friends, I could no longer forbear upon this occasion, to signify unto thee what hath been upon my mind for some time towards thee.

He puts the case of the imprisoned Friends with moderation, giving the facts without comment, the injustice of the charges, the length of time they have illegally been kept in confinement, and how the goods of many poor people have been " miserably spoiled."

He suggests that the Archbishop may not be fully aware of these practices, as to which his conscience is the best judge, and says,

I presume thou lookest upon it as thy chief honour to be reputed a Christian Bishop, deriving thy authority from Christ and his apostles, but they never gave any warrant for such doings, being preachers and practisers of patience and suffering, but never persecutors or causing to rob any of their goods and liberty for conscience sake.

141

He continues :—

I confess the bloody Bishops of Rome gave large precedents of such actions, but then I suppose thou art not anxious to be accounted ane imitator of them in that respect.

He goes on to say that he is confident that the Archbishop is not persecuting the Friends merely for their consciences but because he thinks their principles subversive to the peace of the State, and likely to result in the overturn of established authority " both lawful and laudable." Therefore he brings before him such proofs of their peaceful conduct and patient endurance of wrongs and injustices that he never can deny the knowledge of them, and goes on to utter the warning that,

Should thou be found a positive persecutor of those against whom no wrong of that kind can be alledged, would not that give plentiful occasion for such as desire to represent thy other actions with the worst aspect to show that whatever thou pretends of the State's security, yet thou art a persecutor of pure conscience only.

, He maintains that no persecution or Rigour of the Law can shake their faith, and that they are prepared cheerfully to endure even Death itself, doubting not that God would raise witnesses out of their ashes who will outlive all the violence and cruelty of man.

One passage, which was quoted as prophetic in the light of later events, runs,

And albeit should thyself be most inexorable and violent towards us, thou may assure thyself not to receive any evil from us, there-fore . . . to the God of Truth . . . to whom vengeance belongs, we leave it, who will certainly in his own time and way revenge our Quarrell, whose dreadful Judgement should be more terrible to thee, and much more justly to be feared, than the violent assaults or secret assassinations of thy other Antagonists. That thou may prevent both the one and the other by a Christian moderation suitable to the office thou layest claim to is the desire of thy soul's well wisher.

(Signed) R. BARCLAY.

From the Chappell prison of Aberdeen the 6th of the 1st mo. 1677.

While the Friends still patiently awaited a reply to this appeal, the news came to them of the barbarous murder of the Archbishop, when travelling in his coach on the road to St.

Andrews, in May, 1679. His treachery to the Presbyterian ROBERT
church, which had entrusted its cause to his advocacy, and BARCLAY,
been heartlessly betrayed, had caused him to be regarded with 1648–1690, Urie II.
bitter hatred by the Covenanters, and a body of these, driven
mad by oppression, had taken the law into their own hands,
and avenged their wrongs.

The Friends regarded this as a direct interposition of Providence on their behalf, and pointed out the phrasing of
Robert Barclay's letter as having been inspired.

It is perhaps difficult for us now to understand the eagerness with which points of doctrine were discussed among all
classes and at all times in seventeenth-century England and
Scotland. The religious atmosphere was keenly controversial,
and Fox's simple message that Christ had come not only to
bring forgiveness but to make his dwelling-place in the
hearts of men, enabling them to live pure and holy lives, came
as a great light to many minds confused by elaborate arguments and blinded by obscure interpretations of the Scriptural teaching.

The glimpses of earnest conviction and high spiritual
aspiration that we get, cannot but impress a reader in these
more Laodicean days.

Robert seems to have been a little anxious as to the effect of March, 1677.
his rather lengthy exhortations on the Princess, and in March
he writes again in a more intimate fashion to her, she having
apparently accepted the fact of their relationship, and wished
him to drop the formal style of address.

He appears to deprecate the idea that he should dictate to
her, and explains that he wishes her to have perfect freedom
of choice.

Aberdeen prison

5th of the month March

1677.

DEAR AND WELL-BELOVED ELIZABETH

By thine of the 19th of the last month I receive with gladness the
renewed testimony of thy love and friendship, not because of any
great expectation I have that this essay will produce my outward
liberty, but because it hath pleased God to raise and begett in thee,
that love and regard to his pretious Truth and testimony and that

143

compassion towards His despised witnesses that for their sakes thou not only willingly undergoes this trouble, but runs the hazard of encurring the Court censure, and of bearing a part of that reproach which hath been and always will be the lot of the faithfull, from such as are acted and guided by the spirit of this world.

He goes on to point out that her singular preservation from reproach or censure appears to prove that the blessing of God rests upon her efforts. He recommends her

to wait seriously in the silent place, in a mind willing to obey, for light from the Lord rightly to distinguish between the good and necessary—and the hurtful and unnecessary. It is far from me to require of any, far less of thee, to do anything merely upon my persuasion. My dear friend, the Lord give thee a clear understanding of these things, who knows I use this freedom with thee not to over-drive thee, but of pure love and desire thou mayest not fall short in anything to the hindering of thy growth in righteousness, that thou mayest receive light and grace from God more and more to wax strong therein is the earnest and daily prayer of thy assured friend. R. BARCLAY.

P.S. George Keith, my dear brother and companion in bonds, salutes thee and Anna.

Prince Rupert, moved by Princess Elizabeth's letter and presumably recovered from his " sore legg," petitioned the King on behalf of Robert Barclay, who was released on April 9th, 1677, after five months' imprisonment.

Robert himself always attributed this to the intervention of the Duke of York. The confusion between the two decrees of the Council, spoken of in Colonel Barclay's life, led to his finding himself and his friends at large, and seeing that neither the magistrates nor the sheriff would be responsible for them, possibly through fear of Royal displeasure, they went quietly before a Notary, and protesting that they were freemen, and should be allowed to pass away about their own lawful occasions, were at last permitted to do so.

Other friends attributed this happy result to Court interest, and Princess Elizabeth wrote, " I do love the Duke of York for it."

A rather unexpected friendship had sprung up between Barclay and James Duke of York. Two men holding more diametrically opposite views could hardly be imagined, but there was something in Robert's sincerity of purpose that James admired, and his own bigoted adherence to his Roman Catholic faith cannot but be respected when it is realised that he lost three kingdoms for it.

Robert Barclay always saw that James's determination to allow liberty of conscience to all, though intended to cover " Papists " only, would also include the Quakers, and he believed that James was a good friend to them. But the Duke's limitation of his good offices to Robert and his father, in the letter quoted by Robert on the 17th of the 7th month, 1677, makes it doubtful how far he was disposed to risk popularity on behalf of the Society in general. However, in this case his intervention was successful, and Robert was proportionately grateful.

St. James,
Sept. 12, 1677.

I could not refuse this bearer, Barclay, a Quaker, to write to you in favor of him and his father Colonel Barclay that you would be as favourable to them as you could, as to the inconveniances which may happen to them by reason of their perswasion in point of Religion, and that which makes me write about these two Quakers, is that as this bearer informs me, he is in some way related to our family, one of Sr. Gordoune I thinke he called him Sr. Robert, that came into England with King James, being his Grand or Great Grand father, which if so sure both he and his father will deserve some favor, though that they have the misfortune to be Quakers. This being the only subject of this letter I shall say no more, only to assure you that you shall always find me the same to you.

JAMES.

For the Duke of Lauderdale.

William Penn also corresponded with Princess Elizabeth, and a letter from her acknowledging his, and mentioning Robert Barclay, written from Herwardine (or Herford) on May 2, 1677, shows her humble and devout temperament.

My Freind will tell you that both your letters were very acceptable, together with your wishes for my obtaining those vertues which may make me a worthy follower of our great King and Saviour, Jesus Christ. What I have done for His true Disciples is not so much as a cup of cold water : it affords them no refreshment neither did I expect any fruit of my letter to the Duchess of L, as I have expressed at the same time unto B.F.

But since Robert Barclay desired that I should write it, I could not refuse him, nor omit to do anything that was judged conducing to his liberty, though it should expose me to the derision of the world. But this a mere moral man can reach at ; the true inward graces are yet wanting in

Your affectionate friend,

Elizabeth.

It was not long after his release that Robert again travelled southward in May, to hold a conference with William Rogers of Bristol, who had formed a sect called Separatists in Westmoreland.

In pursuance of his habit of investigating personally all questions of religion, he arranged to meet their leader, and to discuss with him a book called *The Anarchy of Ranters* or, more diplomatically, *Church Discipline*, which Barclay had written.

It might have been expected that such a debate would have been conducted with some heat, but the moderation and calmness of Robert's manner and arguments disarmed Rogers so much that he acknowledged that he had misapprehended a part of the book. But he did not drop his opposition afterwards, and continued the controversy with other Friends, writing again in answer to Barclay's book, so his mildness at this time can only be attributed to Robert's diplomatic handling of the situation.

On July 26, 1677, another journey was taken to Holland, and a ship sailed from Harwich to Brill, carrying George Fox, Robert Barclay, William Penn, George Keith and other leaders. Their object was to organise yearly meetings at Amsterdam, and quarterly and monthly meetings for all the separate Continental countries.

The new movement had immediate success. Only William Penn had any previous knowledge of the Dutch language, but notwithstanding the need for interpreters, George Fox writes in his journal : " There was a mighty concourse, and the Mystery of Iniquity and Godliness were opened and declared in the Demonstration."

The deputation was a powerful one, and the results were ROBERT BARCLAY, 1648-1690, Urie II.
triumphant in more senses than one.

The Friends were not only being persecuted in England and Scotland, but all over the Continent, and in Danzig in par- 1677. ticular they were undergoing heavy suffering. William Penn therefore wrote to John Sobieski, then King of Poland, urging him to cease the persecution, and quoting a noble saying of his ancestor Stephen, " I am King of men, not of consciences, of bodies, not of souls," which appeal is said to have greatly improved their condition.

A characteristic anecdote of Robert Barclay is related by George Fox, which reminds us of Colonel David's energy and determination. George Fox Journal, p. 233.

On their voyage the ship was becalmed within a league of the coast of Holland, and they were obliged to anchor for the night. To be so near the end of the journey and to be vexatiously delayed was too much for the impatience of William Penn and Robert Barclay, all on fire to begin their evangelising work. They therefore persuaded two of the crew to let down a small boat that belonged to the packet and row them to shore ; but before they could get there, the gates of the harbour were shut, and there being no house without the gates they were fain to lie in a fisher's boat all night. As soon as the gates were opened in the morning, " they sent a boat, which brought us to Brill, where the Friends received us with great gladness."

There were a large number of Friends in Holland and they held meetings in Leyden, Harlem, and Amsterdam, where, as Penn wrote, " The Gospel was preached, the dead were raised, and the living were comforted." The dead in this sense referred only to the spiritually " dead in trespasses and sins."

Penn also wrote describing their success in Holland among non-conformists of all sects. " This being the first day of the week, we had a very large meeting again, there coming to it a great concourse of people of several opinions, as Baptists, Seekers, Socinians, Brownists, and some of the Collegians. Robert Barclay, George Keith and I did severally declare the

147

everlasting truth among them . . . and the Meeting ended sweetly and well."

Considering how hotly these various religious sects had opposed the first teaching of the Friends, this is a testimony to the eloquence of the teachers, and the spread of the movement.

Robert Barclay's friendship with the Princess Palatine stood them in good stead, for as soon as she heard of the arrival of the deputation she hastened to invite them to Herwardine, a four days' journey by boat and post wagon.

Robert Barclay and William Penn were at this time both young men, of not more than 30 years of age, but the Princess found " she could speak to them as a scholar to scholars, as a thinker to thinkers, without exaggeration, or uninstructed enthusiasms." They were in addition accustomed to good society, and were both remarkable for personal dignity, and beauty of face and carriage. " The calm nobility of their natures showed the strength of their inward convictions."

It is recorded that they received an invitation to supper and among the guests was a French lady of quality, whose name is not given, " who had come to the meal prepared to criticise and oppose them." After hearing their grave arguments she became " deeply broken, and very affectionately kind and respectful to both William Penn and Robert Barclay."

The Princess's lady in waiting, the Countess of Hornes, was greatly interested and struck by the similarity of the Quaker doctrines to those taught by Monsieur de Labadie, a one-time Jesuit priest, who had formed a sect of " plain people " and attracted adherents.

Robert Barclay, of all people, would have been able to understand the mystical bond that existed between sincere believers in doctrines apparently so widely differentiated in practice, and Penn wrote in his diary, " The Lord was not wanting to us, but we were all sweetly tended and broken together, and virtue went forth of Jesus that day which did not a little pleasure that noble young woman."

After the meal they held a meeting with the Princess

148

Elizabeth, the Countess, and various of their friends, " to ROBERT BARCLAY, 1648-1690, Urie II.
their great satisfaction." When that was over the Countess
appealed to Robert Barclay to hold yet another for the servants
from which the Princess said she would absent herself, " so
as not to cause them embarrassment." To this he gladly
agreed, and so the Court servants had their opportunity of
hearing the Quaker teaching from its two greatest exponents.

The next day was the first of the week, and it being agreed
with the Princess to have another meeting, William Penn
desired that not only as many of her own family, but as many
of the town as would willingly be there might be admitted.
" And thus, William Penn and Robert Barclay had a large
opportunity to preach effectually and to discharge their
hearts."

After the meeting, the Princess came to Robert Barclay,
and taking him by the hand, spoke to him of the sense she had
of the power and presence of God, that had been among them,
" and thus going on she broke forth into an extraordinary
passion, crying out with her hand upon her heart, ' I cannot
speak to you, my heart is too full.' "

They stayed several days in the town, principally employed
in religious exercises, and left, having discharged their
testimony and sown the seed, the results of which are apparent
to this day.

George Keith went on to Germany, where William Penn
and Robert Barclay intended to follow him later. When they
bade farewell to the Princess she burst into tears, crying,
" Come again, before you depart from Germany."

Penn replied seriously, " We are in God's hands, friend
Elizabeth. We cannot dispose of ourselves but we will not
forget thee, nor those belonging to thee."

They were never to meet again, for she died in 1679, but
Penn has recorded the last words she had spoken to him.
" Though I live at a distance, and you should never see me
more, I desire you to remember that I thank you for this
good time, and be assured that though my condition subjects
me to divers temptations, yet my soul hath strong desires 1677.
after the best things."

In fact the Princess was a Quaker in all but name, and if any official lists of converts had been kept at that time her name would doubtless have been among them.

As Robert Barclay travelled home to Scotland, he stopped at Theobalds in Enfield Chase, the former hunting mansion of King James, and wrote to the Princess from there.

> Theobalds near London,
> 12th of the 7th [9th] mo 1677.

DEAR FRIEND,

By thy letter of the last of the month past I understand of the friends being with thee ; and was refreshed by the account they gave me of thy kind and Christian entertainment of them (they having overtaken me in Holland). God will not be wanting to reward thy love as well as to encrease the same. Finding no ready passage streight for Scotland, I came over here ; and albeit I had no great expectation of success, I resolved once more to try thy Cusen the Duke of York. So I told him that I understand from Scotland, that notwithstanding Lauderdale was there and had promised ere he went, to doe something, yet our Friends bonds was rather increased and that now there was only one thing to be done, which I desired of him, and that was, to write effectually to the Duke of Lauderdale, in that stile wherein Lauderdale might understand that he was serious in the bussiness, and did really intend the thing he wrote concerning should take effect ; which I knew he might do, and I supposed the other would answer, which if he would do, I must acknowledge as a great kindness ; but if he did write, and not in that manner, the other might not suppose him to be serious, I would rather he should excuse himself the trouble ; desiring withall to excuse my plain manner of dealing, as being different from the Court manner of soliciting, all which he seemed to take in good part, and said he would so write, as I desired, for my Father and me, but not for the generall, so he hath given me a letter : whether it may prove effectual or not, I cannot determine, but of this thou may hear of hereafter.

I am now entered into my journey, and intend to pass by the way of Ragly.

What thou writest of the Counsellor of the Elector, and the other preachers is very acceptable to me to hear, whose joy it is, to understand that the eyes of any are opened to see the truth as it is in this day revealed.

The rest of the letter contains more personal matter relating to spiritual things, and he reiterates the caution that Elizabeth should not allow her worldly occupations and temptations to ROBERT
BARCLAY,
1648-1690,
Urie II. obscure her seeking the true light. He concludes with

> Thou mayest make mention of my dear and tender love to Anna (the Countess of Hornes) whose servant, as also the French woman, I forget not. To Anna I thought to have written apart, but must now leave it until another opportunity. If thou seest meet to salute that Counsellor of the Elector in my name thou mayest do it. I shall add no more at present, but that I am
>
> Thy Real and unfeigned friend,
> R. BARCLAY.

Another letter from Princess Elizabeth touching on some family matters connected with the Mollisons ends with the words :—

> I hope that you are still in freedom, and that the Duke of York's interest hath been effectual for you and your father. I also recommend to your prayers
>
> Your loving friend,
> ELIZABETH.

This was received in November, showing that Robert's friends were never quite free from uneasiness on his account. He was now enjoying his home and family life at Urie, though the persecution was still raging outside, and he could never have felt quite secure from sudden arrest and imprisonment.

The gaols were full of Friends, and 350 had died in 1678. prison during the reign of Charles II.

In 1678 the ambassadors of the King of France, and those History of
the Friends,
Sewel. of the United Netherlands, with several other potentates, met at Nimeguen to treat about a general peace, and Robert Barclay wrote an epistle to them in Latin, to exhort them to this good work. This tract was entitled " An Epistle of love and friendly advice to the Ambassadors of the several Princes of Europe, met at Nimeguen, to consult the peace of Christendom, so far as they are concerned ; wherein the true cause of the present War is discovered, and means for a firm and settled peace is proposed, by Robert Barclay, a lover and travailer for the peace of Christendom."

It was addressed " To the Ambassadors and Deputies of the Christian Princes and States met at Nimeguen to consult

the peace of Christendom, Robert Barclay, a Servant of Jesus
Christ, and hearty well-wisher to the Christian World, Wishes
Increase of Grace and Peace, and the Spirit of sound judgement, with Hearts inclined and willing to Receive and Obey
the Counsel of God."

Though rather long, the advice is so applicable to the
present day, that it is inserted in full.

AN EPISTLE OF LOVE AND FRIENDLY ADVICE

Let it not seem strange unto you, who are men Chosen and
Authorized by the Great Monarchs and States of Europe to find
out a speedy Remedy for the present great trouble (under which
many of her Inhabitants do groan) as such, whose Wisdom and
Prudence, and Abilitie have so recommended them to the World,
as to be judged fit for so great and Difficult a Work, to be addressed
unto by one, who by the World may be esteemed Weak and Foolish ;
whose Advice is not ushered unto you by the Commission of any
of the Princes of this World, nor Seconded by the Recommendation
of any earthly State : For since your Work is that which concerns
all Christians ; why may not every Christian, who feels himself
stir'd up of the Lord thereunto, contribute therein ?   And if they
have Place to be heard in this Affair who come in the name of Kings
and Princes ; let it not seem heavy unto you to hear him, that comes
in the name of the Lord Jesus Christ.

Know then, My Friends, that many and often times my Soul
has been deeply bowed down under the Weighty Sense of the present
state of Christendom ; and in secret before the Lord I have mourned,
and bitterly lamented because thereof.   And as I was Crossing the
Sea, and being the last Summer in Holland, and some parts of Germany, the Burthen thereof fell often upon me and it several times
came before me to write unto you, what I then saw and felt from
God of these things, while I was in those Parts.   But I Waited, and
was not willing to be hasty, and now being returned to my own
Country and at my own Home, I chearfully accept the fit Season,
which the Lord hath put in my hand, and called me therein.

The Chief Ground, Cause, and Root then of all this Misery among
all those called Christians, is, Because they are only such in Name,
and not in Nature, having only a Form and Profession of Christianity
in Shew and Words, but are still Strangers, yea and Enemies to the
Life and Virtue of it, owning God and Christ in Words, but denying
them in Works.   And therefore the Lord Jesus Christ will not own
them as his Children nor Disciples.   For while they say they are

1678.

152

his Followers; while they preach and exalt his Precepts; while they extol his Life, Patience and Meekness, his self-denying perfect Resignation and Obedience to the Will of his Father; yet themselves are out of it; and so bring Shame and Reproach to that Honourable Name, which they assume to themselves in the face of the Nations, and give an occasion for Infidels (Turks, Jews, and Atheists) to Profane and Blaspheme the Holy Name of Jesus. Is it not so? While upon every slender Praetext, such as their own small Discontents or That they judge the present Peace they have with their Neighbour cannot suit with their Grandeur and Worldly Glory, they sheathe their swords in one another's Bowels; ruine, waste and destroy whole Countreys, Expose to the greatest Misery many Thousand Families; make Thousands of Widows, and Ten Thousands of Orphans; And all this while they pretend to be Followers of the Lamb-like Jesus; who came not to destroy Men's lives, but to save them; The Song of whose appearance to the World was, Glory to God in the Highest, and Good Will and Peace to all Men, Not to Kill, Murther, and Destroy Men, not to hire and force poor Men to run upon and murther one another, meerly to satisfy the Lust and Ambition of Great Men, they being often-times ignorant of the ground of the Quarrel, and not having the least Occasion of Evil Will or Prejudice against those their Fellow-Christians whom they thus kill, amongst whom not one of a Thousand perhaps ever saw one another before. Yea, is it not so that there is only a Name, and nothing of the True Nature of Christians especially manifest in the Clergy, who pretend not only to be Professors but Preachers, Promoters, and Exhorters of others to Christianity, who for the most part are the greatest Promoters, and Advancers of these Wars; and by whom on all such occasions the name of God and Jesus Christ is most horribly abused, prophaned, and blasphemed, While they dare pray to God, and Thank Him for the Destruction of their Brethren Christians, and that for and against, according to the Changeable Wills of their several Princes. Yea, so that some will join in their Prayers with and for the Prosperity of such, as their Profession obliges them to believe to be Heretical and Anti-Christian; and for the Destruction of those, whom the same Profession acknowledges to be Good and Orthodox Christians. Thus the French, both Papists and Protestants, Join in their Prayers and rejoice for the Destruction of the Spanish Papists, and Dutch Protestants. The like may be said of the Danish, Swedish, and German Protestants, as respectively concerned in this matter. Yea, which is yet more strange, if either Constraint or Interest do engage any Prince or State to change his Party, while the same War and Cause remain, then will the Clergy presently

ROBERT
BARCLAY,
1648-1690,
Urie II.

accommodate their Prayers to the Case, In praying for Prosperity to those whom instantly before they wished Ruine ; and so on the contrary.

As in this present War, the case of the Bishop of Munster is manifest. Was there ever, or can there be any horrible profanation of the Holy and pure Name of God, especially to be done by those, who pretend to be Worshippers of the True God, and Disciples of Jesus Christ ? This not only equals, but far exceeds the Wickedness of the Heathens ; For they only prayed such Gods to their Assistance, as they fancied allowed their Ambition, and accounted their Warring a Virtue ; whom they judged changeable like themselves and subject to such Quarrels among themselves, as they that are their Worshippers. But for those to be found in those Things who believe there is but One only God, and have, or at least profess to have, such Notions of His Justice, Equity and Mercy, and of the certainty of his Punishing the Trangressors of the Law, is so horrible and abominable, as cannot sufficiently be neither said nor written.

The Ground then of all this is the want of True Christianity, because the Nature of it is not begotten, nor brought forth in those called Christians, as therefore they bear not the Image, nor bring forth the Fruits thereof. For albeit they have the Name, yet the Nature they are strangers to ; The Lamb's Nature is not in them, but the Doggish Nature, the Wolfish Nature, that will still be quarrelling and destroying, the Cunning, Serpentine, Subtle Nature and the proud Ambitious, Luciferian Nature, that sets Princes and States a work to contrive and foment Wars, and engages People to fight together, some for Ambition and Vainglory, and some for Covetousness and Hope of Gain. And the same Cause doth move the Clergy to concur with their Share in making their Prayers turn and twine ; and so all are here out from the State of True Christianity. And as they keep the Name of being Christians, so also upon the same Pretext each will pretend to be for Peace, while their Fruits manifestly declare the contrary. And how doth Experience daily discover this Deceit ? For how is it brought about ? Is it not when the weaker is forced to give way to the Stronger, without respect to the Equity of the Cause ? Is it not just so, as among the wild and devouring Beasts ? Who when they fight together the Weaker is forced to give way to the Stronger, and so desist, until another Occasion offer ? So, who are found weakest, who are least capable to hold out, they must bear the inconveniency ; and he gets the most Advantage however frivolous, yea however unjust, his Pretence be, who is most able to vindicate his Claim, and preserve it not by Equity, but by force of Arms. So that the Peace-Contrivers Rule is not the Equity of the Cause, but the Power of the Parties.

HISTORY OF THE BARCLAY FAMILY

Is not this known and manifest in many, if not the most of the Pacifications that have been made in Christendom ?

Try and Examine your selves therefore seriously in the sight of God, whether you be Led, Acted, and Influenced in your present Negotiation by the Wisdom of this World, or by the Heavenly and Pure Wisdom of God. If the warring part be removed out of you, then are you fit to consult and bring about the Peace of Christendom. Whereof, and of all those that profess the name of Christ I am

A true Friend and

Hearty Well Wisher

ROBERT BARCLAY.

This came upon me from the Lord to write unto you at Ury, in my native Country of Scotland, the second of the month called November. 1677.

This epistle, together with his *Apology*, was delivered to each of the said Ambassadors.

George Fox also sent an exhortatory letter to them, which was translated and printed in Latin.

Though we have no means of ascertaining how far Robert Barclay's arguments influenced the Ambassadors, before this year came to an end, a Peace was concluded.

The last religious meeting of the Friends in Scotland which was disturbed by the authorities, took place on November 4th, 1679, when all the leaders were once more arrested and imprisoned, but in about three hours they were set at liberty, it was said for fear of Robert Barclay's Court influence, and was possibly in consequence of instructions given to Lauderdale by the Duke of York. 1679.

From this time their religious Assemblies were held at Aberdeen without molestation from the Magistrates, " who having abundantly proved the Patience and Constancy of this People, in religiously assembling to worship God, to be such as their utmost Force and Cruelty could not conquer, forbore at length to repeat their fruitless attempts and quietly to permit what they were fully convinced their Power was unable to prevent." Sufferings of the Quakers, Besse.

Robert Barclay's last letter to the Princess was written from Rotterdam, where he had gone on business. He excuses himself for not going to see her and makes one of his rare

ROBERT
BARCLAY,
1648-1690,
Urie II.

allusions to his own health, which had never been robust and could not have been improved by his labours and imprisonments.

DEAR FRIEND, 6th of the $\frac{5}{mo}$ 1679

Thou may think strange that after so long a silence, I should now apply myself to answer thy last (which came to my hands at a time when I was under great bodily weakness) for which I will not trouble thee with any further apology, than to assure thee that no want of respect or regard to thee, but ane unwillingness to work in mine own will, and a fear in doing rather to hurt than help thee hath hindered me until now, had I given way to mine own Inclinations and to the course of that love which without flattery I may say I have for thee, so as to have exprest but the hundredth part of that concern which frequently possessed me upon thy account. I have overcharged thee with my letters, but knowing it is not the will of man that bringeth about the work of God, I choosed rather to be silent than forward, but being through a singular occasion come to this country, and not having access to make thee a visit, I found a true liberty from the Lord in my spirit thus to salute thee, for herein I have peace before God, that I never sought to gather thee nor others to myself but to the Lord, I pretend to be no seat-master, and disgust all such, my labour is only as ane Ambassador to Instruct all to be reconciled to God, and I desire no more than to be manifest in the Consciences of those to whom I come that I am such, by the answer of that of God there. . . .

Thy sincere and truly affectionate Friend

R. BARCLAY.

The Princess died a few months after this letter had been received.

At the close of 1679 the Duke of York became a member of the Scottish Privy Council, and took up his residence at Holyrood. Robert Barclay, being within reach, was constantly summoned to conference with James, and became an intimate friend, though the constant calls cannot but have been irksome to him, " wearied " as he writes he was with Court life.

1680.

In 1680 he made another journey to Edinburgh and carried out some law business on his father's account. While there he received a friendly letter from the Duke of York from

HISTORY OF THE BARCLAY FAMILY

London, giving him an introduction to the legal authority most likely to be of use to him.

Windsor June 27 1680

I send you here inclosed a letter to the Lord Advocate, as you desired. I chuse to write to him, because I had spoke to him of it, when in Scotland.

You see I do my part, and I make no doubt but he will do his, and then you will have no further trouble in that affair.

JAMES.

Directed for Mr. Barclay.

Robert did not fail to use his influence with the Duke of York on behalf of his friends, and two letters from the Earl of Perth written at this time show that his efforts were appreciated and supported.

From the Earl of Perth, to Robert Barclay of Urie.

SIR,   Edinburgh Oct 13, 1680

I had one indeed from you two weeks ago, but had so little leisure since, that I ventured upon your goodness and took some moments to myself, which should have been yours, could I have wrote as easily as my heart was full of the sense of your kindness.

This goes by Mr. Falconer, an occasion I would not let go without telling you, that your friend here is still mindful of you and your concerns, nor wants he any solicitation to do you all the kindness I could promt him to, for he was as zealous that way as I can be, but no occasion has offered since, and Sir William Purvis is considered as interested in all his proposals : but of this more afterwards. I shall this evening speak to the Duke, of that affair of Calder's and if I cannot get a distinct answer now by the Aberdeen post, you shall have it shortly. Viscount of Arbuthnot shall not be forgot, but you will believe I have some reason to delay it, when I tell you, though I dare not let you know what it is at present : he is well in the Duke's esteem, so the thing will be easy.

I am glad to hear from you, and should be much more so to do you any service ; I hope you think better things of me than that I could be much disappointed with the instability of an human condition. I do not look upon anything here so fixed as worthy of too much concern, or capable to bear weight. I will resolve to be what God pleases, a plowman or Courtier, or what else may be most for His honour. I know this is much too long a letter : forgive me and believe that you have not a faithfuller friend than

Your affectionate friend

PERTH.

157

P.S.—I have spoken to the Duke since I wrote my letter, and he is well satisfied to have a Rentall, though my own opinion is that it should be exactly given, & all the proposed advantages of such a purchase as evident as can be & though I know Calder's humour well enough to foresee how cautious he must appear in this matter, yet I suppose it cannot be absolutely necessary you be at the paines to go to his house for it, he will find if the Interest be so considerable, the Duke will be very frank on it. I wish we had leave to put Tarbet upon it too, for he knows the importance of such a purchase for the ends designed, better than I by far & consequently might make it much more easy on all hands, but this you shall do according to your good pleasure.

The Duke speaks wonderfully kindly of you. Adiu.

Again a few weeks later he writes :—

Edinburgh Nov. 7 1680

SIR,

Last night I had yours of the 17th of last month. It was so slow of coming to me, because I was called out of town to see my wife. I am glad we shall so soon again see you. I wish you a good journey to us. I give you my hearty thanks for your good advice, to every part of which I do entirely agree, and I hope my carriage shall be an argument I do so, whatever happens.

I am glad you come so fully prepared to advise the Duke in that matter your Journey north seems to have some relation to, and that you are of my mind to trust the register with it. I could tell you news if everyone else did not, but I know you will have all here from other friends. You see I am so void of ceremony that you could not wish me more so ; expect then no more formal concluding of letter from

Your affectionate Servant and Cousin
PERTH.

It would seem that Robert's favour with the Duke of York attracted the friendship of the sycophantic courtiers, for Lord Perth's later career was not entirely in accord with the admirable sentiments expressed in this letter, so well adapted to the opinions of his correspondent, for after encouraging Lauderdale in the incredibly base policy of letting loose the savage Highlanders upon the disaffected western shires of Scotland, he turned upon him and disavowed his action.

He supported the Crown, received several legal appointments, and became Lord Chancellor in 1684.

158

He was notorious for having added the thumbscrew to the instruments of torture, and was said to have been very successful in extorting evidence. He became a Roman Catholic in 1684. ROBERT BARCLAY, 1648-1690, Urie II.

The rather cryptically worded letters seem to show that the Duke of York consulted Robert Barclay on matters not always connected with the Friends, and that he leant on his advice. 1680.

Robert had so many Roman Catholic friends, in consequence of his schooldays at the Theological College, that an accusation frequently levelled against him was that he was more in sympathy with the Romish than the Presbyterian Church, but he had seen too much of that teaching to regard it with anything but the sternest disapproval. He said he considered " Persecution and Cruelty the worst part of Popery, and the most contrary to the teaching of Christ." But when dealing with Roman Catholics individually, he wrote also " It hath never agreed with the notions I have of the Christian religion to hate these persons," and no doubt his unswerving sincerity and wise tolerance made his presence very acceptable in those Court circles where suspicion and treachery lurked everywhere, and no man knew whom he could trust.

In 1679, Charles II gave Robert the Charter before referred to under the Great Seal, which erected the lands of Ury into a free Barony, with civil and criminal jurisdiction, "to Colonel David Barclay and his heirs." The grant was undoubtedly due, as it states in the preamble to the Act of Parliament ratifying it, " for the many services done by Colonel David Barclay and his son, the said Robert Barclay, to the King and his most Royal progenitors in the past"; nevertheless, it may be questioned if such an acknowledgment would have been made, however tardily, had it not been for Robert Barclay's influential friends at court. 1679.

Between the accession of James I and the deposition of his grandson, James II, England had greatly increased her trading and colonising interests. The Dutch had been the carriers of Europe and distributed foreign wares of all sorts to every country, planting trading stations in the East, Africa and 1623–1679.

America, and commanding the markets everywhere, but
England entered into competition with them in these years,
and the commercial rivalry became keen.

The Governments of the respective countries went to war
in 1623 and gradually the greater resources and enterprise of
the English traders triumphed, and they rapidly became
possessed of the general carrying trade of the world.

In 1672 England had entirely ousted the Dutch from India
and Africa, and though Southern and Central America had
been largely colonised by the Spaniards and Portuguese, the
northern provinces still lay vacant for settlement.

As early as in 1607 the first emigrant ships had sailed for
Virginia, which became prosperous by the sale of tobacco and
was the first of a long series of successful settlements. In
1620 the Pilgrim Fathers landed in the *Mayflower*, near Cape
Cod, and many isolated and independent communities grew
up in " New England," which greatly encouraged and
increased the natural wealth of the country.

There had been an echo of the Thirty Years War in the beginning of the colonisation of these provinces, for in 1623
Gustavus Adolphus had sent out some of his Swedish subjects,
who had combined with the Dutch, and built Lutheran
churches and towns, with forts for defence against the Indians.

In 1664, when the English conquered the Dutch, they became masters of their Colonial possessions, and the corrupt
Restoration Government regarded them as Royal property and
used them for the enrichment of the courtiers. Charles II
made over the province that lay between the Hudson and the
Delaware estuaries to his brother the Duke of York, who
granted it to Sir George Carteret and Lord Berkeley. It
was named New Jersey in honour of the former, who was a
Jersey man. Lord Berkeley was head of the Fitzharding
family in Gloucestershire.

George Fox had long been considering the formation of a
Colony of Friends in that region, and had discussed it with
William Penn and Robert Barclay. Penn had dreamed of
establishing a refuge in America for sufferers for conscience'
sake ever since his undergraduate days, and was keenly

sympathetic to the scheme. America was incredibly remote in those days, and the project involved labour, time and expense, but he devoted all his energy and courage to the realisation of his dream. In one of his pamphlets he makes a passionate appeal on the part of the Friends, pointing out " the grievous spoils and ruins their harmless neighbours had suffered for twenty years. The flocks have been taken out of the fold, the herd from the stall, sixty pounds have been distrained on a debt for twelve—two hundred for sixty." Indeed the Friends had had more than financial persecution to endure, and notwithstanding the action of King Charles II, who had pardoned and released over four hundred in 1672 by the exercise of his royal prerogative for suspending the penal laws in matters ecclesiastical, the public dissatisfaction was such that he was compelled to recall his proclamation, and their persecution continued through his reign. ROBERT BARCLAY, 1648–1690, Urie II.

Penn's hopes were encouraged to some extent at this time, for the speculative owners of the newly acquired provinces were quite willing that the harsh English penal laws should not exist across the ocean, realising that the persecuted sectarians were the only people likely to colonise them and make them remunerative. It was not until 1679 that his plans were enabled to materialise completely, though in 1677 he had been able to persuade Sir George Carteret to divide his province, retaining himself the eastern and more settled districts, while the Friends took over the western lands, still in the possession of the Indians. 1677.

Penn issued a prospectus, and two hundred and thirty Friends, mostly from Yorkshire and London, at once responded, sailing in the ship *Kent* in the summer of 1677. History of the Quakers, Clarkson.

Clarkson tells that as they were about to weigh anchor, the King's barge was seen approaching. It drew alongside, and the King enquired the object of the voyage, and if all the emigrants were Quakers. On hearing that they were, the King bade them farewell with his blessing. Charles did not encourage intolerance at Court, and however the fashionable world might sneer at William Penn, who had been one of themselves, or turn the cold shoulder to Robert Barclay, they had to conceal their feelings when any of the Royal Family were present.

The *Kent* was soon followed by other ships, and within eighteen months there were some eight hundred Friends in the Colony. They bought a tract of land from the Indians, in exchange for a long list of various articles, including guns, kettles, garments of all kinds, tools, mirrors, glass ornaments, and miscellaneous goods.

They also gave them, unhappily, six ankers of rum, having no idea of the ruin worked by spirits on the Indians, but when it was discovered they at once stopped the sale, with the approval of the more enlightened Chiefs. They settled on the Delaware river, and built a town called Burlington, on the site of which rose Philadelphia, " The City of Brotherly Love."

The purchase or exchange of the land for articles valued by the natives was a statesmanlike action, for though the Friends had legally acquired the province from the recognised English proprietors, it would have been difficult to explain this to the Indians, who were of course the original owners. This judicious treatment retained their goodwill.

When George Carteret died his widow was forced to sell East New Jersey to pay his debts, and in 1681 Penn, with the help of eleven Friends, purchased the entire province. Twelve other Friends, among whom was Robert Barclay, were added as owners, and some of the Scottish nobility who were not Quakers were included in the scheme.

Original
Deed
at Bury Hill.

A council of twenty-four proprietors was formed, those for East New Jersey being appointed in 1684, and those for West Jersey three years later.

Penn was able to contribute largely to the purchase, as his father, Admiral Sir William Penn, had died, leaving him a considerable sum of money, besides which he had a claim on the Crown for £16,000, lent to the impecunious Charles by the Admiral. William Penn desired in lieu of repayment to obtain this tract of land in America and petitioned the King to grant it. After some opposition on the score that Penn was a Quaker, the request was granted, and the Charter submitted for the Royal signature. The King, however, insisted on

naming the new Colony " Pennsylvania," to the vexation of ROBERT BARCLAY, 1648-1690, Urie II.
William Penn, who disliked the appearance of personal vanity, and thought it contradicted his teaching. He had intended to call it " New Wales," being, as he said, " a pretty hilly country," but the Secretary, a Welshman, objected, so he suggested " Sylvania," to which Charles prefixed " Penn." William Penn tried hard to reverse this ruling, even offering the Secretary twenty guineas to have the name altered, and called personally on the King to protest, but Charles only laughed at his scruples, and said it was in memory of Penn's father, whose money had purchased it, and he was forced to consent.

The Province consisted of land, 300 miles by 160, " of extreme fertility, unusual wealth, and richness of all kinds." Penn's ambition was to establish it as a Christian State on the Quaker model, and a strictly democratic basis. Like those of all idealists, some of his plans were unpractical enough and he had to deal with many economic, legal, and financial difficul- Original Deed at Bury Hill.
ties, but he was at last able to draw up a Constitution embodying his dreams. His rules were simple and covered much ground.

The first, as would be expected, was the right to free worship, whereby all who believed in God and accepted the Christian moral code were allowed to hold religious worship after their own fashion.

The second was democratic assembly, with universal suffrage and vote by ballot.

The third, trial by jury, the judges to be elected for two years.

The fourth, no imprisonment for debt, and the fifth, state education for orphans.

The most severe of his laws was that forbidding intemperance, card-playing, swearing and playgoing, with " other evil sports and games." He concluded with the excellent advice that " Whosoever had a desire to be concerned in this intended plantation should weigh the thing well before the Lord, and not headily and rashly conclude any such remove, and see that they did not offer violence to the tender love of their near kindred, but soberly and conscientiously endeavour to obtain their goodwill, and the unity of friends whom they love."

ROBERT
BARCLAY,
1648-1690,
Urie II.

He created a quick market for the lands by publishing in England and on the Continent his liberal scheme of Government, and his intention to try " the holy experiment " of a Colony free for all.

1682.

In 1682, when he crossed the sea to take possession, he found the western bank of the Delaware already populated by a mixed race of Swedes, Dutch, and English. To these, as to settlers from all nations, he conceded equal liberties.

The country was picturesque, rather resembling, in some parts, the Weald of Kent. It had low hills and shallow valleys, rich prolific soil, flowing rivers with occasional cascades adapted to turn mill-wheels and supply factories. Wheat, rye, maize, potatoes, and above all tobacco, grew luxuriantly, and soon orchards, meadows, and woodlands increased its likeness to the English landscape.

When Penn arrived with a party of a hundred Friends in the ship *Welcome*, the celebrated meeting between the new Quaker owners of the Province and the Indians who had become their subjects took place. The Indians, in war paint and feathers, mustered in many thousands and the little band of white men must have appeared very insignificant.

Life of Penn,
Clarkson.

" But they found strength in the righteousness of their cause," and when Penn addressed the multitudes through an interpreter, giving them his message of peace and goodwill, the Chiefs accepted the Treaty he offered. Voltaire, who was certainly not in sympathy with the Quakers, admits " C'est le seul traité entre ces peuples et les Chrétiens qui n'ait point été rompu." A testimony indeed to the unswerving integrity of the Friends.

1682.

At least fourteen hundred Quakers were already settled when William Penn brought a further large company to take possession of the new province in 1682.

This colonisation policy had a great and strengthening effect on the spread of the new teaching. W. C. Braithwaite, in his

History of
the
Quakers,
Braithwaite.

History of the Quakers, says : " Quakerism would have been to the world a half-uttered thing, if its highest forms of expression had been found in the Church organisation of Fox, or the writings of Barclay. It would have produced cloistered

164

saints, and a lofty speculative theory of Christianity but it would not have indicated itself as a Faith able to reshape the whole of Life. In the New World, it addressed itself to this high adventure, and amid much imperfection of execution, supplied the Nations with the inspiring precedent of a Christian State. . . ."

" They laid a sure foundation for the overthrow of negro slavery and caught a glimpse of the task that confronted the world in later years. The Quaker message would have been almost inarticulate on those larger issues had Philadelphia—the City of Brotherly Love—not been born."

As early as 1671 Fox had told the Friends in Barbados, to " train up their slaves in the fear of God . . . and after certain years of servitude they should set them free." This rule was observed by the new colonists until, while trying to improve the condition of their slaves, they perceived the iniquity of the whole system.

Though it is only fair to say that the German emigrants first protested against negro slavery, yet it was the Quakers who first passed a resolution at their annual meeting at Burlington, declaring it morally wrong to hold slaves. In twenty years a large majority set their slaves free, and " refused to be considered members of the same body with any man who held another man in bondage."

Emigration was extensive from England, Ireland, Wales, Holland and Germany, of numbers of persons longing for peace and liberty of conscience, as well as of those with more material aspirations, and William Penn wrote to Lord North, then Lord Chancellor, " I must say without vanity, that I have led the greatest colony into America that ever man did, upon a prosperous beginning."

Robert Barclay's correspondence with the Earl of Perth may have had some connection with the fact that he, as one of the proprietors of the new Colony, among others, pressed Robert to accept the Governorship of East Jersey, as it was still called. The post carried no salary, but he had allotted to him 5,000 acres above his proprietary share, that he might grant to others as he saw fit, and no doubt that power was the chief inducement to him to accept the responsibility.

Charles II confirmed the grant of the Government, and the Royal Commission states that " such are his [R. B.'s] known fidelity and capacity, that he has the government during life ; but that no other governor after him shall have it longer than for three years."

Robert Barclay made it a condition that he was not required to go to America himself. He selected one of the proprietors, Thomas Rudyard, as first resident Deputy Governor, who before long was succeeded by another proprietor, Gawen Laurie, at a salary of £400 a year (representing £1,000 in our money). Robert Barclay applied himself to the organisation at home. A good administrator was needed in England, and the work of finding, supplying and shipping out suitable colonists, which Gawen Laurie wrote was of the first importance, besides arranging for transport, stores, building materials, and the countless necessities for life in a new country, demanded more time and attention than he was accustomed to give to worldly concerns.

When William Penn received his Charter for the grant of the tract of land, he had to give " the fealty of two beaver-skins annually for the undertaking therein contained," and " that no custom or other contribution shall be laid upon the inhabitants or their estates, unless by the consent of the Proprietary or Governor and Assembly, or by Act of Parliament in England." He was empowered to assemble the freemen "in such form as he thought fit, for raising money for the use of the Colony, and for making useful laws."

But he was not without his critics. He was accused of considering the rights of his Colonists and ignoring the just claims of others. He was said to have used his influence with the Duke of York to annex the town of Newcastle, with a territory of twelve miles round, from Lord Baltimore, who had a legal right to it.

The friction and discussion thereby occasioned caused much trouble and delay in settling the affairs of the new Colony, until the two districts were separated under two

Governors. It was also said that while the Quakers held the unpracticable doctrine that war was ungodly, they had no objection to being protected by the arms of others, and even paid a subsidy of three hundred pounds towards the fortification of New York, though under the somewhat transparent pretext that it was for the " relief of the distressed Indians on the frontier of the Province."

William Penn's task was a difficult one. The very virtues of the Quakers, their determination and consistency of purpose, made them a difficult people to govern, and when they became strong enough, they cheated him out of his quit-rents, and refused to pay the imposts they had solemnly promised, so that he personally reaped little but sorrow, disquiet and poverty, and though in the end they returned to their allegiance, he died in ignorance of their tardy repentance.

In the spring of 1683, Robert Barclay and his wife made a journey to London, taking with them their eldest son Robert, (Urie III) then eleven years old. George Keith, who had been a friend of Robert's for many years, and had accompanied him on several of his evangelising tours, had established a Friends' school at Theobalds, fifteen miles north of London, in the open district known as Enfield Chase. There they left the boy and spent the summer in London. Their homeward journey was made in company with Christian's brother Gilbert Mollison, and an intimate friend, Aaron Sonemans, a Dutch merchant, one of the proprietors of New Jersey, now residing in Scotland. On their way the little party had an alarming and tragic adventure.

As they rode soberly along the road leading to Stonegate Hole, between Huntingdon and Stilton, they were suddenly attacked by highwaymen. One of these, judging Robert to be the leader, presented a pistol full at him. He showed no alarm, and calmly took the man by the arm, saying " Friend, how comest thou to be so rude; I know thy business," which so disconcerted the thief that, trembling, he dropped the weapon on the ground, and offered him no more violence. But the other men of the party apparently offered resistance, for Gilbert Mollison was " riffled and rudely used " and Sonemans, more, it was thought, by accident than design, was shot through the thigh and, being with some difficulty brought to Stilton, died in a few days. It is recorded that Christian Barclay afterwards spoke of the deep impression made upon her mind by the fact that her husband had a curious prevision of misfortune before starting, and told her it was his opinion that some unusual trial or exercise was to befall them on that day, but when the affair happened he showed his usual serenity. After having seen his friend buried, they returned home in September.

Robert Barclay the Apologist was of a generous disposition, and his purse always open to any who needed help. George Keith, who had been a keen and zealous preacher and worker for the Society, was at this time in straits for money, and Robert, having been to Edinburgh in the winter and received the repayment of a long-outstanding debt by the Earl of Mar, bestowed the half of it on his old friend.

Another recipient of his bounty was John Swinton, the same who had persuaded Colonel David Barclay to join the Friends when imprisoned with him in Edinburgh Castle in 1676. He had been attainted by the Parliament of Scotland before the Commonwealth, and after the Restoration recommitted to prison. He had in the interim joined the Society of Friends and refused to employ some strong and valid pleas in point of law when required to show cause why he should not receive sentence, saying that at the time his crimes were imputed to him he was " in the gall of bitterness, and bond of iniquity, but that God having called him to the Light he saw his past errors and did not refuse to pay the forfeit of them, even though it cost him his life."

It seems that though his life was spared, his estates were forfeited, for Robert Barclay assisted him with both interest and money, " thus answering practically the apostolic injunction to permit those to reap carnal things who had sown spiritual things to his family."

With all his charities and literary work at home, Robert Barclay took the duties of his Colonial Governorship very seriously, and a letter to his cousin Sir John Gordon in Robert Edinburgh, a lawyer whose brother controlled a fleet of ships for export and import trade, shows his personal attention to detail.

To Sir John Gordon
Advocat in Edinburgh.
Ury, the 4th of the 1st mo 1684.

[It must be remembered that this was before the change of the Calendar, and as Quakers only employed the number of the month, the 1st month was then March.]

DEAR COUSINE,

I suppose thou hast wrott ere now to London, to thy brother George, and proposed to him to bring down his veshell here to carry passengers to East Jersey.

I doubt not but he may make as good a venter that way as any he can propose, and knows how to project a retourn for himself. There will not want passengers, besides those that fills another ship to be hired, and one that is goeing from Glasgow with Maryward, which will be the best way. And besides those George may carry upon thy brother's account and thines, iff he want, it is but getting men from Strathnaver, to cary over at a venter, which is as profitable a commodity as he can trade in ; the sooner something be done in this the better. I expect also from thee a speedy answere as to that part now in thy optione, that thou will determine it one way or other, that I may regulate myself accordingly. If George com with his ship, so as to be ready to goe about Whitsunday, he will be sure to be full, for the other is to come afterwards.

Desir him to call at London to William Bockwra att little St. Helen's over against Leather-sellars Hall in Bishopgait Street, who will give him full informatione in what may be needful unto him.

So, expecting thy care in this, and thatt thou will lett no time be lost, which is the chief point in such caises,

I rest thy affectionate cousine
ROBERT BARCLAY.

It is pleasant to read that with all Robert's devotion to duty, he did not entirely neglect occasional relaxation, for in 1684 he acquired a salmon fishing upon the waters of Don, which doubtless afforded him many hours of peaceful meditation untroubled by persecuting bigots or importunate friends.

The new Utopia exercised its fascination on other members of the family, and Robert's second brother, John, went out among the earlier settlers, and made a home in East Jersey, where he died in 1731, leaving children ; but a heavy family grief fell upon them all, in the death of David, the Colonel's third son, who died on the voyage out in 1685. It took nearly as many months then, as it does days now, and there were many losses of life, through tempests and climatic conditions, with the rough accommodation and food. The death of the promising young man came as a heavy blow to the old Colonel, who had a special affection for this son, and spoke of him on his death-bed.

In 1685 Charles II died, and, in spite of the Test Act and the Exclusion Bill, his brother James Duke of York became the Roman Catholic King of Protestant England. He never concealed his intention of restoring the Roman Catholic religion, but for politic reasons allowed himself to be crowned by the Archbishop of Canterbury, and actually undertook to uphold the Church, for churchmen, he said, were always loyal subjects.

Soon after his Coronation, he went to Mass in state, though for the first few months of his reign he made no change in Charles II's policy, except by the more rigorous prosecution of the Conventicle Acts in Scotland, and the infliction of brutal penalties on all who infringed them.

One result of this policy immediately affected the Barclays.
The Privy Council of Scotland made a general arrest of more than a hundred Covenanters in the southern and western districts, who were accused, from their general principles, of being enemies of the Government, though among them were many women and children. These unhappy people were rudely herded northward and driven into a subterranean dungeon in the castle of Dunnottar, on the borders of the Urie estate.

Though all prisons were gloomy, insanitary, and over-crowded, this place seems to have been incredibly so. It had one window only, opening to the front of a precipice that faces the North Sea, then called the German Ocean. The prisoners had been cruelly beaten and driven all the way, and mocked and jeered at by the northern prelatists, who employed fiddlers and pipers to play scurrilous tunes as Robert Barclay, 1648–1690, they passed, and even when they had arrived at their des- Urie II. tination they found no peace. The guards charged them 1686. exorbitant prices for the merest necessities of life, and even for water. When they complained of this extortion, the soldiers poured the water out on the floor, saying, " If they were obliged to bring water for the canting Whigs they were not bound to afford them the use of bowls or pitchers free."

The crevices in the walls are still to be seen, where many of them had their fingers crushed in with wooden wedges, to guard against attempts to escape.

In this prison, which was for long called " The Whigs' Vault," many died of disease, and others sustained fatal injuries in desperate efforts to get out by the window. A tombstone, with their names inscribed, was erected in the churchyard of Fetteroso by their friends and is referred to in Sir Walter Scott's novel *Old Mortality*. Thirty men and seven women, unable to endure the miseries and tortures of their imprisonment, took the oath of allegiance and ab-juration, but 92 men and 38 women remained true to the Covenant.

Robert Barclay saw in his Colonial powers an opportunity of relieving some of these sufferers. Now that James II's administration had ceased from molesting the Quakers, he turned his attention to the victims of the new persecution, and helped many to escape and find homes in New Jersey. But a number weakened by privation and suffering, died on the voyage out, or of fever, and few ever returned to their native land.

Unfortunately the Castle of Dunnottar, once the property of the Earl Marischal, and now since his forfeiture used as a State prison, though technically included in the Urie estate, was outside the limits of the Barclays' baronial jurisdiction, so they could not legally interfere, though they must both have been deeply shocked by the callous cruelty of the authorities.

The forbidding pile of the old castle still stands, but a

ROBERT
BARCLAY,
1648–1690,
Urie II.

prophecy of Thomas the Rymer written three hundred years before, has been literally fulfilled :—

> Dunnottar, standing by the sea
> Lairdless shall thy land be
> Beneath the sole of thy hearthstane
> The toad shall bring her young ones hame.

William Penn was at this time in the throes of the complicated arrangements surrounding the formation of the new Colony, and like all his friends, consulted Robert Barclay.

Bury Hill
Archives.

Four letters addressed by him to Penn are of exceptional interest, as relating to the early proprietorship of New Jersey and Pennsylvania, but do not come within the scope of this history.

1685

Early in this year, Robert Barclay went to Edinburgh to attend his sister Jean's wedding as third wife to the great chieftain Sir Ewen Cameron of Lochiel. Shortly afterwards her husband was accused of treason, and his powerful neighbour, the Duke of Gordon, seized the opportunity and asserted a fictitious claim to his lands. Lochiel turned to Robert Barclay for that help which was never refused by the generous-hearted Quaker, who applied to several of his influential friends on his behalf.

He found no very warm response, but being himself convinced of the righteousness of his brother-in-law's cause, he urged him to apply direct to King James, and backed his application with his eloquent tongue and ready pen.

The dispute gave Robert considerable trouble, but at last his efforts were successful; his brother-in-law's name was cleared and his property restored.

This business and other acts of charity kept Robert in London for some months, and he saw a good deal of King James, who still " honoured him with great friendship," and showed this in practical form by ratifying and confirming the beforementioned charter granted by Charles II in 1679, giving lawful possession of the lands of Urie to Colonel Barclay and his heirs *in perpetuo*.

The wording of this deed is :

Bury Hill
Papers.

" Att Edinburgh the 15th June, 1685, our Soveraigne Lord with advice and consent of his Estates of Parliament for the good and faithfull services done and performed to his Majesty and His most Royal progenitors by Colonell David Barcklay of Ury, and Robert Barcklay, his eldest lawful sone, in tymes past, by this present ratifies and confirms ane Charter dated August 13, 1679, granted by King Charles II."

Then follows a long list of " landes, maynes, manor-places, house-biggings, yairdes, orchyairds, dowcats (dovecotes), pairtes, pendicles, and pertinentes thereof, and salmond fishings belonging thereto, upon the waters of Cowie, as weel in salt as in fresh water. . . . And all and haill the townes and lands of Maugray, Woodhead, Poubair, Balnageicht, Glechno and Cairnetoune, milne (mill) of Cowie, milne, pleugh, milne lands, multures, sequelles, and knaveship, thereof. . . ."

All of which seems to show that the estate of Urie had not diminished in value under the Colonel's stewardship. Later " the tounes and lands of Redclock, Finlaystoune, Easter and Wester Logies, Montquich called Twilles, Burnlauch, Rorthineck and Corslay, with all their pendicles and pertinents," point to an extensive acreage.

The list winds up with " All and haill the lands and maynes of Dunnottar, All and haill the milne of Stonehyve, landes, multures, etc., etc.," and concludes :

" In the haill heids, articles and clauses thereof, His Majestie with consent of His Estates of Parliament statutes and ordaines the forsaid Generall Ratification to be also valid and sufficient, and of also great force, strenth, and effect to all interests and purposes. . .

" Extracted forth of the Records of Parliament by George, Viscount of Tarbatt, Lord McLeod and Castle-haven, Clerk to His Majesties Parliament, Councell, etc., etc. (Endorsed) Ratificatione. In favour of Collonell David Barclay and his sone. 1685."

It is satisfactory to know that the brave old Colonel lived long enough to see his " good and faithfull services " to the Royal Family adequately acknowledged and recompensed.

Robert's time in London was, however, cut short, for he was hastily summoned home on account of his wife's delicate health and the increasing illness of his father, who was now 76 years of age.

He had been failing in health for some time, and though Robert wrote of him, " There be hardly to be found one of a thousand like to him for natural vigour of his age," he was attacked by a virulent fever, and in a fortnight the noble old soldier of Christ " fell asleep like a lamb, in remarkable quietness and calmness."

1686.   This sorrow, of course, put a good deal of responsibility on Robert's shoulders, and a letter from George Fox, received at this time, had to be put on one side for later attention.

Unworldly though the tenets of the Friends were, and as their leaders undoubtedly struggled to be, they could not be ignorant of the value of Robert's Court influence, and knew his real regard for James II, misguided and imprudent as the King was considered. So at this time, finding themselves involved in legal difficulties, partly in consequence of their refusal to take any oaths in courts of law, they addressed this urgent appeal to him :

" Edmonton. 5th Mo. 1686.
" Dear Friend Robert Barclay,
" With my love to thee, and thy wife and father, and the rest of the Friends in the holy seed of life, that reigns over all, in whom ye have life and salvation, and peace with God.
" The occasion of writing to thee at this time is that Friends are very sensible of the great service thou hadst concerning the Truth, with the King and all the Court, and that thou hadst their ear more than any Friend, and liberty on Friends and Truth's behalf. And now dear Robert, we understanding that the occasion of thy sudden return, concerning the condition thy wife was now in, being now over by her being delivered, I desire thee, and it is the desire of several other Friends that, whilst the door is open, and the way so plain, thou wouldst be pleased to come to London with speed, or as soon as maybe. There is great service in thy coming upon several accounts, more than I shall mention at this time ; and so I hope the Lord will incline thy heart to weigh and consider thy service in it.
" (signed) GEORGE FOX."

This letter, with its somewhat blunt phrasing, was followed by a postscript :

" George Whitehead remembereth his very dear love to thee and thy wife & Father, and desires me to tell thee that the Earl of Middletoun is kind to him and Gilbert Latey in the business relating to the Informers, which is returned with the report of the

Commissioners to the King & by the King referred to the Lord Chancellor. What will be done in it, we hear not at present, but the Report did carry pretty much reflection upon the Informers and diverse of them are convicted of perjury at the last London Quarter Sessions for Middlesex, and since have stood in the pillory."

There was also enclosed another urgent message from the company of Quakers that gathered about their leader, and added their entreaties to his :

" London.   22 of the 5th month 1686.
" Dear Robert,
" The within desire of George Fox is also the desire of us, and we think, of all the Friends here, we therefore hope thou willt do the needful herein.
" We are thy real friends
" JOHN OSGOOD.   FRANCIS CAMFIELD.

" P.S.—George Watt not present, else would have signed, and we are not willing to delay first post."

(John Osgood was a great tobacco merchant, the ancestor of the Osgood Hanburys, of Coggeshall, Essex.)

Though the King had been as good as his word, and religious persecution of the Quakers had ceased on his accession and the publication of his Declaration of Indulgence, Robert realised that the hostility of their opponents, checked in that direction, was finding vent in vexatious legal prosecutions and ruinous fines for non-payment of tithes and other smaller offences, and that the Friends naturally desired a surer basis on which to depend for protection against any revival of the penal laws. They hoped for a radical redress of their wrongs from Parliament, as is shown in a clause in the Address from the yearly meeting in 1687, which says :

" We hope the good effects thereof (the King's Declaration of Indulgence) may produce such a concurrence from the Parliament, as will secure it to our posterity," and they considered that Robert would be their most suitable ambassador. It was important to have sound credentials, as a spurious address, purporting to come from the Society of Friends, had once been presented to the King and done them much damage, until the fraud had been discovered.

ROBERT
BARCLAY,
1648-1690,
Urie II.

1687.

Robert was unable to undertake the long journey again for some months. Another family bereavement befell, in October 1686, when his sister Lucy died at her uncle's house at Cluny, and it was not until the following spring that he was able to arrange his affairs at home and go to London, through Edinburgh. Seventeenth-century travellers found it judicious to travel in company, and Robert joined the party of Viscount Arbuthnot and his wife, who was the daughter of the Earl of Sutherland and Robert's first cousin. It will be remembered that Lord Sutherland had written a pathetic appeal to Colonel David Barclay to intercede with his son-in-law on behalf of his young wife, whom her husband was alleged to be ill-treating ; but as the family party were travelling in company at this time, it is to be hoped that the Colonel's mediation had been successful.

On arrival in London, the business upon which Robert was bound was put in hand, and he laid a statement of the grievances of the Friends before King James. He also finally concluded the difference between the Duke of Gordon and Sir Ewen Cameron, in which the King's interposition was effective.

Life of
Robert
Barclay.

In August 1687 he took his journey homewards by way of Chester, where the King then was, and where he met William Penn and held a large meeting in the " Tennis Court." Unfortunately Robert met with an accident here, and had a fall from his horse which may have had serious effects later.

However, he continued his journey through Lancashire, visiting George Fox at his home, Swarthmore, then riding on to Edinburgh, whence he went on to visit the Earl of Perth, at Drummond Castle.

A letter from him to William Penn about this time shows some depression of spirit and speaks of his bad health, which indeed was not to be wondered at considering his strenuous life in the service of others.

After this he returned to Urie, and no doubt hoped for an undisturbed time to see to his own affairs and rest with his family, now growing up. Among other estate business, he began to build the wall round the Howff burial place, as desired by his father. While digging for the foundations he found several Roman urns, which seemed to indicate that the Romans had themselves used that place as a burying ground. This was of great interest to antiquarians, who had doubted whether they had penetrated farther north than Hadrian's great wall.

He was unable, however, to stay long at home, and in March 1688 we find him again upon the road.

He spent the whole summer in London, " writing and serving his friends to the utmost of his power." He was accompanied by his eldest son, Robert, whom he presented to the King, and who passed much of his time at Court. His school was within an easy ride of London, and the regulations were apparently not unduly strict. He was an attractive boy, and his father's many friends made much of him.

Meanwhile James pursued his obstinate course, notwithstanding prudent counsels, and on April 27th, 1688, his Declaration for Liberty of Conscience was published for the second time, without any concessions to public opinion. It met with considerable opposition from the nation, deeply suspicious of his " Papist " policy, and the Archbishop of Canterbury, with six bishops, boldly declared it to be illegal.

The Quakers, of course, saw the difficulty, but Penn and Barclay both maintained that the danger of Popery could be met by limiting powers and checking usurpations, while the kingdom in general would be relieved of intolerable burdens. King James, not content with appointing Roman Catholics to many places of influence and granting them important privileges, strengthened the distrust of his policy felt by all churchmen, by giving a splendid reception to the Pope's Nuncio at Windsor in the summer, with state equal to that accorded to a foreign Monarch. However, at the same time, he made special concessions to the Friends, ordering many who were still in prison to be released, and any who complained of confiscation of goods to be compensated ; while he treated them through their spokesmen, Robert Barclay and William Penn, with the utmost mildness and courtesy.

Some forty Friends in Norfolk, having applied to the King

ROBERT
BARCLAY,
1648-1690,
Urie II.
1688.

to cause them to be made freemen, he sent an order to the Attorney General, requiring him to appoint his well-beloved subjects freemen of the City of Norwich, " with all the rights and privileges thereunto belonging, without administering unto them any Oaths whatsoever, with which We are graciously pleased to dispense in their behalf."

This concession was, of course, due to the representations of Penn and Barclay, and we can understand how, when all the nation was up in arms against the King, the Quakers invariably expressed gratitude and even affection for him.

The Bishops were still obdurate, and maintained that the repealing of the Test and Penal Laws, which the Declaration involved, was merely opening the great offices of State to the Papists. They refused to sanction the repeal, or read the Declaration from their pulpits, as expressly ordained.

This refusal so angered the King that he sent seven of the Bishops to the Tower.

Strong popular feeling was aroused, and their imprisonment and trial had an important effect on the position of the King.

History of
the Friends,
Sewel,
Vol. i, p. 337.

During their imprisonment King James had tried to win over popular feeling by referring to the religious persecution sanctioned by the Church, and said the Bishops had been responsible for the death of innocent men. This being reported to them, they sent a demand for proofs, and Robert Barclay was deputed to visit them. He was able to show them undeniable evidence of some persons who by order of Bishops had been kept in prison till death, even against the advice of physicians who were not Quakers. They were unable to deny it, but Robert said that since they were themselves under oppression, the Quakers had no intention of publishing such matters, which would only exasperate the King more against them, and it was not the time to rub old sores, since the Bishops themselves showed a disposition to moderate their views and to look more favourably on liberty of conscience.

As this liberty was now enjoyed all over the Kingdom, the Quakers thought it convenient at their Summer Meeting in London to draw up an address to the King to acquaint him with another thing that continued to be troublesome to them, and which had been brought under his notice by Robert the previous year.

" To King James the II over England.

" The humble address of the people called Quakers, from their yearly meeting in London, the sixth day of the month called June, 1688.

" We, the King's loving and peaceable subjects, from divers parts of his Dominions, being met together in this City, after our usual manner, to inspect the affairs of our Christian Society throughout the world, think it our duty to humbly represent to him the blessed effects the liberty he has graciously granted his people to worship God according to their consciences, hath had, both on our persons and estates ; for whereas formerly we had ever long and sorrowful lists brought to us from all parts almost of his territories, of prisoners, and of the spoils of goods by violent and ill men, upon account of conscience ; we bless God and thank the King, that gaols are everywhere clear, except in cases of tithes, and the repair of parish churches, and some few about oaths ; and we do in all humility lay it before the King, to consider the hardships our friends are yet under for conscience sake in these respects, being in the one chiefly exposed to the present anger of the offended clergy, who have therefore lately imprisoned some till death ; and in the other they are rendered very unprofitable to the public and themselves ; for both in reference to freedoms in corporations, probates of Wills and testaments, and administration of answers in Chancery and Exchequer, trials of our just titles and debts, proceeding in our trade at the Custom House, serving the office of Constables, etc., they are disabled, and great disadvantage taken against them, unless the King's favour do interpose ; and as we humbly hope he may relieve us, so we confidently assure ourselves he will ease us what he can.

" Now, since it hath pleased thee O King, to renew to all thy subjects, by thy last declaration, thy gracious assurances to pursue the establishment of this Christian liberty and property upon an unalterable foundation, and in order to it, to hold a Parliament in November next at furthest.

" We think ourselves deeply engaged to renew our assurances of fidelity and affection, and with God's help intend to do our part for the perfecting of so blessed and glorious a work, that so it may be out of the power of any one party to hurt another, on account of conscience ; and as we firmly believe that God will never desert the just and righteous cause of liberty, nor the King in maintaining of it so we hope that by God's grace to let the world see we can honestly and heartily appear for liberty of conscience ; and be inviolately true to our own religion, whatever the folly or malice of some men on that account may suggest to the contrary."

This address was well received by the King, but his power was already tottering, and his reign was nearing its end, for on the day when, amid scenes of immense national enthusiasm, the seven Bishops, after their acquittal, were drawn in triumph through the streets of London, a secret message had been despatched to William of Orange, inviting him to come over and free the country from James's tyranny and the menace of Popery.

William III of Orange, son of William II of Orange and his wife Mary, daughter of King Charles I, had married in 1677 his first cousin, Mary, daughter of James II by his first marriage with Anne Hyde. Princess Mary would have succeeded to the throne of England on the death of James without heirs male, but the firm adherence of her husband to the Protestant religion and his statesmanlike conduct of the war in the Netherlands decided Parliament to invite him to intervene for the restoration of English liberty and the protection of the Protestant religion.

A son, James Francis Edward, had been born to James's second Queen, Mary of Modena, on June 10th, 1688, but his birth had been declared a Papist imposture. Discreditable manœuvres were attributed to the Court party and generally accepted, since, if the heir were acknowledged, a Roman Catholic dynasty would be established. The current rumour that the child had been introduced into the Palace in a warming-pan gave him the nickname of " The Pretender," by which he was known in later years.

Robert Barclay was much grieved and concerned at the grave differences between James II and his Parliament, and though the Quakers took no part in politics, he had many serious discussions with the King upon the situation. Christian Barclay recorded that " they sometimes took agreeable resolutions, but one way or another they were always prevented from being executed." Robert wrote at this time: "I considered it not my busines to make a judgement of these things," but in

180

the *Apology* he says, "The forcing of men's consciences is contrary to sound reason, and the very laws of nature. For man's
understanding cannot be forced by all the bodily sufferings
another man can inflict upon him, especially in matters spiritual. By that course indeed men may be made hypocrites, but
can never be made Christians, and hypocrisy is the worst of
evils, in the matter of religion."

ROBERT
BARCLAY,
1648-1690,
Urie II.

Doubtless his opinion helped to strengthen the King's determination, but if James had employed greater statesmanship,
and modified his policy on the lines suggested by Penn and
Barclay, he might have retained his throne. History, however,
shows his stubborn disposition and lack of understanding of
the national character, which brought about his inevitable
downfall.

Robert Barclay always loyally upheld him and hoped to the
last for a solution of the problem.

1688.

During the last few months of James's troubled and uncertain reign he found time to make a restitution that was long
overdue. Colonel David Barclay had never been reimbursed
for the money paid out of his private pocket to his troop during
the ill-fated "Engagement" to restore Charles I, when he ex-
pended some £400. Doubtless application had been made in
the proper quarters for repayment after the Restoration, but
nothing had been done.

King James, however, realising the debt, gave orders that
Robert Barclay was to receive the sum due, though the gallant
old Colonel had passed away. There should have been interest
for the forty years that had elapsed since 1648, but Robert accepted £300 in full settlement. The acknowledgment of this
debt should have been a complete answer to those who accused
the Colonel of having been in Cromwell's employment at that
time, though Robert still had to make an explanation in his
Vindication, as will be seen.

Secretary's
Papers,
Registry
House, Edin-
burgh, 1688.

At their final parting, he was standing alone with the King at
a window whence they could see a weather-vane, which
showed, in the parlance of the Court, "whether the wind set
from the Papist or Protestant quarter," and James, looking out,
said, doubtless with some bitterness, "The wind is now fair for

the Prince of Orange, his coming over." Robert Barclay said regretfully, "It seems hard that no expedient could be found to satisfy the people." To which the King replied, "I would do anything becoming a gentleman, except to part with liberty of conscience, which I never will while I live," to which Robert Barclay could make no rejoinder.

When, on November 5th, 1688, his fleet of six hundred transports, escorted by fifty men-of-war, anchored in Torbay, the nobility and gentry of the West of England flocked to the standard of the Prince of Orange. They were soon followed by those of the Midland, Eastern and Northern Counties, A great shout for "a free Parliament and the Protestant Religion" rose from all parts of the kingdom. The Royal armies fell back in disorder, and James, abandoning the struggle in despair, took advantage of the means of escape almost openly placed at his disposal, and embarked for France, practically unhindered, on September 23rd.

The House of Peers, the only authority that could legally call Parliament together in the absence of a king, requested William to take on himself the provisional government of the kingdom until one was elected.

When Parliament assembled it drew up a Declaration offering the Crown to the Prince and Princess of Orange. They should be acknowledged as joint Sovereigns, but the actual administration should rest with William alone. William accepted the offer in his own name and that of his wife and declared that the resolve of both was to maintain the laws and govern by the advice of Parliament. One of his first strokes of policy was the passing of the Toleration Act, which voiced the Englishman's conviction that the conscience could not be forced, and may be regarded as proof that the Friends had not suffered in vain— for their passive resistance and heroic endurance had convinced the nation of the injustice and uselessness of laws for controlling belief.

When James II had fled to France, the country breathed again. The Church was now on the side of the Constitution, and the late King's foolish attacks on Protestantism had left him without a party in the State. William III and Mary

182

mounted the throne as joint Sovereigns, and all Englishmen, ROBERT BARCLAY, 1648-1690, Urie II.
Whigs and Tories, Churchmen and Non-Conformists, combined in a great National Party to save Church and Constitution from Popery and Despotism. With the accession of a Constitutional Monarch came the final triumph of Protestantism and the " Glorious Revolution" was completed, almost without bloodshed.

The country being now at peace, Robert Barclay sent his son back to Urie, whither he followed him shortly. He spent two years quietly at home. His strict religious views did not interfere with healthy, simple occupations, and he gives a glimpse of his personal tastes and pastimes in the *Apology*, where he writes, "There are innocent divertissements which may sufficiently serve for relaxation . . . for man cannot be always in the same intentiveness of mind . . . such as for friends to visit one another, to hear or read history, to speak soberly of the present or past transactions; to follow after gardening; to use geometrical and mathematical experiments, and such other things of this nature."

He does not refer to fishing, which was a favourite occupation with the Friends, though they drew a strict line between fishing for food and fishing for sport. The river Cowie abounded in salmon and his boys were all expert anglers. He is also said to have been interested in horse-breeding and used to train young stock himself.

Even now he was not altogether free from slanderous accusations. Though King William was firmly seated on the throne 1689. and Robert had never meddled with politics, his friendship with James II was not forgotten, and his warning to Charles II against "Court parasites" had rankled in some minds. So bitter were the attacks made upon him that he found himself compelled to pen a " Vindication" of his conduct.

This "Vindication" is an explanation by the Apologist of circumstances connected with his intercourse with King James II, and was written in 1689. It is taken from a manuscript formerly at Urie and presented in 1857 or 1858 by the late Hudson Gurney to Arthur Kett Barclay, Bury Hill III.

In it he denies the charge that he is a Papist and argues that

183

his writings must refute that accusation, though he states frankly that it never agreed with the notions he has of the Christian religion to "hate these persons," and that he has a just esteem for the moral virtues of many personal friends of the Popish religion. He deals with the accusation of his interest with the King and says, "I have never found reason to doubt his sincerity in the matter of liberty of conscience," and affirms that his opportunity of frequent access to the King was used to the advantage of his friends and acquaintances, pointing out that he himself had no advantages from his attendance at Court: "I am sure who frequents the Courts of Princes find often more reason for wearying than pleasure, and so it proved often with me, and nothing but to serve my friends obliged me to do so dangerous a drudgery, where people are much more capable to get hurt than good."

He goes on to deny that he had ever received money as a reward for his labours, and says that he had not been to the King on his accession, to testify his respects, nor had he at any time asked any return for his loss of time, and trouble, and neglect of domestic affairs.

He concludes with a prayer for King James, "that God may bless him, and sanctify his afflictions to him, and if so be His Will to take from him an earthly crown, he may obtain through Mercy an Heavenly one."

A touch of genuine personal affection is in the words, "In short I must own, nor will I decline to avowe, that I love King James, and that I wish him well. That I have been sensibly touched with a feeling of his misfortunes, and that I cannot excuse myself from the duty of praying for him."

History
of the
Carnegies,
Earls of
Southesk,
Sir W.
Fraser.

In 1689 there was some country business to be transacted in Kincardineshire, relating to property of which Robert Barclay and his kinsman Sir David Carnegie, second Laird of Pitarrow, were heritors, and Robert writes:

" Ury the 17th of January 1689.

" Friend,

" I am so indisposed I could not come to Drumlithie and hope my man will come so timeously to thee, as to prevent thy trouble of coming from home.

" I have sent thee the raw project, which thou may see, it being ROBERT
the first and only coppy I have, to receive the Amendments of thy BARCLAY,
more mature judgment, which, when thou hast perused and 1648-1690,
corrected, send to Johnstone, that he may transmitt to Oldbairn, Urie II.
when thou and he sees meet: that at least will let those of Angus
know what is our desein. I shall expect my coppy back on the
next week, and the weather being tollerable, iff in health, upon
advertisement will meet thee where thou wilt appoint. This would
be done, as I said next week, that may commission (?) what may be
proper to some in Aberdeenshire.

" Mind my respects to thy Lady, who am thy assured friend,
" ROBERT BARCLAY.

" Doe me the favour to signifie to Johnston that I will expect to
hear from him one day next week at furthest."

The brave and gentle spirit was over-pressed with bodily 1690.
labours and mental exertions, and his strength was failing
fast. A series of meetings had been arranged in Aberdeen,
and Robert, though worn and wearied out, undertook
to attend, to arrange for Friends to visit those scattered
Quakers in wild outlying districts who could not easily reach
the towns. He rode up to the Jaffrays' house, Kingswells,
with some who had been among these itinerant preachers ;
and they sat up late, discussing and arguing. One who
watched him " observed his exalted look, as if he was holding
communing with God, and had lost recollection of the place
and the company, and when roused to take food he barely
tasted it, and bade saddle the horses at once, as he would
fain be at home."

He went back to Ury, though clearly unfit to travel, and
was at once struck down with a violent fever. The end came
a few days later. He was conscious to the last, and gave his
whole mind to comforting the rest, until he had barely strength
to lay his hand on the head of each of his children. He died
on 3rd October 1690, passing peacefully at sunset, with messages of love to all on his lips.

He was described as " a man of eminent gifts and great History of
endowments, expert not only in the languages of the learned, Friends,
but also well versed in the writings of the ancient Fathers, page 358.
and other ecclesiastical writers, and furnished with a great

III.—BB 185

ROBERT
BARCLAY,
1648-1690,
Urie II. understanding, being not only of a sound judgement but also strong in arguments and cheerful in sufferings. Besides, he was of a friendly and pleasant yet grave conversation, and eminently fitted for composing of differences, and he really lived up to what he professed, being of an unblamable deportment, truly pious and well beloved of those he conversed with. And in this happy state, it pleased God to take him away out of this vale of tears, into a glorious immortality, in the prime of his age, not having lived much above the half of the life of a man, as it is commonly accounted, viz. : in his forty-second year.

The last words recorded of Robert Barclay were full of the courageous resignation that he showed in every action of his life. He said " Remember my love to Friends in Cumberland, at Swarthmore (George Fox's home) and to dear George, and to all the faithful everywhere. God is good still : and though I am under a great weight of sickness and weakness in my body, yet my peace flows. And this I know, that whatever exercises may be permitted to come upon me, they shall tend to God's glory and my salvation ; and in that I rest."

1690. He was buried beside his father, on the summit of the hill which Colonel Barclay had chosen for his resting place, looking over his beloved countryside, with its stretches of purple heather, belts of dark pine-trees, and clumps of golden gorse.

The estate had largely recovered from the black days of the Great Rebellion, but a good deal of the land was still to be reclaimed, and the plover and sea-mew flew over it, and the larks soared and nested, almost as undisturbed by human presence as when Colonel David had first ridden over its fields.

No mausoleum then covered the Barclay graves, but the sad and stormy times had passed when the survivors could never be sure that their beloved dead would rest in peace, but might be rudely disturbed by the fierce intolerance of their persecutors, and removed to alien ground.

The memory of Robert Barclay may not be as vivid among

186

the country folk as that of his father, but his life and work in the cause of his religion will never be forgotten. His brilliant intellect, his wide experience, his deep erudition, which might perhaps have gained him more worldly advantages, had all been devoted to this end, while his home life was an example of tenderness, sympathy, faithfulness, and charity. Though he died comparatively young, he established his faith on a firm basis, and through much suffering had attained his goal.

His writings were numerous, and have been referred to, but a collected list may not be out of place here. His first published work was, *Truth Cleared of Calumnies*, followed by *William Mitchell Unmasked*.

He next issued the leaflet entitled, *A Seasonable Warning, and Serious Exhortation to, and Expostulation with the Inhabitants of Aberdeen*.

His next book was his *Catechism and Confession of Faith*, followed by *Theses Theologicæ*. He also published another pamphlet in Latin, to answer some controversial criticism of his *Theses*, by one Nicolas Arnold, Professor of the University of Franquer.

He then wrote a reply to an attack called *Quakerism Canvassed*, written by some students of Divinity, which elicited sincere expressions of regret and admissions of " convincement " from his adversaries ; and in the same year (1676) he published his *Anarchy of the Ranters* (later re-published as *Church Discipline*) and his monumental work *Apologia* in Latin, though this was not translated into English until the following year.

The next book was entitled *Universal Love, considered and established upon its right foundation;* and after that the *Epistle of Love and Friendly Advice to the Ambassadors of the several Princes of Europe, met at Nimeguen, to consult the Peace of Christendom. . . .* " and the long Latin letter he wrote to Herr Adrian Paets, which was the last thing he printed.

His celebrated letter to the Archbishop of St. Andrews was not included among his publications.

ROBERT BARCLAY, 1648-1690, Urie II.

1676-1692.

ROBERT
BARCLAY,
1648-1690,
Urie II.

After his death, his works were collected in 1692 in a folio volume, entitled " Truth triumphant through the Spiritual Welfare, Christian Labours and Writings of that able and faithful servant of Jesus Christ Robert Barclay."

Long after Robert Barclay's death his writings were eagerly read, and devoutly referred to. One John Faldo, a clergyman of the Episcopal Church, who had written two rather bitter books of attack on the Quakers, wrote in 1708 :—

" As I had occasion to be one day in a bookseller's shop, I happened to cast my eye on Barclay's books, and having heard that he was a man of great account among the Quakers, I had a mind to see what their principles were, and what defence they could make for themselves . . . I took Barclay home with me, and I read him through in a week's time, save a little treatise at the end, which I found to be very philosophical, I omitted, but however I soon read enough to convince me of my own blindness and ignorance in the things of God ; there I found a light to break in upon my mind, which did mightily refresh and comfort me . . . and therefore I received the truth with all readiness of mind . . . so that though before I was in great doubt and trouble . . . I was now fully satisfied in my own mind which way I ought to go, and to what body of people I should join myself."

Another opponent, called Evan Jevons, says :—

" When in a wretched and doleful condition of mind, I lighted upon R. Barclay's *Apology for the Quakers*, by the reading thereof I was so well persuaded of their principles, and by turning my mind inward to the Divine gift (according to their doctrine) it gave me victory, in a great measure over our common enemy, banished away my disorderly imaginations, and restored me to my former regularity. I received much satisfaction and comfort to my distressed soul, that thereupon I left the Church of England, and joined myself in Society with them."

The writer goes on to expatiate on the peace and composure of mind that followed on this change of doctrine, and maintains that " As for deserting that Church and Ministry which the Son of God came down from Heaven to establish, I am not conscious to myself thereof for I say that Christ is the head of our Church, and by His Spirit and Grace, the Ordainer of our Ministry."

HISTORY OF THE BARCLAY FAMILY

It was not only among those who held Robert Barclay's tenets that he was honoured and appreciated, for many members of other sects and in the Church of England spoke most highly of him. A learned clergyman named Norris wrote, " Mr. Barclay is a very great man, and were it not for the common prejudice that lies against him as a Quaker, he would be sure not to miss being preferred to the greatest wits the age has produced." And after certain discussions with him, he adds, " I would rather engage with a hundred Bellarmines, Hardings, and Stapletons (all famous controversialists) than with one Barclay."

A Scotch poet, writing of two other famous Barclays, William and John, concludes with these lines on Robert :—

> " But lo a third appears with serious air
> His Princes' darling, and his country's care
> See his religion, which so late before
> Was like a jumbled mass of dross and ore
> Refined by him, and burnished o'er with Art
> Awakes the spirits and attacks the heart."

Among the numerous letters received by Robert's widow, one from George Fox says :—

"Now dear friend, though the Lord hath taken thy dear husband from thee his wife and his children, the Lord will be a husband to thee and a father to thy children, therefore cast thy care upon the Lord, and trust in Him . . . therefore cast thy care upon the Lord, and trust in Him . . . therefore thou and thy family rejoice that thou had such an offering to offer up to the Lord as thy dear husband whom I know is well in the Lord, in whom he died, and is at rest from his labour, and his works do follow him . . . From him who had a great respect for thy dear husband, for his work and service in the Lord, who is content in the will of God in all things, that he doth, and so must thou be, and so the Lord God Almighty settle and establish thee and thine upon the heavenly rock and foundation, and as thy children grow in years they may grow in grace, and so in the favour of the Lord. Amen. George Fox.

P.S. I know thy husband left a good savour behind him, so I desire all you may do the same.

George Fox's few words, dated just two months before his own death, are full of heart, and convey a genuine sense of the special character and value of Robert Barclay's services. "Much more might be written," he says, "concerning this faithful brother in the Lord, and Pillar in the Church of Christ, who was a man I very much loved for his labour in the truth, but I will leave the rest to his countrymen."

Among those who endeavoured to express in writing their admiration for him and sorrow at his loss, one Arthur Forbes of Brux, endeavouring to write a preface to the collected edition " of the works of that faithful servant of the Lord, Robert Barclay of Urie," breaks down after two lines only, and says, " I do confess my mind I cannot raise To give the defunct his deserved praise." And he was no Quaker.

Rowntree says :—

" Robert Barclay rode forth into the fuller day, as it seemed to us before his time, but the members of the Church he loved may make his experience and prayer their own. Good men do not die, Love bridges death . . . and we will adventure with hope and in the spirit and strength of our great Example of Galilee . . . like him to fight the good fight of Faith."

The Countess of Errol, one of the most religious, as well as wise and learned ladies of her time, speaks of Robert with warm affection, saying he was so deserving a friend to herself and her brothers, and how he had always mentioned them affectionately, even when most of the world was railing at them, and that his friendship for them only increased as their misfortunes grew upon them. She begs to be believed to be one who had a real esteem for his virtues " more than it is possible for me to express," and adds, " By the little time I had the satisfaction to see your son, I was very well pleased to see so good an appearance in him of supplying the place of so deserving a father, and it shall be a very acceptable satisfaction to me, to see any of your family at this place, for I am affectionately at your service.

" ANNE ERROL."

HISTORY OF THE BARCLAY FAMILY

In William Penn's testimony to Robert Barclay and George Fox, he says:—

" The overcasting of so many bright stars almost together, and of the first magnitude, in our horizon, from our bodily view, is not the least symptom or token to me of an approaching storm, and perhaps so dreadful that we may have fresh cause to think them happy that are delivered from the toils and miseries that may come."

Robert Barclay, the Apologist (Urie II), and his wife, Christian Mollison, had seven children, of whom three were sons :—

Robert, born 1672, who succeeded his father in the estate of Urie.

David, born 1682, who settled in London and whose descendants, on the failure of the direct line in 1854, became heirs male of Urie.

John, born 1687, who settled in Dublin and died there in 1751. He married firstly Margaret Wilson, by whom he had no issue, and secondly Anne Strettell, daughter of Amos Strettell of Dublin and Experience his wife, by whom he had two sons :—

Robert, born 1717: Tradition has it that he went to The Barclays of New York, Moffat, p. 86. America, and the Barclays of Maryland claim descent from him.

John, born 1723, who severed himself from the Society of Friends and married Anne Cooper of Shraugh, Queen's County, by whom he had one son, John, and four daughters.

—and nine daughters, of whom

Experience m. James Clibborn of Moate, County Westmeath.

Elizabeth m. Edward Scriven of Dublin.

Lydia m. Benjamin Alloway of Dublin.

The four daughters of Robert Barclay (Urie II) were: Patience, who married Timothy Forbes, and Catherine, who married his brother James, sons of Alexander Forbes of Aquorthes; Christian, who married Alexander Jaffray of Kingswells; and Jean, who married Alexander, son of John Forbes.

ROBERT BARCLAY

Robert Barclay (Urie III), eldest son of the great Apologist, was born at Urie on 25th March, 1672, and went to school at Theobalds in Middlesex in 1683, as we have already seen. He stayed there for five years, returning to live at home in 1688 at the age of sixteen, and succeeded his father in 1690.

The many friends and admirers of the Apologist took great interest in his young family, and his son, though only nineteen at his father's death, held a character for gravity and earnestness beyond his years, which caused many of them to correspond and consult with him.

This letter from one David Wallace shows how far from toleration or understanding the " Covenanters " of Scotland remained, and how, notwithstanding the passing of the Declaration for Liberty of Conscience and the Toleration Act of William III in 1689, the Quakers were still subjected to harsh and cruel persecution.

" Hamiltoun, 1691
" The 19 of the 12 month.

" Dear Friend,

" By this my dear love is remembered to thee and thy mother and the rest of the children about you, hoping ye are all well as we are at present, blessed be the Lord for His many mercies and preservation, Who hath been with us hitherto. Glory be to his name for ever.

" Yesterday we were at Glasgow, a city abounding in malice and self-conceit, where Friends being gathered together in the Meeting House, our dear Friend Robert Barrow having prayed and afterwards having spoken a little while, that woman called the Captain with another young man came in with a rable at their back in great noise and confusion, she coming straight to Robert as he was declaring, taking him by the arm and desiring him to go with her, some Friend interposing put her by, then they two chiefly went to and fro, sometimes to one Friend then another, haling at them to be gone, then up comes two Collegians, and there was a great bustle and confusion, & they said they were bound by their Covenant to extirpate Hereticks, for so they judged us. Friends all kept their places pretty well, & Bartholomew Gibson was very valiant for the truth with severall other Friends, but they raged still the more at us, pulling and haling [hauling] & first they pulled down John Miller and dragged him quite downstairs, haling him by legs

and arms, as they did honest old Bartholomew with John Neil, ROBERT
Duncan Morison & Andrew Fitchel, they using the said Andrew BARCLAY,
so hardly in their fury and madness, that he cried out in a loud 1672-1747,
voice " Murther without Law," which so astonished the people Urie III.
without that diverse came running in.   They looked amazed and
confounded themselves for a little time & still there was a great
noise, who brought us all forth to the Clerk's Chamber, all the way
the snowballs went thick among us, then the Provost asked our
names & wherefore we came hither, we told him our names and
the cause of our coming, which was to visit our friends.   He said
we had no Warrant to do so, neither would he suffer us, and commanded to take us away and convey us out of town, and would not ·
consent we should take any refreshment in the town, but that our
horses should be brought to us without the town, upon which
Bartholomew Gibson said, " Thou art recorded both in heaven and
earth as a persecutor " ; then we were conveyed away by the officers
to the Bridge, the balls flying among us though some laboured to
restrain them, but we were all preserved from hurt and harm
outwardly and inwardly, the glory and praise be to our God,
Who bore up our heads with our hearts and minds, so that we were
all well refreshed and our strength was renewed, so that we have
cause to be encouraged, & boldly stand for the Truth on earth."

Robert's mother, Christian Mollison as she was always called, Bury Hill
it not having become the custom in Scotland for the wife to Papers.
adopt her husband's name, had strict ideas of discipline, and in
a letter written to Friends in Aberdeen she gives much sage
advice as to the bringing up of children.   She has definite
notions as to the avoidance of " superfluous words and jesting,
yea, needless words for both old and young," and desires
that " we may all travel more and more into silence."

In John Gratton's journal he says, speaking of a visit to
Urie, " I observed that when the children were up in the
morning and dressed she (Christian) sate down with them
before breakfast and in religious manner ' waited upon the
Lord.' "

It might be expected that as her sons grew up they would find
her rule somewhat irksome, and it speaks well for both mother
and children that they were guided by her teaching and influenced by her principles all their lives.

His father's friend, the Countess of Errol, was in constant
correspondence with Robert and his mother, and pleasant

III.—CC   **193**

messages, gifts of fruit, exchange of recipes for Christian's
Day Book, as well as cordial invitations passed between them.
In one of his letters Robert showed some of the sternness of the
Quaker doctrine, as when he mentions the loss of a child, no
doubt Margaret, who died in 1707, saying, " My wife is much
afflicted by this, which she ought not to be."

He inherited some of his father's gift for dialectical writing
and at times used rather un-Quakerlike terms. In speaking of
a book attacking one of their leaders, Dr. Garden, he said of the
author, " He plays stoutly at Footballe with their name (the
Friends) and without Rime or reason, but ventures not upon one
of their arguments for fear of breaking his shinns. His reason-
ings against are just as convincing as the Hangman's when he
burns a book in the Palace Yard, and his arguments as pungent
as those of a monkey in a glass shop. In lieu of a better jest I
cannot but smile to see how he musters up all his Gingle and
Gorgon to abuse this supposed Antagonist . . . I should
think my time much better employed in cracking of nuts, than
in answering him. . . . In days of yore when people were such
fools as to be priest-ridden, they got a notion in their peri-
craniums that being a clergyman made a gentleman of a scoundrel. But now the world are grown so wise as to see that being
a clergyman often makes a scoundrel of a Gentleman."

Robert Barclay took his duties as a landed proprietor and
feudal baron very seriously, and there are records of the frequent
meetings of the Baron Court, at which he presided with dignity
and diligence. He held strong opinions on the questions of
destruction of " Wodis and dowcattis " [dovecots] and the
" killing of haires, doves, partridges, moore foullis, duke and
drake," and indeed was as severe on the offenders as any sporting squire of fifty years ago on the poaching fraternity. He
saw to it that the poor on the barony were relieved, and later
the payment of " vagabond money " was enforced by law.

His Quaker principles prevented undue severity in criminal
cases, and mutilations for theft were unknown in his jurisdiction. Banishment with forfeiture of " Guids and Geyr " was
the heaviest sentence imposed. He was strict in the matter of
cutting or " casting " of peat or turf, but there is no doubt that

194

much damage had been done to the property by the wanton ROBERT BARCLAY, destruction of tenants, and that the land had been impoverished 1672-1747, thereby, as much against their own interest as that of the owner. Urie III.

As might be expected, he and his mother took a deep interest in the services of the Kirk and spoke out boldly if they were not satisfied with the way they were conducted.

Christian Mollison was descended from a famous soldier, Memoirs of Colonel Mollison, who had distinguished himself in the battle Robert Barclay, of Candia, when besieged by the Turks, and was mentioned in Urie III. Ricaut's history. She was greatly beloved by her family and appears to have combined the gentleness of the Friends with some of her grandfather's fighting spirit, as after her celebrated husband's death we have record of an indignant protest on her part against the doctrines preached in the church of Fetteroso, for which she was " summoned to compeir before the Sheriff of Kincardine, or his deputies, in ane Court to be holden at Stonehyve upon the 20 day of August inst, to answer at the August, instance of the Profiscall for the disturbance of Mr. John Mylne, 1691. Minister at Fetteroso Kirk, in time of Divine Service and administration of the Sacrament."

The summons was served " by delivering and serving off two litterall copies in the lock holl [presumably the letter-box] of the inner Yett [gate] of Urie after the knocking of thrie severall cnocks [knocks]."

It begins :

" Procurator Fiscall contra Christian Mollesson, Ladie of Urie," which appears to have been the form of subpœna.

" At the hearing of the cause, Christian Molleson, Lady Urie . . . acknowledges and confesses that upon the 3rd day she heard a pairt of the sermon silently, and did not offer to sturr, till the Minister comeing doune furth of the pulpit, she desyred him to stay and speak with her, for she hade heard him with patience, and she not taking notice of what he annsred she insisted in her discourse and being interrogat why she did not remove when she was desyred, she ans^{rd} she would not remove till she had declaired her Commission from the Lord, and thereafter she insisted both within and without the church in long continued discourse."

The witnesses say that the Minister refused to be interrupted and that she then addressed the congregation " over the breist

of her loft " calling him " Ane hyreling and much more im-
pertinent discourse "until the lady was removed "furth from the
church to the church yaird." For the " injurious and unroulie expressions by the ladye, she was fined ane hundred pounds Scots."

Notwithstanding her militant qualities, she was greatly
respected and beloved and brought up her numerous family
" in the fear and knowledge of the Lord."

Again, in 1695, in addition to the penalty exacted from
" Lady Ury " for her interruption of the Minister's discourse
in August, 1691, we hear of Robert Barclay and his tutors and
curators being summoned in February to attend " ane court
to be holden within the tolbooth of Stonehyve for his disturbing the people and raising of ane tumult in the Kirk of Fetteroso
in time of divyne service, and interrupting divyne worship,
particularly in the time of singing of psalms upon Sunday last,
by his publict vociferat^{ne}, pretended preaching and his de-
clairing his hereticall and schismatic doctrine of his quaker
principles att that tyme and under the law."

The witnesses stated that—

" The said Robert Barclay of Urie, about the tyme of the reading
of the first lyne of the psalmes, did stand up in his own laft [loft]
upon Sabbath Day, and yt begine and spake ane number of words,
but what they were he could not tell by reason of the tumult, which
his appeairing and publict cryeing and speaking in the Kirk of
Fetteroso then maid, but only in general that he dissuaded the people
from hearing the minister, who he allegst was leading them all the
black gett [gate] and that thereby he interrupted divyne worship
for a short space, while he [spake] himselfe, which is a truth as he
shall answer to God."

" There was no appearance for Robert Barclay, who was
again summoned to appear on February 25, 1695, but there
was again no appearance."

On February 25th, 1695, the Sheriff Deputy having " considered the witnesses' depositions and the Def^r his citations to
have compeired to have heard them and deponed in the matter
within written, and he not compeiring nor his tutors and curators for y^r entreat albeit laudlie [loudly] summoned. In respect
y^r of the Sheriff amerciats the said Robert Barclay in the soume
of fiftie punds Scots to be payed to ye Pro^r fiscal as accords."

HISTORY OF THE BARCLAY FAMILY

The intensity of the bitter feeling against the Quakers was, however, dying down. It may be that in the changing conditions of life, both public and private, the rigid conventions and possibly limited views of the early exponents of their Faith were becoming somewhat modified, and that though the old teaching still held, it was being brought more into line with the social customs of the day; but it is certain that their patience under suffering, and the steadfastness with which they maintained their convictions, gradually made an impression, and gained for them respect even from their opponents.

Whereas, in the early years of the movement, adherence to their religious principles had meant deprivation, if not of liberty, at least of means of livelihood, little by little the personal integrity of the Quakers earned them a reputation for probity and honourable dealing.

George Fox left in his Diary some interesting conclusions upon this point, which have been supported by later experience.

He says, " At the first commencement, when Friends could not put off their hats to people, nor say ' you ' to a particular, but ' thee ' and ' thou,' and could not bow nor use the world's salutations, nor fashions, nor customs, and many Friends being tradesmen of various sorts, they lost their custom at the first, for the people would not deal with them nor trust them. And for a time they could hardly get money enough to buy bread, but afterwards when people came to see Friends' honesty and truthfulness and yea and nay at a word in their dealings . . . and they knew and saw that they would not cozen nor cheat them for conscience sake towards God . . . .So then things altered, and all the enquiry was where was a draper, or shopkeeper, or tailor, or shoemaker, or any other tradesman who was a Quaker, insomuch that Friends had double the trade beyond any of their neighbours."

In 1696 Robert Barclay married Elizabeth Braine. The marriage contract sets out, with much legal circumlocution, how that on " the sixth day of July, Anno Domini one thousand six hundred ninety and six, It was contratted and finally agreed between the parties following, to Witt Robert Barclay

197

of Ury in the Parish of Fetteroso, in the Sherifdom of Kincardine and Kingdom of Scotland Gentleman, on the one part, and Elizabeth Braine lawful daughter to John Braine of the Citty of London, Merchant, with the speciall advise and consent of the said John Braine, her father. And the said John Braine for himselfe and taking burthen upon him for his said daughter on the other part in manner following, that is to say the said Robert Barclay and Elizabeth Braine with consent forsaide bind and oblige them to solemnize and compleat the Bond of Marriage either of them with other to the manner and practise of the people called Quakers, betwixt —— and —— day of next ensuing the date of these presents."

The marriage contract is on stiff parchment, and the writing, though the ink has faded slightly, is perfectly clear. It is a long, verbose document, setting forth the various possessions and properties of the young people and the sums of money to be bestowed by their relatives.

1697. By some mistake the funeral tablet on the wall of the Howff at Urie gives the bride's name as O'Brian.

Early in January, 1697, Robert Barclay received the following letter from his uncle, Sir Ewen Cameron, the great chieftain of Lochiel, who had, it will be remembered, married Jean, younger daughter of Colonel David Barclay, in 1685.

"Locharkrigg,
"Much honoured nephew,   "7 Jan., 1697.
" I have no will that my long silence make us weir [wear] out of acquaintance, for I assure you neither the distance of places or alteration of times will make me forget your parents nor such as is come of them. I am glad to hear that you are well married & that the rest of the children and your Lady are in good health.

"I know your aunt will give an account of her own and her children's condition, I am still a prisoner when there is any news of an invasion, but Sir John Hill who is Governor of Fort William is very civill to me. Your Aunt and I had some expectation of your coming here, but now I fear your Lady will impede it. I will give you no further trouble with this bad hand, only kind respects from my Lady and children to yourself and your Lady though unacquainted and shall be glad to hear all your good healths, and am still to remain

"Your most affec^te Uncle and Servant,
"EWEN CAMERON LOCHIEL."

Lochiel had played a distinguished part in the Civil War and fought with conspicuous bravery against the Parliament. He was knighted in 1681 by Charles II and later refused to acknow- ledge King William, though offered a title and fortune to do so. He took up arms under " Bonnie Dundee," and his wise counsels greatly contributed to the victory of the Highlanders over the King's troops at Killicrankie in 1689. The gallant old man ultimately submitted to the Government and died in 1719, at the age of ninety.

This letter from him to Robert Barclay is interesting, show- ing that Lochiel was still under restraint for his Jacobite opinions.

In 1698 Robert was involved in trouble through an indis- creet acquaintance, whose name seems to have been Hugh Rawson. This man was implicated in Jacobite plots and tried to persuade him to join in restoring King James, talking of the divine right of kings and his duty to James Stuart, who had been his father's friend and benefactor. Robert, however, firmly resisted his arguments, saying he was a loyal subject to King William, and in any case his principles as a Friend would forbid him to rebel against him. He warned his friend that it was dangerous talk, as the Society had many enemies who would be glad of any excuse for annoying his family, and Alexander Jaffray joined him in strongly urging the young man not to embroil them in any way. But he would not listen to reason and openly spoke of King William as the Usurper, boasting that he held a warrant from King James to incite to rebellion.

Robert, therefore, kindly but firmly told him that the house of Urie could no longer shelter an accredited agent of the late King, there for the purpose of stirring up rebellion, and that he must take his departure at once. But his wild talk had been repeated, and that very day news came that a warrant was out for the apprehension of Robert Barclay, Alexander Jaffray and their guest, on the charge of being concerned in a Jacobite plot.

The young man escaped in disguise, but Robert remained quietly at home, and he and Jaffray made no resistance when

ROBERT
BARCLAY,
1672-1747,
Urie III.
the officers of the law arrived to arrest them. They were taken to the tolbooth of Aberdeen under an escort of troopers and lodged in the same prison where Robert's father and grandfather had been confined twenty years before.

They were, however, allowed a decent room and writing materials, and Robert at once wrote to his relative the Marquis of Huntly, asking him to assure the King of his loyalty, and to make it clear that he was not a certain Sir George Barclay who had been prominent in a conspiracy for the assassination of King William in 1696 (a prominent Jacobite whose origin is unknown).

This was a judicious action, for King William, just and tolerant as he was, knew neither of them, and one Barclay was the same as another to him. Lord Huntly explained the confusion of names and interceded so effectively for his kinsman that an order for his release arrived in Aberdeen little more than a month after his committal to gaol. The magistrates of Aberdeen had learned that no Friend was likely to enter into plots against the Government, and he was released at once without question.

About this time Robert Barclay took steps to restore the estate of Urie to its original acreage, following in the footsteps of his grandfather, Colonel David. He repurchased the lands of Finlayson and Redcloak, which had previously been alienated, and at the same time he restored to the Earl Marischal certain detached portions of the Barony that lay within the parish of Dunnottar.

1710.
In 1710 we find Robert taking up the cudgels on behalf of the Friends. They were indignant at the wording of the burghers' oath, and complained at the injustice of the magistrates to them on that account, so they appealed to him for support, and he sent in the following protest.

" The form of the petition given in 29 Nov., 1710, by Robert Barclay of Ury and others of the people called Quakers, sons of burghers, and inhabitants of the said burgh of Aberdeen in behalfe of themselves and others of the friends concerned, mentioning that whairas in the tyme of a severe persecution upon the Quakers in this place there was ane act of counsell made debarring them from

200

being admitted burgess therin, which hath of late been improved ROBERT BARCLAY, 1672-1747, Urie III.
not only with respect to the Quakers but as a further hardship upon
other protestants (witnes the new form of the burger oath printed
last winter) whoever shall owne or profess Quakerisme shall thereby
renounce all benefit and priviledge competent to them as burgesses
this the petitioners humbly conceaved was a depryving them and
others and those who owned or professed Quakerism of their
naturall or civill rights, most of the petitioners being sons of burgess,
and all of them recognised by the Queen and Parliament as protestant dissenting subjects, witnes severall Acts of Parliament, both
befor and since the Union. The pet^{rs} therefore crave that the
present Counsell wd be pleased to rescind the sd Act as contrary
to the liberty and property of the subject, that they and their
posterity might, according to the inclinations of the Queen and
Parliament, enjoy their just right and priveleges, and the petitioners
as in duty bound should ever pray, etc.

> " ROBERT BARCLAY.   ALEXANDER JAFFRAY.
> JOHN SOMERVAILE.   DANIEL HAMILTON."

Another letter from him addressed to the Earl of Mar in 1713.
1713 shows how he was again appealed to by the Friends to
support their claims. He wrote to solicit Lord Mar's interest
in regard to the " right of affirmation " which had been
conceded to the English Quakers and was about to be extended
to the Scots.

The form of it was not acceptable to the Friends north of Bury Hill Papers.
the Tweed, and Robert argued: " Our case is this—we cannot
with freedom take the benefit of the solemn affirmation
formerly granted to our friends in England, and now under
consideration of the House of Commons to be renewed and
extended to us, without it be made easier and more agreeable
to the simple and plain precept of our Lord and Saviour,
Jesus Christ. I beg of thee, with all the earnestness I can,
that if it come your length, thou should become our advocate
for an amendment so as to make it effectual to us, thy friends
in the ancient kingdom, as well as thousands of our brethren
in England under the same difficulty with us, we always being
willing to be subjected, upon the breach of our simple affirmation, to the same penalties by law inflicted upon perjury."

He leaves no stone unturned and at the same time enlists Bury Hill Papers.
the Duke of Argyll's influence in a letter beginning " Hon-

III.—DD

oured Friend Argile," saying that he hopes he will not take it
unkindly that " I, with all respect, become thy Suter in
behalf of myself and friends in this Nation, our case being we
cannot with freedom take the solemn affirmation favourably
granted by the Government in England to our brethren there,
as ane expiring Act resolved to be renewed and now by the
Union extended to us.

" What we, with all due submission, begg, is that ane
Ammendment may be made to render it easy & so of use
to us here as well as thousands of our Brethren . . ."

He goes on to hope that " you that are the Patriots of our
country, will not so far neglect your poor friends in the
antient Kingdom, as not endeavour to get us eased."

The form objected to was, " Upon all occasions, though
never so triffling or small moment when judiciously called
thereto, we can oblidge ourselves solemnly to declare in the
Presence of Almighty God, witness to the truth of what we say."

Though a considerable number of the Quakers agreed to
adopt this form, Robert Barclay held the view that it was
" derogatory to the honour of the King of Kings, to be summoned as a witness in things of such a nature, which it would
be below the dignity of ane earthly King to be," and that to do
so " is our adversaries' oppinion, not ours."

The controversy raged hotly among the Friends, and
Robert wrote with such a caustic pen to the Society in Aberdeen that they replied through George Whitehead in pained
protest: " But your presently proceeding to severe censures,
smiting and prophecying against your Friends and Brethren
do not bespeak that they and the rest of the subscribers etc.,
are in such a low state of humiliation or contrition, as to be so
deeply humbled and brought so low in the dust."

The quarrel looked like a serious breach, but it was apparently pacified, as befitted members of their Society, and we
hear no more of it.

A year later Robert Barclay was himself elected a Burgess
on the terms granted to his father by King James.

At the death of Queen Anne in August, 1714, the prospect
of a German King caused the Jacobite party to redouble their

efforts in the cause of James Stuart, the Pretender, and the ROBERT BARCLAY, 1672-1747, Urie III.
following year found the Earl of Mar at Perth with a force of 6,000 foot and 600 horse. The Government sent the Duke of Argyll to quell the rising, but he was embarrassed by lack of troops. After some months of indecisive actions the northern Jacobites, having been joined by their supporters from the Border and Northumberland, marched south, to meet defeat at the battle of Preston on November 14th, 1715. Almost simultaneously, a Scottish Jacobite force under the Earl of 1715. Mar was defeated at Sheriffmuir.

The hopes of the Jacobites were crushed, but at this inauspicious moment James Stuart, against the advice of his friends, landed at Peterhead on December 22nd, too late to advance his cause. The larger number of his supporters had suffered death or imprisonment and the remainder were greatly disheartened by the retreat of James before a force under Argyll. On February 4th, 1716, the Pretender, abandoning the remnant of his followers to relentless pursuit, left Scotland in haste and secrecy, never to return.

In view of his political opinions and pacifist principles, it is not surprising that Robert Barclay took no part in this ill-judged and tragic rising; nevertheless he must have felt keenly the suffering and sorrow of many of his relatives and friends who were involved.

He seems to have passed these sad times in the improve- 1722. Macfarlane's Geographical Collections, pp. 247-257.
ment of his estates, and a description of the property in 1722 gives a clear picture of his environment. It speaks of the "Mannor Place of Urie" as "being charmingly surrounded with very fine gardens, the south wall of which is washed with the water of Cowie, and the East is so near a large brook that nothing intervenes but a slip of ground planted with fir trees, for a fence to the garden. This brook is well stockt with large fine trouts, and runs through an enclosure of cow pasture.

"It is very healthfully placed upon a gravelly soil, sloping to the south towards the river, so that the gardens are very delightfully placed below one another, quite to the river side, and although standing upon an eminency, which gives it a good prospect of the sea, towards the south west, yet by rising ground to the E. and N., and trees towards the W., is tolerably well guarded from all winds except the S. and S. W.

"The house is an old castle-built house having very thick walls, and is tolerably well repaired, the present owner, Robert Barclay, grandchild to Colonel David Barclay, already mentioned, hath planted a good many trees of several sorts, particularly fir trees, which thrive very well. He is supposed to have near an hundred thousand, which is thought to be the most considerable planting of such firs that is so very near the East sea between the Murray Firth and Dover Castle.

"One remarkable curiosity of planting made by him is not (to) be omitted, viz., upon the N. end of his cherry garden and in view of his windows, he hath planted a piece of ground equal in breadth to his garden, the rows and openings answering to it, with 25 different sorts of barren trees (*sic*) and so exactly regular, that where there is one or more sorts of trees in one place, it hath the same on the opposite side, which with the different colours of the leaves so nicely intermixed and variety of foliage, makes a charming show. He hath made not a quarter of a mile north of the house in a hollow surrounded with rising ground upon all sides but one, a very beautiful pond with two islands in it, planted with trees, in which the wild ducks breed yearly of their own accord. The pond is well stored with fishes, several very fine springs being brought into it, and the rising ground round it planted with trees of various sorts, as elms, birch, and willows near the water, and having a boat in it to go to the islands makes it a very pleasant place.

"He hath also, about half a mile from his house towards the N.-E., a natural pond or loch, in which are very good perch and very large : much frequented with wild ducks, also to the north west of the house he hath a larger loch in which were found an old helmet with a name supposed to be Danish, and shin pieces, which he gave to Sutherland the antiquary, and it is probable that they were by him, with his other antiquities sold to the Faculty Advocates at Edinburgh.

"The advantage of this Estate House being rightly considered in the healthfulness of its situation, the regularity of its gardens, Robert the extensiveness of its enclosures, the nearness of a seaport Barclay, 1672-1747, town, the plenty of fishing, both in salt and fresh water, Urie III. the abundance of game of all sorts both at sea and land, makes it a very delightful habitation.

"It holds of the Crown ; hath 2 yearly fairs belonging to it, where all sorts of cattels and countrey products such as stockins, linen cloaths, etc., are sold, they being kept in a very convenient place above the town of Cowie near the great road, and in a good season, the one being in June, the other in October, and there being no other fairs in the parish, make them well frequented."

Truly a different prospect from the bleak and barren moorland that Colonel David Barclay had viewed with a prophetic eye so many years before.

At the close of 1722 Robert's mother, Christian Barclay, died. *Piety Promoted,* one of the best known of Quaker publications, gives an account of her life and character.

We read that " she was taken ill the 12 of the Ninth month, and from that time continued in a weak state, in which she witnessed many comfortable opportunities ; her concern for the truth and the church's prosperity continued with her to the last, for sickness seemed not to alter her temper or concern: many pious expressions dropped from her during her illness, and He Who had been with her all her life long blessed her with His Presence to the drawing of her last breath, which appeared to be in great peace and quietness, the 14th of the Twelfth month 1722 aged Seventy six years."

For all his gravity and serious view of life, Robert Barclay may at times be found in lighter mood, as, for instance, when in reply to an angry letter from a neighbour, Sir Peter Frazer, he writes in a whimsical strain, though with his usual directness:

" Thy Tragick-comicall letter, that both breathes Fear and denounces Peace, blends Philosophy and Divinity together so that it would need an Aristotle or Aquinas to separate and put them in their right places, but since our modern wittes have concluded the Universe only a hodge-podge, or Congress of Atoms, why should thy epistle not be it in miniature." He remonstrates with Sir Peter for credulity in the matter of finding buried treasure, which he calls " A wille with the Wisp," and says with good temper and some humour, " As to my being no Christian, I acknowledge I received not mine at the Font as thou did, neither did I, after thy example, leave it there, and I doubt not that our Moralls differ as much as our religion." Sir Peter had the reputation of changing sides with ease, for he first sided with William of Orange, then became a Jacobite, then a violent Whig, and went to the Court of Hanover in Queen Anne's reign.

It will be readily understood that Robert Barclay's views did not always correspond to those of his neighbours, some of whom were ready enough to scoff and ridicule, even if they did not go further in opposing him.

Satires and lampoons were so much the mode in those days that few could hope to escape them, and one of these is
among the family papers and appears to refer to a lawsuit brought against Robert by some gentlemen of the locality.

This " Satyr " is headed :

> " The end of September proves the first of Aprile
> When fools goes of errands the time to beguile."

" Ane old squire leads the Vann, his posse attending,
(Old Fullerton)
Three knights and a rable, his rare cause defending.
(Ramsay Bolman, Sir A. G. Ronnerman, Sir Al Barnett, and Sir Jack Fullerton)
Young Hopeful comes next, his heart in his hose,
His brains in his pocket, his witt to expose,
Whilst his dear Dulcinda sits cursing at home
A right hanke of the Noft (?) forestalling her doom.
(His wife, daughter to Ellick)
Chas Leslie for spokesman to open the Case
Bright Turnbull explaining with suitable grace
(Fullerton's factor)
The old Barron supporting, who brays like an ass
Much famed for cunning and a forehead of brass
With witnesses plenty as the Cause doth require
Like those who imployed them, full freighted with Ire,
From the dull swearing Knight, both stupid and keen (?)
(Leys)

HISTORY OF THE BARCLAY FAMILY

To priest angry, and Allan, and little Bob Skeen,
(The Laird of Skeen)
With his Chiefe for to cheer them, his bagpipes in trim
The Maiden Knight, their Conductor, both sleekit and prim.
To destroy a young neighbour, they march in parade,
(Barclay of Urie)
But his vigour proved bright all their force to evade
Thus when fools went their errand the time to beguile
The end of September proved the first of Aprile."

The author was evidently a sympathiser, though he can hardly be classed among the great satirists.

About this time Robert Barclay made some important alterations in the family coat of arms.

The shield had formerly been described as emblazoned with "Three Crosses Patees, with a chevron, and a Mitre for a crest." He now rejected the mitre as being a mark of episcopacy, and assumed for crest a dove with an olive branch in its beak, as more fitting to a man of peace. The chevron he also discarded, it being thought by some to be a mark of cadency (descent of younger sons), though Sir George Mackenzie says in his great work on Heraldry that it was anciently esteemed an ornament only.

The re-arranged coat of arms was then described as " A shield azure, three crosses patées in chief, argent, with Dove and Olive Branch for Crest." In an escrole above, " Cedant arma," and below, " In hac vince."

This alteration in the armorial bearings, however, was never registered with the Lord Lyon, and both crests are used by members of the family.

Robert Barclay interested himself in compiling a record of his ancestors, which, though written during the years we are now reviewing, was not published till 1740, when it was printed by James Chalmer, Printer to the Town and University of Aberdeen. It was entitled,

" *A Genealogical Account of the Barclays of Urie, formerly of Mathers*, extracted from ancient registers and authentick documents, together with

Memoirs of the Life of Colonel David Barclay of Urie, and of his eldest son, the late Robert Barclay of Urie, collected for the Information and Use of their Posterity."

HISTORY OF THE BARCLAY FAMILY

ROBERT
BARCLAY,
1672-1747,
Urie III.

Of the first edition of this book only two copies are known to exist to-day, one in the British Museum, and one in the possession of Lieut.-Col. Hubert F. Barclay, compiler of this History.

A second edition was issued in 1812, with the addition of "Letters that passed between him, The Duke of York, Elizabeth Princess Palatine of the Rhine, Archbishop Sharp, the Earl of Perth, and other Distinguished Characters, containing curious and interesting information never before published." It was printed for the Editor, Mr. Henry Mill, by John Herbert, No. 10 Borough Road, London.

The intention of the author, Robert Barclay (Urie III), has been amply realised, for although the fresh light thrown by modern research has proved him wrong in a few statements, yet his *Genealogical Account* has been invaluable to those of his descendants who have endeavoured to trace the ramifications of the Barclay connections over a period of eight hundred years. The Memoirs of his father and grandfather have been the foundation of all their biographies, and but for his writing, the records of two valuable lives might have been lost to the world.

In 1731 Robert wrote a long letter in connection with his genealogical research to his brother David of Cheapside. He had been working on the family history and stated that he had found " nine distinct Familys of the name of Barclay, none of whom, as I have ever heard, would own themselves to be come of others. Viz : Barclay of Innerkeller, Barclay of Balvaird, Barclay of Pierston, Barclay of Colairnie, Barclay of Kilburnie, Barclay of Brechin, Barclay of Garthie, Barclay of Towie, and lastly Barclay of Urie, formerly Mathers. We being the lineal representatives of that family, our grandfather Colonel David Barclay being the only son of David Barclay the last Laird of Mathers that had any·children. . . For, by a very authentick document, viz. a stated account signed by a public notary, Sherriff's Clerk of the Mearns, I find our grandfather acting as his father's eldest son, heir, and representative, calling his Factors to an account for their

208

Intromissions with the old Estate from the year 1630 untill year
and crop 1650, and receiving as his own the ballance due."

He goes on to say that "five of the nine Familys are now
extinct," leaving Colairnie, Towie and Pierston. " But of
this I am morally sure so far as can be relyed upon authentick
documents that our family of Urie, formerly Mathers, in the
Shire of the Mearns (where never any Gentleman of the
name of Barclay pretended to be or to have been settled except
ourselves, and those who have confessedly come of us) can
boast of this good Fortune, that the male blood of the Barclays
without mixture hath run in our Vains upwards of six hundred
years. Yet of this let us not be so vain as to deserve the lash
of the Satyrist in the universal passion for Satyr,

> By standing for Fame on our father's feet
> And only by Herauldry proved valiant and discreet
> Neither with decent pride to throw our eyes
> Above the Man by their descents less wise
> But rather pass forward in Fame's glorious Chase
> Nor looking backward, and so lose the Race."

By his wife, Elizabeth Braine, Robert Barclay had three
sons and five daughters :

Robert, of whom later.

John, who died young.

David, born April 29th, 1710, died October 10th, 1783. He
married Mary, daughter of John Pardoe of Worcester, by
whom he had issue one daughter Mary, who married
Thomas Wagstaffe and died without issue.

Mollison, who married 1. John Doubleday.
                2. — Strettell.

Elizabeth, known as " Bonnie Betty Barclay," who married Sir
William Ogilvie of Barras.

and three other daughters who died unmarried.

Robert Barclay, third Laird of Urie, died March 27th,
1747, and was succeeded by his eldest son.

III.—EE

ROBERT BARCLAY (ROBERT THE STRONG)

Robert Barclay, the fourth Laird of Urie, known as "Robert the Strong," was born May 20th, 1699. He inherited the physical strength and personal comeliness that had always been characteristic of the Barclays.

The family is described by Alexander Gordon as possessing "a noble physique and fine countenance, strong and active animal spirits, temperament alternating between dashing enterprise and sublime contentment, no corner of the character capable of harbouring a mean thought."

The temperament of the fourth laird perhaps possessed these opposing characteristics in a more marked degree than most of his kindred, and one side of his life contrasts rather oddly with the other.

Following in the steps of his father and grandfather, he was the author of several religious tracts and essays. In 1740 he published a pamphlet upon Faith, "which showed the difference between that which is true and that which is false," a secret that many have wished to know since the days of Pilate. He expressed in it his own joy and happiness in the possession of that Faith, "that he had found alone, being forsaken, by his fellowship therein with that that lived in Dens and Desolate places, and through Death he had found Resurrection and eternal Holy Life."

Yet this pious Quaker gentleman was a "lusty man of his hands" and so celebrated for his feats of bodily strength, and his generosity to those who challenged them, that he was known far and near as "Robert the Strong," and as such is still remembered in tales and legends of that countryside.

The best known story is that while walking in Urie grounds he found a donkey grazing near the roadside. The Laird, who had previously told the tinkers not to graze their animals in the park, promptly threw the cuddy over the wall, 7 to 8 feet high. The tinker thereupon threw the animal back over the wall, and it was again ejected by Robert Barclay. The tinker, who had not seen who put the cuddy out, then called out from the road, "If you are not Barclay, then you are the Deil." What happened to the cuddy is not related; but he took the tinker back to Urie House, and recompensed him handsomely both for his efforts and his loss, saying he had not often met a man able to compete with him in such a feat.

Another story is of a stalwart Highland soldier, called Ian More, or Big John, who had killed a famous English boxer with one blow, and got into disfavour with the military authorities thereby. He elected to cross the park of Urie by a short cut forbidden to trespassers. Confident in his strength, he disregarded this rule, though assured that the Laird was " an awfu' chiel though a Quaker."

Shortly he met Robert Barclay, who told him to turn back, as no one was allowed that way. The soldier good-humouredly refused to retrace his steps, whereupon the Laird, who asked nothing better, challenged him to a wrestling bout, and laid his hands upon his shoulders to enforce his meaning. However, for once he had met his match, and after being twice thrown, he acknowledged that Ian was the better man, and saying " This is the first time, friend, that my back was laid on the grass," he led his opponent to the house, where he fed and entertained him for a fortnight.

He did not succeed his father till 1747, but took an active part in the management of the estate before that date, and is several times referred to in the " Court Book " as " Robert Barclay younger, of Ury."

On July 28th, 1725, in his father's lifetime, he married his cousin Une Cameron, the daughter of Sir Ewen Cameron of Lochiel, the great Chieftain, known as the Black Lochiel. The marriage was conducted after the simple Quaker fashion, as the contract sets forth, " Att Kingwells (the home of the Jaffray family) the twenty eight day of July, XVII^c and twenty fyve years." " It is appointed, contracted, finally ended and agreed upon betwixt Robert Barclay Younger of Ury heretable proprietor of ye landes and other underwritten, eldest lawfull sone to Robert Barclay of Ury procreat between him and Elizabeth Barclay alias Braine his spous, with consent of his said father on the one part, and Mistress Une Camerone, daughter to the deceast Sir Ewen Camerone of Lochiel, procreat betwixt him and umquhill Jean Barclay his spouse on the other part ... and to the effect following that is to say the saids Robert Barclay, younger, and Mrs Une Cameron, are to take and accept one another for their lawfull spouses, and promis to solemnize and compleat the honourable bond of matrimony betwixt (dates) to come and hereafter to treat, love, cherish and entertaine each other, as becometh Christian married persons of their rank and quality during all ye days of their lyftyme. In contemplatione of the which marriage the said Mrs Une Cameron by these presents gives, grants, etc., etc."

It is signed by " R. Barclay Y^{r}, Une Cameron, and R. Barclay, Consenter," with two witnesses, Alex Cadenhead, " Servitor to the within designed Robert Barclay Y^{r}," and John Hunter, Schoolmaster at Kingwells.

It is interesting to note how closely the phrasing of the Quaker contract approaches that of the Church of England marriage service.

In 1745, England and Scotland were profoundly stirred by the attempt of Charles Edward, the grandson of James II, called " The Young Pretender," to attain " three crowns to lay at his father's feet." The incompetence of the " Old Pretender " had disheartened his followers, but his son was a young man of charming appearance and attractive manners, and the smouldering ashes of Jacobitism were fanned into flame. France took up his cause, and sent a fleet from Dunkirk to invade England in 1744, but the ill fate that dogged the Stuarts intervened, and the fleet was wrecked in a terrible storm. However, Charles Edward persevered, though he could only muster enough money to fit out two ships, one of which was disabled by an English cruiser.

On July 25th, 1745, he landed at Loch-nan-Uamh in Inverness-shire, and two important clans, the Camerons, under Sir Donald Cameron of Lochiel, the nephew of Robert Barclay's wife, and the Macdonalds, rallied to his standard. This was followed by a successful capture of two companies of the regular troops, and practically all the clans flocked to join him.

He marched in triumph into Perth, and the campaign was conducted with more spirit than in 1715. " All Jacobites went mad; all doubtful people became Jacobites; all bankrupts became heroes ; and all the fine ladies became passionately fond of the young adventurer," writes Duncan Forbes the historian.

The victory of the Prince's forces at Prestonpans, a result largely due to the gallantry of Lochiel and his clan ; the surrender of Edinburgh, which was achieved by Lochiel with no loss of life ; and Charles Edward's proclamation at the Market Cross there, as James VIII, made him the master of Scotland.

But the prospect was hopeless south of the Tweed, and the overwhelming forces of King George II gathered threateningly round the Scottish army. Charles retired northward, and on April 16th, 1746, the Highlanders stood at bay on Culloden Moor, near Inverness, where they were utterly routed and dispersed with loss of several thousand men. Lochiel was severely wounded, but was rescued by his clansmen and concealed in a cave, until the Young Pretender embarked for France, whither he accompanied him. He was given a regiment in the French service, but died in 1748. His estates were of course forfeited, but were afterwards restored to the family.

The Young Pretender had many romantic adventures before he escaped to France, and after the peace between France and England in 1748 he was expelled by the French. Brokenhearted and unsupported, he became a confirmed drunkard, and soon lost all importance, though after his father's death he called himself King of England.

Strong as must have been the Jacobite enthusiasm of his wife, born a Cameron of Lochiel, the sturdy Laird of Urie was true to his Quaker training, and neither took part on either side nor encouraged his children to do so, though there exists a long list of Scottish Barclays who followed the fortunes of Bonnie Prince Charlie and suffered in many cases for their loyalty.

Robert Barclay lived out his useful and peaceful life, famous

[margin note:] ROBERT BARCLAY, 1699-1760, Urie IV.

ROBERT
BARCLAY,
1699-1760;
Urie IV.

for his strength, but never using it to the hurt or harm of others. He died in 1760, aged sixty-one.

By his wife, Une Cameron, he had four sons and one daughter :—

Robert, who succeeded him.

David, born September 24th, 1737, who, forsaking the Society of Friends, joined the 42nd Highlanders (1st Battalion The Black Watch) and was killed at the taking of Martinique in 1762.

Ewen, or Evan, born October 1st, 1738, died unmarried August 23rd, 1805.

Alexander, died young.

Jean, born March 22nd, 1726, died unmarried in July, 1750.

ROBERT BARCLAY-ALLARDICE, M.P. (Urie V)

By Sir Henry Raeburn

ROBERT BARCLAY-ALLARDICE, M.P.

Robert Barclay fifth Laird of Urie was born on November 17th, 1732. We are told that he also followed the family type and inherited from his father symmetry of form and great muscular power, being over six feet in height and of a handsome presence. His father, the fourth Laird, had not been interested in land-cultivation, and during his lifetime the estates had been allowed to get out of order, but Robert was " a born improver." He had devoted much of his time to the study of agriculture, both in theory and practice, in the best districts of England, and was now able to put his knowledge into operation.

His son, speaking of his father many years later, said : " When he began reclaiming the land the estate of Ury was a complete waste, consisting of baulks and rigs everywhere intersected with cairns of stone and moorland. For twenty years he toiled most indefatigably, and during all that time was never known to be in bed after five o'clock in the morning, winter or summer."

He was the first man who ever sowed a turnip in a field or artificial grasses north of the Firth of Forth. He commenced operations always at the far end, for he used to say " A tired man will struggle hard to reach home." He therefore left the part of the estate nearest to the house to the last, which accounted for the fact that his son when he succeeded complained at first that the place was in the rudest order, but, on taking up his father's task, warmly acknowledged his indebtedness to him.

The fifth Laird not only improved the land but introduced from Norfolk, then the great agricultural school of the Kingdom, both the best implements and a number of Norfolk ploughmen to teach their use.

He brought into a high state of cultivation 2,000 acres, reclaimed 800 from moor and planted 1,200 to 1,500 acres with forest trees. So great was his reputation for his thorough knowledge of agriculture and " the successful manner in which he executed the manifold operations connected with it,"

215

that his practice became the conventional standard over an extensive district, and he, with the Duke of Bedford and Sir Tatton Sykes of Bakewell, were the real founders of British agriculture.

Soon after his father's death in 1760, Robert Barclay bought the property of Arduthie and, by the grants of feu-rights on the estate, laid the foundation of Stonehaven, a well-planned and salubrious town which took the place of the cluster of insanitary old houses and fishermen's cottages which were the old Stonehyve. It contained good streets, churches and banks, and soon had a population of 3,000, which is now nearly doubled.

By unanimous election Robert Barclay represented his native county of Kincardineshire three times in Parliament. It is recorded that so great were his pedestrian powers that he used to walk from Urie to London to take his place in the House of Commons, a distance of 510 miles. On one occasion he accomplished this feat in ten days, and King George III is said to have remarked that he ought to be proud of his Scottish subjects when his Judges (referring to Lord Monboddo) rode on horseback and his Members of Parliament walked.

We learn from a local newspaper of the period that in his Parliamentary life he was distinguished by his loyalty and patriotism and was honoured by the intimate friendship of William Pitt and other great statesmen of the time.

Robert Barclay resembled his forbears in that he was not afraid to express his opinions, as we see by a letter from him to " his constant friend " Sir James Carnegie of Pitcarrow, who but for his attainder would have been 6th Earl of Southesk, in which he gives his views on the legal and medical professions.

He writes, " I had heard that you had been indisposed and mounted my beast next day and came as far as Montrose, not only to enquire after your welfare, but knowing you was upon the point of setting forth for London thought you might want some assistance about any little affairs you had to do in the country." After expressing his agreeable surprise at finding Sir James had already started and he had had his forty mile ride for nothing, Barclay concludes his letter by heartily join- ing in Sir James's prayer that " they might both be delivered from trials, lawyers and doctors, and from having dealings with unreasonable men."

From another letter we learn that Robert Barclay preserved the Quaker tradition in his home life. It was written by his granddaughter, Mrs. Schimmelpennick, and describes a visit which she paid to Urie.

" How delightful to me was the quiet, the spirit of love and order and peace which characterised the household. My grand-father himself presented a striking likeness to William Penn in West's picture of the Treaty with the Indians. He was very cheer-ful, orderly, active acute as a man of business, and most kindly in his consideration and thought for the welfare and happiness of all about him. He gave his charity in a benevolent, considerate and business way, with brotherly kindness he ascertained what would add to the wellbeing of his people, and supplied the want kindly, benificently yet not lavishly, with a completeness that showed his pleasure in giving, yet with an orderly economy.

" He considered himself as a responsible steward, and as his fortune had been the fruit of God's blessing on industry, he desired, remembering the labour of his youth, to reward industry in others, and to make as many hearts as he could light and graceful to God, the Giver, never seeking to fix the eye of the receiver on himself."

Mrs. Schimmelpennick also gives us another intimate detail which is of interest. Though Robert Barclay was only a lad of fourteen at the time of the '45 and his father's Quaker principles did not permit of his taking part in the rising, yet his mother's devotion to the house of Stuart and the heroic adventures of her kinsmen of Lochiel in support of the Young Pretender, must have left a life-long impression on his mind, for his granddaughter tells us that every morning he caused the children to salute the portrait of Prince Charles Edward.

This portrait remained at Urie until 1854, when it passed to Margaret, daughter of the last Laird. It is now in the posses-sion of Lieut. Colonel Hubert F. Barclay.

Robert Barclay (Urie V) was twice married, first to his cousin Lucy, daughter of David Barclay of Cheapside, second son of the Apologist, by whom he had one daughter Lucy,

III.—FF
217

born 1753, who married Samuel Galton of Birmingham, and was the mother of Mrs. Schimmelpennick; and secondly, in 1776, to Sarah Ann, only daughter of James Allardice, heiress of the line of the Earls of Strathearn, Airth and Monteith, when he assumed the name of "Barclay-Allardice" though he seems seldom to have used the double surname. This marriage was dissolved in 1795 and Sarah Ann Allardice married John Nudd, and died in 1833.

By his second wife Robert had eight children, three sons and five daughters:—

Robert, born August 25th, 1779, who succeeded him.

James, born 1784, died 1804 unmarried.

David Stuart, born 1787; joined the same regiment in which his uncle had served at Martinique, the 42nd Highlanders, now 1st Batt. the Black Watch; Lieutenant 1811, Captain 1813, Major of the 28th Foot 1822; died 1826 unmarried.

Anne, born 1777, died young.

Une Cameron, born Sept. 13th, 1778; married John Innes; died 1809.

Margaret, born Oct. 4th, 1780; married Hudson Gurney; died 1855.

Mary, twin with the above, died 1799.

Rodney (a daughter), born April 29th, 1782, died 1853 unmarried.

Robert Barclay, fifth Laird of Urie, died on April 8th, 1797, and was succeeded by his eldest son. His portrait, by Raeburn, is now in the possession of Alexander Barclay-Pierson, of Johnstoun Lodge, Laurencekirk, whose mother was the granddaughter of Une Cameron Barclay, the daughter of Robert Barclay-Allardice, and who married John Innes. There is another portrait at Keswick Hall which may have been taken there by Mrs. Hudson Gurney, his daughter. It is mentioned by Gerard Hudson Gurney in his book *Portraits at Keswick Hall* 1922, and he decides that it is not a copy of the Raeburn and may be by Beechey.

CAPTAIN ROBERT BARCLAY-ALLARDICE (URIE VI)

HISTORY OF THE BARCLAY FAMILY

CAPTAIN ROBERT BARCLAY-ALLARDICE
The Pedestrian

CAPTAIN
ROBERT
BARCLAY-
ALLARDICE,
1779–1854,
Urie VI.

Robert Barclay-Allardice, sixth and last Laird of Urie, was under eighteen years of age when he succeeded to the estates in 1797.

By his father's will he, with his four sisters and two brothers, was placed under the guardianship of no fewer than twelve " curators," six of whom were in Scotland and six in England, namely :

Lord Adam Gordon.
Sir David Ogilvie.
John Durno, advocate in Aberdeen.
James McDonald of Inglismadie.
Joseph Straton of Kirkside.
Ewen Barclay, their uncle.
Samuel Galton, husband of their half-sister, Lucy.
David Barclay of Walthamstow, brother of their father's first wife.
Robert Barclay of Clapham (Bank II).
Robert Barclay, Brewer, of Park Street, Southwark (Bury Hill I).
John Henton Tritton of Lombard Street.
Abel Chapman, merchant, of London.

Cameron, the eldest girl, who had devotedly nursed her father during his last illness, is described as " a worthy and amiable young lady, of excellent principles and judicious conduct." The three younger girls and the two little boys had been placed by their father at schools in England, but Robert and Cameron now wrote to Samuel Galton, the most active of their guardians, saying that they desired that the younger children should return and reside at Urie, where Robert, with great promptitude, had already engaged a tutor with whom to pursue his studies. His guardians, however, decided that he must go to Cambridge, and in accordance with their wishes he entered Trinity College at the end of the October following, from whence he wrote describing his purple gown, " like a beadle in a procession," and his cap with a silver tassel.

The immediate future of the younger girls was the subject

Captain
Robert
Barclay-
Allardice,
1779-1854,
Urie VI. of much anxious correspondence between Lucy Galton and her uncle, David Barclay of Walthamstow. Owing to lack of funds, for reasons presently to be shown, strict economy was necessary, and it was agreed to place them under the " vigilant eye of an able supervisor " in rooms at Moseley, near Birmingham, and the home of the Galtons.

David Barclay of Walthamstow busied himself in finding a suitable person, and " E. Crook " was interviewed by him, made to read portions of prose and verse aloud, and engaged as governess " to superintend the educational and domestic affairs " of his three orphan nieces, at a salary of £50 a year. The old gentleman wrote somewhat racily, describing her as not outwardly attractive, " bearing all the marks of an advanced damsell," but trustworthy, and he had been to the pains of taking places for her and her charges on the Oxford coach, by which they were to proceed to Birmingham.

He was concerned about the health of Mary and Rodney, who had been staying with him at Walthamstow. " Mary looks dismally . . . and Rodney likewise pale and delicate." He advised exercise for them, and recommended that they should make their own beds and do some of the house work, which would also save a second maidservant. He went so far as to despatch a bed, with white dimity hangings, and a mahogany pembroke table as a contribution to their furnishing.

One may well imagine that the poor girls had been unhappy at school and pined for the freedom of their home at Urie. Mary's health did not improve, and she died in the following June.

Robert Barclay (Bury Hill I) and John Henton Tritton were also concerned for the welfare of their wards, but we read that Mr. Abel Chapman was excused from attending to his duties as guardian, as he was seriously occupied in fitting out his " Indian in the Thames " as the Government required troops to be despatched expeditiously. These were the days of the French menace in India and Wellesley's campaign against Tippoo Sultan.

Meanwhile the guardians in Scotland were facing a difficult task. The property was in an excellent state of cultivation, but portions of it were heavily mortgaged, and there was a vast load of debt to be met.

John Durno wrote to Samuel Galton on April 24th, 1779, mentioning debts which he believed to be considerable, and continued :

> " The Land Estates consist of Ury which is entailed, and of Redcloak, Arduthie and Findlaston adjacent and unentailed As also Allardice, Hallgreen and Kinghornie with the command of the Borough of Bervie likewise unentailed. The whole land estates at present yield from £3,400 to £3,500 of yearly rent, and in a year hence when many leases expire will certainly rise to £4000. . . . If possible I declare myself anxious to preserve all the lands. They are in better management than any other lands in Scotland, and if Mr. Barclay's Plan is carried on, will rise very much in their value."

Mr. Durno was, however, too optimistic in his estimate, and finally the Trustees were forced to sell Hallgreen, Kinghornie and Dava, " a part of Allardice," to meet the demands of the creditors. They were united in their decision that " Mr. Barclay's Plan " for the cultivation of the estates, which is frequently mentioned, must be adhered to.

Robert's tutor at Trinity reported well of him, saying : " I am charmed with his disposition and think well of his understanding, his sense is solid and he is fond of good conversation," but the young man himself was not so favourably impressed with university life. He soon left Cambridge and went to live at Urie, where he engaged in the athletic pursuits in which he later became so celebrated.

He had always shown an aptitude for manly sports, and had no doubt been trained by his father, for at the age of seventeen he had won a match for £100, walking six miles within the hour, heel and toe. Two years later he walked seventy miles in fourteen hours on the Croydon Road, beating his opponent by several hours.

He kept a pack of hounds at Urie and took a keen interest in sport of all kinds, as well as the cultivation of his estate, until 1805, when he put it under good management and went into the Army, obtaining a commission in the 23rd Regiment, now the Royal Welsh Fusiliers, serving under Lord Cathcart.

CAPTAIN ROBERT BARCLAY-ALLARDICE, 1779–1854, Urie VI.

" Galton Letters."

221

CAPTAIN
ROBERT
BARCLAY
ALLARDICE,
1779–1854,
Urie VI.

He was promoted Captain and was A.D.C. to Lieutenant-General the (5th) Marquis of Huntly in the Walcheren Expedition in 1809.

The Walcheren Expedition was intended to make a diversion in Northern Germany in favour of the Russians and Austrians, in pursuance of the policy of checking the advance of Napoleon on the Low Countries, but it was mismanaged and utterly failed, and Captain Barclay-Allardice returned home.

He then commanded the local Militia in Kincardineshire, and brought it into a high state of discipline.

His extraordinary strength and endurance in walking won him the title of " The Pedestrian," and he established records that have never been beaten, pre-eminent among which was his feat of walking 1,000 miles in 1,000 hours (one mile in each hour) for a wager of £1,000. This he accomplished in 1809, five days before he set off for Walcheren.

He had not even gone into regular training, and pursued a different system from the only other pedestrian who attempted the task, but nearly died in its fulfilment. This was Richard Hanks, a native of Warwickshire, who performed 1,000 miles in as many hours at Sheffield, in 1850, commencing each mile at the beginning of each hour, whereas Captain Barclay's wager was to walk each mile within each hour, and this permitted him to walk two miles consecutively, and to sleep about an hour and a half at a time. At the end the Captain was doing one mile in twenty minutes, while Hanks took nearly the hour, slept as he walked, or was forcibly kept awake by bodily suffering.

Robert started, on a measured mile on Newmarket Heath, at midnight on June 1st and finished his task on July 12th, about three in the afternoon, among a great crowd of excited spectators, having taken 42 days. No other pedestrian has succeeded in the attempt, but all have given in after 15, 22 or 30 days, from over fatigue. He did not achieve it without

" Pedestrian-
ism," by
Walter
Thom.

pain, for at the end he was so stiff after resting that he had to be lifted to his feet, but after seventeen hours' sleep he had completely recovered. About £100,000 depended on the

CAPTAIN ROBERT BARCLAY-ALLARDICE (Urie VI)
(*The Pedestrian*)

match, which roused much popular enthusiasm and established his fame.

Another of his walks was from Urie to Borough Bridge, in Yorkshire, a distance of 300 miles, in five oppressively hot days.

A match for 5,000 guineas to perform 90 miles in 21½ hours excited great attention. In the preliminary trial he walked 110 miles at a rate equal to 135 miles in 24 hours, on the road from Brechin to Forfar. He gained the 5,000 guineas prize on November 10th, 1801, by an hour and eight minutes.

On another occasion he started from Urie at midnight, walked to Ellon, in Aberdeenshire, where he breakfasted, and returned to Urie by midday. Again he walked from Urie to the house of Dr. Grant at Kirkmichael, a distance of 80 miles; he remained there a day and a night, without going to bed, and walked back home by dinner on the third day, returning by way of Crathynaird, a detour which lengthened his journey by 20 miles. The distance altogether was 180 miles, over bad roads, through the hilly country of Aberdeenshire. Another time he walked 100 miles in 19 hours, and in December, 1806, over one of the worst roads in the kingdom, from Urie to Crathynaird, where he stayed only 50 minutes and walked home. The distance was 28 miles each way, and the time taken, inclusive of stoppages, was 17½ hours, a nett average of 5¾ miles an hour. On this walk he was accompanied by his servant William Cross, who was himself no mean pedestrian.

The Captain once walked from London to Birmingham, round by Cambridge, accomplishing 150 miles in two days, and a few days later returned in the same time by Oxford.

His staying powers were no less remarkable, for in 1807 he covered 78 miles in 14 hours, leaving Urie at 2 a.m., attended a cattle sale 4 miles beyond the Boat of Forbes, where he stayed 5 hours, walking several miles in the fields, and returned home by 9 at night.

The next year (1808) he performed an even more laborious feat. Having gone to Colonel Murray Farquharson's house of Allanmore, in Aberdeenshire, he went out grouse-shooting

CAPTAIN
ROBERT
BARCLAY-
ALLARDICE,
1779–1854,
Urie VI.

" Pedestrian-
ism," p. 114.

Captain
Robert
Barclay-
Allardice,
1779-1854,
Urie VI.

at 5 a.m., and tramped at least 30 miles on the mountains. He dined in the afternoon, and in the evening set off for Urie, a distance of 60 miles, which he walked in 11 hours without stopping. At Urie he attended to his ordinary business and walked 11 miles to Laurencekirk in the afternoon, where he danced at a ball all night, and returned home by seven in the morning. Even then he did not go to bed, but spent the day partridge-shooting in the fields. He had not slept or been in bed for two nights and nearly three days.

He was excessively independent and unconventional in his training, and ate beefsteaks, mutton chops, roast fowls and drank porter and wine on his most strenuous expeditions, but during his 1,000 mile walk he is said to have lost two stone in weight notwithstanding this diet.

His walks caused great excitement, and every house, vehicle and bed for miles round used to be engaged by the crowds who came to watch him.

Not only was he an incomparable pedestrian, but he possessed remarkable fleetness of foot, and easily defeated Mr. John Ward, one of the fastest runners in England, over 440 yards in Hyde Park, his time being 56 seconds. While stationed at Eastbourne with his regiment, he ran two miles in twelve minutes, and one mile in five minutes and seven seconds. He won every match he engaged in, until people left off challenging such a champion.

By the wonderful development of the muscles of his arms he performed astonishing feats of strength. In 1806 he offered a bet that he could lift half a ton from the ground, which he did by procuring a number of weights ascertained to be 21 half-hundredweights, or half a hundredweight over half a ton. He fastened them together with a rope and lifted them clear of the ground. Afterwards with a straight arm he threw a half-hundredweight a distance of eight yards, and put the same weight over his head a distance of five yards.

His most extraordinary achievement was said to be that he lifted Captain Keith of the 23rd Regiment, who weighed eighteen stone, upon his right hand and, steadied by his left, he raised him and set him on a table.

HISTORY OF THE BARCLAY FAMILY

Another of Captain Barclay-Allardice's sporting tastes was his fondness for driving four-in-hand. He often took the reins of the " Defiance " coach which became known as the best appointed four-horse coach in Scotland. A silver bowl, now at Bury Hill, bears the following inscription :—

" Presented by a few well-wishers, this first of July, 1835,
To Robert Barclay-Allardice, Esq.
of Ury, as a mark of public approbation for his splendid exertions in having along with his Partner established between Edinburgh and Aberdeen the Best, Safest and Fastest Public Conveyance of the day, The Defiance Coach."

He drove the Holyhead Mail right through to London, " an unprecedented performance."

He was, as might be expected, an ardent patron of pugilism, then in the height of its popularity, and many of the leading professors of " the Fancy " were trained at Urie. Among them was the great Tom Cribb, who was prepared there for his famous battle with Black Molyneaux, which resulted in Cribb's victory, in 1811. He used to take the men for long tramps in the Highlands, which gave them tolerably severe exercise in keeping up with him. He also trained Alexander Mackay, a Badenoch man, to fight Simon Byrne for the championship, but the fight had a fatal termination, for Byrne killed Mackay with a heavy blow. The story that the Captain challenged Byrne and defeated him is not authenticated.

He was able to hold his own in that as in any other field, for, when a professional pugilist called Fuller gave an exhibition in the Salutation Hotel at Perth and challenged his audience to produce an antagonist on whom to display his powers, Robert took up the gage, and with his superior science soon worsted the prizefighter, who had to acknowledge that he was no match for his renowned opponent.

As Captain Barclay grew older and gave up pedestrianism, pugilism and his other active pursuits, he devoted much time and money to the improvement of the breeding of cattle and sheep, and the annual sale at Urie was for many years the meeting place of the most eminent agriculturalists from all parts of

CAPTAIN
ROBERT
BARCLAY-
ALLARDICE,
1779–1854,
Urie VI.

the kingdom. In 1838 a public dinner was given to him by about two hundred of the gentry and farmers of the Mearns and adjoining counties, where his splendid services to the country were acknowledged. He was honoured as a landowner, as a farmer and as an agriculturalist who had helped to raise Scotland to be the best cultivated country in the world, and above all as a breeder of live stock. " Regardless of expense, he had introduced into the country a breed of cattle, which was unmatched in Scotland, unsurpassable elsewhere. By crossing the short-horned or Durham breed with the breed of the country he had greatly improved upon both and had widely disseminated a most splendid breed of cattle."

In his reply Captain Barclay-Allardice spoke warmly and affectionately of his father, who he held was a " heaven-born improver," and told the story of how, as a young man, he had carried on his back all the way from Aberdeen a bundle of young plants, which he planted in the Den of Urie in spite of the remonstrances of his father (Urie IV), who protested that the " protecting of the plants annoyed the people's sheep."

In the Council Room of the Shorthorn Society there hangs a print of Captain Barclay-Allardice, from the portrait now at Bury Hill, and references to his stock appear in many of the pedigrees of important shorthorns to the present day.

There is much information in Sinclair's *History of Improved Shorthorn Cattle* which will be of interest to cattle-breeders. A detailed account is given of the formation of the herd at Urie.

Direct descendants of the Captain's best cow, " Lady Sarah," are now in the Bury Hill herd.

Sales were held at Urie at various times, after which Captain Barclay entertained the buyers at dinner, followed by whisky punch. It was a habit of his to lock the dining-room door at this stage, so that his guests could not leave early, relays of hot water being handed in through the hatch . . . It frequently happened that they had to find beds where they could at Urie.

226

HISTORY OF THE BARCLAY FAMILY

Many stories are told of him, one being that once, when he was walking, he was overtaken by a cart. The driver, who could not have recognised him, offered him a lift. His reply was, " Do you think I would ? " The driver seems to have made fun of him and driven on, but was overtaken by the Captain on a long hill and challenged to a fight, in which the driver did not get the best of it.

"The Walker," as he was called in the family, used to dine at Bury Hill, the seat ,of his cousin Charles Barclay (Bury Hill II) and thought nothing of walking out from London, a distance of 25 miles, and back again after dinner.

He had something of the Haroun el Raschid disposition, and used to dress up as a tramp or tinker and visit his tenants. According to their conduct to him they found themselves strictly or liberally dealt with later on.

In the year 1841 he paid a visit to the United States and Upper Canada, and published an account of it in the following year. He says in his preface,

" From habitual pursuits, the writer in his visit to the other side of the Atlantic would most probably find his attention peculiarly attracted by agricultural matters. But having been asked to assist a near relative to determine whether an intended purchase of land should be made in the United States or Upper Canada, he was still the more particularly induced to enquire into the situation of rural affairs in those countries."

He consequently made careful investigations and noted those more prominent and important points which appeared sufficient to convey a general view of Transatlantic agriculture.

He gave considered advice on the breeding and crossing of cattle, and spoke of his own experience, which must have been of the greatest value to his listeners. He goes on to mention wages, which were about three shillings a day, with board and lodging to labourers, the hours from sunrise to sunset, and the average rate for mowing wheat or red clover two to three acres per day.

Labour was plentiful, and he said with an improved breed

227

CAPTAIN
ROBERT
BARCLAY-
ALLARDICE,
1779-1854,
Urie VI.
of stock and a better system of husbandry the land could double or treble its value.

The inns were comfortable and the people " sedulous in attention."

He brought letters of introduction to several families, chiefly of the Society of Friends, and, as the lineal descendant of the " Apologist," was welcomed with enthusiastic kindness and hospitality. He said that while staying with Friend T. P. Cope, a leading merchant in Philadelphia, his hostess dressed more in the primitive simplicity of the Quakers than any one he had yet seen, and " evinces much of the kindness and affability peculiar to females of that persuasion."

Philadelphia was a city of special interest for Robert, with his ancestral connections, and he says: "Philadelphia, the metropolis of Pennsylvania, a country which only two hundred years ago—a short space in the history of nations—was in its forest state taken possession of by Europeans. Not by the force of war, but by peaceful negotiation and agreement with the indigenous inhabitants, now appears one of the fairest portions of the earth, rich in everything that pertains to civilized life, and for nothing more remarkable than its many benevolent institutions, proclaiming the philanthropy of its founder, William Penn, and in its neatness, order and decorum owning the influence of that excellent Society of Friends."

On Saturday, July 17th, 1841, he embarked for England, and arrived at Liverpool on July 29th, making a record passage of twelve days from Boston, and only nine days from Halifax. On taking leave, the captain of the ship addressed Captain Barclay-Allardice, jocosely, in these words : " You have now crossed the Atlantic in shorter time than ever it was crossed since the Atlantic was the Atlantic—and you can tack that to the rest of your feats."

Captain Barclay-Allardice did not make any more contributions to literature, as a chapter on " Training," which he wrote for a work on *Manly Sports*, and a few newspaper articles made up the sum of his writings. Though chiefly

228

concerned with farming and athletics, he was no mean classical scholar and had a considerable knowledge of good literature.

An excellent description of this Laird of Urie was written by Mr. Thomas F. Jamieson, LL.D., of Ellon, in Aberdeenshire, who tells us :—

" Barclay, whose appearance I well remember, was a man of medium height, and somewhat over it ; not very square or wide in his shoulders, but with powerful limbs and a body rather round than broadly built. He usually wore knee breeches and top boots, a green coat with gilt buttons and a black beaver hat, which was often decidedly shabby and weatherbeaten, for the Captain didn't carry an umbrella. His countenance was heavy, voice deep, speech slow and deliberate ; he walked with a composed and measured step, his whole bearing and carriage indicating the athletic type of the man."

" Sinclair's History of Shorthorn Cattle."

At the end of April, 1854, he received a kick from a horse, from which he never recovered, and died on the 1st of May. He was buried in the family burying place, called the " Howff," at Urie, where a marble tablet records his life-work.

Robert Barclay-Allardice married in September, 1815, Mary Dalgarno, daughter of Alexander Dalgarno, a merchant in Aberdeen. She died August 30th, 1820, and by her he had issue, besides a younger daughter who died in infancy, a daughter Margaret, born July 4th, 1816. It may be understood that her father's sporting interests made the home at Urie no place for the sound upbringing of a young girl. In spite of the efforts of her aunt, Mrs. Hudson Gurney, to inculcate discipline, Margaret Barclay grew up uncontrolled, and in April, 1840, she eloped with Samuel Ritchie, a sergeant in her father's regiment. He died September 17th, 1845, leaving issue three sons and one daughter. After the death of her father in 1854, Margaret adopted by Deed Poll the name of Barclay-Allardice for herself and her children. Her eldest son, Robert Barclay-Allardice, lived at Lostwithiel and was Mayor of that town. Another son, David Stuart Barclay-Allardice, is living to-day at Providence, R.I., and

CAPTAIN
ROBERT
BARCLAY-
ALLARDICE,
1779–1854,
Urie VI.

has issue. Margaret married, secondly, on July 30th, 1854, James Tanner, a printer in New York, by whom she had one daughter. Margaret Barclay-Allardice died August 7th, 1903.

Captain Barclay-Allardice, sixth and last Laird of Urie, made an attempt to revive the titles of the Earldoms of Strathearn, Airth and Monteith, to which his mother, Sarah Ann Allardice, had a strong claim on the distaff side. She was great-granddaughter of the last Earl of Airth and Monteith, who was descended from David, Earl of Strathearn, eldest son of Robert II by his Queen Euphemia, daughter of the Earl of Ross. Captain Barclay was himself seventeenth in lineal succession from that monarch, but in the legal proceedings he failed to establish his claim, though it was passed by the House of Lords.

It is believed that mortification at his daughter's marriage caused Captain Barclay to forgo any further proceedings. The claim was unsuccessfully revived by Margaret's eldest son, Mr. Robert Barclay-Allardice, some years later.

For nearly two hundred years Urie had remained in the possession of the direct male line of the Barclay family, and it was believed by Charles Barclay (Bury Hill II) to be entailed on the heirs male, but we learn from a letter of Lydia Ann, daughter of Robert Barclay of Clapham (Bank II), that in 1848, when she visited Urie, the matter of selling the place was already in the Laird's mind. Two documents in his own handwriting, found at Urie and now at Bury Hill, prove that he had obtained, as early as 1820, opinions from two learned judges to the effect that he had the power to leave the property to his daughter without being liable in damages to the heirs of entail. At his death he left it to Margaret, but his debts were so enormous that everything had to be sold to satisfy his creditors. The estate was purchased by Alexander Baird of Gartsherrie, whose great-nephew, the first Baron Stonehaven of Urie, is the present proprietor.

Part II, p. 1.

Urie thus followed the fate of Gartley and Mathers, and the senior direct line, descended from the traditional John

230

HISTORY OF THE BARCLAY FAMILY

de Berchlai of Gloucestershire, ceased to hold lands in Scotland.

All the vast properties formerly in the possession of the family, Gartley, Towie, Collairnie, Mathers, Urie and Pierston, have now passed into other hands, and to-day not an acre is held in Scotland by any of the main branches of the Barclay family.

On the death of Captain Robert Barclay-Allardice in 1854, the representation of the family passed to Charles Barclay of Bury Hill, great-grandson of David Barclay of Cheapside, second son of the Apologist, who became " Chief of Mathers and Urie."

Upon the death of the last Laird of Urie, his brother-in-law, Hudson Gurney, and Arthur Kett, eldest son of Charles Barclay (Bury Hill II), went to Urie to settle his affairs, which were in great disorder.

A certain number of old family records, including two charters under the Great Seal of Scotland and the original grant of Mathers in 1351, were brought away. Certain possessions went to his daughter, Margaret Tanner, some of which have now returned to Bury Hill ; but many documents, or what remained of them, which would have been of supreme interest, were undoubtedly lost to the family.

John Barclay, son of Robert Barclay of Clapham (Bank II) in his *Diary of Alexander Jaffray*, states how, in the autumn of 1827, he visited Urie enquiring for records relating to the early days of the Society of Friends. He speaks of manuscripts " to all appearance much neglected " lying in a corner of the Apologist's study, from among which he retrieved a portion of Jaffray's Diary " much injured by time and in parts wholly unintelligible." Patient search, however, revealed other manuscript in the same handwriting " leaf by leaf in a very tattered condition, in the loft of a farmhouse, not far from the old mansion, among heaps of waste paper."

It may well be imagined of what absorbing interest the documents included in those " heaps of waste paper " would have been to future generations.

Before saying farewell to the old House of Urie one more

231

CAPTAIN
ROBERT
BARCLAY-
ALLARDICE,
1779–1854,
Urie VI.

story remains to be related. The reader may form his own judgment on its authenticity. It is to be found in *John Wigham Richardson*, 1911, pp. 37, 38, under date 1849.

"Lindley Murray Hoag, when he visited Aberdeen, expressed a wish to visit Ury, and Captain Barclay hospitably invited him to stop there and sleep on his return journey to the South, adding that by so doing he would see the place both by daylight and by candlelight. It was a raw afternoon in October when Hoag started and by the time the conveyance reached Ury he felt himself thoroughly chilled, and requested to be allowed to go straight to his room and have a basin of gruel in bed. The next morning, at breakfast, they were standing as people do before the fire, when Hoag, looking at an old portrait of the soldier who fought ' ankel deep in Lutzen's blood,' remarked, ' Ah, there is my friend of last night.'

" ' Not quite,' said Miss Barclay. ' That is an ancestor of ours who has been dead nearly two hundred years.'

" ' Oh,' said Hoag, ' he looks like the old gentleman who came into my room last night.'

" At this juncture breakfast was served, and Captain Barclay seemed in deep thought. At last he said, ' Will you please tell me, Mr. Hoag, who it was that came into your room last night and what he was doing there ? '

" ' Well,' replied Hoag, ' I was just going off to sleep when there was a knock at the door and a sweet old gentleman very like that portrait came into the room, and he apologised for disturbing me. He then went round to the foot of the bed and opened a cupboard in the wall at the other side, taking out some old papers which looked like parchments."

" ' Did ye ever hear the like o' that ! ' exclaimed both the Barclays. ' Why, there is no cupboard there.'

Captain Barclay remained thinking, and when breakfast was over he said, ' Mr. Hoag, will you please do me the favour of showing me exactly where the old gentleman found the papers ? '

" They all three went upstairs, and sure enough there was no appearance of any cupboard, but the wall sounded hollow. Barclay tore off the paper and found some wooden boarding. This he broke off with the poker, and an iron door was laid bare. He tried fruitlessly to open this and then sent for a blacksmith, who found and opened a safe door . . . and in the safe were the missing deeds.

" Miss Barclay ever after used to speak of entertaining angels unawares whenever she related the circumstances of Lindley Murray Hoag's visit to Ury."

From this incident it would seem that a portrait of Colonel David existed in 1849, but it has never been traced and there is no other record of it.

The Miss Barclay mentioned can only have been Captain Barclay's sister Rodney.

CAPTAIN
ROBERT
BARCLAY-
ALLARDICE,
1779-1854,
Urie VI.

The name URIE or URY is variously spelt in contemporary records. The compilers of this History have adhered to the former spelling because that was employed by Robert Barclay (Urie III), author of *Genealogical Account of the Barclays of Urie* (1740).

PEDIGREE II.

The Barclays of Bury Hill

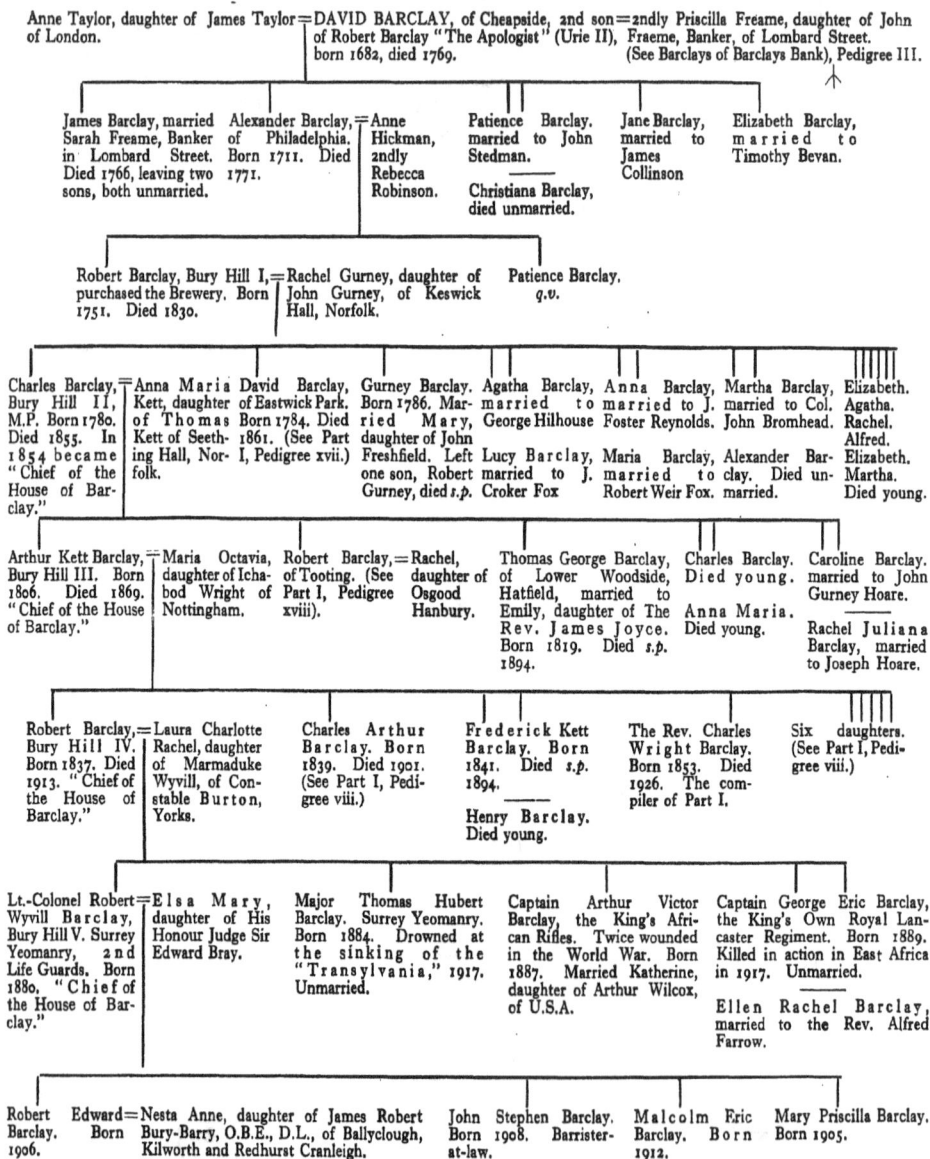

Anne Taylor, daughter of James Taylor = DAVID BARCLAY, of Cheapside, 2nd son = 2ndly Priscilla Freame, daughter of John
of London. of Robert Barclay "The Apologist" (Urie II), Freame, Banker, of Lombard Street.
born 1682, died 1769. (See Barclays of Barclays Bank), Pedigree III.

James Barclay, married | Alexander Barclay, = Anne | Patience Barclay, | Jane Barclay, | Elizabeth Barclay,
Sarah Freame, Banker | of Philadelphia. Hickman, | married to John | married to | m a r r i e d t o
in Lombard Street. | Born 1711. Died 2ndly | Stedman. | James | Timothy Bevan.
Died 1766, leaving two | 1771. Rebecca | ——— | Collinson
sons, both unmarried. | Robinson. | Christiana Barclay,
 | | died unmarried.

Robert Barclay, Bury Hill I, = Rachel Gurney, daughter of | Patience Barclay,
purchased the Brewery. Born | John Gurney, of Keswick | q.v.
1751. Died 1830. | Hall, Norfolk.

Charles Barclay, = Anna Maria | David Barclay, | Gurney Barclay. | Agatha Barclay, | Anna Barclay, | Martha Barclay, | Elizabeth.
Bury Hill II, | Kett, daughter | of Eastwick Park. | Born 1786. Mar- | married to | married to J. | married to Col. | Agatha.
M.P. Born 1780. | of Thomas | Born 1784. Died | ried Mary, | George Hilhouse | Foster Reynolds. | John Bromhead. | Rachel.
Died 1855. In | Kett of Seeth- | 1861. (See Part | daughter of John | ——— | ——— | ——— | Alfred.
1854 became | ing Hall, Nor- | I, Pedigree xvii.) | Freshfield. Left | Lucy Barclay, | Maria Barclay, | Alexander Bar- | Elizabeth.
"Chief of the | folk. | | one son, Robert | married to J. | married to | clay. Died un- | Martha.
House of Bar- | | | Gurney, died s.p. | Croker Fox. | Robert Weir Fox. | married. | Died young.
clay."

Arthur Kett Barclay, = Maria Octavia, | Robert Barclay, = Rachel, | Thomas George Barclay, | Charles Barclay. | Caroline Barclay.
Bury Hill III. Born | daughter of Icha- | of Tooting. (See | daughter of | of Lower Woodside, | Died young. | married to John
1806. Died 1869. | bod Wright of | Part I, Pedigree | Osgood | Hatfield, married to | ——— | Gurney Hoare.
"Chief of the House | Nottingham. | xviii). | Hanbury. | Emily, daughter of The | Anna Maria. | ———
of Barclay." | | | | Rev. James Joyce. | Died young. | Rachel Juliana
 | | | | Born 1819. Died s.p. | | Barclay, married
 | | | | 1894. | | to Joseph Hoare.

Robert Barclay, = Laura Charlotte | Charles Arthur | Frederick Kett | The Rev. Charles | Six daughters.
Bury Hill IV. | Rachel, daughter | Barclay. Born | Barclay. Born | Wright Barclay. | (See Part I, Pedi-
Born 1837. Died | of Marmaduke | 1839. Died 1901. | 1841. Died s.p. | Born 1853. Died | gree viii.)
1913. "Chief of | Wyvill, of Con- | (See Part I, Pedi- | 1894. | 1926. The com-
the House of | stable Burton, | gree viii.) | ——— | piler of Part I.
Barclay." | Yorks. | | Henry Barclay.
 | | | Died young.

Lt.-Colonel Robert = Elsa Mary, | Major Thomas Hubert | Captain Arthur Victor | Captain George Eric Barclay,
Wyvill Barclay, | daughter of His | Barclay. Surrey Yeomanry. | Barclay, the King's Afri- | the King's Own Royal Lan-
Bury Hill V. Surrey | Honour Judge Sir | Born 1884. Drowned at | can Rifles. Twice wounded | caster Regiment. Born 1889.
Yeomanry, 2nd | Edward Bray. | the sinking of the | in the World War. Born | Killed in action in East Africa
Life Guards. Born | | "Transylvania," 1917. | 1887. Married Katherine, | in 1917. Unmarried.
1880. "Chief of | | Unmarried. | daughter of Arthur Wilcox, | ———
the House of Bar- | | | of U.S.A. | Ellen Rachel Barclay,
clay." | | | | married to the Rev. Alfred
 | | | | Farrow.

Robert | Edward = Nesta Anne, daughter of James Robert | John Stephen Barclay. | Malcolm Eric | Mary Priscilla Barclay.
Barclay. | Born Bury-Barry, O.B.E., D.L., of Ballyclough, | Born 1908. Barrister- | Barclay. Born | Born 1905.
1906. | Kilworth and Redhurst Cranleigh. | at-law. | 1912.

DAVID BARCLAY OF CHEAPSIDE

On the death of Captain Robert Barclay-Allardice, without male issue, in 1854, and the consequent failure of the direct line in Scotland, we come south to find the " Chief " of the House of Mathers and Urie in the person of Charles Barclay of Bury Hill (II), the lineal descendant of David Barclay, second son of Robert Barclay, the Apologist.

David Barclay, later known as " of Cheapside," was born at Urie in 1682 and left home when quite a young man, having received the portion of a younger son, amounting to 9000 merks Scots, equivalent to about £500 sterling. He went to London, where he bound himself apprentice to James Taylor, Citizen and Glover, whose daughter Anne he married in 1709. He was associated with his father-in-law in business and became an opulent export merchant.

He joined the Drapers' Company as an assistant in 1729 : was fined £40 for declining to serve as Warden in 1746, and again, in 1756, he paid £20 to be excused serving as Master.

David Barclay lived in one of the finest houses in the City, opposite to the Church of St. Mary-le-Bow in Cheapside.

After the Great Fire of London had devastated the City in 1666, a wealthy mercer, Sir Edward Waldo, had purchased three sites and erected upon them " a great Messuage " known by the Sign of the Bear. Owing to the situation the building commanded an excellent view of the Lord Mayor's procession, and thither in 1671 had come King Charles II and his suite to see the " Show," the first held after the Fire, " setting themselves in a Balcony under a canopy of State."

Subsequent crowned heads also visited the house on the same errand : William and Mary in 1689 ; Queen Anne in 1708 ; and George III and his Queen in 1761, when David Barclay was their host, as we shall presently relate. Tradition tells of a similar visit by George II during the occupancy of David Barclay, but of this no record has been found.

The mansion contained " Warehouse, Counting-houses,

DAVID
BARCLAY OF
CHEAPSIDE,
1682–1769,
Urie IIIb.
parlour and Kitchen on the ground floor, with a large Draw-ing-room and Balcony above." This fine apartment, where the royal guests were entertained, was embellished with beautiful oak panelling and elaborate carving now attributed to Grinling Gibbons. It is interesting to find a reference to this in *The Times* of June 10th, 1861, when

> " A fine old oak panelling of a large diningroom with chimney-piece and cornice to correspond, elaborately carved in fruit and foliage, in excellent preservation, 750 feet superficial, from 107 and 108 Cheapside, London, immediately opposite Bow Church,"

Reminis-
cences
connected
with Old Oak
Panelling,
M. C. Jones.
was offered for sale, and after brisk bidding was knocked down to Mr. C. Jones of Gungrog, Welshpool, North Wales.

An amusing account of the visit of George III to David Barclay in 1761 has been preserved in a letter from John Freame junior, brother of David Barclay's second wife, to his sister Mrs. Mary Plumstead, dated Christmas Day, 1761.

He begins by apologising for touching upon " the stale un-pleasing topick " of the bad times, and goes on to describe " how matters were concluded at Cheapside on the late im-portant day." He says :—

> " that Brother Barclay spared no expense in repairing his house both inside and out, as well as decorating it in a suitable manner for the reception of the Royal Family, and that Lord Bruce came several times to teach them their duty and to give directions about the apartments and furniture (all very grand). But the head of the house was firm on the matter of their costume, and insisted that the family should be dressed as " Plain Friends." This instruction, he says, " was an exciting time to several of them," but they had to comply, and when the sons were dressed in plain cloth, and the daughters in plain silks, with dressed black hoods, he admits that " on the whole they made a genteel appearance, and acted their part in the masquerade very well." So that the Testimony of the Apology appeared to be maintained.

The King was most gracious, and asked to have the family presented to him, and they were permitted to have the honour to kiss his hand without kneeling (an instance of such condescention as never was known before.)

After the introductions, during which His Majesty saluted my sister (Mrs. David Barclay) and the girles, he same honour was conferred on them by the Queen, and others of the Royal Family. A copy of the Apology was then presented to the King, after which he discoursed familiarly with his host, Sister Barclay being quite spent with the fatigue of the day, and having begged the favour of the Queen to dispense with her further attendances.

In the interval the Queen with others of the Family refreshed themselves with the repast provided for them in the back parlour and the kitchen, which was elegantly set off for the occasion, and it being I suppose a great Novelty to them, were delighted with the Entertainment.

On the King going away, he thanked Brother Barclay for his entertainment, and politely excused (as he was pleased to say) the trouble they had given. This condescention (I am told) so affected the old man that he not only made a suitable return to the compliment, but, (like the good patriarche of old) prayed that God would please to bless him and all his family, which was received by him with great goodness.

So of course, (in my estimation) things in general must have been well conducted."

This letter shows us that the Royal Visit was long expected and carefully prepared for, and disproves a widely circulated story which declares it accidental, and relates how the King and Queen were one day driving down Cheapside when the horses took fright and were stopped by David Barclay, who said, " Friend George, wilt thou not bring thy wife Charlotte into my house to recover from her alarm ? "—which would certainly have been quite unpremeditated.

Another tale sounds more like the sturdy independence of the old Quaker. King George is reported to have offered him preferment at Court for his son, but David declined it, saying that he intended to bring him up in honest trade.

This is probably more correctly described by Mr. M. C. Jones, who says in his short account of David Barclay :—

" Then he somewhat reluctantly attended at Court to pay his respects, the King shook him warmly by the hand, and asked him what he intended to do with his son, probably John, adding ' Let him come here, and I will provide him with profitable and honourable employment.' But the honest Quaker replied cautiously

237

that he feared the air of the Court might not agree with his son. So George showed no offence, and said, ' Well David, you know best—you know best,' and John was established in the sound business of John Freame, goldsmith, which afterwards became Barclay's Bank."

There is another amusing letter, believed to have been written by one of David's daughters. In it she expresses her admiration and approval of the splendour surrounding Royalty, in spite of the simplicity and strictness of her up-bringing. She is " in raptures, not only from the brilliancy of her (the Queen's) appearance," but by " that inexpressible something that is beyond a set of features . . . she is vastly genteel, with an air . . . truly majestic. Her hair, which is of light colour, being in what is called Coronation ringlets, has a circle of diamonds. Her clothes, which were as rich as gold and silver and silk could make them, were a suit from which fell a train supported by a little page in scarlet and silver. The lustre of her stomacher was inconceivable . . . on which was represented, by the vast profusion of diamonds placed on it, the magnificence attending so great a Prince— who, I must tell you, I think a fine personable man. I doubt not that the novelty of our appearance aroused her curiosity, for amidst such a profusion of glitter, we must look like a parcel of nuns." She tells us " an opportunity was made for introducing ' my little darling ' [Lucy, later Galton] with Patty Barclay and Priscilla Bell [later Wakefield] who were the only children admitted " and remarks that the sweet face of her little " Miss " made such an impression on the Duke of York that " I rejoice she was only five, instead of fifteen."

This letter, dated November 13, 1761, was published nearly fifty years later in the *Gentleman's Magazine*. David Barclay of Walthamstow, who was then nearly eighty, wrote some interesting additions to it :—

" To receive instructions on the occasion, I was desired to go to the lord who was to be in waiting, and he informed me that the King was sensible of the trouble which he should give, and directed him to enquire—What compensation would be satisfactory ? Whether the honour of knighthood would be acceptable ? To which I replied my father did not desire any other compensation than the

ROYALTY AT DAVID BARCLAY'S HOUSE IN CHEAPSIDE

satisfaction he should receive by accommodating the king and the royal family."

The worthy family were left in " Astonishment at their Condescension," and it is to be feared that the sober Quaker tenets must have sustained something of a shock.

The affair seems to have caused no little stir, for in a work entitled *George III and His Family* it is again referred to.

" Though both their Majesties considered their visit to the honest Quaker as devoid of etiquette, yet his family contrived to maintain an elegant decorum without infringing upon their own primitive simplicity . . . The King's example of kissing all the fawn-coloured ladies was followed by the Princes, his brothers, and his Royal uncle."

A little granddaughter of David Barclay amused the company by apologising for not making a curtsey, as her grandpapa would not permit it, but the objection of the " Friends " to " bend the knee to Baal" was met by the kindly old King by absolving them from kneeling in his presence, as is mentioned in John Freame's letter.

As so large a company was assembled on this occasion it is not surprising that many would-be guests were disappointed. In the *Lord Mayor of London*, by Harrison Ainsworth, there is a dialogue between the Lord Mayor and the Duchess of Richmond, in which the lady expresses disappointment at not being invited to Mr. Barclay's, and rather grudgingly accepts the Lord Mayor's offer of a seat " nearly opposite his house." From there she observes and admires the crimson damask hangings, and even gets a glimpse of Mr. Barclay himself.

Unfortunately the Lady Mayoress, making her obeisance to their Majesties from her coach, caught her towering headdress in the window, which " caused their Majesties great amusement until the footman relieved her dilemma."

We find Mr. Barclay's house again mentioned in the *Annual Register* of 1761, by a writer who says :—

" The Royal cavalcade set out from the Palace about 12, but, would you believe it, by mismanagement of those who should have cleared the way of hackney coaches and obstructions, it was nearly

HISTORY OF THE BARCLAY FAMILY

four hours before the Royal Family got to Friend Barclay's house opposite Bow Church."

It will be remembered that David Barclay of Cheapside received a letter upon the lineage of his family from his brother, Robert Barclay, Urie III, author of the *Genealogical Account*. This research into their history appears to have led David to erect the Mausoleum or Howff over the graves at Urie, and in it a stone bearing the following inscription :

ANNO 1741 CONDITUM

AUSPICIO ROBERTI BARCLAY DE URY

SUMPTIBUS AUTEM FRATRIS SUI

DAVIDIS BARCLAY MERCATORIS LONDINENSIS

AD MAJORUM CINERES TEGENDOS.

A letter from him to his son David, enclosing a copy of the *Apology*, was found among the latter's papers at Keswick Hall, and it is so full of advice worthy of the good old Quaker that it is worth while including it here.

" It is a satisfaction to me that it pleased God so to bless my endeavours in the World, yt I have been able to do for thee agreable to my wishes. By which with Industry and Honesty I hope it may be sufficient for thee to improve upon, so that thou may by the permission of Providence lay a Foundation for a Happy Life, as well as be enabled to assist and help others especially those of my family, Where thou ought always to look on thyself as a Father in some respects.

The Dependance I have of this made me the more willing to do everything on my part for thee, beyond what would have been expected from me everything considered. Thy Care, Capacity & Industry in Business is very agreeable to me, Yet in my Approbation there is more wanting to compleat thee. & to render thee fitt to encounter the variety of uncertaintys generally met with in this world.

What I have to recommend to thee is a humble regard for God which will bring thee to a solid concern on a Religious account. I think it very becomming thee as thou art a grandchild of R Barclay who wrote so excellent a system of our Principles, to give them a serious perusall, sure if thy Worthy Grandfather took the Labour and Paines to write so excellent a Book, its very hard if thou should not think it once worth reading over, by which thou may have a just Notion of the principles thou by education professes. I need not tell thee Men of Sense of all professions value his Writings. In my

240

opinion, its very unbecomming a Man not to know, as well as to be DAVID acquainted with his Principles, as to be able to say something for BARCLAY OF them in conversation, and the best way to be so qualified is to read CHEAPSIDE, the Apology. I intend the one of them for that end, and desire 1682–1769, thou may read it over seriously & give me thy thoughts of it, thou Urie IIIB. will also find great advantage and Benefitt in reading the Scriptures especially the New Testament, altho too much neglected and over-slited by the generallity of the young folke of this age, yet will be found always was of great worth & value to those who desire the best things, such as Righteousness and Truth, wch are really ties of Good in themselves & what will support thee, if thou happily lays hold of them, when other accidents in Life such as Riches or even Health & Strength of Youth itself may and will fail, often when least looked for. But Goodness is really substantial and Solid, and what will accompany a good man to his grave, yay even beyond it.

I remember to have observed thee touched with a sence of that which is good in thy very young days. I beg thou may not overgrow that sence of the best things, nor neglect its Calls, but lay hold of it having just regard to the Shinings of that Delight which will clearly show thee ye way thou ought to walk in. In other times it may be the small still voice behind thee saying this is the way, Walk in it, and if thou pays a just regard to this glorious principle in thyself, it will discover to thee everything that is evil, and will strengthen and enable thee, there being sufficiency in it not only to resist Evil, but to do good. My son, believe me this Moniter is beyond all teachers in the world it being always with thee. Thou never did Evil but thou wast checked thereby nor Good but it gave thee joy and satisfaction. Now if thy father who loves thee very well was always with thee it would not render thee any way safe without this prin-ciple, because I could not perceive the thoughts of thy heart, but this witness being placed for and by God who knows all things. The clear Shining of it is adhered to give thee oportunity to chuse the direct and only safe Path to happiness here and hereafter. O that thou may chuse to serve and obey God above all. That servitude carries its own reward with it, of Peace and Joy far exceeding the joys of this world. I must declare that so far as I have been preserved, its been by taking due heed of this principle. Therefore it is I, in Fatherly affection, recommend thee to lay hold of it now in thy Youth, whereby thou may prevent further trouble, which every Soul that sinneth must know before they can witness peace with God their Creator. For they that go into any Bad Road must tread all that way back through Repentence, ere they get into the Path of Happiness.

III.—II   241

DAVID
BARCLAY OF
CHEAPSIDE,
1682–1769,
Urie IIIB.

These things I offer to thy consideration in the affection of a Brother rather than the authority of a Parent, hoping my advice will not be slighted, because I do not constrain my Son, a method I always avoided, Many Fathers take Bonds of their children to keep them in subjection to their Wills, but I chuse ye Bond of affection, when thats lost they are lost to me.

I shall conclude with most Prayers to ye Father of all our Mercy that thou may be so happy as to prefer the best things which will be ye continual delight of thy affectionate Father · D.B."

The result desired by this letter was most certainly achieved as is shown in the life of the recipient.

David Barclay of Cheapside died at his country house, Bush Hill, Winchmore Hill, Middlesex, on March 18, 1769, and was buried in the graveyard attached to the Quaker Meeting House there, where his tombstone and those of several of his descendants are still to be seen.

It is interesting to record that Bush Hill had previously been the home of his wife's grandfather, John Freame, senior.

David's fortune at his death was worth no less than one hundred thousand pounds, including the freehold estate of Bush Hill, which he left to his second surviving son, David (of Walthamstow). Among several legacies he bequeathed the sum of £500 to his great-nephew, and son-in-law, Robert Barclay (Urie V), thus returning to the Scottish estate his original patrimony of 9000 merks.

By his first wife Anne Taylor, who died December 3, 1720, David Barclay had two sons and four daughters.

> James, married Sarah Freame and became a banker in London. He died of consumption in 1766 and was buried at Winchmore Hill. He had issue two sons, Joseph, died 1797, and Alexander, died 1812, both unmarried, and one daughter, Anne, who married James Allardice of Allardice, County Kincardine, and was the mother of Sarah Anne, second wife of Robert Barclay, Urie V.
>
> Alexander, born 1711, went to Philadelphia where he married. He was grandfather to Charles Barclay (Bury Hill II) Chief of Mathers and Urie, and will be dealt with later.
>
> Christiana, died unmarried.
>
> Patience, married John Stedman.
>
> Jane, married James Collinson.
>
> Elizabeth, married Timothy Bevan.

242

DAVID BARCLAY OF WALTHAMSTOW AND YOUNGSBURY

AFTER ZOFFANY

HISTORY OF THE BARCLAY FAMILY

On August 8, 1723, David Barclay married, as his second wife, Priscilla, daughter of John Freame, banker, of London. She was the niece of Sarah Freame (Sally), the wife of his eldest son James, which complicated the relationships of the two families. On the death of her brother John in 1766, she became sole heiress of the banking business in Lombard Street, now known as Barclays Bank.

By his second wife David Barclay had two more sons who both became partners in the Bank :

> John, born 1728, known as " of Cambridge Heath." Married Susannah Willett and was the progenitor of the important branch known as the " Barclays of the Bank," an account of whom will be given in due course.
>
> David, born 1729, known as " of Walthamstow and Youngsbury." Died 1809 without male issue.

Also six more daughters :

Catherine, married Daniel Bell of Tottenham.
Lucy, married Robert Barclay, fifth Laird of Urie.
Caroline, married John Lindoe of Norwich.
Priscilla, died unmarried.
Richenda, married Nathaniel Springall.
Christiana (second of this name), married firstly Joseph Gurney, secondly John Freame, and thirdly Sir William Watson.

DAVID BARCLAY OF WALTHAMSTOW AND YOUNGSBURY

David Barclay of Walthamstow and Youngsbury in Hertfordshire was second son of David Barclay of Cheapside by his second wife, Priscilla Freame.

For many years he was a merchant in London and became a partner in the Bank in Lombard Street in 1776.

He was stated to be one of the most influential men in the City. He had an estate in Jamaica and owned many slaves, all of whom he emancipated at considerable loss to himself, and instructed in trades and handicrafts before settling them in America.

An interesting episode in his life is found in his action as an intermediary between Benjamin Franklin and Lord North's

Ministry in negotiating for a reconciliation between Great
Britain and the American Colonies in 1774-5. David Barclay
took the initiative in this matter by calling on Franklin with
reference to a meeting of merchants to petition Parliament,
and urging that Franklin might achieve the great merit of
contriving some means of averting the impending calamity
of Civil War.

Franklin found the Ministry difficult to convince, but drew
up a plan of reconciliation, which David handed to Lord Hyde.
Ministerial conferences took place upon this plan, and at one
time it looked as if the mediation of the " Friends " might be
successful. But Franklin wrote to Barclay saying " that he
was sure that the Ministry would rather give him a place in a
cart to Tyburn than any other place whatever, and that he
overestimated his power to assist." So all the conferences and
negotiations ended in nothing.

The following letter, which appeared in the *Public Advertiser* of January 17, 1775, shows us how deep was David
Barclay's concern for those who were suffering through the
prevailing depression in trade.

" There having appeared a letter in the London *Evening Post* of
Saturday last, dated from Leeds the 9th instant and signed by the
Mayor, with several other gentlemen, calling on me ' to set forth
so much of the Contents of a Letter ' which I read at the King's
Arms on the 4th inst., in compliance with that request, and in
Justification of my own Conduct, I give the Public the following
Extract, viz. :

' Leeds, 28th December, 1774.

' The unhappy Differences betwixt Great Britain and America
throws the Merchants in this Country into great Inconveniences,
and the Manufacturers into great Distress. There are now a great
many Cloth Dressers in this Town out of Employ, and a much
greater Number of Cloth-makers, such as Carders, Spinners and
Weavers in the Country adjacent. The Poor's Rate at Dewsberry is
already got up to Eight Shillings in the Pound, and at Betley,
Heckmondwicke, and the other Towns thereabouts, the Poor's Rate
is nearly as much, and it is my firm Belief that if the Trade to
America is shut up until this time Twelvemonth, all the Rents of
the Lands and Houses in the above Townships will not be sufficient
to support the Poor alone. I wish our Rulers, who are at the

Head of Affairs would spare a Day to visit a few of the poor Cottagers, and see for themselves the Manner in which they live, their poor Diet, their wan Looks, their ragged Cloathing, their starved Children, it might be a better Guide to 'em in ordering of Affairs than their always being in, and seeing nothing but Affluence and Plenty ; but as this I fear is not likely to be the Case, and as this Country now feels the bad Effects of the Stop to America, if any Thing can be done to obtain Redress, it is a Pity but it was done.

' If the Merchants of London petition Parliament for a Repeal of those Acts that are the Cause of the Difference, the Merchants and Manufacturers of this Country will be glad to join in a Petition to the like Import, provided the Merchants in London should think it necessary ; for people at this Distance cannot so well judge what is expedient as you that are upon the Spot. I therefore could wish we had the Direction of the Merchants in London what to do ; for if there is the least Prospect of doing Good, our Endeavours should not be wanting.'

I think it proper to add, that I have writ to the Author of the above, desiring that he will avow its Contents to the Mayor, and the rest of the Gentlemen who signed the Letter from Leeds.

DAVID BARCLAY."

Cheapside, Jan. 16,
   1775.

" Instead of making those he loved dependant on his future bounty," writes his biographer in the *Morning Chronicle*, " David Barclay became the executor of his own Will, and by the most magnificent aid to all his relatives, lived to see the maturity of all those establishments which now give such importance to his family. Charitable and philanthropic objects had in him a munificent benefactor, and honest desert a helpful friend." He spent fifteen hundred pounds a year, for several years, in starting a House of Industry at Youngsbury, but succeeded ultimately in organising a system of management that made it self-supporting.

He was also one of the Trustees for the famous Quaker school at Ackworth.

On the death of the Brewer Henry Thrale, husband of the celebrated Mrs. Thrale, afterwards Mrs. Piozzi, his business was offered for sale and furnished an opportunity for investment. David Barclay of Walthamstow arranged for the purchase of the Anchor Brewery, in Southwark, and put his

DAVID
BARCLAY OF
CHEAPSIDE,
1682–1769,
Urie IIIB.

245

nephew Robert Barclay, son of his half-brother Alexander, into the firm.

The letter he received from his father, David of Cheapside, which has already been quoted, bore fruit in an excellent memoir of the Apologist, published by David Barclay of Walthamstow in 1802.

He was described as " a man who for the integrity of his heart, soundness of his understanding and general philanthropy of his breast, had few equals."

We have already recorded the interest he took in his orphan nieces, daughters of Robert Barclay (Urie V).

During his later life the struggle of William Wilberforce and his fellow workers, Clarkson, Sharp and Buxton, for the emancipation of the slaves was at its keenest, and the Society of Friends was closely associated in the crusade. David Barclay, in his sympathy with the oppressed and needy and his strong antipathy to slavery, had already, as we have noted, freed the slaves on his estate in Jamaica, and he, together with the family circle resident at Clapham and his kinsfolk the Buxtons and Gurneys, brought all his influence to bear to gain the desired end. The old man must have rejoiced to see, in his seventy-ninth year, the law for the suppression of the Slave Trade pass the legislature.

In *Bell's Weekly Messenger* of Sunday, June 4th, 1809, appeared the following notice :—

"Died. On Tuesday (May 30th) at Walthamstow David Barclay Esq. in the eighty-first year of his age, the last grandson of Robert Barclay of Urie, who wrote the celebrated Apology for the People called Quakers."

He was buried near his father at Winchmore Hill.

David Barclay was twice married, firstly to Martha Hudson, by whom he had an only surviving daughter, Agatha, who became the wife of Richard Gurney of Keswick Hall, Norfolk; and secondly to Rachel Lloyd of Birmingham, by whom he had no issue.

At his death his large fortune, including his interest in the Brewery of Barclay, Perkins and Co., went to his daughter, Agatha, and her husband, Richard Gurney. At their death

246

it descended to their son, Hudson Gurney the millionaire, whose wife, Margaret Barclay, was a sister of Robert Barclay-Allardice of pedestrian fame, the last Laird of Urie.

DAVID BARCLAY OF CHEAPSIDE, 1682–1769, Urie IIIB.

A good portrait of David Barclay of Walthamstow, after Zoffany, hangs in the dining-room at Bury Hill, of which many excellent mezzotints are to be found.

Among the family papers at Bury Hill there is an interesting correspondence between David Barclay of Walthamstow and the descendants of John, the second son of Colonel David Barclay (Urie I), who, as we have seen, emigrated to East New Jersey. This John was the great-uncle of David of Walthamstow.

In the year 1802 the consent of the living heirs of John Barclay of East New Jersey was necessary to the release of certain lands from the entail of Urie. The deed was duly sent out to Perth Amboy and signed by all concerned. It is seen in the letters that David of Walthamstow, with his usual generosity, sent out a sum of five hundred dollars and also a parcel of books to be divided among his cousins in the American colony.

In due course each of these cousins wrote to him thanking him for his gift and telling him of their circumstances. One of them enclosed a genealogical tree giving all the descendants of John Barclay (Urie IIB) in America, which is still preserved at Bury Hill.

PEDIGREE III.

The Barclays of the Bank.

Anne Taylor, daughter of = DAVID BARCLAY of Cheapside, 2nd son = 2ndly, Priscilla Freame, daughter James Taylor of London. of Robert Barclay "The Apologist" (Urie II). of John Freame, Banker of (See Barclays of Bury Hill, Born 1682. Died 1769. Lombard Street. Pedigree II.)

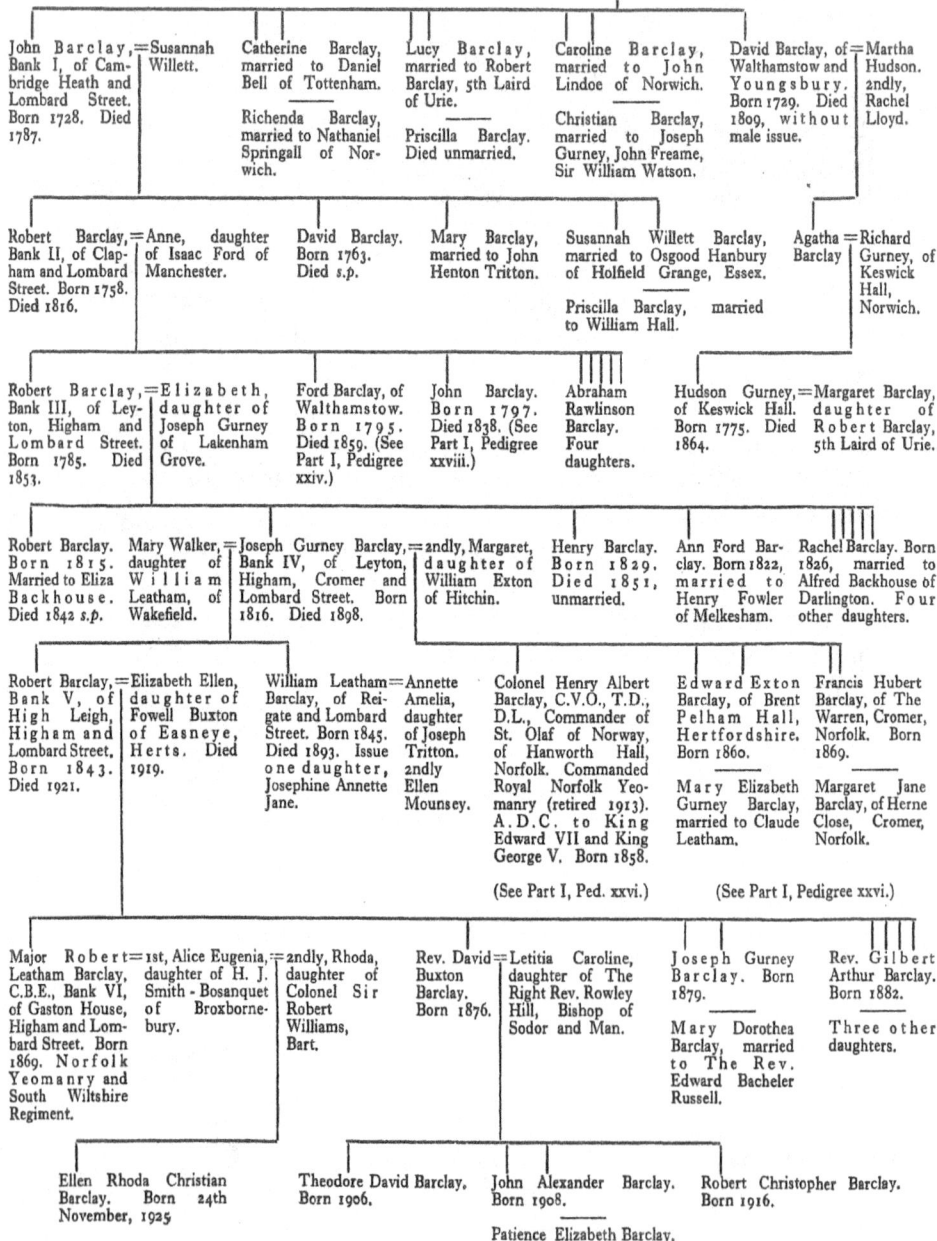

John Barclay, = Susannah Willett. Bank I, of Cambridge Heath and Lombard Street. Born 1728. Died 1787.

Catherine Barclay, married to Daniel Bell of Tottenham.

Richenda Barclay, married to Nathaniel Springall of Norwich.

Lucy Barclay, married to Robert Barclay, 5th Laird of Urie.

Priscilla Barclay. Died unmarried.

Caroline Barclay, married to John Lindoe of Norwich.

Christian Barclay, married to Joseph Gurney, John Freame, Sir William Watson.

David Barclay, of = Martha Walthamstow and Hudson. Youngsbury. 2ndly, Born 1729. Died Rachel 1809, without Lloyd. male issue.

Robert Barclay, = Anne, daughter Bank II, of Clapham and Lombard Street. Born 1758. Died 1816. of Isaac Ford of Manchester.

David Barclay. Born 1763. Died s.p.

Mary Barclay, married to John Henton Tritton.

Susannah Willett Barclay, married to Osgood Hanbury of Holfield Grange, Essex.

Priscilla Barclay, married to William Hall.

Agatha = Richard Barclay Gurney, of Keswick Hall, Norwich.

Robert Barclay, = Elizabeth, Bank III, of Leyton, Higham and Lombard Street. Born 1785. Died 1853. daughter of Joseph Gurney of Lakenham Grove.

Ford Barclay, of Walthamstow. Born 1795. Died 1859. (See Part I, Pedigree xxiv.)

John Barclay. Born 1797. Died 1838. (See Part I, Pedigree xxviii.)

Abraham Rawlinson Barclay. Four daughters.

Hudson Gurney, = Margaret Barclay, of Keswick Hall. daughter of Born 1775. Died Robert Barclay, 1864. 5th Laird of Urie.

Robert Barclay. Born 1815. Married to Eliza Backhouse. Died 1842 s.p.

Mary Walker, = daughter of William Leatham, of Wakefield.

Joseph Gurney Barclay, = 2ndly, Margaret, Bank IV, of Leyton, Higham, Cromer and Lombard Street. Born 1816. Died 1898. daughter of William Exton of Hitchin.

Henry Barclay. Born 1829. Died 1851. unmarried.

Ann Ford Barclay. Born 1822, married to Henry Fowler of Melksham.

Rachel Barclay. Born 1826, married to Alfred Backhouse of Darlington. Four other daughters.

Robert Barclay, = Elizabeth Ellen, Bank V, of High Leigh, Higham and Lombard Street. Born 1843. Died 1921. daughter of Fowell Buxton of Easneye, Herts. Died 1919.

William Leatham = Annette Barclay, of Reigate and Lombard Street. Born 1845. Died 1893. Issue one daughter, Josephine Annette Jane. Amelia, daughter of Joseph Tritton, 2ndly Ellen Mounsey.

Colonel Henry Albert Barclay, C.V.O., T.D., D.L., Commander of St. Olaf of Norway, of Hanworth Hall, Norfolk. Commanded Royal Norfolk Yeomanry (retired 1913). A.D.C. to King Edward VII and King George V. Born 1858.

(See Part I, Ped. xxvi.)

Edward Exton Barclay, of Brent Pelham Hall, Hertfordshire. Born 1860.

Mary Elizabeth Gurney Barclay, married to Claude Leatham.

Francis Hubert Barclay, of The Warren, Cromer, Norfolk. Born 1869.

Margaret Jane Barclay, of Herne Close, Cromer, Norfolk.

(See Part I, Pedigree xxvi.)

Major Robert = 1st, Alice Eugenia, **Leatham Barclay, C.B.E., Bank VI,** of Gaston House, Higham and Lombard Street. Born 1869. Norfolk Yeomanry and South Wiltshire Regiment. daughter of H. J. Smith - Bosanquet of Broxbornebury. = 2ndly, Rhoda, daughter of Colonel Sir Robert Williams, Bart.

Rev. David = Letitia Caroline, **Buxton Barclay.** Born 1876. daughter of The Right Rev. Rowley Hill, Bishop of Sodor and Man.

Joseph Gurney Barclay. Born 1879.

Mary Dorothea Barclay, married to The Rev. Edward Bacheler Russell.

Rev. Gilbert Arthur Barclay. Born 1882.

Three other daughters.

Ellen Rhoda Christian Barclay. Born 24th November, 1925.

Theodore David Barclay. Born 1906.

John Alexander Barclay. Born 1908.

Robert Christopher Barclay. Born 1916.

Patience Elizabeth Barclay.

THE BARCLAYS OF
THE BANK

JOHN BARCLAY OF CAMBRIDGE HEATH

John Barclay, eldest son of David Barclay of Cheapside by his second wife Priscilla Freame, was born in 1728, and was the progenitor of the large branch known as the Barclays of the Bank.

As we have already mentioned, he was present with his family when King George III visited his father's house in Cheapside to view the Lord Mayor's Show in 1761, being then about thirty-three years of age. The King is said to have offered him a position at Court, which the old Quaker, his father, would not permit him to accept.

At this time he appears to have been engaged in the family business at 108 Cheapside, and, after his father's death in 1769, he and his nephew Robert Barclay (Bury Hill I), carried it on together for some years.

John Barclay was also concerned in the banking business in Lombard Street, but the exact date on which he became a partner in the firm is uncertain. In *The History of Barclay's Bank* the date is given as 1785, but from a " Memorandum of Agreement " dated London, November 16th, 1781, it would appear to have been considerably earlier.

This document, now among the records at the Anchor Brewery, Southwark, is of considerable interest, giving many details of John Barclay. It is signed by David Barclay of Walthamstow, Silvanus Bevan, and Robert Barclay (Bury Hill I), the original partners in the Brewery, and by John Barclay. The witness to their signatures is Robert Barclay, eldest son of John, later known as of Clapham (Bank II). He signs " Robert Barclay jun." It is divided into thirteen heads, and provides as follows :—

1. That John Barclay (Bank I) and Robert Barclay (Bury Hill I) shall continue the concern at 108. John Barclay two thirds and Robert Barclay one third.

III.—KK   249

JOHN
BARCLAY,
1728–1787,
Bank I.

2. That the Firm shall be " John and Robert Barclay & Co."
and that Nathaniel Springall shall be a nominal partner and
receive five hundred pounds per annum.
(Nathaniel Springall was brother-in-law of John Barclay.)

3. That John Barclay shall have the management and shall
consult David Barclay (of Walthamstow) on material points.

4. That John Barclay shall have a " RESOURCE " of ten
thousand pounds from Barclay, Bevan, Barclay & Benning
whenever the business at 108 needs it.
(This mention of two Barclays in the name of the Bank
proves that John was a partner there before the year 1781.)

5. That John Barclay shall receive from the partners in the
Brewery the £6,000 that he had advanced towards the
purchase of the same.

8. That the partners in the Brewery shall be bound to admit
John Barclay into partnership if he shall see fit to retire from
or sell the business at 108.

11. That Silvanus Bevan shall have the power to admit his son into
the Brewery.

13. That John Barclay may invest ten thousand pounds in the
Brewery for the benefit of his wife and family after his death,
at ten per cent.

It is seen by the deeds of the Anchor Brèwery that John
Barclay never exercised his option to become a partner in
that concern, but during the last year or two of his life devoted
all his energies to the Bank in Lombard Street. As the
business in Cheapside was mainly export to America, it
declined considerably during the years of the War of Independence, and on the acknowledgment of the Declaration of
Independence by Great Britain in 1783 it ceased to become
profitable and was wound up.

The following extract from the records of the banking
business, then styled " Barclay, Tritton and Bevan," affords
an amusing contrast to the imposing personnel of 54, Lombard
Street, to-day :—

History of
Barclays
Bank,
Matthews
and Tuke,
p. 40.

" Towards the end of the eighteenth century the staff of Barclays
consisted of three clerks, and on the appearance of the third as a
new clerk coming to the office for the first time, he was dressed after
the following fashion : he wore a long flapped coat with large
pockets, the sleeves had broad cuffs with three large buttons, somewhat like the coats worn by the Greenwich pensioners of the

present day, an embroidered waistcoat reaching nearly down to his knees, with an enormous bouquet in the buttonhole; a cocked hat, powdered hair with pigtail, a bag wig, and a golden-headed cane, similar to those subsequently carried by footmen to ladies of rank. This gentleman, who cut so curious a figure, remained in the house many years, and died at a very advanced age, much respected by his employers."

John Barclay of Cambridge Heath, Hackney, married Susannah Willett, and had issue, two sons and three daughters.

Robert, born in 1758, who succeeded him.
David, born in 1763, died young.
Mary, known as " Patty Barclay," married John Henton Tritton, afterwards a partner in the Bank.
Priscilla, married William Hall.
Susannah Willett Barclay, married Osgood Hanbury of Holfield Grange. An interesting account of this wedding is preserved in a contemporary newspaper. It runs as follows :—

" August 19th 1789.

" This day was married in the Quaker's Meeting in Gracechurch Street Osgood Hanbury, a Banker in London, to Miss Susannah Barclay, daughter of the late John Barclay and niece to the present David Barclay. . . . The gentleman is son of the late Osgood Hanbury of Holfield Grange in the county of Essex, and grandson of the late John Hanbury, well known throughout Europe, as the greatest Tobacco merchant of his day, perhaps in the world. This gentleman, although one of the people called Quakers, was no less remarkable for this connection and intimacy with the first nobility of the kingdom, particularly with the old Duke of Newcastle, the very learned Lord Grenville, Gregory Sharpe, Sherlock Bishop of London, Hoadley Bishop of Winchester, Sir Charles Hanbury Williams, his relation, and most of the Lords spiritual and temporal of the Newcastle and Pelham administration. The Lady receives additional honour from being a descendant of Robert Barclay, author of the Apology for Quakers, as of that Philanthropic, steady and persevering Friend to the cause of distressed human nature the Negro Slaves of America.
" It is no wonder such connections should bring to the Meeting an assemblage of the first ranks of fashion and property now in the Metropolis. There were present and signed the Parchment of the solemnization of the marriage the French Ambassador, the Duke de Montmorency with the Duke de Luxemburg, several French Marchionesses, Lady Dunmore, the right Honble Brother to the

HISTORY OF THE BARCLAY FAMILY

Duke of ——, whose name I have forgotten . . . several of the late
governors of the West Indian Islands and of the Colonies in America.
" The beautiful neatness in dress and person of several of the
Quaker females must have impressed the foreign nobility with just
ideas of the superiority of elegant simplicity when compared with
the high polish of Gallic ornament.
" There was a suite of between 30 and 40 Carriages of the near
Relations of the new married party which were distinguished very
eminently in figures and beautiful propriety, the inexplicable
sublimity of the line ' simplex munditus.' "

This Susannah Willett Barclay was the great-great-grand-
mother of Hubert Frederick Barclay, the compiler of this
History, through his grandmother Rachel Hanbury of Holfield
Grange.

John Barclay of Cambridge Heath died in 1787, and he and
his wife Susannah were interred in the burial ground adjoining
the Quaker Meeting House at Winchmore Hill, where their
tombstones may still be seen.

Many of John Barclay's possessions, including china, his
walking-stick, and a silver candlestick which he presented to
his wife on the day of their marriage, are now at Gaston
House, the home of Robert Leatham Barclay, the present
head of this branch of the Barclay Family.

ROBERT BARCLAY OF CLAPHAM

Robert Barclay, eldest son of John Barclay of Cambridge
Heath and his wife Susannah Willett, was born in 1758,
probably at 108 Cheapside, where his father was engaged in
the family business.

Of his youth and education we have no record. As we
have already noticed, he was witness, at the age of twenty-
three, to the " Memorandum of Agreement " concerning the
business at 108 Cheapside and the Anchor Brewery, in 1781,
when he signed as " Robert Barclay Junior," his first cousin
Robert of Bury Hill being Robert Barclay Senior.

Robert (Bank II) was a staunch Quaker and became one
of the leaders of the Society. He married, about the year
1784, Anne, daughter of Isaac Ford of Manchester, " a descend-

252

ROBERT BARCLAY OF CLAPHAM (BANK II)

AND

HIS WIFE, ANNE

ant of the ancient family of Ford of Forde Green, County Robert Barclay, 1758–1816, Bank II. Stafford." Although a member of the Society of Friends, this lovely girl, who was famed for her beautiful hair, had, very naturally, a partiality for raiment becoming to her beauty and seems somewhat to have scandalised the staid members who approved of more sober garb, for she earned for herself the sobriquet of " the gay Quakeress."

Robert also was possessed of unusually good looks. He and his bride went to reside at Clapham, where his first cousin Robert (Bury Hill I), son of his uncle Alexander of Philadelphia, was already established, with his wife Rachel, in " The Terrace." Thus began the formation of the delightful family circle, of both Bury Hill and Bank cousins, which lasted so many years and from which sprang so many philanthropic and scientific activities.

So far as can be ascertained Robert Barclay was engaged in the banking business in Lombard Street all his life, but does not seem to have been a partner in the firm until the death of his uncle David of Walthamstow in 1809. His father, John of Cambridge Heath, died in 1787, as we have seen, but there is no mention of Robert becoming a partner at that time.

Robert Barclay was from his early manhood deeply interested in the science of astronomy. He built an observatory in his grounds at Clapham, where his half-cousin, Thomas Collinson, son of Jane Barclay of Cheapside and James Collinson, was his fellow worker.

The following letter from Thomas Collinson at the Chapter Coffee House, to Robert Barclay, Clapham Common, dated December 3rd, 1783, may be of interest to readers who also study the heavens, though it is not unlikely that the claims of the earlier students may be considered somewhat extravagant :—

" . . . However, I ventur'd to pass Saturday night last with Herschel in the open space till midnight—in which situation I seldom suffer. His late finish'd great Telescope I turn'd to several parts of the Heavens but found no Place without Stars, not even near the Horizon—a circumstance which distinguishes his Instrument from any other hitherto made—The Moon appear'd thro' it too

ROBERT
BARCLAY,
1758-1816,
Bank II.

light to be contemplated with safety to the Eyes and we had too little time to put on the greater magnifying Powers to diminish the splender. We therefore contented ourselves with his first made large Telescope, which showed us Orion gloriously and unified all we saw thro' yours. Double and double-double Stars it showed us to great advantage and we beheld divers Nebulae, or radiant spots in the Heavens so thickly sown with Stars that they appear'd like glittering dust. We also saw the new Comet and the Georgium Sidus. But instead of going on with telling you what I saw, it will be of more consequence to inform you of what he has seen. In a small portion of the Galaxy, twelve degrees broad by three degrees long, he counted forty-three thousand stars, and in various other parts of the Heavens there seems particular systems of Stars which seem to have reference to each other. Then another system, and so on without end. His discoveries in Mars are wonderful. He has not only ascertained its Equatorial and Polar Parts, but has discerned both Poles involved in Snow—And even more than that: he has beheld this Snow diminish and increase as each pole has been turn'd towards or from the Sun. While spots have likewise been visible in the Tropical Regions such as the snowy summits of our Andes would exhibit to an observer at a great distance from our Earth. He has seen so much as to enable him to ascertain diurnal Revolution of Mars, and to calculate the Sun's Declination there on the 25th September last &c. In Jupiter's Belts and Spots he has seen very extraordinary changes and Peculiarities and distinguish'd (what I believe no man has done before him) one of Jupiter's Satalites on his Body, it happening to have a dark broad Belt behind it. The shadow also of this Satalite appear'd on the Planet at the same time.

On Saturn he has discovered Belts and Spots as on Jupiter and also is enabled to make this mathematical conclusion: "That Saturn is posited exactly in the Focus of its Ring, by which means it has all the solar light and heat possible.

" His discoveries in the Moon are in no wise inferior. He has *plainly* discover'd a *Volcano* there. It was burning whilst he beheld it. He even traced the Lava—nor has he stopped there. He has seen a conical Mountain form'd near it that did not exist before, &c., &c. . . ."

Rachel
Gurney,
of the Grove,
Pease.

Robert Barclay, in the closing years of his life, had a town house in Tavistock Square, where Rachel Gurney of Lakenham Grove stayed in May, 1813.

He died at his house on Clapham Common on January 25th, 1816, and was buried beside his wife in the graveyard at

HISTORY OF THE BARCLAY FAMILY

Winchmore Hill. The house at Clapham still stands and is now part of " The Hostel of God," a convalescent home. Robert Barclay (Bank II) and his wife Anne Ford, who died in 1801, had four sons and four daughters :

Robert, born 1785, who succeeded him.

Ford, born 1795, married Esther, daughter of William Foster Reynolds of Carshalton, who died in 1889, aged 90 years. He lived first at Tooting and then at Forest Place, Walthamstow, where he died in 1859. He and his wife were buried at Winchmore Hill. His eldest son,

Henry Ford of Monkhams, Woodford, Essex, born 1826, died 1891. Married, in 1848, Richenda Louisa, daughter of Samuel Gurney of Ham House, by whom he had five sons and three daughters. His eldest son,

Colonel Hugh Gurney Barclay, M.V.O., of Colney Hall, Norwich, born 1851, is the present head of his branch of the family. He entered the Norwich Bank in 1875, and was appointed one of the original Directors of Barclays Bank, Ltd., in 1896. He married, in 1880, Evelyn Louisa, daughter of Sir Stuart Hogg. High Sheriff of Norfolk in 1905, commanded the 3rd/4th Norfolk Regiment in the Great War. He has issue. (See Pedigree xxiv, Part I.)

John of Croydon, third son of Robert Barclay (Bank II), born 1797. He was twice married: first, in 1820, to Georgina, daughter of Major Thomas Hill, by whom he had issue, some of whom are now living in New Zealand ; secondly, to Mary, daughter of William Moates, by whom he had issue. (See Pedigree xxviii, Part I.) John Barclay was a leader in the Society of Friends. He collated and published, in 1833, *The Diary of Alexander Jaffray*, who had been a close associate of his great-great-grandfather, the Apologist. He died 15th of the 6th month 1838 and was buried at Winchmore Hill.

Abraham Rawlinson died, in 1829, unmarried.

Mary, married Hubert John Barclay Galton.

Elizabeth Lucy, married, in 1823, Henry Birkbeck.

Susannah, died unmarried.

Lydia Ann, born 25th of the 10th month, 1799, was a remarkable woman, noted for her " untiring zeal for the prosperity of Zion." She was " recorded a minister in the Society of Friends on the 24th of the 12th month, 1835," and in that capacity, in spite of feeble health, travelled in many parts of the British Isles. She resided at Croydon, Reigate and

255

ROBERT
BARCLAY,
1758–1816,
Bank II.

Aberdeen, and in 1854 moved to Cockermouth, where she died in the following year. Her letters were published in 1862.

ROBERT
BARCLAY,
1785–1853,
Bank III.

ROBERT BARCLAY OF LEYTON

Robert Barclay (Bank III), eldest son of Robert Barclay and his wife Anne Ford, was born at Clapham in 1785.

It will be remembered that Robert Barclay (Bury Hill I) had married, in 1775, Rachel, sister of Joseph Gurney of Lakenham Grove, and a very close friendship existed at this time between the three families and led to more than one love affair.

Rachel
Gurney,
of the
Grove,
Sir Alfred
Pease.

In 1813 Robert Barclay (Bank III) became deeply attached to Elizabeth, the third of Joseph Gurney's six lovely daughters. The progress of the romance was a subject of eager interest to her sisters. Robert was very much in love, but Elizabeth was not to be hurried, and on Christmas Day, 1813, Rachel, her nineteen-year-old sister, was waiting expectantly to hear that " Robert's fate is decided," intending " when it is to write him a letter of *condolence*."

Early in January, Joseph Gurney and Rachel paid a visit to Darlington, and on their return journey were snowed up at Swaffham for three days. They were able at length to reach The Grove in a waggon with four horses, preceded by another waggon, with seven horses, filled with men to cut through the drifts. Rachel's health was permanently undermined by the exposure.

Meanwhile Robert was waiting in great suspense for Elizabeth's answer, and Jane took pity on him and wrote to explain the reason for her sister's indecision and was able to give him hope. Her father notes in his diary, " Dear Elizabeth's consent to his advances is serious in prospect, but not unpleasant." At length Robert gained her promise, and in March Rachel was able to write to her future brother-in-law reporting Elizabeth " blooming " and " agreeable and sweet-tempered—in short, I think she will make a tolerably nice wife."

The lively sisters commanded him to attend weddings in

order to " learn his lesson," for " he has no idea what he has to say or do."

On May 10th the young lovers appeared before the Norwich Monthly Meeting to give formal notice of their intention to marry, and the wedding took place at Lakenham Grove on June 29th, 1814.

During the year just recorded another romance had been followed with interest by the girls at The Grove. Gurney Barclay, third son of Robert Barclay (Bury Hill I) and of their aunt Rachel Gurney, a most beloved cousin, had been anxious to marry Mary Freshfield, also a cousin of the Gurneys, but the lady refused him, greatly to the indignation of Rachel, who wrote from Tavistock Square, where she was staying with Robert's parents in May, 1813, " when I see Gurney both at home and abroad it makes me *stamp, stamp* again, to think that our dear Mary should lose such a prize." This letter is an interesting one for other reasons, for in it she mentions that she has dined with the Barclays (Bury Hill II) at Clapham, and has called at Fulham on " Lady Barclay, who is a beautiful but not *wholy* agreeable-looking woman" (this was, no doubt, Margaret Hodgson, second wife of Bury Hill I); " we met Margaret (daughter of Urie V and wife of Hudson Gurney), Gatty Hanbury (sister of Hudson Gurney, wife of Sampson Hanbury of Poles and grand-daughter of David Barclay of Walthamstow), Mr. and the Misses Barclays " (Bury Hill I and his daughters). This family gathering serves to show how well the various branches were acquainted. Rachel continues : " I have seen the Exhibition of Sir Joshua Reynolds' painting, the Park, the wonders of Bond Street, the Duke of Kent, and enough to astonish a poor country girl," and concludes with a ridiculous description of Robert Barclay, " I suppose Bessy wants to hear of her beau . . . he has a noble pair of mustachios, and altogether looks rather Esau-like, for he has a plentiful head of hair, which I think, Bessy, thou mayst put in better order."

Soon after her sister's wedding Rachel Gurney's chest delicacy increased, as she whimsically put it, " a snowdrift can knock on the head in a minute a multitude of wise plans."

ROBERT
BARCLAY,
1785–1853,
Bank III.

She was ordered by the doctors to try " the close air of London City," and in November, 1814, went to stay at " Brick Lane," Spitalfields, with the Fowell Buxtons. There she received a letter from her cousin, Gurney Barclay, " He says that the Burdettites are determined to rouse an opposition, though at the same time they say they have not the slightest chance of success, and it is only to trouble Charles and cause him expense." (Charles Barclay, Bury Hill II, was standing for Southwark.) Gurney says, " They are a sad, blackguard set, and when it was proposed to set on foot subscriptions, they could only raise £16 to defray the expenses of the Election. Burdett says he will not stand nor pay, nor canvass, and if they chuse to return him he will not go to the house ! . . . Charles' election is secure . . . David (of Eastwick Park) says Elizabeth shall go to see Charles chaired, and wear the blue and orange cockade; but she remains true to her own party, and says she never could stoop to put on those colours she has always been taught to despise so much . . . (Charles) is a most courteous canvasser ; they say that ' No Porter at 5½d. ' is written all over the walls."

After Mary Freshfield had refused him, the attachment between Gurney Barclay and Rachel grew warmer. Her sister Jane had, it is said, given her heart to his brother David (afterwards of Eastwick Park), but a tenet of the Society of Friends forbade marriage between first cousins, a rule against which Joseph Gurney was a strong protester, " as unwarranted by Scripture or primitive Christian practice." Jane was eventually won by her faithful suitor Henry Birkbeck, but her short married life ended with the birth of her first child. Her husband afterwards married Elizabeth Lucy, sister of Robert Barclay (Bank III).

The brief romance of Rachel and Gurney Barclay was destined to be ended tragically soon, but meanwhile his devotion brought him constantly to The Grove. Verses written by him and preserved for us by Sir Alfred Pease, who has dealt so charmingly with the story of " Rachel Gurney of the Grove," serve to show their happy intercourse.

" IL PENSEROSO."

ROBERT
BARCLAY,
1785–1853,
Bank III.

Go, happy wreath, round Rachel's brows
    Entwine thy arms, and shed
The peace that only virtue knows
    Within her silent bed.

Go, happy wreath, and soft embrace
    Her locks of golden hair ;
With magic spell for ever chase
    The dreams of anxious care.

Let no disturbing thoughts intrude
    To break her peaceful rest :
No passions move her tranquil mood,
    Or agitate her breast.

But o'er her mind, and thro' her frame
    A gentle sleep dispense :
Sleep such as only angels claim—
    The sleep of innocence.

With fairy forms of fond delight
    Each silent hour employ,
And gild each vision of the night
    With gleams of tempered joy.

Go, happy wreath, round Rachel's brows
    Entwine thy arms and tell
That he whose heart the gift bestows,
    Is one that loves her well.

" L'ALLEGRO."

Once going to bed, our Rachel said,
    This ribband's out of fashion ;
Then swift as thought, the monster caught,
    And snapped it in a passion.

Repenting then, she seized her pen,
    And cried, the devil burn ye
This very night, I swear I'll write
    And order one from G-rn-y.

259

Down sat the dame, with looks of flame
    And thoughts intent on plunder,
And crammed the page with words of rage
    And paragraphs of thunder.

The frightened slave, too weak to brave
    Commands so high and mighty,
Scarce dared to stop, to take a drop
    Of gin or aqua vitæ.

But hurried forth, east, west and north,
    Searched ev'ry hole and corner,
From Rotten Row to Stratford Bow,
    For ribbands to adorn her.

Now worn to death and out of breath
    He humbly sends his duty,
And hopes the boon, despatched so soon
    May please capricious beauty.

But clouds of sorrow were gathering fast over the family at The Grove. Rachel's two young brothers were taken from them within a little over a year of each other, and she herself was rapidly failing. After visits to Devonshire and Brighton which availed nothing, she, with her sister Jane and her cousin Priscilla of Earlham, journeyed to Nice, Gurney and his sister Agatha, afterwards Mrs. Hilhouse, meeting them at Avignon in November, 1816. Four months later Gurney, " always a faithful and watchful steward," met the sorrowing parents at Antibes " with latest accounts from Nice." He returned shortly afterwards to England as escort to Priscilla Gurney, leaving A. Rawlinson Barclay, brother of Robert Barclay (Bank III), to give what help and support he could. It was not for long. On June 1st, 1817, Rachel Gurney passed from pain to peace, at the age of twenty-three.

Robért Barclay and his bride began their married life in " a house on the north side of Russel Square." It had a garden " extending a hundred feet at the back, and was open behind across Tavistock Square to Hampstead." Here their first child, Robert, was born in April, 1815.

HISTORY OF THE BARCLAY FAMILY

Elizabeth was much beloved by her husband's family and became a notable housewife. Her sister-in-law, Lydia Ann, writing many years later, says :

" I highly approve and advise to all the keeping of a correct system of accounts, by which they may see what they spend in each branch, what should be retrenched, and what may be properly devoted to the help of others. I was taught it first by my dear sister-in-law, Elizabeth Barclay, then followed the practice when living with my dear brothers and sisters together in Russel Square, and afterwards when keeping my dear brother A. R. B.'s house at Forest Place (at his special desire)."

Robert Barclay was engaged in the family business in Lombard Street and became a partner in the Bank at his father's death in 1816.

He was an active Quaker, and, like all the " circle " at Clapham, took great interest in philanthropic activities. He was also a keen sportsman and enjoyed the shooting over the estate at Higham which formed a part of his wife's marriage portion.

The following letter from Joseph Gurney to his daughter Elizabeth Barclay bears upon this subject :

" My dear Elizabeth,   11.10.1824.

Be not cross, I beseech thee. Men's business is to furnish supplies, and if a good wife loves and delights a little in the order and ornament of her house and does not want her husband *at all times to be with her* and direct in it, do suffer that a husband also has some pride and pleasure in his investments and in the growth and ornament of the improvements under his hands, and be united in the endeavour so far to accede to the taste and business one of another, as that whilst he loves the indulgence of a well ordered family, thou mayst also make his path easy in taking an interest in its progress—a visit now and then to Higham on the way thus be pleasant to both of you. I would not have chosen for him a spot apart as this is from our home interests, but circumstances, not choice, having brought it forward, I think it need not make that inroad into your domestic association which thy *crossness* forbodes, and it probably affords a better security for investment in Land than others he might have made choice of. I am, however, most willing that he should relinquish it if it be so agreed between you—indeed I have both felt and fear'd it might involve him in more trouble

261

and thought than was profitable, if not in more temptation than might in the end be rightly resisted, and on these grounds alone I would be satisfied with the prudent counsel of his uncle. The result seems to be that he is the more " bitten " by it, and we must after all judge for ourselves.

"Thou art acquainted, no doubt, with the history of our introduction to this possession—A part of the settlement to thee and thy children was placed on mortgage upon it ; the interest began to accumulate and expenses of Inclosure with others upon the property with the strange involvment of the Owner of it, made it but policy to get the possession by purchase. To the Settlement I shall add £6,000, which may secure thee in thy £100 every half year (if it be a separate appropriation to thyself), and for this reason thou wilt have full liberty to dun thy husband. Dear Hannah's life being spared to us, I mean to do the same for her, and carry both into effect as a New Year's arrangement. So far I think it right for thee to be acquainted with the bearing of the thing inasmuch as thy inheritance is concerned. But it by no means binds it to this Estate, though from present prospects it would be difficult perhaps for Robert to find a more eligible investment. . . ."

An amusing record remains to us of an incident during Joseph Gurney's tenure of the Higham estate. Being a Quaker and a pacifist, he was somewhat disconcerted to learn that the flints from Higham were being sold " for military purposes." In reply to his protest, his agent, James Crowe, wrote the following letter :

"12th February, 1805.

"I certainly shall not think it necessary to *ascertain* the guns to which any flints may be put which may come out of the lands at Higham—it appears impossible to me to trace them. It is, however, a laborious work and not apparently profitable either to my body or soul. Robinson, or whoever is the maker, will no doubt sell his manufacture to any person whatever that will buy and pay for it ; therfore *he* could not inform me what use will be made of them. Iron ore, as it may be converted into Iron proper for casting cannon, etc., and wood, as it may be converted afterwards into charcoal and then into gunpowder used for improper purposes, are two staple articles equally objectionable in my mind ; but I feel no objection to the sale of these articles found to be my property. I beg, dear Sir, to assure you I have still a perfect deference for your opinions, they are proceeds from the purest spring, I have no doubt ; but I

am satisfied, and shall desire Mr. Brown to give leave to the ROBERT
man of Flint to begin under some bargain for a short time, and BARCLAY,
take the first opportunity of making such enquiries as may be 1785–1853,
useful, as nothing in such a bargain can militate against your Bank III.
opinions. . . .

P.S.—I am persuaded the flints at Higham are of a very superior quality and in great abundance, and on part of the land (in particular) we had in exchange from King—the north side of the turnpike road—if I were to hazard an opinion of the use intended to be made of this manufactory, I should incline to think they were for the use of sportsmen, and that a sale for them was to be found in most parts of the world—the Army agents seldom purchase the best of *any* commodity, I believe."

This property, which Robert Barclay (Bank III) was the first of his family to possess, is held to-day by his great-grandson, Robert Leatham Barclay (Bank VI).

It cannot be stated in what year Robert Barclay went to Letters live at Knotts Green, Leyton ; but in 1832 Lydia Ann of
Lydia Ann Barclay, his sister, was staying there with him and wrote to Barclay. her brother, A. Rawlinson, giving her idea of an old maid's life, as hers was likely to be.

After the death of his wife in 1835, Robert Barclay continued to live at Knotts Green with his unmarried daughters until his death in 1853. He was buried in the graveyard at Winchmore Hill.

Robert Barclay and his wife Elizabeth Gurney had three sons and six daughters :

Robert, born April 20th, 1815, married in 1842 Eliza Backhouse, and died six months later, without issue.

Joseph Gurney, born 1816. (Bank IV.)

Henry, born 1829, died 1851 unmarried.

Jane Mary, born 1818, died 1899 unmarried.

Elizabeth Gurney, born 1820, died 1845 unmarried.

Ann Ford, born 1822, died 1913. Married Henry Fowler of Melksham.

Emma Lucy, born 1823, died 1847 unmarried.

Rachel, born 1826, married Alfred Backhouse of Darlington.

Louisa, born 1834, died 1847.

JOSEPH
GURNEY
BARCLAY,
1816–1898,
Bank IV.

JOSEPH GURNEY BARCLAY

Joseph Gurney Barclay, second son of Robert Barclay of Leyton, and his wife Elizabeth Gurney, was born at 13, Russell Square in 1816.

He was brought up in the principles of the Society of Friends, and was educated, together with his elder brother and his cousin Daniel Gurney, by a private tutor at his home, Knotts Green. Cambridge University had not at this time opened its doors to Quakers.

Robert Barclay (Bank III) early introduced his two elder sons into the Bank as Junior Partners, and for many years Joseph Gurney was largely responsible for the management of the business.

He married, in 1841, Mary Walker, daughter of William Leatham of Wakefield.

Letters
of
Lydia Ann
Barclay.
p. 275.

In the following year a great sorrow overtook the family in the death of his elder brother Robert, " a most sweet young man " who was regarded as of great promise in the Society of Friends. He married, early in 1842, Eliza Backhouse, but almost immediately his health gave cause for grave anxiety and he succumbed to a hæmorrhage. There is a touching record of the many young friends who had been present on his wedding day attending his funeral exactly six months later.

On the death of his father in 1853, Joseph Gurney succeeded to the properties of Knotts Green, Leyton, and Higham, and to the whole Barclay interest in the Bank, now " Barclay, Bevan, Tritton and Company."

In 1850 his wife Mary died, leaving him two young sons, and in 1857 Joseph Gurney entered upon a second marriage with Margaret, daughter of William Exton, whose family were Quakers and Bankers at Hitchin in Hertfordshire.

Joseph Gurney Barclay attended assiduously to his business, driving up from Knotts Green to Lombard Street each day behind his trotting Norfolk cob.

To all the banks the year 1866 was one of great difficulty, and the sudden failure of the bill-broking firm of Messrs.

Overend and Gurney, with liabilities of eleven million Joseph sterling, caused a panic in the City. Messrs. Overend and Gurney Barclay, Gurney were connected in business with the Norwich Bank 1816–1898, and many of Joseph Gurney Barclay's relations were heavily Bank IV. involved. It was a time of grave danger to the firm at 54, Lombard Street, and the restoration of confidence was due to his calmness, generosity and business acumen. The evening of Black Friday is still remembered. At Knotts Green Mrs. Joseph Gurney Barclay waited hour after hour for her husband's return, pacing the hall in her anxiety, with her two young sons, who had taken advantage of her distraction to steal unreprimanded from their beds, sliding down the banisters. At length he arrived, and said : " The worst day the City has ever known ; but we are all right."

In addition to his business labours, Joseph Gurney Barclay devoted much attention to philanthropic activities. He was for long connected, among other societies, with the London City Mission, and for years acted as Treasurer to the British and Foreign Bible Society.

Possessed of great wealth, his charities, though unostentatious, were on a munificent scale.

Joseph Gurney was a good sportsman and an excellent shot, but an incident in his youth is said to have left him with a shrinking from fire-arms which he found hard to overcome. Together with his father, Robert Barclay (Bank III), he was out shooting at Higham ; and as the elder man was reloading, his gun went off accidentally and blew a round hole in the wide brim of the Quaker hat he was wearing. He was quite unmoved and continued his day's sport, but his son never forgot his father's narrow escape, and was always nervous before a day's shooting.

Joseph Gurney Barclay was deeply interested in literature and scientific pursuits, particularly that of astronomy, which interest was shared by his kinsman and contemporary Arthur Kett Barclay of Bury Hill. For many years an expert astronomer was resident at Knotts Green, where there was a fine telescope.

The happy life of the family there was constantly shared

by well-known philanthropists who were their intimate friends, and although himself unconnected with political life, Joseph Gurney was a close friend of John Bright, who had married a sister of his first wife and often spent week-ends with him, being known to the children as " Uncle Bright."

In the summer he and his family used to move to Cromer, the gathering place of innumerable relations, Barclays, Buxtons and Gurneys in particular. He lived first at " The Warren," and later built " Herne Close " moving there himself, while " The Warren " was at the disposal of his sons and their growing families. In his later life he had a house at Brighton, where he spent some of the winter months.

He retired from business in 1896 after the great amalgamation which converted the old family firm into " Barclay & Co., Ltd." He died two years later, aged eighty-one years.

Joseph Gurney Barclay was a man of great qualities of mind and heart, of sweet temper and great serenity. He remained a member of the Society of Friends to the end of his life. Times were changing fast and none of the younger generation of the Barclays adhered to Quaker ways. Many of the older generation also were by this time attending services of the Church of England. Except for his sisters, who survived him and were faithful to the Society and its dress, Joseph Gurney was the last of the old order, whose lives were pleasant and prosperous, whose beneficence ameliorated the lot of thousands, and who remained, in spite of great riches, simple and single-hearted servants of the God in whom they trusted.

Knotts Green, like so many spacious houses, was submerged in the advancing tide of greater London. It is now Livingstone College, for the training in elementary medicine of missionaries going to the tropics. Joseph Gurney Barclay's grandson, Robert Leatham Barclay, is now Treasurer of the Institution (1933).

Margaret Barclay survived her husband for seven years and died on the 25th June, 1905. A woman of great lovingkindness and boundless generosity, she was a friend to all, and her familiar figure, in her little chaise with its piebald pony led by a groom, is a well-loved memory in Cromer.

HISTORY OF THE BARCLAY FAMILY

By his first wife, Mary Leatham, Joseph Gurney Barclay had two sons : JOSEPH GURNEY BARCLAY, 1816-1898, Bank IV.

Robert, born 1843, Bank V.

William Leatham, born 1845, died 1893, the first of his family to enter Cambridge University. Became a partner in Barclay, Bevan, Tritton & Co. in 1880 and retired in 1888 on the amalgamation with Ransom, Bouverie & Co. Married 1st, in 1872, Annette Amelia, daughter of John Tritton, died 1873, by whom he had one daughter, Josephine Annette Jane. Married 2nd, in 1877, Ellen, daughter of Jaspar Mounsey, by whom he had no issue. He remained a Friend to the end of his life.

By his second wife, Margaret Exton, Joseph Gurney Barclay had four sons and two daughters :—

Colonel Henry Albert Barclay, C.V.O., T.D. (1909), of Hanworth Hall, Norfolk, born 1858. Deputy Lieutenant for Surrey and Norfolk. Raised and commanded The King's Own Royal Norfolk Yeomanry, retiring in 1913. A.D.C. to King Edward VII, 1907 to 1910, and to King George V, 1910 to 1925. Commander of the Order of Prince Olaf of Norway. Married, in 1881, Marion Louisa, only daughter of Francis Hoare of Hampstead and Cromer, has issue two sons and two daughters :

The Rev. Humphrey Gordon Barclay, C.F., M.C., born 1882. Married Beatrice Evermar, daughter of Benjamin Bond Cabbell of Cromer Hall, Norfolk, has issue two sons and three daughters.

Lieut.-Colonel Joseph Francis Barclay, T.D., born 1883. Commanded The King's Own Royal Norfolk Yeomanry. Was at the landing at Gallipoli in the World War. Married Constance, daughter of Arthur Flower. Has issue four sons.

Eugenia Barclay, married Lieut.-Colonel Gerald Bullard, T.D. (1915), and has issue one son and one daughter. Colonel Bullard died in 1932.

Margaret Barclay.

Edward Exton Barclay of Brent Pelham Hall, Hertfordshire, born 1860. Has for many years been Master of the Puckeridge Hounds. Became a partner in the Bank in 1886, retired with his father in 1896, on the great amalgamation. Married 1st, in 1883, Elizabeth Mary, daughter of William Fowler of 43 Grosvenor Square, by whom he has issue

HISTORY OF THE BARCLAY FAMILY

JOSEPH
GURNEY
BARCLAY,
1816–1898,
Bank IV.two sons and one daughter. Married 2nd, Elizabeth Mary, widow of Henry John Fordham and daughter of Marlborough Robert Pryor of Weston Park, who died without issue.

Alfred Gordon Barclay, born 1866, died in infancy.

Francis Hubert Barclay of The Warren, Cromer, born 1869. Educated at Trinity Hall, Cambridge. Married, in 1900, Hannah Maude, daughter of Edward North Buxton, who died in 1932, and has issue.

Mary Elizabeth Gurney Barclay, married, in 1886, Claude Leatham, son of W. H. Leatham of Hemsworth Hall, Yorkshire.

Margaret Jane Barclay of Herne Close, Cromer.

(See Pedigree Part I, page xxvi).

ROBERT BARCLAY

ROBERT
BARCLAY,
1843–1921,
Bank V.Robert Barclay of High Leigh, Hoddesdon, Higham, Tarvie in Perthshire, and The Grove, Cromer (Bank V), eldest son of Joseph Gurney Barclay and his wife Mary Leatham, was born December 13th, 1843, and educated at Tottenham and London University.

He became a partner in Barclay, Bevan, Tritton & Co. in 1866 and took an active part in the business, being elected a Director in 1896.

In 1868 he married Elizabeth Ellen, daughter of Thomas Fowell Buxton of Easneye in Hertfordshire.

A good man of business and a shrewd judge of character, Robert Barclay was, like his forbears, a man of strong Christian principles. He was brought up as a Friend, though later he withdrew himself from the Society. He succeeded his father as Treasurer of the British and Foreign Bible Society and was concerned in many philanthropic and missionary associations. He was a liberal supporter of all local institutions for the welfare of those in need in Hoddesdon and elsewhere. High Sheriff for the county of Hertfordshire in 1893, and Chairman of the Bench of Magistrates at Cheshunt.

Robert Barclay retired from business in 1910, and died in 1921, leaving three sons and three daughters :—

Robert Leatham Barclay, Bank VI, born 1869.

The Rev. David Buxton Barclay, born 1876. Married in 1901 Letitia Caroline, daughter of the Right Rev. Rowley Hill, Bishop of Sodor and Man, and has issue :
    Theodore David, born 1906.
    John Alexander, born 1908.
    Robert Christopher, born 1916.
    Patience Elizabeth, born 1911.
Joseph Gurney Barclay, born 1879. Married 1st, in 1903, Gillian, daughter of Henry Birkbeck, by whom he has issue one son ; 2nd, in 1917, Gwendolin Rose, daughter of Dr. Watney, by whom he has issue three sons and one daughter.
The Rev. Gilbert Arthur Barclay, born 1882. Chaplain to the Forces in the Great War. Married, in 1912, Dorothy Catherine Topsy, daughter of C. T. Studd, and has issue two sons and two daughters.
Mary Dorothy, married the Rev. Edward Batcheler Russell.
Clemence Rachel, married the Right Rev. Edward S. Woods, Bishop of Croydon.
Rachel Elizabeth Barclay, died August 1932.
Christina Octavia Barclay.

ROBERT LEATHAM BARCLAY, C.B.E.

Robert Leatham Barclay of Higham, and Gaston House, Hertfordshire, eldest son of Robert Barclay (Bank V) and his wife Ellen, was born on March 30th, 1869.

Educated at Harrow, 1883/6, and Trinity College, Cambridge, he took his degree of M.A. in 1893.

Robert Leatham entered the Bank in 1890 and became a Director in 1910.

Liberal Candidate for Stowmarket Division, 1910. Acted as Honorary Treasurer of the Young Men's Christian Association, 1913–1917.

Served in the Great War, 8th Wiltshire Regiment, King's Own Royal Norfolk Yeomanry, Tank Corps and Home Depot. Major on the Staff of the War Office, 1917–1919, receiving the O.B.E. and C.B.E. Army Agricultural Committee, and present Chairman of the United Services Trustee.

High Sheriff of Suffolk, 1921, and Deputy Lieutenant. Honorary Treasurer to the Church Missionary Society from 1923.

On succeeding to his father's estate, Robert Leatham Barclay conveyed the house of High Leigh to the First Conference Estate Company, and it continues to be the headquarters of their useful work.

Robert Barclay is interested in farming, having two thousand acres in hand at Higham ; he is president of the Suffolk Agricultural Association (1933).

He married firstly, in 1898, Alice Eugenia, daughter of Horace J. Smith-Bosanquet, who died in 1918 without issue ; secondly, in 1924, Rhoda, daughter of Colonel Sir Robert Williams, Bart., of Bridehead, Dorchester, by whom he has one daughter, Ellen Rhoda Christian, born 1925.

Robert Leatham, the present head of his branch of the family, is, as we have traced, the sixth in direct descent of the " Barclays of the Bank."

It is little more than two hundred years since a goldsmith's business in Lombard Street admitted a Barclay into partnership. Messrs. Freame & Gould was then a mere shop with two or three assistants ; but by degrees this developed into a banking business second to none in the City. Its widespread connection with other banks was largely a Quaker and a family one, and was conserved and cemented by the sound business instincts of the Partners. These, in their successive generations, were invariably chosen for their high moral character no less than for their commercial sagacity.

To-day it stands as one of the largest banks in the world, with a capital, in the British business alone, of over £15,000,000, with branches all over England and Wales and subsidiaries in Scotland, Egypt, Palestine, East, West and South Africa, and the West Indies.

Barclay's Bank and Barclay's Brewery are outstanding examples of great commercial and industrial undertakings in England which owe much of their successful development to Scotsmen who came south to engage in trade.

We must now return to the eldest son of David Barclay of Cheapside, to continue the descent of the senior line.

ALEXANDER BARCLAY OF PHILADELPHIA

By T. Hudson

THE BARCLAYS OF
BURY HILL

ALEXANDER BARCLAY OF PHILADELPHIA

Alexander Barclay was the eldest surviving son of David Barclay of Cheapside, by his first wife Anne Taylor, and was born in the year 1711.

On the failure of the Scottish line in 1854, the two sons of his brother James having died unmarried, the descendants of Alexander became the heirs male of Mathers and Urie and Chiefs of the House of Barclay.

As a young man Alexander seems to have been extravagant and rather a disappointment to his father. He ran quickly through the monies which were left him by his mother, and finally went to America to help with his father's export business. He also held the appointment of " Comptroller of the Customs of Philadelphia." The commission to him as " Comptroller of all the Rates and Duties and Impositions arising and growing due to His Majesty at Philadelphia in Pennsylvania in America," dated at the Custom House, London, 5th August 1749, will be found in the Penn. Archives, 3rd Series, Vol. VIII, p. 667.

Very shortly after his arrival in America Alexander married Anne, daughter of Robert Hickman, Citizen and Cabinetmaker of London, and his wife Patience. She was staying with her uncle, Mr. John Hyatt, an Englishman engaged in a very large copper manufactory. He lived in Front Street and was Sheriff of the City and County of Philadelphia about the year 1744, and at this time he sent for his niece from England. He became very much attached to Anne and at his death left her the chief part of his property. Penn. Magazine. Vol. V, p. 96.

Alexander and Anne had two children :

Robert (Bury Hill I), born in 1751, of whom later.
Patience, born 1752, who married 1st (1772) Joseph Warrell, and 2nd (1780) Reynold Keen. She died 4th January 1781.

Alexander married secondly, on the 8th February 1759, Rebecca Robinson, widow of Peter Robinson and daughter of Peter Evans, Sheriff of Philadelphia. They had no issue.

Alexander Barclay died in 1771. The following is an extract from the *Pennsylvania Gazette* of Thursday, 17th January of that year :—

" Last Saturday morning died Alexander Barclay, Esq., Comptroller of His Majesty's Customs for this Port ; a gentleman who was greatly esteemed by the Trading part of this City as a good officer, and by all his private acquaintances as a benevolent and honest man. He was the son of David Barclay merchant of London, and grandson of the famous Apologist, Robert Barclay of Urie."

The memorial tablets to Alexander Barclay and his wife Anne are still to be seen in Christ Church, Philadelphia.

Their portraits, by Thomas Hudson, hang at Bury Hill. They are depicted in Quaker costume, which shows that at that time they still adhered to the Society of Friends. The following letter from Phineas P. Bond is among the papers at Bury Hill. He was British Consul at Philadelphia. The letter is dated 25th June 1794, and is addressed to Robert Barclay (Bury Hill I).

" It is presumed that you have a picture of your mother, which is a most striking likeness. She was a lady very greatly esteemed and was very amiable. She died in the prime of life, much lamented. Your sister Patience was a year old when you lost your mother."

ANNE HICKMAN, WIFE OF ALEXANDER BARCLAY
OF PHILADELPHIA

By T. Hudson

HISTORY OF THE BARCLAY FAMILY

ROBERT BARCLAY OF BURY HILL

ROBERT
BARCLAY,
1751-1830,
Bury Hill I.

Robert Barclay of Bury Hill was the only son of Alexander
Barclay of Philadelphia and his wife Anne Hickman. He
was born in Philadelphia 15th May, 1751, and baptised on
12th June of the same year.

His mother died 18th June 1753 and his father married
again, as we have seen, in the year 1759.

In 1763, when he was but twelve years old, he was sent to
England to his uncle David Barclay of Walthamstow, who,
having divested him of the gold lace on his coat, declared
him to be a Quaker.

He was educated at Wandsworth and there is now at Bury
Hill one of the prizes that he gained at that school. It was
evidently a prize for French, and the writing in it says :—

" Ce livre est le prix de la Diligence de Robert Barclay, obtenu
à Wandsworth le 12 Juillet 1765."

On the completion of his education he entered the business
in Cheapside, his grandfather, David Barclay of Cheapside,
having left him a partnership in trust.

When quite young he fell in love with his cousin Agatha,
the daughter of his uncle David, but owing to the near
relationship and the fact that the young lady was not a
" Friend," their engagement was not permitted.

After his father's death in Philadelphia in 1771, Robert
returned to America with the object of settling up his estate.
He remained there about two years. It was at this time that
he made the acquaintance of his cousins at Perth Amboy, the
descendants of his great-uncle John Barclay (Urie IIb).

In 1775, shortly after his return to London, he married the
beautiful Rachel Gurney, daughter of John Gurney of Keswick
Hall, Norwich, and his wife Elizabeth, daughter of Richard
Kett of Norwich. Her eldest brother, Richard Gurney
of Keswick, had recently married Agatha Barclay, Robert's
first love, and afterwards inherited his father-in-law's share
in the Brewery of Barclay, Perkins and Co. Her second
brother was John Gurney of Earlham whose wife, Catherine

III.—NN   273

Bell, was granddaughter of David Barclay of Cheapside. John Gurney was the father of some very remarkable daughters including Elizabeth Fry and Hannah, Lady Buxton. The third brother was Joseph Gurney of Lakenham Grove, whose daughter Elizabeth married Robert Barclay (Bank III).

Robert Barclay continued to live in Cheapside, engaged in the family business at 108, until the close of the War of Independence in 1783, when it was wound up.

As has been before stated, in the year 1781 the Anchor Brewery came into the market, and he, as trustee for his uncle, David Barclay of Walthamstow, with Silvanus Bevan and John Perkins, purchased it from the executors of the late Henry Thrale. The principal executor, the great Dr. Johnson, offered to sell it to Mr. John Perkins, the head clerk, if he could find parties to unite in producing the requisite funds. Mrs. Perkins having been the widow of Timothy Bevan, grandson of David Barclay of Cheapside, it was suggested that he should have recourse to her connections, and Silvanus Bevan, David Barclay of Walthamstow and Robert Barclay (Bury Hill 1) became the first partners with John Perkins.

Southwark had been noted for its ales as early as the days of Chaucer, who mentions the " ales of Southwark."
Dr. Johnson had been interested in the Brewery through his long friendship with the Thrales, and eight years previously he had written that " Thrale pays £20,000 a year to the Revenue and has four vats, each of which holds 1,600 barrels, above a thousand hogsheads."

The great man was present at the sale, with his ink-horn and pen hanging by a piece of string from his button-hole. He took a keen interest in the business, and enunciated the well-known phrase : " We are not here to sell a parcel of boilers and vats, but the potentiality of growing rich beyond the dreams of avarice."

The price paid to the executors of Henry Thrale was £30,000, and Dr. Johnson seemed to approve of the connection, for he remarked affably to Robert " that he had heard that he devoted time to reading," and advised him to persevere,

BURY HILL

From an engraving by W. Bray

for " no character was more to be esteemed than one where literature and commerce went hand in hand." He also wrote to John Perkins, saying, " With good wishes for the prosperity of you and your partners, of whom, from one short conversation, I could not judge otherwise than favourably."

In 1781, Robert Barclay moved from Cheapside to Clapham. Here, in spite of taking an active part in the management of the Brewery, he found time for the scientific pursuits which had interested him from an early age, and to develop a taste for gardening.

He also purchased Northrepps Hall, near Cromer, where he and his growing family used to spend every summer amid a happy circle of their many Gurney cousins. Very many years after, sitting in the dining-room at the Hall, Catherine, Lady Buxton, recounted to one of Robert Barclay's descendants the sad story of his little daughter Lucy, who was sternly reproved by her father and sent out of the room in disgrace because she would not drink her beer, saying she hated the taste of it.

Northrepps Hall was afterwards sold to Richard Gurney of Keswick.

In 1805, Robert Barclay became tenant of Bury Hill, Dorking, which house, with seven hundred acres, he subsequently purchased from the Earl of Verulam in 1812.

He was Master of the Worshipful Company of Brewers in 1813, but his enthusiasm for horticulture led him to make over to his eldest son the active share in his business and he " devoted himself on an increasingly large scale to the cultiva- tion of rare and beautiful exotics . . . . This interest had already led to his becoming acquainted with the leading British horticulturists and botanists of the time, such as the elder Aiton, Sir Joseph Banks and William Curtis. He ' strenuously advised Curtis,' as Sir William Hooker records, ' to the publication of the *Botanical Magazine*, and foretold the great success it would experience from the British public. He was one of the original Fellows of the Linnean Society of 1788. . . . He gave attention to the study of botany and to experiments in agriculture. By a lavish expenditure of skill

and wealth he endeavoured to add to the great natural beauty
of his estate. To the existing range of glass-houses, which
he used as a conservatory, were added hot-houses for the
occupation of plants from the tropics. In the outdoor
garden, besides a wealth of hardy plants, was an unusually
large proportion of half-hardy subjects, the successful cultivation of which demonstrated the skilful methods of their
owner and his gardener, Cameron. Some of the trees he
planted in 1815 are still there. Many of his choicest treasures
came from his friend Charles Telfair, of Mauritius, who in
his turn was the recipient of equally generous gifts from
Barclay. In one of the letters from Telfair to his friend
mention is made of blessings conferred by Barclay on Mada-
gascar, where 'your apples, pears, and plums are now in
great abundance in the markets of the capital, and add to
the subsistence as well as the luxuries of a numerous people,
and to the countless generations which will succeed them.'

"An artist was kept by Barclay to draw the new and rare
species as they came into flower, and these drawings were
freely distributed for reproduction in botanical periodicals. . . .

"He realised the value of books in the successful study of
plants, and his collection of works on natural science was
among the finest in the kingdom. It was sold soon after his
death for more than a thousand pounds. . . . Wallich, the
great Indian botanist, appropriately commemorated him in
'Barclaya,' a genus of water-lily."

Robert Barclay remained a member of the Society of
Friends and brought up his family in its principles. He was
closely associated with his relatives the Gurneys, together
with the Buxtons and other families whose names are well
known in philanthropic circles.

Like his uncle, David Barclay of Walthamstow, he was
greatly concerned for the emancipation of slaves, and followed
with active interest the work of William Wilberforce which
was crowned with success in 1807.

He also devoted attention to the question of education,
and the first schools for the poor in his neighbourhood were
founded by him, with the co-operation of his daughters.

276

HISTORY OF THE BARCLAY FAMILY

By his wife, Rachel Gurney, who died in 1794, Robert Barclay had fifteen children, of whom six died in infancy. (See Pedigree D. Part I, p. viii.)

Charles, born 1780, who succeeded him.

David, born 1784, died 1861, " of Eastwick Park." He married Maria, daughter of Sir Hedworth Williamson, and had issue, Hedworth David, Robert William, David, Maria Dorothea and Elizabeth Ann.
(See Pedigree G. Part I, p. xvii.)

Gurney, born 1786, died 1820, stated to have been killed in a duel in Phœnix Park, Dublin. (See also under Robert Barclay, Bank III.) His miniature by Engelhart is at Bury Hill. He married Mary Freshfield and had issue one son, Robert Gurney Barclay, who married Henrietta Wyvill and died without issue. Mary Freshfield married secondly Lieut. Colonel Delancy Barclay, C.B., Aide-de-Camp to H.M. King George IV., a direct descendant of the Rev. Thomas Barclay of Albany, New York, q.v. He was in the Grenadier Guards and fought at Waterloo. He was buried in the family vault of the Barclays of Bury Hill, at Wotton, and having been an immensely tall man his coffin always projected from its niche.

Alexander, died unmarried.

Agatha, married George Hilhouse.

Lucy, married J. Croker Rox.

Anna, married J. Foster Reynolds.

Maria, married Robert Weir Fox.

Martha, married Colonel John Bromhead.

Late in life Robert Barclay married Margaret Hodgson, " a lady long associated with the family, of amiable manners and invariable kindness." She survived her husband and died at Sondes Place, Dorking, 17th January, 1837, aged seventy-three.

Robert Barclay lived to the age of seventy-nine years, dying at Bury Hill in 1830. He was buried with his Quaker forbears, at Winchmore Hill.

Several portraits of Robert Barclay are to be seen at Bury Hill, the most notable of which is by Sir Henry Raeburn (See illustration). There is also a portrait by Gilbert Stewart, an American artist, of his wife Rachel Gurney with two of her daughters, Lucy and Maria.

CHARLES BARCLAY

Chief of the House of Barclay

Charles Barclay of Bury Hill, eldest son of Robert Barclay (Bury Hill I) and his wife Rachel Gurney, was born in Cheapside on December 26th, 1780, just before his parents moved to reside at Clapham. He was educated first at the school his father had attended at Wandsworth, and later at Alton in Hampshire.

An amusing incident is related of him in his boyhood. His first cousin Elizabeth Gurney, afterwards Elizabeth Fry, exhibited the youthful ardour of her Republican sympathies by riding through Norwich wearing the tricolor cockade, the new badge of Revolutionary France, which seriously displeased Charles. They were both about fifteen years old at the time, so that even as a boy Charles showed that respect for the Constitution which became marked in later years.

He and his brothers and sisters were brought up as Quakers, but when England was threatened by the increasing power of Napoleon and invasion was feared " his patriotism exceeded his zeal for the old worship of his forefathers" and he joined the local militia raised for the defence of his country. His sisters remained Friends, though one of them married a soldier.

On August 1st, 1804, at the age of twenty-four, he married Anna Maria, eldest daughter of Thomas Kett of Seething, a lineal descendant of Robert Kett, leader of the " Norfolk Rebellion " in 1549. Charles and his wife lived for a time in his father's house at Clapham, where so many of his relatives resided, and here their eldest son was born, but he purchased a house for himself there in 1808.

Like his father and great-uncle he took a prominent part in the Anti-Slavery Campaign, and, with the many supporters of the movement who were his near neighbours, formed the " Clapham Society " for advancing the cause. A seal used at this time is still at Bury Hill. It is engraved with the

CHARLES BARCLAY, M.P. (Bury Hill II)

By E. U. Eddis

figure of a slave, kneeling on his right knee, with chains attached from his wrists to his ankles, and bears the motto,

" Am I not a man and a brother ? "

Charles had early entered the Brewery, and soon after 1812 his father's retirement from active participation in its affairs threw the main responsibility for its management upon his shoulders.

He was, however, able to find time to take up political work and in 1815, in spite of strong democratic opposition, was returned Member for Southwark in the Tory interest. He supported Sir Robert Peel, but did not achieve re-election in 1818 and remained out of Parliament for some years.

He and his family enjoyed country life in Suffolk, spending every summer at his house at Henstead, near Beccles. They left Clapham about 1823, and moved to London, 43 Grosvenor Place.

In 1826, Charles Barclay returned to the House of Commons as Member for Dundalk, having purchased the seat, as was the custom before the Reform Bill.

He was still actively engaged in his business and was Master of the Brewers Company in the same year.

By this time his sons were growing up and, finding Henstead too far from London, he rented Betchworth Castle, near Dorking, a fine sporting estate of some three thousand acres. He did not live there very long, however, as upon the death of his father in 1830 he succeeded to the estates of Bury Hill.

Four years later, upon the fall of the Whig Ministry, it was understood that Sir Robert Peel was to form an administration, and Charles Barclay, a warm admirer of his policy, was induced to stand for West Surrey. After a lengthy canvass he was elected, a success due in large measure to the personal exertions of his sons. His youngest son, Thomas George, then a boy of fifteen, used in his old age to recount amusing stories of the appalling bribery of the election, when pound notes were slipped into the housewife's teapot (the " teapot vote ") and voters were handed half a five-pound note on mounting the hustings and received the other half on descending, if they had " voted straight."

In 1838 Charles Barclay retired from Parliament, his health having suffered from the late hours of the House and from the strain of great anxiety in regard to his wife, who was gravely ill. She died on March 15th, 1840.

After her death Charles Barclay, accompanied by George and his daughter Juliana, went abroad, spending the following winter in Italy. Returning to Bury Hill, he busied himself in the improvement of the house and estate, planting many conifers which flourish to-day. He built the Home Farm and Chadhurst and experimented in improved methods of farming and the Norfolk system of land drainage. He also built Westcott Vicarage and schools, and was largely responsible for the erection of Westcott Church, and Coldharbour and Holmwood schools.

He was High Sheriff of Surrey in 1842, and President of the Board of Governors of Guy's Hospital from 1848 to the end of his life.

After the marriage of Juliana in 1847, his son Arthur Kett Barclay with his wife and family went to live at Bury Hill. The old gentleman was regarded with affection mingled with awe by his grandchildren, to whom he was known as " The Patriarch."

It has already been recorded that, at the death of his kinsman Captain Barclay-Allardice (Urie VI) in 1854, Charles Barclay, as heir male, became " Chief of the House of Barclay."

In the following year, when riding in the grounds, his cob was startled by a hunted deer springing out of covert, and the resultant fall gave him a shock from which he did not recover. He died within a few weeks of his seventy-fifth year, and was buried in the family vault at Wotton.

By his wife, Anna Maria Kett, Charles Barclay (Bury Hill II) had four sons and three daughters :

Arthur Kett, born 1806, who succeeded him.

Robert, born 1808, died 1843. Head of Harrow School and a member of the Cricket XI in 1825. For details of his early life see under his brother Arthur Kett (Bury Hill III). Robert was a man of great height and possessed of exceptional powers of body and mind, a good sportsman and a brilliant shot. He entered the firm of Barclay Bros., in

ROBERT BARCLAY (Bury Hill I)

By Sir Henry Raeburn

Austin Friars, in 1830, and was appointed a Director of the Bank of England about the year 1841. He had made an especial study of international finance and, although so young, his opinion seems to have carried weight. He succeeded his father as a Director of the Imperial Insurance Company and occupied a prominent place on that Board. He was a keen gardener, and one of the earliest growers of orchidaceous plants. His untimely death at the age of 35 cut short a brilliant career. He died at his house, The Grove, Lower Tooting, and was buried in the family vault at Wotton. By his wife, Rachel, daughter of Osgood Hanbury of Holfield Grange, and granddaughter of John Barclay (Bank I), whom he married January 25th, 1830, Robert Barclay had two sons and two daughters:—

CHARLES BARCLAY, 1780–1855, Bury Hill II.

Hanbury, born 1836, died 1909, married Adeline Henrietta Barclay of Bury Hill, his first cousin, and had issue, of whom the eldest is Hubert Frederick Barclay, compiler of this History.

Charles, born 1837, died 1910. Harrow School Cricket XI, 1856/7, Trinity Coll., Cambridge. Married 1875, Charlotte Cassandra, daughter of Benjamin Cherry of Brickendon, Hertford, and had issue. His only son, Charles Roger, Lt. Northumberland Fusiliers, was killed in action near Reddersburg, S.A., April 4th 1900.

Anna Maria, married in 1852 Sampson Hanbury, died 1877.

Emily, married in 1862 F. Hayward Joyce, Vicar of Harrow, died 1922.

Mrs. Robert Barclay died in 1895. (See Pedigree F, Part I, p. xviii)

Charles, born 1810, died at Harrow 1823.

Thomas George, born 1819, died 1894 without issue. Married Emily, daughter of Rev. William Joyce, Vicar of Dorking, and sister of F. Hayward Joyce. Resided at Lower Woodside, Hatfield. Master of the Brewers Company in 1863.

Caroline, married in 1837 John Gurney Hoare of Hampstead. Their grandson is Sir Samuel Hoare, P.C., C.M.G., C.S.I., present Secretary of State for India.

Rachel Juliana, married in 1847 Joseph Hoare of Hampstead, brother of the above.

Anna Maria, who died young.

An excellent portrait of Charles Barclay (Bury Hill II) by Eddis hangs at Bury Hill. A picture of Anna Maria Kett and her sister (Mrs. Thompson) is in the possession of F. Maltby Bland, Esq. of Inglethorpe Manor, Wisbech.

ARTHUR
KETT
BARCLAY,
1806–1869,
Bury Hill
III.

ARTHUR KETT BARCLAY

"CHIEF OF THE HOUSE OF BARCLAY"

Arthur Kett Barclay, of Bury Hill, eldest son of Charles Barclay (Bury Hill II) and Anna Maria Kett his wife, was born at Clapham Terrace, the home of his grandfather, (Bury Hill I), on June 20th, 1806. He succeeded his father in 1855.

From a manuscript written by him on the death of his younger brother Robert, we learn not only many incidents of their childhood, but of the very deep affection that existed between them. The slight difference (only two years) in their ages made it possible for them to be close companions both at home and at school.

In 1808 his father purchased a house on Clapham Common, where, for the greater part of the year, the family resided. Each autumn for many years was spent in Norfolk or Suffolk. Arthur Kett well remembered the

" annoyance of the two long days travelling, at first in one well-filled carriage and latterly in two, when the quietest child was promoted to the honour of sharing the chariot of the parents. Quiet was not Robert's characteristic quality, and it is on record that during one of these journeys much surprise was manifested at his unusual stillness, till it was discovered that he had made entry with his foot into a huge jar of honey and was sedulously employed in conveying from his shoe to his mouth the spoil he had so ingeniously acquired."

In 1813 the two brothers were sent together to a small school at Stockwell kept by a Mr. Everington, " an irritable and injudicious master, and no school could have been worse conducted." Twice the little boys escaped, by climbing the playground paling and letting themselves down by their pinafores. Robert, though younger, was the more valiant-hearted, and led the way, encouraging Arthur by anticipations of a good tea at home. The first time their mother was alone and they were not punished, merely handed over to the pedagogue who came to fetch them ; but the second time

282

their father was at home and they were forced to return without tea and with " such admonitions as they deserved."

They were, however, removed from the school after a few months and spent the autumn at Henstead, near Beccles, under the tuition of their mother and two brothers who kept a school at Wangford.

" Our Mother's taste for History and Poetry and her unremitting attention and care probably then laid the foundation of a love for these subjects and excited our imaginations under the best and most judicious control. At this time, or possibly a little later, we knew most of Scott's ballads, much of the earlier romance poetry, and were conversant with the Iliad and Odyssey in Pope's translation, and well instructed in Northern Mythology as well as that of Greece and Rome.

" I believe a sound knowledge of the principles of religion had by this time been induced. It was never a subject injudiciously and unseasonably obtruded, but our excellent Mother never lost a opportunity of impressing upon us the value of its truths, and a constant habit of reading the Bible to our Father on Sunday evenings was preserved through many years."

At the end of the year the brothers were sent to a school at East Sheen kept by Dr. Pearson, who was an able astronomer, and his influence laid the foundation of the interest in that study which was so marked in Arthur in later life.

Among their school fellows were two sons of the Duke of Wellington, and Arthur writes :

" The Duchess used frequently to come and see them, and at last the Duke himself returned after Waterloo. When he came we were all turned out on the lawn to receive him with our puny cheers ; and well I remember how, with our heads full of Robin Hood and Amadis de Gaule, we could hardly realise to ourselves the greatest man in the world, as we were told he was, in the thin, quiet looking individual in a blue coat and loose trowsers, the latter then worn by boys only, the fathers of all probably wearing the top boot, and leather breeches."

Here, although he had been vaccinated, Robert contracted smallpox, and his case excited great interest among medical men. He soon recovered, but shortly after both brothers were seriously ill with measles. They were removed home

ARTHUR
KETT
BARCLAY,
1806–1869,
Bury Hill
III.
and devotedly nursed by their father and mother. During their convalescence, their mother, having " devoted herself to mastering the rudiments of the Latin Grammar," was again their teacher, and so marked was her success that on their return to school they had lost no ground.

Leaving this school, they and their younger brother Charles shared a tutor, Mr. Lunn, of whom Arthur Kett gratefully stated he derived the greater part of the knowledge he possessed.

The home life of the family was exceedingly happy, and he describes not only his studies, but the pleasures of holidays devoted to sport ; cricket and riding, " attending the shooters" and " visits to the sea beach at Bennacre "; the rapture of games of chivalry in suits of " lead paper " made by their mother and " correctly fashioned from engravings in Grosse's ' Antiquities.' We were almost as conversant with hawberk, plate mail and almain rivets as Dr. Meyrick himself." The evenings were often spent in " the exercise of capping verses and in various games to improve the memory." This pastime seems to have descended in the family, for the children of Robert's son Hanbury were also skilled in it in their childhood.

In 1819 Arthur and Robert went to Harrow, then at the height of its reputation under Dr. George Butler, and here, two years later, they were joined by their brother Charles. Arthur found the study of Latin and Greek distasteful, being more interested in science and astronomy, and his brother Robert progressed more rapidly. It was perhaps for this reason that his parents removed him from school in 1822.

The next year the family suffered a sad loss in the death of Charles, a boy of twelve, from pneumonia subsequent on a chill contracted by jumping into " Ducker " when overheated from strenuous exercise, to retrieve the knife of a school fellow.

Arthur Kett was then placed with a private tutor, Mr. Taddy, at Northhill, under whose care he remained until Christmas, 1824, when he commenced work at the Brewery, living during the week at his father's town house in Grosvenor Place.

Robert left Harrow about this time and went for two years to a private tutor at Bovingdon, near Hemel Hempstead, where he enjoyed shooting over ". a large tract of unpreserved ground " and frequently sent his brother a " neat little box, made by himself, containing snipes, partridges and other spoils."

A serious accident from the bursting of a powder flask incapacitated Arthur during the summer of 1825, and he notes that " the winter produced the eventful panic when for a time credit was almost annihilated and the greatest commercial difficulties ensued." It will be remembered that this was the result of a great rush to invest in Joint Stock Companies promising a high rate of interest. The wildest schemes were rife and loans were granted to half the States in the world. Paper money was issued by the banks to an extent far beyond what was prudent, and in the subsequent panic fifty banks shut their doors and more than two hundred merchants became insolvent.

The following year Arthur Kett made a tour through the west of England and Wales with his friend Mervyn Crawford, from which he returned to Henstead, where he found " our old friend David Barclay (Urie VIc), now a Captain in the 28th Regiment," and passed a merry winter in the pleasures of society, both in their own neighbourhood and Norwich, before returning to Grosvenor Place and the active duties of business.

In 1827 the brothers spent some months in Scotland, where they journeyed from island to island amongst the Hebrides, and visited Urie, where they received a hospitable welcome from Captain Barclay (Urie VI).

A journal kept at this time records the prowess of Robert with a gun and his great walking powers.

Shortly afterwards the younger brother entered the firm of Barclay Brothers, and the two lived happily together at Grosvenor Place, spending the week-ends at Betchworth Castle, not far from Bury Hill, which their father had taken in order to be nearer his boys than he would have been at Henstead. In 1828 Arthur Kett became a partner in the Brewery.

This pleasant life was, however, soon to be interrupted, for

HISTORY OF THE BARCLAY FAMILY

ARTHUR
KETT
BARCLAY,
1806–1869,
Bury Hill
III.

Robert met Rachel Hanbury and fell deeply in love with her. Their mutual attachment was declared and there was no obstacle to their union except Robert's youth, and his father decreed that he must see a little more of the world before thinking of marriage, so sent the brothers abroad.

They visited Norway, Sweden, Finland, St. Petersburg, and then, " placing their carriage on a sledge, set out for Moscow," eventually returning home by Smolensk, Warsaw, Prague, Dresden, Berlin, Brussels, Lille and Calais. Arthur's journal records that during the latter part of the journey they travelled day and night " in order to try to keep pace with Robert's anxious wish to return, and on the 25th day of January, 1830, we drove up to the door at Betchworth in the same little carriage which we had taken from England, wrapped in the furs and Russian dresses which had enabled us to bear the cold of one of the most severe winters known for years."

Shortly after their return, Robert was admitted into partnership with his uncle David Barclay (of Eastwick, Bury Hill IIB) and Robert Foster Reynolds, constituting the house of business of Barclay Brothers, Merchants. His wedding took place in the following February.

In October of the year 1830 the grandfather, Robert Barclay (Bury Hill I), died, and, Arthur Kett's father suceeeding to the estates, the family moved to reside there.

The young man interested himself in resuscitating the Surrey Yeomanry Cavalry, a task which he carried through with zeal and efficiency.

The following extract from Arthur Kett's diary gives us a glimpse of his doings at the time of the Coronation of William IV in 1831.

" September 5th. (To London on the (Horsham) Coach.)

In town all dull except for prepaiations for the Coronation ; which already begin to spread their ephemeral structure against the swarthy architecture of Parliament Street.

September 6th.

Hard work all day (at the Brewhouse) and then visited the world at the Athenæum, where they have determined to put up benches to see the Procession on Thursday, and to admit ladies introduced by members. Walked back again to ye Boro to bed.

286

HISTORY OF THE BARCLAY FAMILY

Thursday 8th.

ARTHUR KETT BARCLAY, 1806–1869, Bury Hill III.

Dies alba notanda lapilla. . . . 5 a.m. commenced the crush of carriages, the throng of humanity. After surveying ye long train of vehicles and their enclosures of feathers, diamonds and wigs, resought my warm nest and snoozed till eight, dreaming of the sleepless wretches " dreeing their weird in the cloistered aisles," when I betook myself to the Athenæum where were Uncle David (of Eastwick), his two boys (Hedworth and Alexander), the Hudson Gurneys, McInnes and hundreds of friends and acquaintances more. . . . That old fox, the Dean of Carlisle (what a bore is a half dabbler in science knowing nothing, a pretender to literature and sleek-faced divine). Just as we were going to begin breakfast Mrs. Gurney began to regret the loss (waste) of a lady's ticket, a peer's, which she had in her reticule and which she could not find anyone to take. I immediately replied, " Give it to me, and I'll be the lady to go in with it," thinking that so late in the day that if there was room the doorkeepers would not be particular.

With extreme exertion I squeezed thro' the dense mob and made my way to the Strand, from whence I made my way by water to the Brewhouse, donned my uniform, and after having astonished the murky countenances of the Borovians with ye nodding plumes and gilded broderie like a chevalier of Elizabethan age, took boat for Westminster. Arrived there, my stout rowers, leaving the vessel, made way for me thro' the crowd to the doors of the Abbey, when the " Admit Miss Gurney " safely introduced the rather unfeminine Cornet Arthur Barclay.

I scrambled up the rather unpromising wooden staircase and made my way thro' plumes and diamonds, swords and sabretaches, till I attained a vacant bench ; and then for the first time I felt I was safe and turned my eyes to gaze. Would that I were Philippe de Comines, or that more ancient author who had the good fortune to be able to describe the " Champ de Drap d'Or," then might I try to recount the blaze of beauty and the glare of jewels that met my sight.

My lucky position was in the north transept. The front rows were occupied by the peers, and those immediately behind by the fortunate few who possessed peer's tickets. On the opposite side were the Peeresses, and proud must anyone present have been to think he was an Englishman on viewing the noble bank of " Ladies fair " reaching from the floor high up towards the fretted roof. The blaze of diamonds in ye distance gave a sort of mirage effect particularly striking : the individual persons were lost in the dazzling total, and it was with almost a feeling of giddiness that one viewed the splendid assemblage where the richest decorations of female beauty vied with the proudest memorials of military honour.

HISTORY OF THE BARCLAY FAMILY

ARTHUR
KETT
BARCLAY,
1806–1869,
Bury Hill
III.

The *Gazette* gives details of the august ceremony ; the noble majesty of the King and ye graceful dignity of ye Queen, etc., etc.

His Majesty, poor man, looked woefully encumbered with his robes and bustled about with an air worthy of gentle King Jamie ; every movement expressed a wish that his canvass was furled and that he had made port. The Queen in all moved a sovereign, grace, elegance and self-possession united. The Hommage was interesting . . . it was gracefully done by the D. of Devonshire, awkwardly by most and none more so than Lord Grey . . . cavalierly by the D. of Wellington, with his coronet tossed on like a forage cap and whose proud eye seemed to intimate " It's your turn now to endanger old England's peace and tranquility, but a stronger hand at the tiller will be wanted yet."

Among the Peeresses none shone to greater advantage than the young Duchess of Richmond. She sat between the Dow^r Duchess and the Duchess of St. Albans, and two better foils could not have been found for her youthful and elegant appearance.

After the ceremony was over and nothing but the receiving of the Sacrament remained to be performed, I scrambled over the back rails of the platform, and, letting myself down into the stream below, gained the door and made my escape long before the throng commenced, and passing by Storey's Gate into the Park, made for ye Athenæum by the new steps opened to-day from the bottom of Waterloo Place. Here, to the greatest advantage, I saw the returning procession, the effect of which was good and noble.

Public opinion was not pleased by the prominent part taken in it by the Fitz Clarences and this has been given as the reason why the Princess Victoria was not present at the ceremony. The D. of Cumberland was received with marked groans and hisses and no one cried " God bless him."

The day was most unpropitious, torrents of rain fell at intervals and sorely discomforted the full dress appointments of the officers on duty. Nothing could exceed the good order and tranquility of the people, even the rain did not put them out of temper, and not a murmur was audible except with regard to the D. . . ."

Arthur Kett Barclay adds that he perambulated the West End with his uncle David and his two boys and saw the display of fireworks in the evening, and under date the day following comments on the

" dull aspect of the relicts of the festival. The vacant seats in process of being removed . . . the long-snuffed candle ends, the burnt out lamps and the grim transparancies hating the light of day . . .

288

and in animate life the fevered eye of alcoholic intoxication and the dull vacant expression of half slept-off beer ! "

" Southwark felt not the excitement " and after a few hours at the Brewhouse he started for Betchworth.

Within a month excitement of a different kind occupied Arthur Kett's attention, for on Saturday, October 8th, 1831, his first thought on waking was, " That the Reform Bill had been thrown out by a majority of 41." Riots broke out in various parts of the country, and on the 14th he notes further details of a row at Derby and the burning of Nottingham Castle by the mob. Rumour was active, and possibly no more accurate than it is to-day.—" Mobs in Bristol. Slaughter by the military, Town sacked and Bishop's palace burned to the ground . . . some killed and many wounded by the sabres of the 14th and 3rd Dragoons who behaved well." By November 4th trouble had begun nearer home, for he records " rumours of a large seizure of arms near Lambeth and of a plot to burn down Lambeth Palace . . . something appears to be dreaded, as special constables are being sworn in in the Boro' and in the City." He determined not to go down to Bury Hill, but looked over the arms stored in the Armoury at the Brewhouse. He found " 35 muskets, about 20 swords, two large bundles of boarding pikes, 4 small cannons and plenty of grape shot and ball cartridges. I trust we shall not have to use them."

The following day, anticipating a visit from the mob, he and T. Perkins

" marshalled our disposable force here, amounting to more than 150, into gangs, each commanded by from three to four Clerks as officers, and arranged a regular plan of defence in case of necessity. In the course of the day George Perkins called to tell me that the services of the London troops of the Surrey Yeomanry Cavalry were accepted for Monday. Artillery and troops have come to town and the 9th Lancers are at the Mews in Pimlico."

On November 7th Arthur turned out early and found all quiet in the Boro' and elsewhere. At eleven he joined the Surrey Yeomanry at the Boro' Sessions House and marched to the riding school in Stamford Street, where they were

joined by the Clapham and Vauxhall troops. Cartridges
were distributed, but after waiting all day they were dis-
missed by a letter from Sir Willoughby Gordon with praises
and thanks for their activity, somewhat disappointed, evidently, by the flatness of the termination of their service.
By the next day, though still full of troops, the town was
quiet enough.

On November 8th, 1833, he was gazetted a Captain in the
Surrey Yeomanry Cavalry, and remained Captain of the
Dorking Troop for many years.

His work at the Brewery does not seem to have been exacting,
for in 1832–3 he was again abroad for a year, and in the
winter of 1834–5 he and his brother Robert threw themselves wholeheartedly into the task of canvassing for their
father, who was candidate for the West Surrey Division
in the election which followed the dismissal of the Whig
Ministry by William IV, "when the long-crushed Conservative Party began again to raise its head." Robert took the
management of the Chertsey voters, while Arthur was allotted
the more southern part of the county. He records that their
days "were spent on horseback seeking out voters widely
spread over the unenclosed heaths, or calling from house to
house in the towns . . . the reaction so much talked about
did not appear to have reached the ignorant and miserable
voters of the wild parts of Surrey, and there it was that our
personal influence was made to tell and we succeeded in
turning many a vote to our side, and by good-humoured
reasoning and constant attention to counteract the acts of our
vigilant opponents." Success attended their efforts and the
Radical candidate, Mr. Long, was defeated by thirty votes.

In December, 1836, Arthur Kett Barclay married Maria
Octavia, daughter of Ichabod Wright, of Mapperly, Notting-
ham, and the young couple resided in the family house at
Grosvenor Place.

Within a month of their wedding Arthur Kett was indignant to find that, entirely without permission, he had been
left guardian to four orphan cousins, the pitiful children
of the marriage of his aunt Martha and Colonel Bromhead.

His beautiful young wife Octavia insisted on taking charge of the half-witted twin girls, one of whom died young, and the other, after leaving school, found a home with her sister Lucy, who had been adopted by their aunt, Mrs. Weir Fox. The boy, Alexander, being about the same age as Thomas George, was brought up at Bury Hill, and became a clergyman.

Leaving London after a short time, Arthur Kett Barclay and his wife moved to a house called The Grove, at Lower Tooting. Here they were within easy distance of Clapham, where not only his brother Robert, but many other relatives resided, and in a pleasant family circle the years passed happily, and Arthur found time to pursue his scientific interests. He left Tooting in 1838 and went to reside at Norbury Park, near Croydon, and Robert succeeded him at The Grove. After his mother's death in 1840 his father's failing health necessitated his being much at Bury Hill, where he built the Observatory, and for his valuable astronomical researches was invited to become a Fellow of the Royal Society. He also belonged to many other learned associations, becoming one of the trustees for the Great Exhibition of 1851.

In 1843 an overwhelming sorrow fell upon him in the death of his beloved brother and companion Robert, whose widow and four children became his constant care.

As has already been recorded, the death of Captain Barclay-Allardice, fifth Laird of Urie, occurred in 1854, and Arthur's father, Charles (Bury Hill II), became Heir Male of the line. His poor health necessitated Arthur Kett undertaking all business connected with the settlement of his affairs and the sale of Urie. Charles died in the following year, and Arthur Kett succeeded to the estates of Bury Hill, where he had been living with his father since 1847.

Three years later, in 1858, he matriculated his arms at the Lyon College. Documents preserved at Urie and Bury Hill were submitted to the Lord Lyon and claim established to the Arms as borne by Colonel David *anno* 1666. A patent of confirmation was issued declaring Arthur Kett Barclay

ARTHUR KETT BARCLAY, 1806–1869, Bury Hill III.

Deed of Matriculation, Bury Hill.

291

HISTORY OF THE BARCLAY FAMILY

ARTHUR
KETT
BARCLAY,
1806–1869,
Bury Hill
III.
" Heir Male and Representative of the Family of Mathers, now the First or principle Family of the Name existing," and entitled to the distinction of supporters to his shield as used by his ancestors. The same Coat of Arms was assigned and ratified to him under the following description :

" Azure a chevron, and in chief three crosses patées argent. Above the shield is placed a Helmet befitting his degree, with a Mantling azure, double argent, and upon a wreath of his liveries is set for crest a Bishop's Mitre affrontée with tassels flottant upwards or, and in an escroll above the same this motto, " IN CRUCE SPERO," and upon a compartment below the shield are placed for Supporters Two Savages wreathed around the loins with Oak Leaves, and holding on their exterior hands Clubs erect all proper, but which distinction of Supporters is limited to the said Patentee and the heirs male of his Body."

There is no mention of the Dove and the Olive Branch, which had been introduced by Robert (Urie III), but it is borne at the present time, together with the Mitre, as double crest, by the Chief of the Family and by many of its members.

Arthur Kett Barclay took an active part in the management of the Brewery, being Master of the Brewers' Company in 1840, but nevertheless found time for many and varied interests. His sound knowledge, not only of astronomy but also of geology and chemistry, gave him a prominent place in the scientific world of his day ; he was indefatigable in promoting the establishment of the Surrey Rifle Volunteers ; he was Justice of the Peace and Deputy Lieutenant for Surrey; but at the early age of fifty he began to be disabled by threatened paralysis. His sound constitution and strong spirit fought against its advance, but for two years before his death, in 1869, he was a complete invalid.

He was a man of noble and unselfish character, strong religious principles, just and calm judgment, and was sincerely mourned by all who knew him.

His wife Octavia survived him for many years, dying at the age of ninety-five at the house of her daughter, Mrs. Lea Wilson, in Nottingham, on the 19th October, 1902. She was a beautiful artist in water colour, and many of her pictures remain to-day at Bury Hill.

292

HISTORY OF THE BARCLAY FAMILY

By her Arthur Kett Barclay had five sons and six daughters :—

Robert, who succeeded him.

Charles Arthur, born 1839, died 1901. Married in 1864 Rhoda, daughter of John Bentley of Lancashire, and had issue.

Frederick Kett, born 1841, died without issue 1894.

Charles Wright, born 1853, died 1926. Vicar of Little Amwell, Hertfordshire, compiler of Part I of this History. Married Florence, daughter of the Rev. S. B. Charlesworth, and a well-known novelist, and had issue.

Henry John, who died young.

Harriet Maria, born 1842. When little more than a girl she decided to dedicate herself to evangelistic work. In a day when such a course was almost unheard of, she deliberately forwent wealth and comfort in order to take the Gospel message to the poor, the outcast and the foreigner. She went to Bermondsey in south-east London, where she still lives in her house " Urie," near St. James's Church ; and to-day, having attained the great age of ninety-one years, she is still continuing the noble work to which her long life has been unfalteringly devoted.

Rachel Caroline, born 1844, died 1888. Married Colonel Sir James Gildea, C.B.E., K.C.V.O., C.B.

Adeline Henrietta, born 1846, died 1899. Married her first cousin Hanbury Barclay and was the mother of the compiler of this History.

Emily Octavia, born 1847, died 1926. Married His Honour Sir Reginald More Bray, Judge of the High Court.

Margaret, born 1848, died 1915. Married Sir Arthur Clay, Bart.

Neville Juliana, born 1851, died 1933. Married the Rev. Charles Lea Wilson.

(See Part I. Pedigrees, pp. viii–xvi.)

ROBERT BARCLAY

" CHIEF OF THE HOUSE OF BARCLAY "

Robert Barclay, of Bury Hill, eldest son of Arthur Kett
Barclay and his wife Maria Octavia Wright, was born at the
Grove, Tooting, in 1837.

In January 1851 he entered Harrow School, first as a Home
Boarder, living with his aunt Mrs. Robert Barclay, and later
at the Head Master's House. He remained there four years
and then passed on to Trinity College, Cambridge, where he
took his degree, B.A., in 1859, and M.A. in 1862.

He was a keen athlete and ran second in the quarter mile in
the " Cambridge University foot races " in 1857, and first
in the quarter mile in his College races in the same year. His
time cannot have equalled the record of to-day, as he ran in
flannel trousers tucked into his socks.

On leaving Cambridge Robert Barclay began work at the
Brewery, but found time to take an active interest in the
Local Volunteers, being gazetted Lieutenant in the 14th
Company of the Surrey Rifle Volunteers in 1860, and in the
following year he and his brother, Ensign Charles Arthur,
were attached for training to the 3rd Battalion Grenadier
Guards.

In 1861 Robert Barclay was appointed a Director of the
Royal Exchange Assurance Company, which position he held
until his death.

In 1868, when troubles in Ireland and consequent Fenian
outrages in England caused acute alarm, special constables
were called for for the protection of London, and Robert
Barclay, with others from the Brewery, was sworn in at
Southwark.

He succeeded his father in the estate at Bury Hill in
1869, and from that time onward took a keen interest in
local and county affairs, being Chairman of the Dorking
Conservative Association for many years, Deputy Lieutenant
for the County of Surrey, Justice of the Peace, and High
Sheriff in 1878.

294

HISTORY OF THE BARCLAY FAMILY

In 1877 he married Laura Charlotte Rachel, daughter of Marmaduke Wyvill of Constable Burton and Denton Park, Yorkshire. ROBERT BARCLAY, 1837–1913, Bury Hill IV.

The fourth generation of his family to hold the office, Robert Barclay was Master of the Worshipful Company of Brewers in 1871. The fifth generation was represented by his nephews, Hubert Frederick in 1905 and Edwyn Frederick in 1919 and 1920.

In the closing years of last century Robert Barclay made considerable alterations and improvements in the mansion at Bury Hill, rebuilding and heightening the two wings and thereby adding to the dignity and proportion of the whole.

He was " Warden of Great Account " in 1905, the year of the inauguration of the scheme of extensive restoration of the Church of S. Mary Overy (Southwark Cathedral) in which he was actively concerned. It will be remembered that it was in this ancient edifice that James I, King of Scotland, while a prisoner in England in 1423, was married to the Earl of Somerset's daughter, Lady Joan Beaufort, his " milk white dove," whose courtship he recorded in " The Kingis Quair." Part II, page 92.

Robert Barclay took an active share in the management of the Brewery, becoming Chairman when the business was reconstituted a Limited Company in 1896, and retaining that office until 1911.

He died at Bury Hill in 1913 and was buried in the churchyard at Westcott.

He was a man of retiring disposition and great kindness of heart, and will long be remembered for his unobtrusive but unfailing generosity to all in need.

By his wife Rachel, Robert Barclay had four sons and one daughter :—

Robert Wyvill, born 1880, who succeeded him.
Thomas Hubert, born 1884, educated Harrow and Trinity College, Cambridge. Major The Surrey (Queen Mary's Own) Yeomanry. Drowned on active service in 1917.
Arthur Victor, born 1887, educated Harrow and Trinity College, Cambridge. 2nd Lieutenant The Surrey (Queen Mary's

295

Regiment) Yeomanry and The King's African Rifles in the Great War. Was severely wounded. Married Katherine, daughter of Arthur Wilcox of U.S.A. and has issue two daughters.

George Eric, born 1889, educated Harrow and R.M.C. Sandhurst. Captain King's Own Royal Lancaster Regiment, attached to The Nigeria Regiment. Killed in action in East Africa, 1917.

Ellen Rachel, married in 1922 the Rev. Alfred E. Farrow, Vicar of S. Cuthbert's, Sheffield.

LIEUTENANT-COLONEL ROBERT WYVILL BARCLAY

" Chief of the House of Barclay "

Robert Wyvill Barclay, the present Chief of the House of Barclay and fifth of Bury Hill, eldest son of Robert Barclay of Bury Hill (IV) and his wife Rachel, was born 23rd November 1880.

Educated St. David's, Reigate, private tutors, and Trinity College, Cambridge. Distinguished athlete, created a record by winning the 100 yards and ¼-mile races against Oxford for three consecutive years, 1902–1904. Was in the Oxford and Cambridge Athletic Team for the ¼-mile race against Toronto and McGill Universities at Montreal, ran second, and against Yale and Harvard Universities at New York, ran third, in 1901, also, in 1904, against Yale and Harvard at Queen's Club London, when he was second in the 100 yards and the ¼ mile.

Joined the Hampshire Carabineers Yeomanry Cavalry in 1900 and transferred to the Surrey Imperial Yeomanry on their formation in 1901.

After leaving Cambridge he entered Barclay's Brewery and became a Director in 1911.

He succeeded to Bury Hill on the death of his father in 1913. Deputy Lieutenant for Surrey 1921, High Sheriff of Surrey 1923.

At the outbreak of War commanded a Squadron of Surrey (Queen Mary's Regiment) Yeomanry, later went as second in command to the Reserve Regiment for a short time, with Headquarters at Bury Hill, then promoted to T/Lieut.-Colonel to Command the 2nd Reserve Regiment, shortly afterwards called the 3/1 Surrey (Q.M.R.) Yeomanry. In 1916 transferred to the 2nd Life Guards and served in France and Belgium to the end of the War.

Married, in 1904, Elsa Mary, only daughter of Sir Edward Bray, County Court Judge, and has issue :—

> Robert Edward, born 1906, thirty-first in descent from Roger de
> Berchelai of Gloucestershire. Educated at Harrow and

ROBERT
Wyvill
BARCLAY,
1880–
Bury Hill
V.

Trinity College, Cambridge. Captain in the 98th (Surrey and Sussex Yeomanry, Queen Mary's) Brigade, Royal Artillery, Territorial Army. Married in 1932 Nesta Anne, daughter of James Robert Bury-Barry, O.B.E., D.L., of Ballyclough, Co. Cork, and Redhurst, Cranleigh, Surrey.

John Stephen, born 1908. Educated at Harrow and Trinity College, Cambridge. Barrister-at-law.

Malcolm Eric, born 1912. Educated at Harrow and Trinity College, Cambridge. 2nd Lieutenant 98th (Surrey and Sussex Yeomanry, Queen Mary's) Brigade, Royal Artillery, Territorial Army.

Mary Priscilla Rachel, born 1905.

HISTORY OF THE BARCLAY FAMILY

During the lifetime of the present holder of Bury Hill, the ROBERT WYVILL BARCLAY, 1880- Bury Hill V. world has been convulsed by the Great War, 1914–1918. It is fitting that special mention should be made of those of the Barclay family who laid down their lives for their country.

RAFE HEDWORTH MYDDELTON, born 1892. Only son of Major Hedworth Trelawny Barclay, and great-grandson of David Barclay of Eastwick Park (Bury Hill IIB). Educated at Rugby, gazetted 2nd Lieutenant in the 60th Rifles, K.R.R.C., June, 1914. Killed in action at the Battle of the Aisne, September 14th, 1914, aged 22 years.

COLIN EDWYN, born 1893. Eldest son of Edwyn Frederick Barclay, and grandson of Charles Arthur Barclay (Bury Hill IVB). Educated at Harrow. Captain in the Royal Field Artillery. Severely wounded, losing his leg, at the Battle of Ypres, 1915. Died, February 25th, 1921, aged 28 years. 1914 Star and Croix de Guerre.

DAVID STUART, born 1897. Third son of Colonel Hugh Gurney Barclay, M.V.O., of Colney Hall, Norwich, and great-grandson of Ford Barclay of Walthamstow (Bank IIIB). Educated at Eton. Lieutenant in the Scots Guards. Severely wounded and blinded in his first engagement, the Battle of the Somme, 1916. Died on April 24th, 1917, aged 20 years.

GEOFFREY WILLIAM, born 1891. Second son of Edward Exton Barclay, M.F.H., of Brent Pelham Hall, and grandson of Joseph Gurney Barclay (Bank IV). Educated at Eton and Cambridge. Joined the 1st Battalion Rifle Brigade, August 1913. Was in the Mons Retreat. Severely wounded in 1915. On recovery returned to the 1st Battalion Rifle Brigade as Major, and was in command of the Battalion for some months. Killed in action near Ypres, July 28th, 1916, aged 24 years. Military Cross, mentioned in despatches May 31st, 1915.

GEORGE ERIC, born 1889. Fourth son of Robert Barclay (Bury Hill IV). Educated at Harrow and Royal Military College Sandhurst. Gazetted to the King's Own (Royal Lancaster Regiment). Attached to the 2nd Nigeria Regiment,

West African Field Force 1912, Cameroons Campaign, 1915-6. In May 1916 he came home on leave and returned to Nigeria in October en route for East Africa, attached to the 4th Nigeria Regiment. Killed in action near the Rufigi River on January 24th, 1917, aged 27 years. Mentioned in despatches May 30th, 1917.

DAVID FREDERICK, born 1894. Second son of Lieut.-Colonel Hubert Frederick Barclay, and great-grandson of Robert Barclay (Bury Hill IIIB). Educated at Harrow. In Canada at the outbreak of war, he came to England with Strathcona's Horse. Transferred to 4th Bedfordshire Regiment and chosen to proceed to West Africa in 1915. Served, together with his cousin George Eric, in the 2nd Nigeria Regiment, West African Field Force, in the Cameroons Campaign, at the close of which he returned home and was given a Regular Commission in the Queen's Bays with eighteen months' seniority. France March 1917, Battles of Cambrai and the Somme. Killed by a sniper's bullet in the trenches north of Hamel on April 2nd, 1918, aged 23 years.

GEORGE REINHOLD, born 1881. Son of Sir Thomas Barclay, Knight, of Bonvil, Cupar, Fife—cadet of Collairnie. Educated at The Bell Baxter Institute, Cupar, Fife; Westminster School; Edinburgh University. Student at Lincoln's Inn and Ecole de Droit, Paris. Inns of Court Rifles. Musketry Instructor 1914. Liaison Officer Belgian Headquarters Staff and Intelligence Corps. Promoted Captain. Killed at Courtrai, October 30th, 1918, aged 37 years.

THOMAS HUBERT, born 1884. Second son of Robert Barclay (Bury Hill IV). Educated at Harrow, and Trinity College, Cambridge. Surrey (Queen Mary's Regiment) Yeomanry 1903, Captain 1913. Served with his Squadron in the 27th Division in France, Belgium and Salonika. Major, Divisional Staff. Rejoined Squadron in Salonika. Home on leave April 1917. Returned in H.M. Transport *Transylvania*, which was sunk by enemy torpedo in the Mediterranean, May 4th. Thomas Hubert reached a raft, but subsequently realising that it was overloaded with men whom he had rescued, he swam behind it, and with Captain A. R. Hill endeavoured to guide it in a rough sea. Being a powerful swimmer he could have saved himself, but remained to help his comrades. After three and a half hours rescue came, but he died of exhaustion, May 5th, 1917, aged 33 years. Captain Hill was picked up unconscious, but survived. Thomas Hubert was buried with full military honours in the Church at Savona. His Majesty the King posthumously awarded him the Board of Trade Silver Medal for Gallantry in Saving Life at Sea.

ROBERT
WYVILL
BARCLAY,
1880–
Bury Hill
V.

" IN CRUCE SPERO." " CEDANT ARMA."

" IN HAC VINCE."

LIST OF PEDIGREES

PART I

The Earlier House of Berkeley to the Sixth Generation

Certain genealogical data of the Scottish Barclays in these pedigrees have been proved erroneous by more recent research. The reader is referred to the amended pedigrees contained in Part II.

PART II

LIST OF PEDIGREES

PART III

INDEX

INDEX OF NAMES
Barclays, Barklys, Berchelais, Berclays
Berkeleys, etc.

Barclay, James, s. of David, Collairnie XI, ii, 325, 326

Barclay, James, s. of David, Collairnie XII, ii, 331

Barclay, James, grandson of David, Collairnie IX, ii, 316

Barclay, James, s. of David, Mathers XI, ii, 191, 201 iii, 14

Barclay, James, s. of David, Urie IIIB, iii, 242, 271

Barclay, James, s. of James (1636), ii, 326

Barclay, James, grandson of Patrick, Gartley XVII, ii, 142

Barclay, James, s. of Patrick, Towie XIV, ii, 220

Barclay, James, s. of Patrick, Towie XV, ii, 228

Barclay, James, s. of Patrick, Towie XXIII, ii, 267, 269, 270, 273

Barclay, James, s. of Dr. Peter (1749), ii, 270

Barclay, James, s. of Robert, Urie V, iii, 218

Barclay, James, s. of William, ii, 144

Barclay, James John, s. of James (1782), ii, 277

Barclay, James William, M.P. (1907), ii, 199

Barclay, Jane, dau. of David, Urie IIIB, iii, 242, 253

Barclay, Jane, dau. of James (1718), ii, 270

Barclay, Jane Mary, dau. of Robert, Bank III, iii, 263

Barclay, Janet, wife of Rev. Adam, Gartley XXII, ii, 149

Barclay, Janet, wife of David, Collairnie IX, ii, 314, 315, 317, 336

Barclay, Janet, wife of Patrick, Towie XV, ii, 227

Barclay, Janet, wife of Patrick, Towie XVII, ii, 238, 243

Barclay, Janet, wife of Thomas (1580), ii, 181, 191

Barclay, Janet, dau. of William, Pierston III, ii, 353

Barclay, Janet, wife of William, Pierston VI, ii, 354

Barclay, Jean, dau. of David, Collairnie IX, ii, 316

Barclay, Jean, dau. of David, Collairnie XII, ii, 331

Barclay, Jean, dau. of David, Urie I, iii, 26, 90, 97, 172, 212

Barclay, Jean, dau. of Gavin (1592), ii, 356

Barclay, Jean, dau. of John, Collairnie XIIIB, ii, 338

Barclay, Jean, wife of John (1672), Collairnie XIIIB, ii, 338

Barclay, Jean, dau. of John, Towie XXII, ii, 263

Barclay, Jean, dau. of Robert, Urie II, iii, 191

Barclay, Jean, dau. of Walter, Towie XVI, ii, 235

Barclay, Jean, dau. of William (1677), ii, 264

Barclay, Jean, wife of William, Pierston VIII, ii, 356, 357

Barclay, Jean, of Cairness, ii, 150

Barclay, Jessie, wife of John (1816), ii, 273

Barclay, Johann Ludwig, s. of Johann Stephan (Russia) II, ii, 283

Barclay, Johann Stephan (Russia) II, ii, 281, 283

Barclay, Johann Wilhelm (Russia) IV, ii, 284

Barclay, Johanna, dau. of Rev. Patrick, Towie XXV, ii, 269

Barclay, John, iii, 189

Barclay, John (1723), iii, 191

Barclay, John, Bank I, iii, 237, 243, 249–253, 281

Barclay, John, Collairnie XIIIB, ii, 331, 332, 334–336, 338

Barclay, John, Collairnie XIIIBB, ii, 338, 339

Barclay, John, Collairnie XVI, ii, 336

Barclay, John, Johnston I, ii, 176, 179, 180, 182, 183, 198 ; iii, 17

Barclay, John, Johnston III, ii, 194–96 ; iii, 20, 46, 53

Barclay, John, Mathers IVc, ii, 163, 165

Barclay, John, Pierston V, ii, 350, 353, 354

Barclay, John, Towie XXII, ii, 265, 266

Barclay, Rev. John, Towie XXIV, ii, 267

Barclay, John, of Perth Amboy, iii, 26, 90, 94, 96, 97, 169, 247, 273

Barclay, John, s. of Alexander, Mathers VII, ii, 172

Barclay, John, s. of Andrew (1621), ii, 239, 240, 242, 279, 282, 285 (Russia)

Barclay, John, s. of David, Collairnie V, ii, 306, 308

Barclay, John, s. of David, Collairnie X, ii, 321, 323

Barclay, John, s. of David, Mathers XI, ii, 191, 199

Barclay, John, s. of George, Mathers X, ii, 181

Barclay, Bevan, Tritton and Co., iii, 264, 267, 268
Barclay Bros., iii, 280, 285, 286
Barclay, Perkins and Co., iii, 246, 273
Barclay-Pierston, Alexander, iii, 218
Barclay de Tolly, Prince Alexander Magnus Friedrich von Weymarn, ii, 286, 290
Barclay de Tolly, Alexandrine, wife of Prince Ernst Magnus, ii, 290
Barclay de Tolly, Prince Ernst Magnus, ii, 285, 286, 289, 290
Barclay de Tolly, Field-Marshal Prince Michael Andreas, ii, 243, 268, 279, 284–287, 289, 290
Barclay, Tritton and Bevan, iii, 250
Barclay-Maitland, Hon. Charles, ii, 258, 259
Barclay-Maitland, Charles, s. of Isobel, ii, 259
Barclay-Maitland, Isobel, dau. of Sir Alexander Innes-Barclay, ii, 256, 258, 259
Barclay's Bank, Ltd., iii, 255
Barkly, Sir Henry, i, xvi, 34, 70 ; ii, 74, 181
de Berchelai, Alice, dau. of Roger III, i, xvii
de Berchelai, Eustace, i, xvii
de Berchelai, John, Towie I, ii, 343 ; iii, 231
de Berchelai, Ralph, i, xvi, 11, 13, 18, 24, 89
de Berchelai, Rissa, wife of Roger I, i, 13, 14, 19, 90
de Berchelai, Roger I, i, vii, xvi, xviii, 7–14, 16, 18–20, 22, 24, 35, 50, 52, 68, 71, 87–90, 92, 93, 95, 100–102 ; ii, 3, 5 ; iii, 297
de Berchelai, Roger II, i, xvii, 18, 22–26, 28, 32, 52, 54, 70, 71, 91–93, 95–98, 100, 102
Berclay, Alexander, Gartley XIII, ii, 303
Berclay, Alexander, Mathers III, ii, 156, 159, 160, 165
Berclay, Archibald, Kilbirnie VI, ii, 345, 346
Berclay, Christian, dau. of John, Towie XII, ii, 221
Berclay, David, Collairnie IV, ii, 156, 162
Berclay, David, Kilbirnie IV, ii, 345
Berclay, David, Ladyland I, ii, 345, 347, 352
Berclay, David, Mathers IV, ii, 159, 160, 163–165, 167
Berclay, David, grandson of David, Collairnie I, ii, 298
Berclay, David, s. of Hugh, Collairnie IIB, ii, 303, 305

Berclay, Duncan, ii, 110
Berclay, Elizabeth, wife of David, Mathers IV, ii, 160
Berclay, George, Mathers V, ii, 160–162, 165, 167, 217, 299
Berclay, Helen, wife of Alexander, Mathers III, ii, 159
Berclay, Helen, wife of David, Ladyland I, ii, 347.
Berclay, Hugh, Kilbirnie V, ii, 345, 347
Berclay, James, son of Walter, Towie XI, ii, 218
Berclay, John, Kilbirnie VII, ii, 345, 346
Berclay, John, Ladyland III, ii, 346–348
Berclay, John, Towie XII, ii, 218–222
Berclay, John, s. of Alexander, Mathers III, ii, 159, 299
Berclay, John, grandson of David, Collairnie I, ii, 298
Berclay, Margaret, dau. of William, Collairnie III, ii, 304, 306
Berclay, Marjorie, dau. of John, Towie XII, ii, 220, 221
Berclay, Marjory, Kilbirnie VIII, ii, 346, 347
Berclay, Patrick, of Bretherton, Mathers IVB, ii, 90, 161–163, 165–167, 299
Berclay, Rachel, dau. of John, Towie XII, ii, 220
Berclay, Robert, s. of William, Collairnie III, ii, 304, 305
Berclay, Walter, Gartley XIV, ii, 111–113
Berclay, Walter, Gartley XVI, ii, 113–115
Berclay, Walter, Towie XI, ii, 167, 213, 215–218
Berclay, Walter, Towie XIII, ii, 117–119, 219, 221–224
Berclay, William, Collairnie III, ii, 298, 301–306
Berclay, William, Gartley XV, ii, 112–114
Berclay, William, Towie X, ii, 303, 304
de Berclay, Agnes, wife of Alexander, Gartley XIII, ii, 110
de Berclay, Alexander, Mathers I, i, xiii, xviii ; ii, 304
de Berclay, Alexander, s. of William, Towie IX, ii, 209–217
de Berclay, Andrew, Gartley XII, ii, 210
de Berclay, David, Brechin I, ii, 76, 80–87, 103, 154
de Berclay, David, Brechin II, ii, 78, 80, 87, 88, 90, 94, 105, 153, 298
de Berclay, David, Collairnie I, ii, 76–79, 297–301, 309

319

320

INDEX OF NAMES
General

323

Bernard the Priest, i, 10, 24, 44, 88
Berry, Elizabeth, wife of George (1850), ii, 275
Berry, Emma, wife of Dr. George (1818), ii, 275
Berta, dau. of Guerinfridus, i, 90
Bethune, Elizabeth, wife of William, Collairnie XB, ii, 315
Bethune, Family of, ii, 324
Bevan, Elizabeth, dau. of David, Urie IIIB, iii, 242
Bevan, Silvanus, iii, 249, 274
Bevan, Timothy, iii, 242, 274
Bigland, —, i, 84
Bilton, Mr., iii, 48
Birkbeck, Elizabeth Lucy, dau. of Robert, Bank II, iii, 255, 258
Birkbeck, Gillian, wife of Joseph Gurney (1879), iii, 269
Birkbeck, Henry, iii, 255, 258
Birkbeck, Jane, iii, 258
Biset, Family of, i, 21
Biset, Sir Thomas, ii, 77
Bisey, Family of, ii, 18
Bisset, Alexander, ii, 192
Bisset, George, ii, 226
Black Douglas, Family of, ii, 115
Black Prince, The, i, 67, 80
Blackburn, John, ii, 308
Blaikie, William Garden, ii, 275
Blair, Agnes, ii, 347
Blair, David, ii, 348, 353
Blair, John, ii, 347, 351, 353
Blair, Richard, iii, 33
Blair-Wilson, Charles, ii, 275
Blair-Wilson, Ethel Maud, dau. of George (1850), ii, 275
Blanche, dau. of Henry IV, i, 85
Bland, F. Maltby, iii, 281
Bockwra, William, iii, 169
Bohun, Humphrey de, i, 72
Bohun, William de, ii, 104
Boivill, Helyas de, i, 42
Bolman, Ramsay, iii, 206
Bompart, Admiral, ii, 271
Bond, Phineas P., iii, 272
Bonvile, Family of de, ii, 209
Bonvile, John de, ii, 209, 210
Bonvill, David de, ii, 216
Booker, Elizabeth, dau. of Dr. John (1755), ii, 269
Booker, Rev. Ray, ii, 269
Borlase-Warren, Sir John, ii, 271
Borswell, David, ii, 321
Borth, J., iii, 39

Bortyque, —, ii, 137
Bosco, William de, ii, 33, 34, 45
Botetourte, John, i, 61, 62
Bothwell, Earl of, ii, 185
Bothwell, Francis, Earl of, ii, 325
Bothwell, James Hepburn, Earl of, ii, 135, 136, 320, 322 ; iii, 19
Bottiler, Thomas de, i, 76
Boulton, Henry, ii, 341
Boulton, Maria, wife of George Perks, ii, 341
Bowman, David, ii, 323
Boyd, Adam, ii, 353
Boyfis, ii, 18
Boyle, Jean, wife of William, Pierston VIII, ii, 355–357
Boyle, John, ii, 356
Boyle, Marion, ii, 356
Bradeley, Richard de, i, 101
Braine, Elizabeth, wife of Robert, Urie III, iii, 197, 198, 209, 211
Braine, John, iii, 198
Braithwaite, W. C., iii, 164
Braker, John, ii, 242
Bray, Sir Edward, iii, 297
Bray, Elsa Mary, wife of Robert Wyvill, Bury Hill V, iii, 297
Bray, Emily Octavia, dau. of Arthur Kett, Bury Hill III, iii, 293
Bray, Sir Reginald More, iii, 293
Brechin, Bishop of, ii, 104 ; iii, 22
Brechin, Alexander, Bishop of, ii, 237
Brechin, David de, ii, 68
Brechin, Sir David de, ii, 80
Brechin, Gregory, Bishop of, ii, 33, 34
Brechin, Henry de, ii, 47, 79
Brechin, Margaret de, ii, 79
Brechin, Philip, Bishop of, ii, 155
Brechin, Turpin, Bishop of, ii, 30
Brechin, William de, ii, 47, 60
Brechin, Sir William de, ii, 79
Bressie, Capt., iii, 48
Brewers' Company, The, iii, 281, 292, 295
Brienne, John de, ii, 50, 51
Bright, John, iii, 266
Bristol and Gloucestershire Archæological Association, i, xv
British and Foreign Bible Society, iii, 265
Brittany, Countess of, ii, 16
Brockhurst, Rebecca, wife of George (1782), ii, 341
Brogane, Henry de, ii, 211
Broghill, Lord, iii, 54
Bromhead, Alexander, iii, 291
Bromhead, Colonel John, iii, 277, 290
Bromhead, Lucy, iii, 291

Bromhead, Martha, dau. of Robert, Bury Hill I, iii, 277, 290
Brown, —, iii, 263
Brown, Alexander, ii, 273
Brown, Isabella, wife of William (1834), ii, 273
Brown, John, iii, 125
Brown, Dr. John, ii, 275
Brown, Sir John, ii, 333
Brown, Marion, ii, 333
Bruce, Agnes, wife of Ninian, Pierston II, ii, 352
Bruce, Christina, ii, 211
Bruce, David, ii, 104
Bruce, Edward, ii, 74, 76, 119
Bruce, Elizabeth Thompson, wife of Charles James de Tolley, Towie XXIX, ii, 278
Bruce, Family of, ii, 85
Bruce, Grizel, wife of Rev. John, Towie XXIV, ii, 267
Bruce, Lord, iii, 236
Bruce, Marjory, dau. of Robert Bruce, King, ii, 84, 89, 153
Bruce, Mary, ii, 153
Bruce, Muriella, ii, 154
Bruce, Nigel, ii, 67
Bruce, Robert, ii, 267
Bruce, Rev. Thomas, ii, 278
Brugge, Edmund de, i, 82
Brugge, Thomas de, i, 86
Brus, Isybella de, ii, 47, 56, 79
Brus, John de, ii, 84
Brus, Robert de, ii, 47
Bruys, Family of de, ii, 18
Brydges, Family of, i, 74
Brydges, Giles, i, 86
Buchan, Alexander Comyn, Earl of, ii, 79
Buchan, Christiana, Countess of, ii, 146, 230, 231
Buchan, Earl of, ii, 222, 226, 239
Buchan, Elizabeth, Countess of, ii, 299
Buchan, Isabella, Countess of, ii, 67
Buchan, James, Earl of, ii, 247
Buchan, John, Earl of, ii, 224, 299, 303
Buchan, John Comyn, Earl of, ii, 98
Buchan, John Stewart, Earl of, ii, 215
Buchan, Robert, Earl of, ii, 141, 146
Buchanan, George, ii, 354
Buckingham, Family of, i, 75
Bullard, Eugenia, dau. of Henry Albert (1858), iii, 267
Bullard, Gerald, Lieut.-Col., iii, 267
Bullock, Dom William, ii, 84, 85
Bundane, John, ii, 244

Burke, Sir Bernard, i, 8
Burnell, Robert, Bishop of Bath and Wells, i, 75
Burnet, J., ii, 195
Burnet, Robert, iii, 83
Burnet, Sir T., ii, 195
Burnett, George, ii, 26
Bury-Barry, James Robert, iii, 298
Bury-Barry, Nesta Anne, wife of Robert Edward (1906), iii, 298
Butler, Dr. George, iii, 284
Buxton, —, iii, 246
Buxton, Lady Catherine, iii, 275
Buxton, Edward North, iii, 268
Buxton, Elizabeth Ellen, wife of Robert, Bank V, iii, 268, 269
Buxton, Family of, iii, 246, 266, 276
Buxton, Fowell, iii, 258
Buxton, Hannah Maude, wife of Francis Hubert (1869), iii, 268
Buxton, Lady Hannah, iii, 274
Buxton, Thomas Fowell, iii, 268
Byrne, Simon, iii, 225
Bysset, Walter, ii, 40
Cabbell, Beatrice Evermar, wife of Humphrey Gordon (1882), iii, 267
Cabbell, Benjamin Bond, iii, 267
Cadenhead, Alex, iii, 212
Caenmoir, Edward, s. of Malcolm, ii, 11
Cairale, Alexander, ii, 170
Caldair, William, ii, 232
Calder, —, iii, 157, 158
Caldwell, Robert, iii, 191
Callender, Earl of, iii, 11, 17, 28
Calvin, John, iii, 125, 129, 130
Cambron, Sir John de, ii, 62, 64
Camden Society, The, i, xiv
Cameron, —, iii, 276
Cameron, Sir Donald, iii, 212, 213, 217
Cameron, Sir Euan, iii, 26
Cameron, Sir Ewen, iii, 97, 172, 176, 198, 199, 211, 212
Cameron, Family of, iii, 212
Cameron, Hugh, ii, 34
Cameron, Jean, dau. of David, Urie I, iii, 26, 97, 172, 212
Cameron, Richard, iii, 68
Cameron, Une, wife of Robert, Urie IV, iii, 211, 213, 214
Camfield, Francis, iii, 175
Campbell, Alexander, ii, 183
Campbell, Archibald, ii, 177
Campbell, Family of, iii, 13
Campbell, Helen, ii, 354
Campbell, Sir Hugh, iii, 63

Darenthal, Stephan, ii, 283
Darnley, Lord, ii, 125, 135, 136 ; iii, 19
David, brother of Griffin, Prince of Wales, ii, 52
David I, King, ii, 11, 12, 19, 21, 26, 27, 298
David II, King, i, xiii ; ii, 82–86, 89, 102–106, 154, 155, 209
David of Lochore, ii, 51
David, Prince of Wales, i, 75
Davidson, Dr., ii, 214–216
Davidson, Duncan, ii, 223
Davidson, William, ii, 137
Deane, Major-General, iii, 43
Debonaire, Louise, wife of John, great-grandson of Patrick, Gartley XVII, ii, 124
Dempster, James, ii, 193, 230
Dena, i, 11, 88
Despencer, Sir Edward de, i, 67
Despencers, Family of Le, i, 77
Devonshire, Duke of, iii, 288
Devorguila, wife of John de Baliol, ii, 39
Dickson, Dr., ii, 45
Dishington, Family of, ii, 324
Donald, Lord of the Isles, ii, 214, 215
Donaldson, James, ii, 191
Dorscheus, Johannes Georgius, ii, 281
Doubleday, Mollison, dau. of Robert, Urie III, iii, 209
Douglas, Agnes, ii, 347
Douglas, Alexander, ii, 167, 217
Douglas, Anne, daughter of David, Mathers XI, ii, 200, 201
Douglas, Archibald, ii, 171
Douglas, Archibald, Earl of, ii, 299
Douglas, Sir Archibald, ii, 83
Douglas, Catherine, ii, 93
Douglas, Earl of, ii, 312
Douglas, Earls of, ii, 115
Douglas, Family of, i, 21 ; ii, 85–87, 89, 91, 154, 172, 174, 324
Douglas, Helen de, wife of David, Collairnie I, ii, 299
Douglas, Helen, wife of David, Ladyland I, ii, 347
Douglas, Helen, wife of Patrick, Towie XIX, ii, 251
Douglas, Hugh, ii, 85
Douglas, James, Earl of, ii, 211
Douglas, James, ii, 91, 347, 352
Douglas, Sir James, ii, 82, 86
Douglas, Jean, ii, 177
Douglas, John, ii, 86, 195
Douglas, John, of Tilliwhilly, ii, 200, 201
Douglas, Jonet, Lady Glamis, ii, 177, 179

Douglas, Margaret, ii, 319, 347
Douglas, Margaret, Countess of, ii, 211, 212
Douglas, Margaret, wife of David, Collairnie VI, ii, 308, 309
Douglas, Robert, iii, 53
Douglas, Sir Robert, ii, 29
Douglas, William, ii, 84, 86, 87, 101–103, 195, 319
Douglas, William, Earl of, ii, 115, 211
Douglas, Sir William, ii, 85, 86, 177, 299, 320
Drauyer, Anna Dorothea, wife of Rev. Thomas, ii, 337
Draycote, Family of, ii, 58, 59
Dreux, Count de, ii, 53
Drimming, John, ii, 69
Drummond, Alexander, ii, 183
Drummond, Anna, wife of Patrick (1600), ii, 239, 243, 245
Drummond, Lord David, ii, 243
Drummond, George, ii, 183
Drummond, Sir John, ii, 238
Drummond, Margaret, ii, 238
Drummond, Patrick, ii, 183
Drury, David, ii, 319
Duddingstone, George, ii, 325
Duddingstone, James, ii, 270
Duddingstone, Margaret, wife of Dr. Peter (1780), ii, 270
Duddingstone, Mary, wife of Dr. John (1765), ii, 269
Duff, Helen, wife of Sir Alexander Innes-Barclay, ii, 257, 258
Duff, James, ii, 257
Duff, Jean, ii, 257
Duff, John, ii, 146
Duff, William, ii, 257
Dugdale, Sir William, I, xv, 33, 42, 52
Dunbar, Family of, i, 21
Dunbar, Sir James, ii, 173
Dunbar, Patrick de, ii, 104
Dunblane, Bishop of, ii, 51
Duncan, Earl, ii, 18, 22
Duncan, Elizabeth, ii, 145
Duncan, Elspeth, dau. of Rev. Patrick, Towie XXV, ii, 269
Duncan, father of King Malcolm, ii, 6
Duncan, George, ii, 270
Duncan, Isabella, dau. of Rev. Patrick, Towie XXV, ii, 269
Duncan, Jane, dau. of James (1718), ii, 270
Duncan, John, ii, 145, 230, 243
Duncan, Rev. John, ii, 269
Duncepouche, David, i, 40, 93
Dunfermline, Abbot of, ii, 104, 302

Falside, Thomas de, ii, 155
Fantosme, Jordan, ii, 14
Farquharson, Col. Murray, iii, 223
Farrow, Rev. Alfred E., iii, 296
Farrow, Ellen Rachel, dau. of Robert,
  Bury Hill IV, iii, 296
Fentoun, Janet, ii, 113
Ferdinand of Styria, Emperor, iii, 1-3, 25
Feria, Duchess of, ii, 139
Fernie, Family of, ii, 324
Ferny, Arthur, ii, 308
Ferrieres, Henry de, i, 6
Fife, Duncan, Earl of, ii, 297
Fife, Isabella, Countess of, ii, 88, 297
Fife, Malcolm, Earl of, ii, 45
Fife, William, Earl of, ii, 297
Findlater, Earl of, ii, 256
Findlater, James, Earl of, ii, 259
Fitchel, Andrew, iii, 193
FizArthure, Nigelle, i, 40, 92
Fitzclarence, Family of, iii, 288
Fitzhardinge, Elena, wife of Roger IV,
  i, 41, 45, 47
Fitzhardinge, Elias, i, 40, 92
Fitzhardinge, Family of, i, 14 ; iii, 160
Fitzhardinge, Jordane, i, 40, 92
Fitzhardinge, Maurice, i, 10, 36, 39, 41,
  43, 47, 91, 92
Fitzhardinge, Robert, of Bristol, i, xvii,
  15-17, 35-41, 43-45, 49, 91-94, 100
Fitzherbert, Adam, i, 6
FitzNeal, Richard, ii, 17
Fitzosborn, Earl William, i, xvi, 8, 10,
  12, 16, 18 ; ii, 5
FitzRalph, Roger, i, 24
FitzRobert, Richard, i, 40, 92
FitzStephen, Ralph, i, 44
Flanders, Baldwin, Count of, ii, 7
Flawford, Thomas de, ii, 297
Fleming, David, ii, 155
Fleming, Sir David, ii, 85, 87, 88, 91
Fleming, Family of, i, 21 ; ii, 85
Fleming, Jean, dau. of David, Brechin I,
  ii, 85, 87, 91
Fleming, Jean, dau. of David, Towie VIIв,
  ii, 94
Fleming, Sir Malcolm, ii, 83
Fleming, Sir Robert, ii, 85
Fleming, Thomas, ii, 105
Flower, Arthur, iii, 267
Flower, Constance, iii, 267
Fodringhay, Family of, ii, 209, 210
Fodringhay, Sir William, ii, 210
Forbes, Alexander, iii, 191, 221, 228, 229,
  245, 267

Forbes, Arthur, iii, 190, 223, 247
Forbes, Sir Arthur, iii, 45
Forbes, Catherine, wife of George, Gartley
  XIX, ii, 130
Forbes, Catherine, dau. of Robert, Urie II,
  iii, 191
Forbes, Sir Charles, ii, 3
Forbes, Christian, dau. of John, Towie XII,
  ii, 221
Forbes, Duncan, ii, 149 ; iii, 213
Forbes, Elizabeth, wife of Patrick, Towie
  XV, ii, 228, 229
Forbes, Family of, i, 20 ; ii, 3 ; iii, 6, 76
Forbes, James, ii, 247, 248 ; iii, 191
Forbes, Jean, dau. of Robert, Urie II,
  iii, 191
Forbes, John, ii, 149, 197 ; iii, 23, 138, 191
Forbes, Jonet, ii, 143
Forbes, Jonet, wife of Walter of Bath-
  nagoak, ii, 125
Forbes, Margaret, ii, 247
Forbes, Marjorie, wife of Rev. Adam,
  Gartley XXII, ii, 149
Forbes, Master of, ii, 177
Forbes, Patience, dau. of Robert, Urie II,
  iii, 191
Forbes, Patrick, ii, 147
Forbes, Timothy, iii, 191
Forbes, William, ii, 149
Ford, Anne, wife of Robert, Bank II,
  iii, 252, 255, 256
Ford, Family of, iii, 253
Ford, Isaac, iii, 252
Fordham, Elizabeth Mary, née Pryor, wife
  of Edward Exton (1860), iii, 268
Fordham, Henry John, iii, 268
Fordun, Sir John, ii, 86
Fordun, John of, ii, 100
Fordyce, Capt. Dingwall, ii, 278
Forret, Family of, ii, 324
Fotheringham, Thomas, ii, 94
Fowler, Ann Ford, dau. of Robert, Bank
  III, iii, 263
Fowler, Elizabeth Mary, wife of Edward
  Exton (1860), iii, 267
Fowler, Henry, iii, 263
Fowler, William, iii, 267
Fox, George, iii, 31, 39, 65, 78, 86, 103,
  104, 119, 121, 123, 126, 127, 129, 143,
  146, 155, 160, 164, 165, 174-176, 186,
  189-191, 197
Fox, Maria, dau. of Robert, Bury Hill I,
  iii, 277
Fox, Robert Weir, iii, 277
Fox, Mrs. Weir, iii, 291

Innes, Anne, ii, 257
Innes, Cosmo, i, 21
Innes, Elizabeth, ii, 222, 255–257
Innes, Family of, ii, 214
Innes, Sir George, ii, 249, 255–257
Innes, Isobel, wife of Adam, Gartley XXIII, ii, 150
Innes, James, ii, 219, 220, 222
Innes, Jean, ii, 257
Innes, Jean, dau. of Walter, Towie XVI, ii, 235
Innes, John, ii, 232 ; iii, 218
Innes, Sir John, iii, 24
Innes, Laird of, iii, 12
Innes, Robert, ii, 235
Innes, Sir Robert, ii, 214, 219, 220
Innes, Thomas, ii, 214
Innes, Une Cameron, dau. of Robert, Urie V, iii, 218
Innes, Walter, ii, 123, 223
Innes, William, ii, 228
Innes, Sir William, ii, 262
Innes-Barclay, Sir Alexander, ii, 256, 258
Innes-Barclay, Helen, wife of Sir Alexander, ii, 257, 258
Innes-Barclay, Isobel, dau. of Sir Alexander Innes-Barclay, ii, 258
Innes-Barclay, Jean, wife of Alexander Innes-Barclay, ii, 258
Innes-Barclay, Jean, dau. of Sir Alexander Innes-Barclay, ii, 258
Innocent, Pope, i, 31, 98
Innocent IV, Pope (1250), ii, 11
Irvine, —, ii, 219
Irvine, Mr. (1792), ii, 207
Irvine, Anne, dau. of David, Mathers XI, ii, 201
Irvine, Alexander, ii, 137, 141, 146, 223
Irvine, Jonet, wife of David Barclay of Mearns, ii, 168, 171, 172
Irvine, Robert, ii, 201, 233
Irving, Sir Alexander, iii, 22
Isabel, wife of Robert Bruce, King, ii, 70
Jaffray, Alexander, iii, 76, 114, 116, 117, 191, 194, 199, 201, 231, 253
Jaffray, Andrew, iii, 82, 84, 90, 94, 112, 114, 138
Jaffray, Christian, dau. of Robert, Urie II, iii, 112–114, 191
Jaffray, Family of, iii, 185, 211
Jaffray, James, ii, 194
James I, King of Scotland, ii, 19, 90–94, 110, 159, 163–166, 194, 196, 345 ; iii, 295
James II, King of Scotland, ii, 112, 113, 115, 167, 306, 345 ; iii, 54, 62

James III, King of Scotland, ii, 115, 116, 171, 306, 345
James IV, King of Scotland, ii, 117, 118, 125, 173, 217, 310
James V, King of Scotland, ii, 119, 126–129, 174, 176, 177, 181, 220, 221, 226, 228, 230, 310–312, 314, 315, 317, 348
James VI, King of Scotland, ii, 121–123, 125, 136, 148, 184–186, 188, 192, 193, 231, 237, 238, 243, 244, 246, 325, 328, 350, 355–357 ; iii, 1, 4, 5, 19, 129, 159
James II, King of England, iii, 134, 144, 145, 150, 151, 155–160, 166, 170, 172, 174–184, 199, 202, 212
Jameson, Barbara, wife of James Barclay (1635), ii, 325
Jamieson, Thomas F., iii, 229
Jardyne, Alexander de, ii, 216
Jeayes, Mr., i, xv
Jedburgh, Abbot of, ii, 51
Jevons, Evan, iii, 188
Joan, wife of Alexander II, ii, 40
Joan, wife of David II, ii, 81, 83
Joan, sis. of Henry III, ii, 38
Joan, Queen, wife of James I of Scotland, ii, 110
John of Fordun, ii, 51, 53
John, King, i, 55, 71 ; ii, 36–38
John le Scot, ii, 37
Johnson, Dr., iii, 274
Johnston, —, ii, 223
Johnston, James, ii, 116, 220
Johnston, William, ii, 220
Johnston of Warriston, iii, 5
Johnstone, —, iii, 185
Johnstone, Crowder, ii, 248
Johnstoun, George, ii, 194
Johnstoun, William, iii, 15
Johnstoun, Laird of, iii, 12
Joleta, wife of Alexander III, ii, 53
Jonah, ii, 207
Jones, C., iii, 236
Jones, M. C., iii, 237
Jorwult, Llewellyn ap, i, 54
Joyce, Cornet, iii, 27
Joyce, Emily, wife of Thomas George (1819), iii, 281
Joyce, Emily, dau. of Robert (1808), iii, 281
Joyce, Rev. F. Hayward, iii, 281
Joyce, Rev. F. William, iii, 281
Judith, dau. of Adelidis, i, 90
Kay, Sir Brooke, ii, 269
Kay, Capt., ii, 269

336

340

Pitcarne, Henry, ii, 310
Pitcarrn, H. Carnegy, iii, 53
Pitt, William, iii, 216
Pittars, A. Carnegy, iii, 46, 56
Planché, J. R., i, 12
Planta, Hugh de, i, 42, 43
Plumstead, Mary, iii, 236
Pluscarden, Thomas, Prior of, ii, 108
Pont, Timothy, ii, 343, 347
Pope, Alexander, iii, 283
Port, Adam de, ii, 15
Postoyle, ii, 46
Prevost, Sir George, ii, 271
Pride, Colonel, iii, 32
Pryor, Elizabeth Mary, wife of Edward
    Exton. (1860), iii, 268
Pryor, Marlborough Robert, iii, 268
Purvis, Sir William, iii, 157
Quarritch, Bernard, i, 47
Quincey, Orabilis de, ii, 23
Quincey, Robert de, ii, 23, 24
Quincey, Roger de, ii, 22, 39
Quincey, Roger de, Earl of Winchester, ii,
    52
Quincey, Saher de, Earl of Winchester,
    ii, 23
Raeburn, Sir Henry, iii, 277
Rafe of Tweley, i, 40, 92
Rait, David, ii, 172, 179, 188, 195
Rait, Mary, wife of David, Mathers IX, ii,
    176, 188
Rait, Thomas de, ii, 90
Rait, W., iii, 46
Rait, William, ii, 172, 188, 189, 195
Rait of Halgreen, ii, 176
Ramsay, Alexander de, ii, 87, 88, 102, 309
Ramsay, Archibald, ii, 172
Ramsay, David, ii, 195
Ramsay, Elizabeth, ii, 77
Ramsay, Elizabeth, wife of David, Col-
    lairnie I, ii, 297
Ramsay, Family of, ii, 18, 324
Ramsay, G., iii, 46, 53
Ramsay, Isabella, Countess of Fife, ii, 77
Ramsay, Ionete, ii, 310
Ramsay, Katherina, dau. of Alexander,
    Mathers VII, ii, 172
Ramsay, Sir William de, ii, 88, 297, 298
Ramsay, Sir William, Earl of Fife, ii, 77
Ramsey, William, iii, 46
Randall, Thomas, ii, 74
Randolph, Family of, ii, 110
Randolph, Regent to David II, ii, 82, 83
Randolph, Richard, ii, 110
Randolph, Thomas, ii, 76

Randolphi, Richard, ii, 303
Randulpho, ii, 46
Rankine, Patrick, iii, 50
Ransom, Bouverie and Co., iii, 267
Ranulf, Earl of Chester, i, 70
Rawson, Hugh, iii, 199
Red Douglas, Family of, ii, 115
Reginald, s. of Roderick of the Isles, ii, 102
Reginald of St. Walery, i, 32
Reid, Anna, wife of George Barclay (1660)
Reid, Margaret, wife of William, Towie
    XX, ii, 253
Reid, Patrick, ii, 150
Reid, Thomas, ii, 199
Remigius, Bishop of Lincoln, i, 6
Renny, Thomas, ii, 193
Reynolds, Anna, dau. of Robert, Bury
    Hill I, iii, 277
Reynolds, Esther, wife of Ford (1793), iii,
    255
Reynolds, J. Foster, iii, 277
Reynolds, Sir Joshua, iii, 257
Reynolds, Robert Foster, iii, 286
Reynolds, William Foster, iii, 255
Ricart, Robert, i, 33-35, 37
Ricaut, iii, 195
Richard I, King, i, 46, 48, 49, 71; ii, 19, 83
Richard II, King, i, 19, 84; ii, 90
Richard, Duke of Normandy, i, 90
Richardson, Wigham, iii, 232
Richelieu, Cardinal, iii, 5
Richmond, Duchess of, iii, 239, 288
Ridal, Patrick de, ii, 45
Riddell, Ann, wife of David, Collairnie
    XII, ii, 327, 331, 332, 338
Riddell, Jean, ii, 327
Riddell, John, ii, 220
Riddell, Sir John, ii, 327, 338
Riddell, Maria, wife of Andrev (Russia),
    ii, 240, 242, 279
Riddell, Patrick de, i, 46
Rigbie, Alice, wife of George (1679), ii, 341
Ritchie, Margaret, dau. of Robert, Urie VI,
    iii, 229
Ritchie, Samuel, iii, 229
Rizzio, David, ii, 136
Robert Bruce, father of King Robert
    Bruce, ii, 56
Robert Bruce, King, i, 21, 62; ii, 4, 43,
    55-57, 67-70, 73-77, 79-82, 99-101, 153,
    237
Robert II, King, ii, 209, 210, 212; iii, 230
Robert III, King, ii, 156, 159, 194, 196, 302
Robert of St. Maryes, i, 40, 92
Robertson, Dr. Arthur, ii, 340

William IV, King, iii, 286, 288, 290
William, son of Baldwin, i, 42
William the Lion, King, i, 45, 46; ii, 5, 8, 12–20, 22–30, 32–34, 36, 37, 39, 45, 55, 56, 61, 79, 153, 156, 192
William of Malmesbury, i, 1, 21, 35
William, son of Henry II, i, 40, 92
William of Tullibardine, ii, 135
Williams, Sir Charles Hanbury, iii, 251
Williams, Rhoda, wife of Robert Leatham, Bank VI, iii, 270
Williams, Col. Sir Robert, Bart., iii, 270
Williamson, Sir Hedworth, iii, 277
Williamson, Maria, wife of David (1784), iii, 277
Wilson, Barbara, wife of Patrick, Towie XXIII, ii, 267
Wilson, Rev. Charles Lea, iii, 293
Wilson, Isobel, wife of Patrick (1696), ii, 265
Wilson, Mrs. Lea, iii, 292
Wilson, Margaret, wife of John (1687), iii, 191
Wilson, Neville Juliana, dau. of Arthur Kett, Bury Hill III, iii, 293
Wimberley, Capt. Douglas, ii, 113, 119
Wimmeston, Lawrence de, ii, 297
Winchester, Hoadley, Bishop of, iii, 251
Windus, William, ii, 232, 233
Winton, Earls of, ii, 23, 156
Winton, William de, i, 99
Wirfaut, Roger, ii, 35
Wiseman, William, ii, 76
Wishard, John, ii, 28
Wishart, iii, 36
Wishart, Anna, ii, 325
Wishart, Catherine, wife of Alexander, Mathers VI, ii, 168
Wishart, Sir George, ii, 325

Wishart of Pittarrow, ii, 179
Wisnod, i, 11, 89
Wiston, Henry de, ii, 36
Wolsey, Cardinal, ii, 126
Wood, Mr., ii, 29
Wood, Alexander, ii, 182
Wood, Elizabeth, wife of George, Mathers X, ii, 181, 182
Wood, James, ii, 185
Wood, Patrick, ii, 182, 183, 186
Wood, William, ii, 185, 186
Woodrow, iii, 68, 69, 89, 116
Woods, Clemence Rachel, dau. of Robert, Bank V, iii, 269
Woods, R. Rev. Edward S., Bishop of Croydon, iii, 269
Worcester, Bishop of, i, 70
Worcester, Prior of, i, 73
Worcester, Simon, Bishop of, i, 24, 25
Worcester, Tilhere, Bishop of, i, 1
Worcester, St. Mary's, Prior of, i, 72
Wright, Andrew, ii, 111
Wright, Ichabod, iii, 290
Wright, John, ii, 303
Wright, Maria Octavia, wife of Arthur Kett, Bury Hill II, iii, 290, 291
Wright, Thomas, ii, 110
Wygorn, Simon, Bishop, i, 96, 98-100
Wyntoun, Andrew de, ii, 261, 262, 302, 303
Wyntoun, Chronicler, ii, 101
Wyntoun, Family of, ii, 324
Wyvill, Henrietta, wife of Robert Gurney (1816), iii, 277
Wyvill, Laura Charlotte Rachel, wife of Robert, Bury Hill IV, iii, 295, 297
Wyvill, Marmaduke, iii, 295
York, Archbishop of, ii, 86
York, Duke of, ii, 335 ; iii, 208, 238
Zoffany, John, iii, 247

PLACE NAMES

Abbotshall, ii, 324

Abdie, ii, 331

Aberbrothoc, ii, 292

Aberbrothwick, iii, 67

Aberchirder, ii, 222

Aberdeen, ii, 30, 61, 62, 68, 69, 74, 86, 98, 108, 110, 112–114, 117, 118, 130, 132–134, 136, 144, 147, 154, 156, 158, 167, 177, 184, 187, 194, 199, 212, 215–217, 219, 221, 223, 224, 226, 228, 230, 231, 233, 234, 237, 244, 248, 251, 262, 264, 273, 275, 312 ; iii, 8, 13, 14, 17, 76, 78–80, 82–84, 86–89, 94, 97, 108–110, 115, 117, 119–121, 130, 136, 138, 140–143, 155, 157, 185, 187, 193, 200, 202, 207, 219, 225, 226, 229, 232, 256

Aberdeen Castle, ii, 61, 98

Aberdeen Cathedral, ii, 117, 157, 228

Aberdeen, College Green, iii, 78

Aberdeen Grammar School, ii, 275

Aberdeen, King Edward's Church, ii, 119

Aberdeen, King's College, ii, 144, 148–150, 216, 250, 263, 269 ; iii, 2

Aberdeen, Marischal College, ii, 270, 273, 275, 277, 278 ; iii, 117

Aberdeen, Robert Gordon's College, ii, 224, 254, 259

Aberdeen, St. Nicholas, ii, 111 ; iii, 117

Aberdeen, The Tollbooth, iii, 82, 83–87, 130, 138, 200

Aberdeen University, ii, 119, 216, 275 ; iii, 121, 207

Aberdeenshire i, xvii, 20, 21 ; ii, 3, 4, 39, 44, 99, 119, 148, 197, 203, 210, 214, 223, 224, 226, 227, 229, 234, 238, 249, 278, 338 ; iii, 10, 185, 223, 229

Aberluthnot, ii, 168, 179, 182, 188, 189, 194, 195, 198, 199

Abernethy, ii, 7

Achlowne, ii, 211

Acholt, i, 26, 28, 30, 98–100

Achorteis, ii, 232 ; iii, 76

Acknowe, ii, 150

Ackworth, iii, 245

Acton Burnell, i, 75

Adamton, ii, 347, 348, 353

Africa, iii, 159, 160

Agilgirg, ii, 30

Ailsa, Rock of, ii, 349

Airdrie, ii, 307

Airth, iii, 218, 230

Aisne, R., iii, 299

Albamarla Castle, i, 90

Albany, Fort Orange, ii, 336

Albany, U.S.A., ii, 337

Albany, U.S.A., St. Peter's Church, ii, 337

Aldmyll, ii, 226

Alford, ii, 148

Allanmore, iii, 223

Allanton, ii, 340

Allardice, iii, 221, 242

Almonsbury, i, 10, 38, 87

Alnwick, i, 45 ; ii, 11, 15

Alton, iii, 278

Altyre, iii, 20

Alwerdene, ii, 26

America, iii, 97, 160, 161, 165, 166, 191, 243–245, 247, 250–252, 271, 273, 296

America, U.S.A., ii, 271 ; iii, 227

Amiens, i, 90

Amsterdam, iii, 122, 129, 146, 147

Andes, The, iii, 254

Angers University, ii, 123

Angus, ii, 19, 20, 30, 38, 80, 104, 174 ; iii, 36, 52, 54, 185

Annandale, ii, 67

Anstruther, ii, 327

Antibes, iii, 260

Antioch, ii, 81

Antigua, ii, 340

Appleby, ii, 15

Aquorthes, iii, 191

Arbornie, iii, 191

Arbroath, ii, 19, 26, 29, 32–36, 43, 80, 98, 111, 140

Arbroath, Abbey of, i, 46 ; ii, 19, 20, 25, 30, 32, 34, 37, 60 ; iii, 292

Archindrane, iii, 15

Arcoch, ii, 351

Ard, ii, 108

Ardit, ii, 307

Ardlane, ii, 227, 230, 236, 247

Ardross, ii, 324

Ardrossan, ii, 8, 343

Arduthie, iii, 216, 221

Are, ii, 345

Argyllshire, ii, 76

Arkinholm, ii, 115

Arlingham, i, 24

Arlington, i, 10, 87

Arnage, ii, 264

Arngask, ii, 333

Arroth, ii, 90

Ashelworth, i, 10, 38, 87

Ashloune, ii, 149

Brothoc, R., ii, 20
Brubtoune, ii, 199
Brucklay, ii, 278
Bruntsfield, ii, 335
Brussels, iii, 286
Brux, iii, 190
Brydskirk, ii, 354, 355
Buchan, ii, 39, 47, 70
Buckhoff, ii, 285
Buckingham, ii, 64
Bucky, ii, 183
Burford Lodge, ii, 341
Burly, ii, 319
Burleigh, ii, 322, 324
Burlington, iii, 162
Burgh-on-Sands, ii, 67
Burialdales, ii, 251, 257
Burnlauch, iii, 173
Bury Hill i, xiii, xviii ; ii, 151, 155, 173, 199, 201 ; iii, 20, 21, 34, 35, 94, 115, 225-227, 230, 231, 247, 253, 272, 273, 275, 277-282, 286, 289, 291, 292, 294, 295, 297
Bush Hill, iii, 242
Buthlaw, ii, 150
Bynnie, ii, 323
Byres, The, ii, 311
Caddell, ii, 183
Caen, ii, 16
Cairnbarrow, ii, 338
Cairnhill, ii, 353
Cairness, Jamaica, ii, 150
Cairnetoun, iii, 173
Caithness, ii, 39 ; iii, 28
Calais, i, 80 ; ii, 85 ; iii, 286
Calder, ii, 94
California, ii, 278
Camalynes, ii, 265
Cambrai, iii, 300
Cambridge, iii, 223
Cambridge Heath, iii, 243, 249, 251-253
Cambridge University, iii, 264, 267, 294, 299
Cambridge University, Trinity College, iii, 219, 221, 269, 281, 293, 295, 297, 298
Cambridge University, Trinity Hall, iii, 268
Cameroons, iii, 300
Camistoun, ii, 162
Camme, i, 10, 24, 59, 87 ; ii, 58, 59
Camnay, ii, 166
Canada, iii, 300
Canada, Upper, ii, 271
Canal-Bank, ii, 351
Candia, iii, 195

Cannaline, ii, 251
Canterbury, ii, 19, 20, 38, 93, 151, 255
Cape Cod, iii, 160
Caprieston, ii, 352
Caprington, ii, 45
Carberry Hill, ii, 136, 320
Carbis Dell, iii, 32
Cardrono, iii, 15
Cardross, ii, 81
Carentowe, iii, 93
Carisbrooke Castle, iii, 27
Carlisle, ii, 12, 14, 15, 126, 137 ; iii, 30
Carny, ii, 63, 68, 73, 76, 77, 97, 297, 324
Carney Berclay, ii, 76, 79
Carny Murthac, ii, 76, 79
Carrick, ii, 67
Carrickfergus, iii, 106
Carse of Gowrie, ii, 69
Carshalton, iii, 255
Carskerdo, ii, 306, 309, 311
Carslogie, ii, 321
Caskiben, ii, 116
Castle Gordon, iii, 18, 22
Cavers, ii, 299
Cepeham, i, 12
Ceres, ii, 306, 321
Chacepot, i, 56
Chadhurst, iii, 280
Chamberlain Newton, ii, 25
Chanrie of Rosse, iii, 17
Chapel, ii, 272
Châtelherault, i, 67 ; ii, 131
Cheltenham, i, 68
Chepstowe, i, 9
Chertsey, iii, 290
Cheshunt, iii, 268
Chester, iii, 176
Chevvy Chase, ii, 91
Chilcote, Manor of, i, 70, 71, 73, 82, 84, 85
Chiveley, i, 99
Cirencester, i, 85
Clapham, iii, 219, 230, 231, 246, 249, 252, 253, 255-257, 261, 275, 278, 279, 290, 291
Clapham, The Hostel of God, iii, 255
Clapham, The Terrace, iii, 253, 282
Clapham Common, iii, 281, 253, 254
Clayhanger, i, 23, 95, 96
Clayhills, ii, 233
Cleeve, i, 81
Cleish, ii, 305, 324, 328
Clifton, i, 24
Clinger, i, 10, 88
Cloberhill, ii, 351
Closingarthe, ii, 345

AAA

355

Forgrund, ii, 46
Fort William, iii, 198
Forth, Firth of, ii, 54 ; iii, 215
Forth, R., ii, 19, 66, 90, 116, 156, 318
Fortreve, ii, 39
Forth-Ramsay, ii, 308
Forthar-Ramsay, ii, 310
Fortrie, ii, 128
Fortrose Castle, iii, 17
Fotheringhay, ii, 37, 142, 183
Fotheringhay Castle, ii, 246
Foulcausey, ii, 328
Foulzie, ii, 118, 119, 141, 146, 180, 225
Foxeledge, i, 12
Frampton Cotel, i, 61
France, ii, 289 ; iii, 25, 100, 151, 182, 212, 213, 278, 297, 300
Franquer University, iii, 187
Fraserburgh, iii, 16
Freland, ii, 308, 309, 317, 327
Frenchie, ii, 146
Frendraught, ii, 219, 233
Fulemont, ii, 220
Fulham, iii, 257
Fullarton, ii, 348
Fyndachtie, ii, 146
Fyntrie Gask, ii, 70
Fyvie, ii, 208, 222, 231, 233, 236, 251
Gaillard, Château, ii, 65, 83, 84
Gala, Vale of, iii, 14
Gallipoli, iii, 267
Galloway, ii, 17, 22, 38, 39, 54, 76
Gallows Hill, ii, 20
Galston, ii, 82
Gamrie, ii, 227, 242, 243
Garden, ii, 324
Garioch, The, ii, 108, 210–212, 214–216, 221, 226, 228
Garlogy, ii, 217
Garry, ii, 128
Gartley, i, xvii, 20, 21 ; ii, 3–5, 7, 8, 13, 35, 41, 43, 98, 101, 102, 107, 109, 112–114, 116–119, 125, 130, 132, 135, 142, 143, 146–150, 186, 214, 215, 223, 239, 263, 312 ; iii, 208, 230, 231
Gartley Castle, ii, 135
Gartsherrie, iii, 230
Garvah Hill, ii, 160
Garvock, ii, 161
Gaston House, iii, 252
Gatchirst, ii, 345
Geicht, ii, 248
Geneva, iii, 99
Germany, ii, 241, 282, 287 ; iii, 2, 20, 25, 149, 165, 222, 241

Girth of St. Duthace, ii, 75
Givons Grove, ii, 341
Glamis, ii, 209, 210
Glasgow, ii, 26, 34, 195, 200, 297, 348, 355, 357 ; iii, 5, 104, 169, 192
Glasgow Castle, ii, 349
Glashlie, ii, 323, 328
Glass, ii, 118, 150, 225
Glechno, iii, 173
Gledoich, ii, 324
Glenbervie, ii, 160–162, 166, 170, 172, 195
Glendowachy, ii, 222
Glenducky, ii, 302
Glenfargt, iii, 53
Glenferkeryn, ii, 34
Glenferyn, ii, 30
Glen Livet, ii, 143, 187
Glenluce, ii, 60
Glen Tilt, ii, 120
Glesbanyn, ii, 46
Glithnow, iii, 20
Gloucester, i, 6, 9, 23, 32–34, 42, 49, 52, 56, 57, 59, 61, 71, 72, 77–79, 85, 98; ii, 11, 59 ; iii, 160
Gloucester, St. Peter's Abbey, i, 18, 19, 22, 23, 25, 26, 34, 42, 46, 53, 57, 71, 75, 95, 96
Gloucestershire, i, vii, xiv, xvi, 1, 6–8, 11–13, 18, 20, 46, 63, 67, 68, 70, 73, 75–82, 84, 86, 98 ; ii, 5, 8, 58, 59, 81 ; iii, 67, 231, 297
Goldsmith's Hall, iii, 13
Goodtrees, ii, 339
Gordonstoun, iii, 19, 22, 26, 32, 60, 70, 90, 98, 99, 101, 102
Gossington, i, 10, 87
Gossnaegh, ii, 341
Goveny, ii, 118
Gownis, ii, 137
Gowrie, ii, 39
Graham, ii, 109
Grampian Hills, iii, 26
Grange, ii, 237, 320
Granton, ii, 131
Grantuly, ii, 112, 113
Great Exhibition, The, iii, 291
Greece, iii, 283
Greenock, ii, 346
Greenwich, iii, 250
Hache, i, 67
Hackney, iii, 251
Haddenrigg, ii, 128
Haddington, ii, 38, 40, 55
Haddo, ii, 223, 264
Hadrian's Wall, iii, 177

357

358

359

360

LIST OF SUBSCRIBERS

Lieut.-Colonel Robert W. Barclay
Robert Leatham Barclay, Esq.
Charles Herbert Barclay, Esq.
Colonel Hugh Gurney Barclay, M.V.O.
The Rev. Charles Wright Barclay
Edwyn Barclay, Esq.
Lieut.-Colonel Hubert F. Barclay
Mrs. Joseph Gould
Captain Alexander H. Barclay. *The Queen's Bays*
Miss Constance Barclay
Miss Helen B. Barclay
Major Hedworth T. Barclay
Robert Cochrane Barclay, Esq.
Thomas Barclay, Esq., *Edinburgh*
Captain Walter Patrick Barclay. *The Black Watch*
Mrs. Blair Wilson
Miss Maria Barclay
C. H. StJohn Hornby, Esq.
Captain Arthur Victor Barclay
Major Cameron Barclay
The Rev. Cyril C. Barclay
The Rev. David B. Barclay
Miss Emily Barclay. *Philadelphia*
Edward Exton Barclay, Esq.
F. H. Barclay, Esq.
The Rev. G. A. Barclay
Colonel Henry Albert Barclay, C.V.O.
Major H. D. Barclay
Mrs. Michael Waterhouse
H. Ford G. Barclay, Esq.
Hugh Lloyd Barclay, Esq.
Miss Joanna Barclay. *Quebec*
Miss Josephine Barclay
J. Gurney Barclay, Esq.

LIST OF SUBSCRIBERS

Miss Marion Barclay
Mrs. Adolphus Tilney
Mrs. Robert Leatham Barclay
Robert William Alan Barclay, Esq. *New Zealand*
W. S. Barclay, Esq.
W. J. Barclay, Esq. *Vancouver*
The Countess of Strathmore and Kinghorne
Lady Proctor Beauchamp
The Right Rev. The Bishop of Monmouth
F. L. Bland, Esq.
Mrs. William Bradshaw
F. E. Bray, Esq.
Mrs. Frances Moon Butts. *Washington City*
Desmond Gurney Buxton, Esq.
Sir Felix Clay, Bart.
Mrs. Dimsdale
Mrs. Douglas
Mrs. Farrow
Mrs. Barclay-Graham
Mrs. Grant. *Edinburgh*
Mr. and Mrs. W. Cecil Harris
Lady Hoare
Miss Hoare
Mrs. StJohn Hornby
Sir Archibald Mitchelson, Bart.
Mrs. Lea-Wilson
The Hon. T. T. Parker
The Lord Wakefield of Hythe
Dorothy, Lady Kennard
The Rev. D. Barclay Mellis
E. G. Wheler-Galton, Esq.
John Bland, Esq.
W. Foster Reynolds, Esq.
Samuel Gurney, Esq.

LIST OF SUBSCRIBERS

H. C. Green, Esq.

F. Bayard Rives, Esq.

Michael Barclay, Esq.

Robert Valentine Berkeley, Esq.

Robert Francis Barclay, Esq., M.A., LL.B. *Glasgow*

Miss R. Mary Barclay, LL.B., M.D. *Edinburgh*

Mrs. Abbot

Charles James de Tolly Barclay, Esq.

Eric Fitzhardinge, Esq.

Mrs. Thomas Golding. *Southern Rhodesia*

Charles Malcolm Barclay Harvey, Esq., M.P.

Schuler L. Parsons, Esq. *South Carolina*

Mrs. Walker

Sir Arthur Worley, Bart.

Robert Cross, Esq.

John M. Hogge, Esq.

Charles J. Peter, Esq. *Vancouver*

Prince Barclay de Tolly

Commonwealth of Australia Parliamentary Library, Canberra F.C.T., Australia

Library of Congress, U.S.A.

The Friends Reference Library

John Hopkins University Library, Baltimore

The Mitchell Library, Glasgow

New England Historical and Genealogical Society

New York Public Library

St. Louis Public Library

The Signet Library, Edinburgh

Toronto University Library

Yale University Library

Mrs. W. J. Barclay

THE
ARDEN PRESS

W · H · SMITH AND SON LTD
STAMFORD STREET
LONDON · S · E

www.ingramcontent.com/pod-product-compliance
Lightning Source LLC
Chambersburg PA
CBHW071829270326
41929CB00013B/1938